Making Contact

Making Contact

MAPS, IDENTITY, AND TRAVEL

Glenn Burger,
Lesley B. Cormack,
Jonathan Hart,
and Natalia Pylypiuk,
editors

THE UNIVERSITY OF ALBERTA PRESS

Published by
The University of Alberta Press
Ring House 2
Edmonton, Alberta T6G 2E1

Copyright © The University of Alberta 2003

Published in association with the Medieval and Early Modern Institute at the University
of Alberta.

National Library of Canada Cataloguing in Publication Data

Main entry under title:

Making contact

Papers from a conference held Oct. 1–3, 1998 at the University of Alberta.

Includes bibliographical references and index.

ISBN 0-88864-377-2

1. Intercultural communication—History—Congresses. 2. America—Discovery and
exploration—Congresses. I. Burger, Glenn, 1954–

HM1211.M34 2002   303.48'2'09   C2002-910888-8

The University of Alberta Press is committed to protecting our natural environment. As part of
our efforts, this book is printed on stock produced by New Leaf Paper: it contains 100% post-
consumer recycled fibres and is acid- and chlorine-free.

Copyediting by Jill Fallis.
Design and layout by Carol Dragich.
Printed and bound in Canada by Friesens, Altona, Manitoba.
∞ Printed on acid-free paper.

The University of Alberta Press acknowledges the financial support of the Government of
Canada through the Book Publishing Industry Development Program for its publishing
activities. The Press also gratefully acknowledges the support received for its program from the
Canada Council for the Arts.

The volume is supported by a grant in aid of publication from the Social Sciences and
Humanities Research Council of Canada.

THE CANADA COUNCIL | LE CONSEIL DES ARTS
FOR THE ARTS | DU CANADA
SINCE 1957 | DEPUIS 1957

Canada

Contents

Part One

SPATIAL AND TEMPORAL MAPS:
Mappaemundi and Calendars

List of Illustrations

Contributors

Glenn Burger is associate professor of English at Queens College and the Graduate Center of the City University of New York. He is the editor of *A Lytell Cronycle*, Richard Pynson's translation of Hetoum's *La Fleur des histoires de la terre d'Orient*, author of a number of articles on Chaucer and queer theory, and coeditor (with Steven F. Kruger) of *Queering the Middle Ages*. His book about sexuality and nation in the Canterbury Tales, titled *Chaucer's Queer Nation*, is forthcoming from the University of Minnesota Press (2003).

Lesley B. Cormack teaches in the Department of History and Classics at the University of Alberta. Her research interests include history of geography in early modern England, images of empire, and the social context of the scientific revolution. She is the author of *Charting an Empire: Geography at the English Universities, 1580–1620* (1997).

Paul W. DePasquale teaches in the Department of English, University of Winnipeg, and works mainly in the areas of Aboriginal literature and early modern culture, with an emphasis on early colonialism and representations of Aboriginal peoples. In 1998–99, he was a Fulbright visiting scholar at Harvard University. Of Mohawk and European backgrounds, Paul is a member of the Six Nations Reserve in Ontario.

David Frick is professor of Slavic Languages and Literatures at the University of California, Berkeley. He is the author of studies in the history of Polish Bible translation in the Reformation and the Counter-Reformation, investigations of border-crossings in early modern Poland-Lithuania, and a biography of the Orthodox archbishop of Połock and convert to Greek Catholicism, Meletij Smotryc'kyj (d. 1633). His current work examines neighborhoods and networks in seventeenth-century Vilnius.

Jonathan Hart teaches in the Department of English, University of Alberta. He has been a visiting fellow at Harvard, Cambridge, Princeton and elsewhere and has written a number of books, including *Theater and World: The Problematics of Shakespeare's History* (1992), *Northrop Frye: The Theoretical Imagination* (1994), *Breath and Dust* (2000), *Representing the New World* (2001), *Dream China* (2002) and *By Speech or Signs* (2002).

Steven F. Kruger is professor of English at Queens College and the Graduate Center of the City University of New York. He is author of *Dreaming in the Middle Ages* and *AIDS Narratives: Gender and Sexuality, Fiction and Science*, and coeditor of *Approaching the Millennium: Essays on 'Angels in America'* (with Deborah R. Geis) and *Queering the Middle Ages* (with Glenn Burger). His current book project is *The Spectral Jew*, on medieval Jewish/Christian relations.

Rick H. Lee is a doctoral student in the department of English at Rutgers University. He is writing a dissertation on representations of identity and generational consciousness in twentieth-century gay male life narrative and autobiography.

Nakai Ayako is a professor of Comparative Culture at Aoyama Gakuin Women's Junior College in Tokyo. She also teaches German Literature at the University of Tokyo. She is the author of *Novalis to shizen shimpishisō* [*Novalis and the Tradition of Nature Mysticism*] (Tokyo: Chōbunsha, 1998). She is working on *Nature Mysticism in European Intellectual History from Renaissance to Romanticism*.

Natalia Pylypiuk is associate professor of Ukrainian in the Department of Modern Languages and Cultural Studies at the University of Alberta. Her publications have focused on Early Modern literature and especially on Hryhorij Skovoroda, an eighteenth-century philosopher. Her current book project is *The Rhetoric of Vision* in the oeuvre of Skovoroda and Vasyl' Stus, a Ukrainian dissident who died in the Gulag. Since 1995 she has been the Book Review Editor of *Canadian Slavonic Papers*.

Scott D. Westrem is professor of English at The Graduate Center and Lehman College of the City University of New York. His recent work includes *The Works of John Chalkhill*, co-edited with Charles Ryskamp (Princeton/The Roxburghe Club, 1999); *The Hereford Map: A Transcription and Translation of the Legends with Commentary* (Brepols, 2001); and *Broader Horizons: Johannes Witte de Hese's Itinerarius and Medieval Travel Narratives* (Medieval Academy of America, 2001). He was associate editor of *Trade, Travel, and Exploration in the Middle Ages: An Encyclopedia* (Garland, 2000). A monograph on the map that is the focus of his article is forthcoming from the University of Minnesota.

Linda Woodbridge, professor of English at the Pennsylvania State University, is author of *Women and the English Renaissance: Literature and the Nature of Womankind, 1540-1620* (1984); *The Scythe of Saturn: Shakespeare and Magical Thinking* (1994); and *Vagrancy, Homelessness, and Renaissance Literature* (2001); and coeditor of *True Rites and Maimed Rites: Ritual and Anti-Ritual in the Age of Shakespeare* (1992). She is past president of the Shakespeare Association of America.

Richard A. Young is professor of Spanish and Latin American Studies at the University of Alberta. His current research interests focus mainly on Argentina, in particular on tango and on representations of urban life in contemporary fiction. He is author of *Octaedro en cuatro tiempos: texto y tiempo en un libro de Cortázar* (Ottawa, 1993) and editor of *Latin American Postmodernisms* (Rodopi, 1997). He has been editor of *Revista Canadiense de Estudios Hispánicos* since 1996 and is currently editing another volume of essays for Rodopi to be titled *Music, Popular Culture, Identities*, which appeared in 2002.

Preface

JONATHAN HART

he Medieval and Early Modern Institute would like to thank, on behalf of the coeditors, all those who contributed to the development of the exploration of this topic and collection, the contributors to the volume, the Social Sciences and Humanities Council of Canada, the University of Alberta, and the University of Alberta Press. These collections take time, care and cooperation: in Chaucer's words, "Of sondry folk, by aventure yfalle/ In felaweshipe, and pilgrimes were they alle."

Acknowledgements

This volume is the result of a rich interdisciplinary collaboration, begun with the founding of the Medieval and Early Modern Institute (MEMI) at the University of Alberta and continued through the hosting of a conference in 1998 with the theme "Making Contact." The conference was very successful thanks to the organizational skills of Glenn Burger and Jonathan Hart, then the co-directors of the Institute. In the creation of this volume, the four editors have had the privilege of working with a host of innovative scholars in a variety of disciplines and in the process have negotiated contacts among, between, and within disciplines and cultures. Reflecting the interdisciplinary spirit of the Institute and this publishing project, as well as the productive dialogue that developed among all four editors while working on the volume, this collection is framed by an introduction written by Lesley Cormack and Natalia Pylypiuk and a conclusion with a different point of view (originally the introduction) written by Jonathan Hart. Thus a dialogue occurs at the beginning and end as well as within the collection.

Making Contact is a testament to the richness of the contributions and to the intricacies and challenges of collaborative and interdisciplinary work. The book contributes to the debate on the boundaries between disciplines and between the Middle Ages and the early modern period, between historical and theoretical perspectives. May the readers enjoy these essays as much as we have.

We have accumulated many debts in the creation of this volume. First, we would like to thank the Faculty of Arts at the University of Alberta, who helped create MEMI to encourage interdisciplinary work in various fields in Alberta and elsewhere. We thank the many members of MEMI who gave us their time, energy, and advice, and we thank the participants and the speakers at the conference. We acknowledge the financial aid we received from the Social Science and Humanities Research Council of Canada, both for the conference and for the publication itself. The University of Alberta Press, particularly the former director, Glenn Rollans; the current director, Linda D. Cameron; the Chair of the Academic Committee, Rod Macleod; and our editor, Leslie Vermeer, have been extremely supportive. Without them, this project would be materially and intellectually diminished. We are very grateful for the advice and suggestions of the volume's two anonymous reviewers. Especially, we thank the contributors to this volume, and our families and friends, who have lived with this project far longer than they might have had any reason to expect.

Introduction

Contact and Identity

LESLEY B. CORMACK AND NATALIA PYLYPIUK

[W]hen we are trained in a discipline, we put on a set of conceptual lenses which limit even as they focus. Most of us have worn these lenses so long that we cease to be aware that they exist. They are crafted through long years of apprenticeship as we absorb, often unconsciously, attitudes and ways of speaking that determine not only the answers we accept, but the questions we ask and the rhetoric we use to ask them ... Only when we try to have conversations across disciplinary boundaries do we realize that different lenses are polarized in different ways.[1]

As scholars of the medieval and early modern world, we spend most of our lives working with our various conceptual models. Although we often recognize the important and interesting work in areas of study close to but not our own, we rarely have the opportunity to consider the models employed by our colleagues or to shift our focus. This volume invites us all, first, to be aware that the lenses we employ have a particular polarization, and second, to discover the manner in which the lenses of others are polarized. As the historical actors that inhabit the following pages can attest, we only come to know ourselves through contact and interaction with 'the other.' This is as true for twenty-first-century scholars as it was for thirteenth-century Jewish and Christian polemicists or for sixteenth-century European explorers and missionaries.

This volume places in immediate proximity the conceptual lenses of scholars whose individual disciplines embrace territories, temporal frameworks, languages, and cultures that do not frequently come into contact at specialized professional forums. It developed on the initiative of the Medieval and Early Modern Institute, which was organized in 1997 with the explicit goal of facilitating interdisciplinary contact among various departments comprising the Faculty of Arts at the University of Alberta. This book arises from a conference that was held on 1–3 October 1998 with the support of Canada's Social Sciences and Humanities Research Council, the Conference Fund of the University of Alberta, the Faculty of Arts, and the departments of English, History and Classics, and Modern Languages and Cultural Studies.

The double title of that conference—"Making Contact: Natives, Strangers, and Barbarians"—might have evoked images of the ineluctable conflict between the Old and the New worlds or between dominant and subjugated cultures. However, the ideologically neutral noun *contact* served to attract, as the organizers had intended, papers devoted to a wide spectrum of topics and disciplines, the juxtaposition of which fleshed out not only the contradictions but also the complementarity and interdependence among various scholarly methodologies. The result was a meeting that went beyond our expectations, for it attracted Canadianists, Europeanists—including experts on Central and Eastern Europe—and scholars whose research involves the Orient and the Hispanic world. Moreover, the participants included those interested in textual sources as well as those looking at material evidence. We were truly making contact. The excitement of that conference, where we crossed boundaries, negotiated terrain, and tried to understand 'the other,' led us to consider subjects we had long ignored. By placing together seemingly distant areas of study, this book uncovers the rich tapestry of contacts that made up the everyday of medieval and early modern life.

In *Making Contact: Maps, Identity, and Travel*, we have resisted presenting a linear narrative, since such a limited perspective ignores the complex and interconnected lives and stories, the situated messiness of the pre-modern world.[2] In this resistance, we have followed the lead of interdisciplinary approaches represented in the collections *Text and Territory* and *The Post-Colonial Middle Ages*.[3] In making our selection, we were also guided by the desire to complement rather than duplicate these recent efforts. Consequently, this volume focuses on the negotiations that went on in the daily lives of pre-modern societies and the multicultural, multi-religious, multi-regional world they constituted, as well as on the manner in which such negotiations are being read today. We used as our organizing principle the important ways in which contact with contrasting 'others' shaped the identities of both individual and corporate 'selves' over a span of approximately five centuries. Thus, North and South as well as East and West are juxtaposed in this volume. The boundaries that separate the medieval from the early modern[4] within our individual scholarly practices are also ignored, allowing these terms, along with others such as "pre-colonial" and "colonial," to serve merely as conceptual tools rather than universalizing temporal markers.

We are aware of the fact that 'identity' is a troubled conceptual vehicle. But we agree with Lisa Malkki that "identity is always mobile and processual, partly self-construction, partly categorization by others, partly a condition, a status, a label, a weapon, a shield, a fund of memories, et cetera."[5] In other words, individuals create their identities while simultaneously expressing—albeit unconsciously— aspects of their society through social contact at home and abroad. In this volume both types of contact are explored, and all chapters address the relationship between contact and identity in a variety of ways. In one case, the contact 'abroad' is as imaginary as it is real, because it is mediated through a cartographic depiction of a highly fantasized Africa. In another case, contact 'at home' represents post-modern recreations of a narrative stemming from a sixteenth-century Spanish contact abroad, thus reminding us that "[t]he discourse of history as well as myth is simultaneously a discourse of identity."[6]

Contemporary sociologists suggest that both place of origin and displacement inform the construction of identity. We propose that the latter need not be only territorial; it could also be social, temporal, and linguistic.[7] The tensions between the two—place of origin and displacement—lead to a complex repertoire of loyalties, or attachments, that govern the formation and reformation of identity. This repertoire is in constant fluctuation. Several of the authors in this volume examine such fluctuations in the lives of individuals whose identities were shaped through contact with others and constantly changing personal and social boundaries. This led to anxieties about the creation of 'the self' and 'the other.' In some cases, it led to real or perceived transgressive identities. Some of the actors discussed in this volume came to discern their own identities, in an increasingly subjective world, through their contact and negotiation with 'the other.'

Thus, the themes of boundary and continuity are important for these chapters, as they are for the scholars investigating them. Liminality has proven to be an important factor in postcolonial studies of pre-modern worlds, since it is often at the boundaries that transgressive behaviour and new identity formation can take place.[8]

ဆင်္ချ

This book is divided into three parts. The first—Spatial and Temporal Maps: *Mappaemundi* and Calendars—considers how unexplored space stimulated the imagination of late medieval cartographers and the manner in which divergent calendrical allegiances affected the everyday life of an early modern urban environment. Both chapters in this part examine contacts within and across intellectual, religious, and material cultures, and the manner in which they shaped the identity of the participants.

In "Africa Unbounded on an Unstudied European *Mappamundi* (ca. 1450) and in Related Cartography," Scott Westrem demonstrates in exemplary fashion the rich resources provided by maps. The first scholar to have done so, he examines the African part of the world as depicted in an intriguing fifteenth-century map, which is currently housed in the James Ford Bell Library at the University of Minnesota. Drawing on European intellectual traditions and Arabic ones alike, this map reveals the cultural, scholarly, and ideological interconnections among fifteenth-century geographers and cartographers. As well, it shows the negotiations taking place in this period between "new" Ptolemaic mathematical cartography, which involved plotting places in a precise location on the globe, and the older *mappamundi* tradition, which sought to depict lived and ideological space.

The Bell Map combines information about this southern part of the world—Westrem rightly avoids calling it "Africa" in some modern sense—with older legends and expectations. He depicts an intellectual tension between traditional knowledge of the "monstrous" races of the south and newer information filtered through travellers' reports. The result is a map in which abundantly illustrated vignettes of political and social mores conceal a paucity of information about Africa. Westrem points out that there is much less real information on the African section of the map than on the European (the Asian is lost to us), a situation that would continue for at least five hundred years of cartographic history. As Westrem says, "The pictures ... appear where other kinds of data were unavailable, and it has long been Africa's fate to be richly illustrated in European cartography, which seems to be marked by a particular vulnerability to *horror vacui*."

Maps such as the Bell Map were never used to find one's way and so should not been seen as direct tools for mediating contact between the hemispheres. Rather, this map and Westrem's chapter point to the intellectual contacts between different scholarly communities and different traditions, and to the interaction, across time and space, of different peoples. Maps such as the Bell Map would colour the physical contacts between peoples, just as the myth of the Golden Age would inform the discursive strategies of reportage about the Americas. As an artifact, the Bell Map reflects more accurately the mindset of its creators than the African continent it purports to represent. This is a theme that surfaces in the third part of this volume, especially in Richard A. Young's discussion of Alvar Núñez Cabeza de Vaca's narrative on his experiences in the New World.

The idea that cultures represent "discrete, object-like phenomena occupying discrete spaces"[9] is probably a modern fiction. In "The Bells of Vilnius: Keeping Time in a City of Many Calendars," David Frick considers the day-to-day encounters within one locality that accommodated Poles, Lithuanians, Germans, Belarussians and Ukrainians, Jews, and Tatars. This case-study focuses on the tensions created in the mid-seventeenth century by the use of various calendars in private and public life at a time when the Counter-Reformation was gradually making its progress in the Polish-Lithuanian Commonwealth. Frick demonstrates the manner in which ethnocultural differences—significantly informed by, or subsumed under, religious identities (Roman Catholic, Greek Catholic, Orthodox, Calvinist, Lutheran, Jewish, and Muslim)—were negotiated in the interest of civic stability. This is especially important if we recall that the social and religious discontent among the largely Orthodox population of Ukraine engulfed, by the late 1640s, the Polish-Lithuanian polity in serious civil strife. Whereas the latter has attracted considerable attention from various scholarly perspectives, the relatively harmonious interactions in urban environments have not.

Frick investigates the manner in which the close proximity of several ethnic[10] and religious communities in the royal city of Vilnius shaped the civic behaviour of those communities and, by implication, their shared identity. He considers as well the major players who preserved the differences that potentially undermined life together. The traditions of toleration—established in the Grand Duchy of Lithuania before the introduction of Christianity in 1386 and the concomitant dynastic union between the duchy and the Kingdom of Poland—were a contributing factor to the city's stability. These traditions were initially sustained by the culture of tolerance among the commonwealth's nobility, i.e., the *szlachta,* which erased some of the differences between Catholics and Protestants. But, in the day-to-day encounters among burghers, the guilds played a significant role in finding practical solutions. Viewing contact as contamination, priests and ministers understandably sought to protect confessional boundaries, especially within family life and social intercourse. The guilds—interested as they were in the sharing of power—formulated, on the other hand, statutes and rituals that took into account the authenticity of 'others,' thus promoting conviviality among men labouring together. It is this factor, as Frick's detailed investigation of archival material suggests, that generated civic patriotism in Vilnius and kept religious violence at a relatively low incidence. Frick's discussion has serious implications for the study of culture and identity as a set of negotiations between the private and public spheres of life.

Identity, be it individual or collective, is never fixed and "is inconceivable without difference."[11] It is a constantly evolving process affected by the presence of 'the other.' The second part of this volume—Identities and Subjectivities: Jews, Buddhists, Christians, and Vagrants—is devoted to this matter. These three chapters explore the contradictions that arise when 'the self' and 'others' live in proximity or come into contact for the first time, but distrust or fail to respect the authenticity of the 'others,' while being troubled by their reciprocally evolving 'selves.'

In "(De)Stabilized Identities in Medieval Jewish-Christian Disputations on the Talmud," Steven F. Kruger examines the tensions between lived reality and ideological distance. Using a series of medieval disputations taking place in Barcelona and Paris between Christians and Jews in the thirteenth century, he shows that Jewish identity and its continued development in post-biblical times were sources of anxiety for Christian leaders and intellectuals. The latter viewed the historical Jews of the Hebrew Bible as representing an identity that, while giving rise to their own, they had disavowed. In the intervening millennium, Judaism had also evolved considerably, a fact that disoriented Christian thinkers.

In Christian Europe there were major persecutions of Jews during the Middle Ages. And yet during this period both groups lived in close proximity, with Jews employing Christian servants, engaging in business transactions with Christians, and often living co-operative lives not unlike those of seventeenth-century Vilnians. Christian thinkers and leaders perceived a tension between the contemporary Jews—with whom they lived—and the historical Jews, as they had constructed them and from whom they had descended. Contemporary Judaism was best observed in the Talmud, a dynamic and growing body of Jewish laws and exegesis that demonstrated the living nature of Jewish culture. Consequently, in the struggle to separate the historical from the contemporary Jew, the Talmud became the focus of Christian attacks, both rhetorical and real.

In examining these conflicts, Kruger reveals the fluidity of Christian and Jewish identities. Historically, Christians came into being because of Jews, but still defined themselves as "not Jewish."

By extension, Jews living in a predominantly Christian Europe were perpetually made aware of ways they were, and were not, Christian. The disputations employed the services of converted Jews to argue for Christianity; nonetheless, religious leaders constantly worried about the possibility of backsliding converts or Christians being enticed into Jewish "heresies." The seeming stability of these religious communities thus concealed a deep anxiety about the mutable nature of identity and a fear of the potential temptations that could affect its transformation. Linda Woodbridge's chapter discusses a similar anxiety governing the relationship between the rich and the poor in early modern England, where distrust of those "passing" as gentry evoked the medieval Christian fear of the converso.

Nakai Ayako's "Jesuit Missionaries and the Earliest Contact between European and Japanese Cultures" focuses on the critical role that individuals play when, in their function as emissaries for their own culture, they encounter for the first time radically different societies. Nakai compares and contrasts the reactions to Japan by the Basque missionary Francis Xavier and his successors: the Italians Alessandro Valignano and Gnecchi-Soldo Organtino, and the Portuguese Luis Frois and Francisco Cabral. Although there were serious differences of perception among the first four, they nonetheless tended to respect the education, intellectual curiosity, and politeness of their Japanese hosts. At the same time, Xavier cunningly exploited the Japanese emphasis on honour over wealth and strict dietary laws, in order to promote Christianity through the concept of humility and ascetic practices. While undoubtedly mercantile considerations and their goals as missionaries led some Jesuits toward strategies of tolerance, their own writings suggest that they were also genuinely curious about, and respectful of, the host culture. It was this that lent comparative success to their evangelizing efforts.

Frois learned Japanese, acted as interpreter for visiting Jesuits, and wrote a comparative study of European and Japanese cultures as well as a voluminous history of Japan. Organtino also learned the language, studied Buddhist texts, and dressed and ate like the Buddhists priests with whom he conversed—but even Valignano, who supported the adoption of Japanese customs, saw Organtino's type of acculturation as too much of a compromise, thus perhaps betraying his own anxieties about identity. Nonetheless, he also censured the policies of Cabral who, by contrast, never learned the language of his new environment although he spent thirteen years in Japan. Governed by the very arrogance against which the self-reflecting Xavier had warned in his letters, Cabral distrusted Japanese politeness from the beginning. He went so far as to argue against teaching Latin or Portuguese to Japanese converts for fear that they would understand the conversations of the Jesuits and learn to disrespect European missionaries. Cabral also did not wish the Japanese converts to become Jesuit priests. This suggests that he too had concerns about the mutation of identity caused by the close contact between such different cultures.

Nakai suggests that a more nuanced perspective on cross-cultural contact can be obtained once scholars engage in case-studies facilitating a detailed comparison of similarities and differences among the principle actors, their attitudes, and their behaviour. The typology of approaches toward the 'other,' which Nakai proposes in her essay, would also be useful in other contexts. Thus, for example, the attitude of Piotr Skarga, among the most prominent Jesuit theologians in Vilnius, toward the language and culture of the Orthodox Ruthenians (i.e., Ukrainians and Belarussians) was not unlike that of the arrogant Cabral *vis-à-vis* the Japanese.[12] The complexities involved in all types of contact require that the scholar carefully distinguish between individual perspectives and group ideology. The role of the latter also receives attention in this volume's last chapter where Richard A. Young considers early Spanish accounts of the New World. As Young posits, the results of an encounter are predicated by the motives leading to it. In other words, is discovery or conquest and subjugation the primary impulse behind the encounter?

The last chapter in this part makes a fascinating case for the parallels between attitudes towards New World natives and the treatment of vagrants in early modern England. In "Vagrants Meet Nomads: Rogues, Aborigines, and Elizabethan Subjectivity," Linda Woodbridge argues that there are at least four important ways in which these two groups—vagrants and nomads—were perceived as inherently similar: in their foreignness, their sexual promiscuity, their intrinsic mobility, and their secrecy and hiddenness. The foreignness of non-European natives was obvious, but followed a pattern that had variously described English vagrants as Irish, Welsh, or gypsy, rather than as the poor English they largely were. Both groups were renowned—in travel literature and in rogue literature—for the presumed immodesty of their public and sexual behaviour. Vagrants were seen as inherently dangerous because they had no fixed domicile. Commonwealth men, as well as later Elizabethan reformers, articulated great anxiety about the growing numbers of vagrants and "masterless men." This resulted in a series of acts concerning the poor, none of which reduced the numbers of the poor nor did much to stop the movement of the armies of migrant workers sojourning across England.[13] Likewise, natives at best aroused suspicion and at worst were considered subhuman for their nomadic ways and lack of a fixed address. Indeed, sixteenth-century imperial discourse relied on a "sedentarist metaphysics,"[14] declaring that the natives of the Americas did not own the land, because they had not settled and improved it, and therefore the settlement of these lands by Europeans was legitimate and not open to challenge.[15] Most important for Woodbridge, both vagrants and aborigines were seen as duplicitous, hiding their thoughts, station in life, and state of health—in short, their very identities.

This anxiety about the hidden nature of vagrants and natives, Woodbridge argues, was exacerbated by, and contributed to, the growing sense of subjectivity in the early modern period. To a degree, the development of an interiority to religious and intellectual life also allowed people to concern themselves with the deceptive exteriority of others' lives: who knew what evil lurked in the heart of men? Thus, "closeting and nosiness were mutually constitutive"; that is, just as individuals gained a sense of their own private relationship with God and with their own thoughts and actions, so they became concerned with what that relationship and those thoughts and actions might be for others. Within this context, Woodbridge discusses the problems of clothing, of language, of feigned illness, and of class mobility. Was this perhaps the root of the many sumptuary laws, of a fascination with "thieves' cant," and with stories of the unveiling of impostors? The behaviour of the English brings to mind the nosiness of their counter-parts in Vilnius, who—as Frick points out in his study—were not averse to cruelly mocking their neighbours whenever the latter were caught "preparing the wrong foods at inappropriate times."

Woodbridge looks at the increased interest by early modern intellectuals and writers in firsthand observation, or the rhetorical claim that seeing is believing.[16] This was an age that relied on the discourse of empiricism in science, travel literature, and rogue literature. Although the reality was much more complex, what was at stake was the unmasking of hidden corruption in other worlds and other people, while projecting the integrity of the narrating persona.

Probably at the heart of Woodbridge's argument is the anxiety over authenticity, over the act of "passing" as something or someone else. That is, inhabitants of early modern England frequently worried that people, and things, would not be as they seemed. Men might be women, women might be men, respectable people might be vagrants, invalids mere dissemblers. Just as Kruger shows the anxiety over the converted Jew and with the contemporary Jew who did not correspond to his historical counterpart, so Woodbridge indicates that the early modern English feared the individuals they encountered were other than they appeared.

❧❦

Contact with the past is mediated through documents and eyewitness reportage. The third part of the volume—Travel to the New World: The Early Modern and the Postmodern—focuses on individuals who produced accounts of early contacts with societies whose perspectives on 'the self' and 'others' are irretrievably lost. The theme of cultural assimilation, which surfaces in the preceding chapters, is further explored here. The three contributors to this part investigate the ways in which early modern authors constructed their identities through negotiation of 'the self' with 'the other,' but for various reasons were unable to proclaim the validity of this process or to document everything they experienced. All three contributors emphasize the need to remain cognizant of the contexts in which such reportage was created, the horizon of expectations of the audience for whom they were intended, and the limitations inescapably imposed upon their authors by the ideologies and narrative conventions of their time.

Early sixteenth-century explorers needed a comparative framework in order to understand the peoples and places they contacted. Many scholars have pointed to the similarities between the literature of first contact and earlier European treatments of the Golden Age, thus positing that explorers found the classical age through traversing space rather than time.[17] Without altogether dismissing such views, Paul DePasquale's "Re-writing the Virginian Paradise: the Conflicted Author(s) of a Late Sixteenth-Century Travel Account" argues that European observers were instead motivated by the instructions they had received as well as by the mercantilist ambitions engendering such instructions. Narrators like Arthur Barlowe (who reported on the early encounters with the Algonquins in what today is North Carolina) were more concerned with potential commodities for exploitation, as well as whether the natives would be amenable to trade, rather than with descriptions of arcadia's recovery.

Just as missionary zeal and economic motives were seamlessly conjoined in Francis Xavier's instructions to his fellow Jesuits bound for Japan, both the classical model of 'the other' and the more immediate urge to exploit the Americas were not necessarily contradictory. They probably coexisted in the minds of early observers of the New World and informed their narrative modes. After all, an expectation of a peaceful arcadia might have made European audiences in some way more predisposed to trade. Certainly, Barlowe's wonder at the lush vegetation and sincere hospitality of the native women reflects both a recognition of the economic potential of this new continent and a seemingly genuine excitement over having recuperated a long-lost Edenic community.

DePasquale indicates that Barlowe also acknowledges the dangers of this early contact and that his narrative shows a tension between the luxuries of plenty and the hazards of unknown enemies. This is especially evident in the differences between the behaviour of men and that of women, since the latter are shown as welcoming and hospitable, while the former are depicted as threatening and unreachable.

Texts such as Barlowe's (and those by Pierre-Esprit Radisson and Núñez, discussed subsequently in this part) were probably subject to the mediation of a publisher or translator. Barlowe's account of Virginia appeared in the 1589 edition of *Principall Navigations*, written and edited by Richard Hakluyt. Inasmuch as the latter's aim was to promote the opening of this new continent, DePasquale argues that much of the immediacy of Barlowe's original tale may have been altered in the process. Thus, parts of the story that might have revealed ambivalence about the venture—in terms of danger or difficult contact, as well as whether the lands were as fertile as imagined—could have been edited out. This is, of course, highly speculative, but it does remind us of the many layers through which accounts of contact were probably filtered. At the same time, DePasquale reminds us that there was real contact at the beginning of this process, and argues that this face-to-face interaction deserves our attention. This was true for Barlowe, just as it proved to be for Núñez and Radisson. While studying the lenses through which these explorers viewed their new worlds, we must also bear in mind that real people saw and affected each other through everyday exchanges, and thus their identities were often reshaped under unexpected conditions.

Rick H. Lee's contribution, "Stylizations of Selfhood in Pierre-Esprit Radisson's *Voyages*," considers a neglected and poorly understood figure in the history of early Canada. Notwithstanding his key role in the establishment of the Hudson's Bay Company, Radisson's accounts of his travels, written in the mid- to late 1660s, have been largely undervalued by historians and literary scholars alike. Lee suggests that the investment of the latter in contemporary Canadian cultural politics has prevented a nuanced discussion of the implications that Radisson's complex repertoire of identities poses to today's reader. A Frenchman, Radisson described his first four voyages in English; but three years before becoming a British subject, he recounted the last two in French. In his various encounters, Radisson intermittently identified himself as French, English, or Indian.

Lee focuses on Radisson's story about his first voyage. This, the least studied of the accounts, describes his captivity and subsequent adoption by a group of Iroquois from May 1652 to October 1653. Lee proposes that the disruptions of structural and temporal logic evident in the work reflect, on one level, their author's struggle to reconcile the process of accommodation to another culture. On another level, they reveal his sense of self at the time of writing, along with his recollection of the self in captivity.

A remarkable transfiguration of the narrative self in the account of the first voyage concerns the manner in which Radisson's descriptions of the Iroquois change over time. At the beginning of the account the Iroquois are referred to as "Barbars," "dogges," and "devils," but after being initiated into the tribe, Radisson articulates filiation to his adoptive family and willingness to participate in their war. The former may have been predicated by the repertoire of insulting epithets available during this period and the latter by the need to survive. Radisson also describes how his adoptive community reacted to the differences between his physical appearance and theirs, differences that led them to invest considerable effort in making him look like one of them. One wonders whether this particular section in Radisson's reportage records an initiation ritual, an attempt on the part of the Iroquois to make 'the other' like 'the self' by erasing the former's external differences.

Lee reminds us of the dangers of literal readings of travel accounts and suggests useful interpretive strategies that can assist the historian and the student of culture to appreciate the complexities of assimilation as well as the fluid nature of identity. The latter is made especially problematic when authors, like Radisson, are torn apart by multiple loyalties or by the need to cater to a community whose native tongue is different from their own. For this very reason, Lee's discussion, like Frick's, is of direct relevance for those who study contemporary multicultural environments.

This volume concludes with the chapter "Re-reading the Past: Cabeza de Vaca in History, Fiction and Film." Here Richard A. Young considers scholarly treatments and postmodern recreations of Los naufragios [The shipwrecks], an eloquent account detailing the inauspicious exploratory journey that the Spaniard Pánfilo de Narváez led to the Florida coast in 1528. Written by one of four survivors of this expedition, Alvar Núñez Cabeza de Vaca, this story was published in two slightly different versions, the first in 1542 and the second in 1555.

Notwithstanding the remarkably critical stance of Núñez toward the imperial project that had been at the core of the failed expedition, well into the nineteenth century Los naufragios was subjected to readings governed by the framework of the Spanish discourse of discovery and conquest. Originally submitted as a report to colonial authorities in Santo Domingo, the first redaction of the story, now surviving only in a summary, was probably motivated by the desire—on the part of the survivors—to secure recognition and rewards for services rendered to the Spanish crown. In this context, it is worth noting that some scholars attributed similarly practical motives to Radisson's English-language account of his first voyage, an argument persuasively disputed by Lee.

The published version of the account by Núñez outgrew the self-serving motives of the report and developed into a polyvalent narrative that more recent scholarship has seen as an individual Christian's progress from darkness to illumination or as a type of hagiography. Alternately viewed as an indictment of the conquest or as a tract promoting peaceful conversion, *Los naufragios* was shaped by the literary conventions available to Núñez in the mid-sixteenth century.

Both of the creative responses to *Los naufragios* that Young analyses were motivated by the celebrations of the quincentenary of Columbus's voyage. The first, published in 1992, is the novel *El largo atardecer del caminanate* [The long twilight of the wanderer] by the Argentinean Abel Posse. Conforming to the postulates of the so-called new historical novel, Posse questions the ability of historical discourse to function as reliable representation. His novel, told from the point of view of a senescent Núñez, has the protagonist admit that his original account was fraught with omissions predicated by the kind of self-censorship that the prevailing ideology and, above all, the Inquisition imposed on him. This then motivates an account, on the part of the fictional Núñez, of the daily contacts he had with the native people among whom he lived for six years and whose cultural practices he adopted. In this manner, argues Young, Posse casts doubt not only on the veracity of *Los naufragios*, but also on the historiography of the conquest and colonization.

The second work discussed by Young is Nicholas Echevarría's *Cabeza de Vaca*, a Spanish-Mexican film released in 1990. Like Posse's novel, this film posits the survivors' assimilation to indigenous culture, a reality that they ultimately conceal through the fabrication of fantastic stories because they suspect that the horizon of expectations of the compatriots—whom they finally rejoin—would prevent the accommodation of what was truly experienced.

The past is also an 'other.' Young's discussion succinctly identifies the difficulties we face when seeking to understand a culture that preceded our own, especially if its native actors were not in the position of recording their reception of early contacts. As foreigners, authors of eyewitness accounts—including the Spaniard Núñez—approached people and phenomena they did not understand and, more than likely, were changed by them and by what they saw. However, the manner in which their experiences would be articulated depended not only on motives leading to the contact, but also on the discursive traditions and, implicitly, the epistemologies organizing perception—their own and that of their intended audiences. According to Young, similar factors govern today's historical investigations or artistic re-creations of the past. At best, we can expect such writing to be a truer reflection of 'the self' than of 'the other' or, more accurately, a depiction of what we believe happened in the past rather than what actually happened.

Young's paper also suggests that identities are continually reshaped. The fact that descendants of the colonizers and the colonized have recently re-created—more than once—the story of Núñez in order to fill in the "gaps" of the original suggests that constructing the past brings emotional comfort precisely because it sanctions reinterpretation. Although borne by the past, identity need not be enslaved by it. Alternately, nostalgia for what Núñez might have "omitted" may be viewed as a search for origins, for a reconciliation of the postcolonial present with historical experience.[18]

All three chapters in the final part confront the fact that the eyewitness authors were, in the first instance, prepared to observe in a particular manner and, in the second instance, writing for particular audiences. Thus, their creation of identity through contact was doubly mediated, and, as Young reminds us, continues to be read through differently polarized lenses.

In November 1493, Christopher Columbus, leading a ragged band of sailors and adventurers, set foot on Dominica and proclaimed its control by the king and queen of Spain.[19] In doing so, he "made contact" with the Arawak Indians and signed their death warrant.[20] This, however, was neither an isolated event nor some late fifteenth-century innovation. Rather, medieval and early modern history is a narrative about continual encounters across—as well as within—cultures, religions, classes, and geographical regions. This book investigates some of these contacts and how they shaped identities and subjectivities. Many more such interactions, including those between the Islamic world and the North, between men and women, between East and West, deserve to be explored in close proximity. Equally worthy of investigation is the manner in which language differences were negotiated during first encounters, as well as the implications that such encounters have for the ethical and philosophical study of culture.

The contributors to *Making Contact* provide an important reminder that 'the self' and 'the other' need not remain as unproblematized terms of opposition. Ideally, they ought to be perpetually questioned.[21] By viewing the medieval and early modern world as an interconnected and interdependent set of spaces, and by keeping sight of the individual, the artificial unity of each of these terms falls apart. This opens up the exploration of the processes behind the production of identity, processes that resist an isomorphic equivalence between space and culture.

NOTES

1 N. Katherine Hayles, "Deciphering the Rules of Unruly Disciplines: A Modest Proposal for Literature and Science," in *Literature and Science,* ed. Donald Bruce and Anthony Purdy, Rodopi Perspectives on Modern Literature, vol. 14 (Amsterdam and Atlanta, GA: Rodopi, 1994), p. 25.

2 David Livingstone, *The Geographical Tradition: Episodes in the History of a Contested Enterprise* (Oxford: Blackwell, 1992), talks about the interwoven reality of the world.

3 See Sylvia Tomasch and Sealy Gilles, eds., *Text and Territory: Geographical Imagination in the European Middle Ages* (Philadelphia: University of Pennsylvania Press, 1998) and Jeffrey Jerome Cohen, ed., *The Postcolonial Middle Ages* (London: St. Martin's Press, 2000).

4 We have chosen the term "early modern," rather than "Renaissance," as a more inclusive term, less charged with the ideology of high culture. This term, "early modern," however, is a good illustration of the polarized lenses we all wear, since it means something quite different for scholars of English literature, for example, than the long *durée* of the social historians.

5 Lisa Malkki, "National Geographic: The Rooting of Peoples and the Territorialization of National Identity among Scholars and Refugees," *Cultural Anthropology* 7, no. 1 (1992): 37.

6 Jonathan Friedman, "Myth, History, and Political Identity," *Cultural Anthropology* 7, no. 2 (1992): 194.

7 On "displacement," see Carol Breckenridge and Arjun Appadurai, "On Moving Targets," *Public Culture* 2, no. 1 (1989): i–iv. We have opted for this term, rather than "deterritorialization," because of its metaphoric amplitude.

8 John Gillies, *Shakespeare and the Geography of Difference* (Cambridge: Cambridge University Press, 1994), argues that transgressive behaviour was possible in liminal frontier space, such as Mark Antony's Egypt. Likewise, Cohen, *Postcolonial Middle Ages*, makes the same case for transitional space rather than hard boundaries in understanding medieval contact. See also Edward W. Soja, *Postmodern Geographies: The Reassertion of Space in Critical Theory* (London and New York: Verso, 1989), and James W. Flanagan, "Postmodern Perspectives on Premodern Space," paper delivered at the Annual Congress, Federation of Humanities and Social Sciences, Sherbrooke, QC, 1999.

9 Akhil Gupta and James Ferguson, "Beyond 'Culture': Space, Identity, and the Politics of Difference," *Cultural Anthropology* 7, no. 1 (1992): 7.

10 We use the designation "ethnic" as do social anthropologists when referring "to aspects of relationships between groups which consider themselves, and are regarded by others, as being culturally distinctive." See Thomas Hylland Eriksen, *Ethnicity and Nationalism: Anthropological Perspectives* (London and Boulder, CO: Pluto Press, 1993), p. 4.

11 See I.B. Neumann and J.M. Welsh, "The Other in European Self-Definition: A Critical Addendum to the Literature on International Society," *Review of International Studies* 17, no. 4 (1991). See also Anthony Pagden, *The Fall of Natural Man* (Cambridge and New York: Cambridge University Press, 1982), and Gillies, *Shakespeare and the Geography*.

12 For a discussion of Skarga's attitudes toward the Ruthenians, see Borys A. Gudziak, *Crisis and Reform: The Kyivan Metropolitanate, the Patriarchate of Constantinople, and the Genesis of the Union of Brest* (Cambridge, MA: Harvard Ukrainian Research Institute, 1998), pp. 83–86.

13 Paul Slack, *The English Poor Law 1531–1782* (Cambridge: Cambridge University Press, 1995), and A.L. Bier, *The Problem of the Poor in Tudor and Early Stuart England* (London: Methuen, 1985).

14 We borrow this term from Malkki, "National Geographic," p. 31.

15 Anthony Pagden, *Lords of All the World: Ideologies of Empire in Spain, Britain and France c. 1500–c. 1800* (New Haven: Yale University Press, 1995).

16 Svetlana Alpers, *The Art of Describing: Dutch Art in the Seventeenth Century* (Chicago: University of Chicago Press, 1983), talks about the connections among such ideas, the growth of realism in Dutch art, and natural philosophy.

17 For example, Harry Levin, *The Myth of the Golden Age in the Renaissance* (London and Bloomington, IN: Indiana University Press, 1969).

18 We are borrowing from David Lowenthal's concept of heritage as nostalgic mythology of "origin and continuance." See his *Possessed by the Past: The Heritage Crusade and the Spoils of History* (New York: The Free Press, 1996), especially p. 128.

19 Stephen Greenblatt, *Marvelous Possessions: The Wonder of the New World* (Chicago: University of Chicago Press, 1991).

20 Alfred W. Crosby, *Ecological Imperialism: The Biological Expansion of Europe 900–1900* (Cambridge: Cambridge University Press, 1986).

21 We are borrowing here the conceptual model proposed by the anthropologists Gupta and Ferguson, "Beyond 'Culture'," pp. 13–15.

Part One

Spatial &
Temporal Maps

MAPPAEMUNDI
AND CALENDARS

The Bell Mappamundi. *Courtesy of the James Ford Bell Library, University of Minnesota; used by permission.*

Africa Unbounded

On an Unstudied European *Mappamundi* (ca. 1450) and in Related Cartography

SCOTT D. WESTREM

Are you there, Africa with the bulging chest and
oblong thigh? Sulking Africa, wrought of iron, in the
fire, Africa of the millions of royal slaves, deported
Africa, drifting continent, are you there? Slowly you
vanish, you withdraw into the past, into the tales of
castaways, colonial museums, the works of scholars....

These words of plaintive interrogation belong to the character Félicité in Jean Genet's drama of revolt *The Blacks*, which premiered in Paris in 1959.[1] Their sympathetic lushness may make us so drowsy that we fail to notice the extent to which her lamented Africa's "bulging chest and oblong thigh" depend on our imagining the world as depicted according to the map projection devised by Gerardus Mercator in 1568. Other cartographical schemes that attempt a more exact relationship between space on a page and actual land area—or that run a central meridian through, say, Thailand or Costa Rica—depict an Africa that, by contrast, seems to suffer from anorexia or curvature of the spine.[2] Moreover, in Félicité's view, the enslavement and deportation of noble millions make a "drifting continent" of Africa, contradicting what some geologists

3

contend is the Americas' status as a meandering land mass and conforming to modern Western notions of global land distribution.[3] A place that exists only as research topic, collectable artifact, and orally transmitted tale, we are subtly (and doubtless unwittingly) given to understand by Genet, must be pre- or at least aliterate, and hence we can expect little else than that Africa should vanish into a vague past.

Félicité's elegy on the theme of Africa echoes many another European attempt to record the story of territory south of the Mediterranean, some of which lack her good intentions. The fact that, until relatively recent times, no single name was used for the territory—ancient, medieval, and early modern writers variously and inconsistently employing "Aethiopia," "Libya," and "Africa"— suggests that this story lacked clear character or plot.[4] This differs from a European stance toward Asia that meant to "[deal] with it by making statements about it, authorizing views of it, describing it, by teaching it, settling it, ruling over it: in short,…dominating, restructuring, and having authority over" it. This well-known definition of orientalism by Edward Said posits a totalizing approach to the East that differs from the somewhat less strident European treatment of Africa before the mid-1500s.[5] Yet even if medieval "Austrinalism" seems unlikely to become the next theoretical neologism, the ways in which Europe did, in fact, go about "describing" and "restructuring" the South during the Middle Ages bear considering, even if I do so conscious of my own participation in a process that would further encourage Félicité to mourn Africa's reduction to a work of scholarship.

It is ironic that Genet's play, born of a desire to portray the physical and cultural vitality of African people and regarded as stunningly avant-garde when it was first performed, sounds so dated and paternalistic today, only some four decades later. We should be mindful of Genet's intention, and his lapses, in considering a different kind of text that seeks to represent Africa in global terms: a little-known, mid-fifteenth-century world map that is the product of a circle of innovative scholars interested in astronomy and geography. This *mappamundi* is an early witness to the widespread recovery of Ptolemaic geographical principles by the European intelligentsia during the later Middle Ages and, at the same time, a purveyor of an ancient and hackneyed image of Africa.

The map (see page 2) was acquired in 1960 by John Parker, then curator (now curator emeritus) of the James Ford Bell Library, a collection of rare books and manuscripts at the University of Minnesota, where it is found today. Purchased from August Laube, an antiquarian dealer in Zürich, the map has an otherwise unknown provenance (Laube is now dead and his firm has been dissolved).[6] Its existence has been noted by only three scholars: Marcel Destombes, John Parker, and David Woodward; in 1992, an image of it appeared without any discussion in a popular book on the lost island of Atlantis.[7]

Originally a representation of the world, in the circular format adopted for most known medieval *mappaemundi*, the Bell Map (as I will henceforth style it) is today only a fragment of the original. What survives is an irregularly shaped rectangle of vellum (fine parchment), about as large as a legal-size sheet of paper, with a bulge near the lower-right corner: it measures 330/334 mm x 223/238 mm (13½ in. x 9–9½ in.). The sheet has been trimmed all around with a rather blunt knife, resulting in the loss of text and image on each of the four sides. Part of the round edge of the earth is visible at the upper-right, and the curvature of its arc makes it possible to calculate that the original terrestrial diameter was approximately 500/510 mm (20 in.). Several additional arcs in the upper-right corner—extending the design another 90 mm (3½ in.)—are all that remains of a series of concentric circles ringing the earth. This was once a cosmological display, an attempt to render planets and the fixed stars in a geocentric universe.[8] The additional space required for these rings would have required an image measuring at least 60 cm (2 ft.) on each side, not including extra marginal space. This means that while only about one-quarter of the original vellum sheet survives, the Bell Map today preserves almost forty percent of the originally depicted surface of the earth, with a considerable amount of the lost matter being the surrounding heavenly spheres.

Nevertheless, the Bell Map is indeed fragmentary. The terrestrial land mass was almost certainly not divided into specifically named "parts," or *partes* (to employ the Latin word that classical and medieval geographers used—not synonymously—for what we today call "continents"). An anachronistic nomenclature is helpful, however, in making it clear to the modern viewer that the surviving depiction preserves almost all of Africa, has lost almost all of Asia, and shows Europe south of a line running approximately from Northern Ireland through Bohemia to the north coast of the Black Sea. Despite its current incompleteness, however, the Bell Map contains important information about its origins and purpose.

First of all, paleographical evidence indicates that the map was assembled between ca. 1440 and ca. 1460, by a cartographer who was probably a native speaker of German with an Austro-Bavarian dialect, a clear aspect of which (*p* for *b*) is evident in the vernacular legend "n'purh" [= n*urem*purh] (Nuremberg) and even the Latin provincial designation "pritania" (Brittany). The handwriting is that of a southern German from ca. 1450, and it is more reliable as a marker of the date of composition than are the legends themselves, which must be read with a critical eye. Although the Canary Islands are described as being "recently discovered," we cannot conclude that this drawing was made in the first decade of the fifteenth century, when this much-heralded event took place.[9] Similarly, the identification of Constantinople as "capital of the Greeks" does not prove that the map pre-dates 1453, since Turkish domination there was long held in Europe to be a temporary misfortune.[10]

Second, the map is a product of what might be called luxurious cartography. Its surface is vellum: in its original state it was presumably a single sheet of carefully cured animal skin the size of a small tablecloth. It is richly and colourfully painted. Waterways—oceans, seas, and rivers—are teal, with striation representing the action of waves. Mountain ranges appear as a brownish wash. Cities are specifically located with black dots, many of them adjacent to an architectural design consisting of some combination of towers, domes, and smaller buildings, decorated mostly in white, red, and black. The civic depictions of the fabled Isle of the Dead (at top-centre) and Cyprus (near the left edge, one-quarter of the way from the bottom) include archways that still glimmer with silver. Ringing the outer rim of the earth are semicircles, only one of which, at the map's top-centre edge, is (almost) complete. Within it is represented the head and torso of a young man with an ochre-coloured hat and flowing fair hair, wearing a red jacket over a teal-collared shirt. He, like figures in the three other surviving semicircles, is an anthrovent, the personification of one of the twelve primary and secondary winds identified by medieval (and later) geographers and cartographers. At the map's upper-left corner, one of these surrounding semicircles intrudes into the round earth (a signal that this indicates Auster, the primary wind from the south); the vellum is now flecked in white and ochre but it appears to have been decorated originally with gold that has been scraped away. The Bell Map is thus a cartographical gem that was produced at considerable expense, although whether its first owner was clerical or secular is unknown.

Other key features of the Bell Map include its orientation to the south (its world looks more familiar to an Amero-European today if it is turned upside-down). This is one of several indications that Arabic science may have had some influence on the map's production. Another is the extension of the earth's land mass in the southern hemisphere almost to the Antarctic pole, an image verbally underscored, somewhat obscurely, by a fragmentary legend.[11] Most world maps produced in Europe before the later 1400s were oriented, literally, to the east, and they represent territory inhabited by humans as being largely or exclusively north of the equator, following theories of climate zones, developed by the ancient Greeks, that held the equatorial region to be a torrid belt whose heat made life impossible. During the Middle Ages, European scholars rarely availed themselves of the hugely important—if by this time largely inactive—scientific information-gathering found in Arab (and usually Arabic) sources, which included data about the east African coastline that patently challenged zonal assumptions. The map may thus be something of an aberration in what Bernard Lewis has characterized as an atmosphere of profound, mutual disinterest in western Christian and Muslim communities for nearly a millennium after the Hejira—a third feature of its significance.[12]

From the standpoint of the history of cartography, however, the map's most remarkable characteristic may be the many dots that serve to mark the exact locations in space of some eighty-one cities. These dots—as well as the design's overall frame, its orientation, the text of its many legends, and the representations of cities and peoples—link the Bell Map to the Vienna-Klosterneuburg school of geographical science, the importance of which to the history of geography was the subject of a monograph by Dana Bennett Durand, whose historical findings remain largely unchallenged half a century after they were published.[13] (His conviction that the fifteenth-century scholars who are the subject of his study illustrate "the complex process by which the science of the Middle Ages was transformed into that of the modern world" assumes a kind of historical intellectual progress that is no longer taken for granted, however.)[14]

Durand amassed considerable evidence that, during the early 1400s, technologies of measurement and theories of spatial representation based on mathematical and astronomical data were developed by a loosely connected group of clerics, principally resident at the great Augustinian foundation at Klosterneuburg but also working in Benedictine monasteries from eastern Austria to Bavaria, together with professors at universities from Vienna to Bamberg. In so doing, Durand argued, they revolutionized the way that geographies were written and maps were drawn. Major figures at this school were already active and teaching by 1406; the most important work occurred during the period from 1420 to 1440. Among the principal scientific influences was the second-century polymath Ptolemy, whose Greek *Geography* began to circulate in Europe around 1407 in Jacopo Angelo's Latin translation, after having been largely lost or linguistically unavailable for almost a millennium. Ptolemy's argument that places in the "real" world can and *ought* to be located on a map by means of calculations, together with his thousands of co-ordinates fixing such places, found receptive readers among the Vienna-Klosterneuburg scholars, who developed their own schemes for recording geographical data. Ptolemy himself appears on the Bell Map: he is a tall figure wearing a crown at the upper-left edge of the fragment, adjacent to a legend whose placement appears to indicate a serious misunderstanding of his theory of the extent of the earth's land mass.[15]

Durand argued that intellectuals within the Vienna-Klosterneuburg circle had, by 1425, constructed a world map using a co-ordinate system. This design was copied with embellishments by one "Magister Reinhard" during his residence at Salzburg between 1434 and 1436.[16] These maps (and, records suggest, several others) are lost, but Durand identified two later, somewhat hybrid, exemplars that do survive: the Walsperger Map of 1448 and the Zeitz Map of ca. 1470.[17] The Bell Map is a *third* member of this cartographical family, in its original state slightly larger than Walsperger's sizable production, and, unlike its siblings, richly illuminated. Durand also uncovered a manuscript with descriptive material, lists of toponyms, and tables that record both legends and a set of numerical calculations of latitude and longitude.[18] The calculations—which form sets of co-ordinate tables—together with a jumbled version of Ptolemy's *Cosmographia*, were copied out by Fridericus Amann, a Benedictine monk at St. Emmeram's in Regensburg, between 1447 and 1455.[19] These data prove that precision applied equally to the location of individual cities and to the "sprawl" of rivers and mountain ranges; they also contain specific instructions that would have enabled an artist to render people and other design features. For example, the Bell Map somewhat obscurely depicts a human reclining supine with a large object overhead. The adjacent legends—"Latipedia" and "These [people] lie protected from the rain under a foot"—clarify the image somewhat, but a notation in one of Amann's texts is far more helpful: "In Latibedia there are people with only one broadly extended foot, whom one depicts with a right foot."[20] Within what Durand called the Vienna-Klosterneuburg "map corpus," as it existed around 1450, the Bell Map was certainly not unique in its decoration; at the same time, among late medieval world maps (as opposed to navigational charts), it is unusual for its representation of scale, as registered most obviously in the accuracy (from a modern perspective) of its coastlines.

The representation of the Latipedian humanoid, together with other designs on the Bell Map, particularly in Africa, may serve to remind us of its more traditional qualities as well. Religious concerns—even sectarianism—very much occupy the cartographer. Almost every architectural design representing a city has at least one tower surmounted by either a cross or a crescent, identifying it as Christian or non-Christian (but not necessarily Muslim, since some crescents designate a place whose inhabitants practise pagan behaviours).[21] The map records (along its left edge) the pathway taken by the Children of Israel on their flight from Pharaoh.[22] At the same time, it should be noted that the Bell Map appears to be less polemical than are other texts related to the Vienna-Klosterneuburg school. For example, it nowhere offers a moral judgement about inhabitants of places, as evidently did the one that, according to Amann's record, depicted the "poz [böse] hayden" (evil heathens) of Magrabia.[23]

Somewhat more telling about the cartographer's attitude toward areas of the world remote from central Europe is the fact that, except for the anthrovents, all the people found on the surviving fragment are in what we today would call Africa. Both text and image highlight their oddity. These populations are definitely not monsters—their cities are illustrated with the buildings of civilization and they profess religious creeds—yet they do seem monstrous. Some are eerily misshapen: the artist decorates a human body with a goat's head, a fox's tail, and a lion's head, as adjacent legends prescribe.[24] One of the map's largest, most distinctive paintings shows a woman wearing a flowing blue gown with a high bodice; her head, which is now faint except for a glaring set of eyes, sprouts five (perhaps six) extensions that resemble feathers. A nearby legend identifies her as "Pallas, said to have nine heads." This information is clarified by a notation at approximately this same place on the mostly undecorated Walsperger Map: "Pallas had nine heads: three human, six serpentine."[25] Other Africans, such as the sun-worshippers mentioned above (and perhaps all those whose cities are topped by crescents), are spiritually benighted, while a society that decapitates its king after he has ruled for one year would have aroused a considerable *frisson* in royalist Europe of the Middle Ages.[26] Unlike the *monstruosi populi* who inhabit southern lands on some of the most famous *mappaemundi*, however, these strange folk (except for the sciapod) are not drawn from the ancient catalogues of wonders compiled by encyclopaedists like Solinus and Isidore of Seville. Instead, the sources for their physical and social deformity are the Latin *mirabilia*, folk-tales, and vernacular romances such as *Herzog Ernst*.[27]

The Bell Map's pictures serve an obvious practical purpose: they occupy space that was mysterious to the cartographer and just about anyone else in fifteenth-century Europe. Although some two-thirds of the land area on the surviving map would today be designated African, fewer than one-third of its legends are found in this territory. The distribution of these bits of explanatory text is indeed illuminating, as the following list indicates. It records the numbers of legends found in each of the geographical areas displayed on the fragment today. (Medieval geographers conventionally placed Egypt within Asia and grouped Mediterranean islands separately from Europe, Asia, or Africa; thus these areas are treated as distinct units.)

Africa	41
Asia	11
Egypt	10
Europe	79
Mediterranean islands	6
Outer cosmological rings	5

Africa not only has surprisingly few legends, the ones that exist emphasize its strangeness by highlighting its peculiar people in relation to what medieval Europeans would have taken as markers of civilization. It has designated ten cities and thirteen regions or kingdoms, but also eleven people(s), including Ptolemy, the hapless king, drowned Pharaoh, and serpentine Pallas. By contrast, Europe's seventy-nine legends identify sixty cities, fifteen regions or kingdoms, one island, two waterways, and one historical event (the discovery of the Canary Islands [see note 9]). The pictures, in other words, appear where other kinds of data were unavailable, and it has long been Africa's fate to be richly illustrated in European cartography, which seems to be marked by a particular vulnerability to *horror vacui*.[28]

The Zeitz Map, which has no decoration whatever, fills much of the territory at its top (south) with lengthy texts, most of them identifying curious population groups. The Walsperger Map has some empty space in central Africa, but that is surrounded by mountains and waterways. The Bell Map's somewhat contradictory character—an intelligent, even avant-garde representation of the world whose cartographer has presented the Africa of myth and folk-tale— is by no means idiosyncratic. When Ptolemy's *Geography* was first printed (entitled *Cosmographia*), with copperplate maps, by Arnold Buckinck at Rome in 1478, and with woodcut maps, by Lienhart Holle at Ulm in 1482, Africa was still home to Ethiopian fish-eaters ("Ichthophagi Aethiopes"), ostrich devourers ("Struchophagi Aethiopes"), and cannibals ("Anthropophagi Aethiopes").[29]

In making this latter point, I have employed—with obvious ambivalence—a continental terminology that is under challenge.[30] Indeed, the Bell Map itself makes no clear division of its depicted earth into *partes*; names of provinces and kingdoms are given in red ink, but no hierarchically superior nomenclature can be found (or remains, at any rate) on the fragment.[31] The word *Affrica* does appear twice: once in its Roman political sense designating a "kingdom" that approximates modern-day Tunisia ("Affrica regio") and, also in conformity with classical ideas, naming the southwesterly wind that "whips up pestilence" ("Affricus pestilencias conflat").[32]

The Bell Map's characterization of Africa as home to physically and socially bizarre humans does correspond to a "continental discourse" that was employed during the later Middle Ages, however. In their brief survey of the "Architecture of Continents," Martin W. Lewis and Kären E. Wigen trace competing twofold and threefold systems for dividing the earth's landmass; they point out how the "elegant geometrical models" of the Greeks were inherited by medieval Europe "in a calcified and increasingly mythologized form."[33] Theoretical reasoning based on the harmonies of numbers that underlay "proofs" that the earth has two or three (or four) principal land areas was replaced by tendentious suppositions, such as those advanced in the mid-1300s by the Benedictine Ranulph Higden in his popular universal history, the *Polychronicon*, in which he attempted to prove, on moral grounds and somewhat reluctantly, that Africa ought to be treated as one of the earth's three *partes*. Higden's argument deserves to be cited in its entirety.

> Asya is moost in qua*n*tyte. Europa is lasse / and lyke
> in nombre of people. But Affryca is lest [least] of alle
> the .iii. partyes / bothe in place and in nombre of
> people. And therfore some men that knewe men and
> londes acou*n*ted but two partyes of the erthe
> oonly.Asya and Europe[.] And they acou*n*ted that
> Affryca is narowe in brede [distance from north to
> south] & euyll doers / corrupte ayer / wylde bestes &
> venemous dwellen therin. Therfore they that acounte
> Affryca the thyrde parte acounte not by space and
> mesure of lengthe and brede. But by dyuerse

dysposycions better and worse and departe Affryca
fro Europa and Asya as a sore membre *that* is not fro
membrys that ben hole and sounde & in good poynt
at the best. Also Affryca in his kynde hath lasse space.
And for the sturenes ['sternness': severity, inclemency
of climate (*inclementia caeli*)] of heuen it hath the
more wyldernes. And though Affryca be lytyll.it hath
more wyldernes and waste londe / for grete brennyng
of the hete of the sonne. Thenne [*read*: sun, than]
Europa for all the chele [chill] and grete colde that is
therinne. For why all that lyueth & groweth maye
better endure with colde than with hete. But mesure
ruleth bothe. ¶Plinius libro .vi. Therfore it is that
Europa nouryssheth and bryngeth forth fayr men
larger and gretter of body myghtyer of strengthe /
hardyer and bolder of herte and fayrer of shappe than
Affryca. For the sonne berne alwaye abydeth vpon
the men of affryca / and draweth out the humours &
maketh hem short of bodyes / blacke of skyn / crypse
of here [curly of hair]. And by drawyng out of
spirites maketh hem cowarde of herte. The contrarye
is of northeren men. In the colde without stoppeth
smale holes and porus [pores] / and holdeth the hete
within / & so maketh hem fatter gretter [taller] &
whyter within / & so hardyer & bolder of herte.[34]

After observing that knowledgeable authorities refuse to give Africa
equal status with Asia and Europe because it is "lytyll" in size and
sparse in population, Higden adopts an attitude of geographical
determinism to argue the opposite. He claims that Africa's location
renders it more vulnerable to wretched weather, which has left much
of the territory a wilderness inhabited by venomous animals and evil
people. These insalubrious qualities—Higden compares Africa to a
"sore member" on an otherwise healthy body—constitute the most
compelling reason to think of it as, in effect, a third continent.
Indeed, Higden does all he can to refute one solution advanced by
other geographers—that Africa should be considered an extension
of Europe—by dwelling on difference. Immoderate heat, he says,

causes Africans to lose vital bodily "humours" through the pores of their skin, rendering them small, scrawny, black of hue, curly-haired, and cowardly, whereas the relative chill of Europe produces people who are handsome, strapping, hardy, courageous, and white because their small skin pores prevent body heat from escaping. Africa is accounted a continent, but only because no one else wants it, no one else can identify with its inhabitants.

The Bell Map does not textually or visually convey the racist perspective that underlies Higden's analysis, but its vignettes of Africans depict them as lacking a certain moderation, even if here they are depicted with light skin, blond hair, and fine European fashion. Though only the fragment of a *mappamundi*, it bears witness to late medieval Europe's reclamation of Ptolemaic scientific cartography, its appropriation of Arabic empirical geography (possibly by members of the intellectual circle that produced it), and its incipient colonization in the Atlantic. In the area in which its cartographer lacked knowledge, however, the map borrows from a fund of ancient prejudices, telling the story of an Africa that is, as Félicité put it in Genet's play, a "drifting continent, ... withdraw[ing] into the past."

NOTES

1 Jean Genet, *The Blacks: A Clown Show*, trans. Bernard Frechtman (New York: Grove Press, 1960), p. 77. The play was originally published as *Les Nègres: clownerie*, ed. Marc Barbezat (Décines [Isère]: L'Arbalète, 1960). Its first performance was at the Théatre de Lutèce in Paris on 28 October 1959. Félicité's speech in the original is as follows:

> Tu es là, Afrique aux reins cambrés, à la cuisse oblongue? Afrique boudeuse, Afrique travaillée dans le feu, dans le fer, Afrique aux millions d'esclaves royaux, Afrique déportée, continent à la dérive, tu es là? Lentement vous vous évanouissez, vous reculez dans le passé, les récits des naufragés, les musées coloniaux, les travaux des savants ...." (p. 111)

2 Perhaps the best-known "revised" world map scheme is the Gall-Peters projection, but this gives to Africa an "attenuated, stretched look," as Mark Monmonier puts it in a trenchant attack on what, in his estimation, is cartography based on "preposterous assertions"; see *How to Lie with Maps* (Chicago: University of Chicago Press, 1991), pp. 96–98 (citations from pp. 97 and 98), and figure 7.7. Note also his discussion of "equal-area" map projections and ways in which the Mercator projection has been "abused," on pp. 10–14, 94–96, and in figures 2.5–2.6, 7.5–7.6.

3 On the construction of "continents" in Western thought, see Martin W. Lewis and Kären E. Wigen, *The Myth of Continents: A Critique of Metageography* (Berkeley: University of California Press, 1997). A crucial part of the authors' argument is that "[o]ur flawed metageography has become a vehicle for displacing the sins of Western civilization onto an intrusive non-European Other in our midst" (p. 68). In my discussion here I am fully aware of—but cannot entirely avoid—a principal concern of their book, which is the danger of dividing the world into neat halves: "West" versus "non-West" or "East" (pp. 6–7 and passim).

4 In their chapter "The Architecture of Continents," Lewis and Wigen demonstrate how various were European constructs of the earth's land mass (*The Myth of Continents*, pp. 21–31, and invaluable footnotes on pp. 214–19 nn. 1–68). The subject is central to Benjamin Braude's book in progress, *Sex, Slavery and Racism: The Secret History of the Sons of Noah*, to be published by Alfred A. Knopf. Among other insightful contributions he makes in this work, some of which I was able to read in manuscript in February 2000, Braude challenges the "myth" of a tripartite continental system based on the distribution of land to Shem, Japheth, and Ham according to Genesis 9:18–19 and 10:32; he expands significantly on his article "The Sons of Noah and the Construction of Ethnic and Geographical Identities in the Medieval and Early Modern Periods," *The William and Mary Quarterly*, 3rd ser., 54, no. 1 (January 1997): 103–41.

5 *Orientalism* (1978; reprint New York: Vintage, 1979), p. 3. Oumelbanine Zhiri sees a more active Europe in the sixteenth century than I do. She contends that Johannes Leo Africanus, born at Granada around 1490 and reared in north Africa, belongs to the "prehistory" of a European orientalism directed south rather than east. She argues further that his attempt to make Arab civilization comprehensible to European readers, coupled with their own misreadings, contributed to "the systematic exploration and colonization of Africa" (Zhiri, "The Frontiers of Leo Africanus," typescript, p. 3 [received March 1999]). This revises (and intensifies) somewhat the approach she takes in her books, *L'Afrique au miroir de l'Europe: Fortunes de Jean Léon l'Africain à la Renaissance* (Geneva: Droz, 1991) and *Les Sillages de Jean Léon l'Africain du XVIᵉ au XXᵉ siècle* (Casablanca: Wallada, 1996).

6 See Scott Westrem, *Learning from Legends on the James Ford Bell Mappamundi*, The James Ford Bell Lectures 37 (Minneapolis: Associates of the James Ford Bell Library, 2000); appendix 1 contains a transcription and translation of the 152 legends (or inscriptions) on this map, which is also the subject of a monograph I am completing for publication by the University of Minnesota Press, offering more detailed information about its acquisition, text and design, and relationship to other cartographical works (see n. 17, below).

7 The map's purchase was announced by John Parker, in "A fragment of a fifteenth-century planisphere in the James Ford Bell Collection," *Imago Mundi* 19 (1965): 106–07. Its two brief mentions are by Marcel Destombes in *Mappemondes A.D. 1200–1500: Catalogue préparé par la Commission des Cartes Anciennes de l'Union Géographique Internationale*, Monumenta Cartographica Vetustioris Aevi A.D. 1200–1500, vol. 1, ed. Roberto Almagià and Destombes, *Imago Mundi*, supp. 4 (Amsterdam: Israel, 1964), pp. 214–17 [52.11] (with a black-and-white reproduction [plate xxxii]); and David Woodward, "Medieval

Mappaemundi," in *Cartography in Prehistoric, Ancient, and Medieval Europe and the Mediterranean,* The History of Cartography, vol. 1, ed. J.B. Harley and Woodward (Chicago: University of Chicago Press, 1987), pp. 286–370, esp. pp. 316–17, 358 (also listed in appendix 18.2, p. 366). A photograph of the map appeared with no commentary in Geoffrey Ashe, *Atlantis: Lost Lands, Ancient Wisdom* (London: Thames and Hudson, 1992), p. 32. See also Westrem, *Learning from Legends,* pp. 3–10 and 21–29.

8 Other well-known displays of this kind include the third and fourth panels of the Catalan Atlas of ca. 1375, a vignette in the lower-left corner of the Fra Mauro Map of ca. 1459, and Giovanni di Paolo's *The Creation of the World and the Expulsion from Paradise,* painted at Siena after 1420 (New York, The Metropolitan Museum of Art). See also the masterful "reconstruction" of a *mappamundi* painted in 1345 for the communal palace at Siena (Marcia Kupfer, "The Lost Wheel Map of Ambrogio Lorenzetti," *Art Bulletin* 78, no. 2 [June 1996]: 286–310).

9 The legend reads "Insula canaria nouiter inuenta" (note the treatment of the toponym as a singular noun). The Castilian conquest of the Canaries, begun in 1402 by the Normans Jean IV de Béthencourt (1360–1422) and Gadifer de La Salle (ca. 1340–1422), and the islands' colonization, which began in 1405, were widely praised as heroic feats; see the popular French poem *Le Canarien,* completed by 1420 and greatly revised around 1490 (ed. Elías Serra Rafols and Alexandre Cioranescu, 3 vols. [Las Palmas: La Laguna, 1959–65]).

10 A legend adjacent to "Grecia Jmperiu[m]" reads "constant[inopolis?] caput grecorum."

11 The legend, which runs in an arc, has two lines, both of which are cut off at both ends by the fragment's edge. What survives reads "[pl?]aga australis uel alie[nus?] / [inhabitabilis prop?]ter nimium calorem ex" (The southern [region?] or other ... [is uninhabited on account of] great heat [from the sun?]).

12 Bernard Lewis, *The Muslim Discovery of Europe* (New York: Norton, 1982), passim (see esp. pp. 73, 81, 300); see note 16, below.

13 Dana Bennett Durand, *The Vienna-Klosterneuburg Map Corpus of the Fifteenth Century: A Study in the Transition from Medieval to Modern Science* (Leiden: Brill, 1952). Durand's book is the published version of his dissertation, submitted to Harvard University in 1934; the world war and Durand's decision to enter the foreign service rather than the academy delayed its appearance for over a decade (it was typeset in 1940). He did not know of the Bell Map's existence. Durand's work may warrant rigorous re-examination, however; see note 16, below.

14 Durand, *The Vienna-Klosterneuburg Map,* p. 29. His confidence at having found the "missing link" between medieval and modern cartography may be questioned today, or at least acknowledged to promote a pejorative view of *mappaemundi* as being unscholarly or intellectually vacant (C. Raymond Beazley refused to discuss them in his three-volume *The Dawn of Modern Geography* [London: 1897–1903; reprint New York: Peter Smith, 1949]). But the implication of Durand's book's subtitle was for George Bingham Fowler one good reason to give it lavish praise in his review in *Speculum* 32, no. 2 (1957): 359–63.

15 The legend reads "Ptholomeus ponit 180 gradus terre habitabilis" (Ptolemy reckons the inhabitable earth [to extend] 180 degrees [within the 360 degrees marking the spherical earth]). The placement of the legend near the southern extreme of the earth's surface (i.e., at the top of the map) suggests that the cartographer assumed Ptolemy's calculation to be of the earth's north-to-south extent and not, as was the case, of its expanse from east to west (a generous measurement that, combined with Ptolemy's similarly erroneous underestimate of the earth's size, prompted Christopher Columbus to assume that he could sail westward from Iberia and reach Asia in only a few weeks). The tradition from which the Bell Map comes correctly understood Ptolemy's figure (Durand, *The Vienna-Klosterneuburg Map*, pp. 176–77, 372–73). The depiction of a crowned Ptolemy reflects medieval Europe's general confusion of the Alexandrian astronomer with the earlier kings of Egypt. Patrick Gautier Dalché analyses nineteen references to the *Geography* in Western sources written from the early fifth to the fourteenth centuries by way of demonstrating that Ptolemy's work was never completely forgotten in Europe, and that its content may have been known in some form to such influential writers as Roger Bacon; see Gautier Dalché, "Le souvenir de la *Géographie* de Ptolémée dans le monde latin médiéval (VIe–XIVe siècles)," *Euphrosyne: Revista de Filologia Clássica*, n.s. 27 (1999): 79–106, at pp. 80, 105–06.

16 Durand, *The Vienna-Klosterneuburg Map*, pp. 209–17; see also pp. 27–29. Gautier Dalché has recently questioned Durand's assumptions that the co-ordinate tables were used in connection with map production, and that the cartographer Nicholas Germanus (who produced Ptolemaic maps before the age of printing) was linked to the Vienna-Klosterneuburg circle. Moreover, he doubts Durand's contention that the data or maps linked to this school show Arabic influence. In his judgement, Durand frequently makes gratuitous conjectures and rarely offers solid evidence for his attributions; see Gautier Dalché, "Pour une histoire du regard géographique: Conception et usage de la carte au XVe siècle," *Micrologus* 4 (1996): 77–103, at pp. 85, 93–95. Gautier Dalché's criticisms of Durand do not affect my central premise, which is that the Bell Map, particularly in its representation of Africa, is cartographically sophisticated but textually naïve.

17 Andreas Walsperger's map is now at Vatican City, Biblioteca Apostolica Vaticana, MS Pal. lat. 1362b; it measures 75 cm x 59 cm (29 ¼ in. x 23 in.) and its depicted earth has a diameter of 42.5 cm (16 ½ in.). Walsperger explicitly links its production to Ptolemy's geographical work (in one legend he calls his map "facta ex cosmographyca ptholomey"). The Zeitz map is bound into a volume containing, among other texts, a manuscript copy of Ptolemy's *Geographia* [entitled *Cosmographia*]; it is Zeitz, Stiftsbibliothek, MS lat. hist. 497, fol. 48r. The Zeitz Map has been trimmed (in binding, presumably) on the left and right (east and west) sides, with loss of text and image; its vertical diameter is 22.5 cm (8 ⅞ in.). A transcription of Walsperger Map legends by Konrad Kretschmer is unreliable; see Kretschmer, "Eine neue mittelalterliche Weltkarte der vatikanischen Bibliothek," *Zeitschrift der Gesellschaft für Erdkunde zu Berlin*, 3rd ser. 26 (1891): 371–406 (legends recorded here are my own readings and translations). It is the subject of a brief essay (and black-and-white illustration) in Roberto Almagià, *Planisferi, carte nautiche e affini dal secolo XIV al XVII esistenti nella Biblioteca Apostolica Vaticana*, Monumenta Cartographica Vaticana, vol. 1, ed. Roberto Almagià (Vatican City: Biblioteca

Apostolica Vaticana, 1944), pp. 30–31 and plate xii. A small colour illustration is in Harley and Woodward, *Cartography in Prehistoric*, plate 21. No transcription exists of Zeitz Map legends; an image of it can be found only in Durand's book (*The Vienna-Klosterneuburg Map*, plate xvi).

18 The numerical units (found in five cosmographical texts) represent a co-ordinate system that is not derived from Ptolemy. The tables include five columns of numbers. The first three record longitudinal locations, which are measured in terms of *signa* (of which there are eleven for the entire earth), *gradus* (there are thirty degrees in each sign), and *minuta* (sixty within each degree). The last two are latitudinal calculations, in *gradus* and *minuta* alone.

19 Durand's appendices 11–17 (*The Vienna-Klosterneuburg Map*, pp. 371–501) contain his transcriptions of Amann's remarkable collection of texts (and other related material). Amann's work (1447–55) is found in Munich, Bayerische Staatsbibliothek, clm. 14583, fols. 98r–v, 222r–77v, 286r–98r, 300r–312r, and 315r–19r; and clm. 14504, fols. 103v–105r.

20 The Latin legend on the Bell Map is "Hy latent sub pede ex pluuia." The Middle High German of Durand's manuscript text reads "der in Latibedia da seint leut nur mit Aim füsz praiten der ain gemalt mit aim rechten füß" (*The Vienna-Klosterneuburg Map*, p. 449 [Durand prints the umlaut as a superscript *e*]). Notice of a human population equipped with a single foot, which makes possible rapid locomotion and umbrella-like protection from the hot sun (not rain), dates at least to Herodotus (between 443 and ca. 425 B.C.E.); they are more generally called *sciapodes* and *monoculi* (by writers well known to medieval readers, such as Solinus and Isidore of Seville).

21 A crescent stands atop a tower next to the legend "Hy solem colui et pro deo adorant" (These ones worship the sun as [their] god). Neither cross nor crescent is associated with the large architectural construct on "Insula iouis et immortalitatis" (The island of Jove and of immortality). In one legend in the margin of his map, Walsperger notes that he uses red dots to identify Christian cities and black dots for heathen ones. This kind of symbolism is a feature of the late Middle Ages; of many hundred architectural designs on the Hereford Map (ca. 1300), for example, only seven are shown with a cross (none has a crescent), and of these only two are explicitly Christian towns; see Westrem, *The Hereford Map: A Transcription and Translation of the Legends with Commentary*, Terrarum Orbis 1 (Turnhout: Brepols, 2001), pp. xxxix–xl and n. 69.

22 The route is drawn in below a legend recording "Submersio pharonis" (The drowning of Pharaoh). The pathway of the Exodus is also shown on the Hereford Map (Westrem, *The Hereford Map*, pp. 125–26, 128–29, 164–65 [legends 278, 287, 381]).

23 Durand, *The Vienna-Klosterneuburg Map*, pp. 449, 452.

24 The legends read "Hy habent capita caprina" (These ones have the heads of goats); "Hy habent caudas wlpium" (These ones have the tails of foxes); and "Hy habent capita leonum" (These ones have the heads of lions). The map's image of a sciapod has already been noted (see n. 20, above).

25 The Bell Map has "Pallas fertur nouem habuisse capita"; the analogous statement on the Walsperger Map is "Pallas nouem habuit capita tria humana

sex serpentina." Amann records a *people* named "Balas" who "habent 3 menschen antliß und 6 slangen heuptner" (have three human faces and six serpents' heads); Durand, *The Vienna-Klosterneuburg Map*, pp. 451, 452.

26 On sun-worshippers, see note 21, above. Near the southern coast of Africa, a rather large painting shows a man with a crown kneeling and facing away from a smaller man who raises a sword over his right shoulder; the adjacent legend reads "Hic rex post an[n]um decollatur" (Here the king is beheaded after one year). Both men are dressed like stylish Europeans, in smart, red, waist-length tunics and knee-high boots, the executioner's being blue on his right foot and red on his left. The misshapen humans and the anthrovents are similarly dressed. Rudolf Wittkower notes that the fabulous races in a fifteenth-century manuscript copy of Thomas of Cantimpré's *Liber de monstuosis hominibus* (1237–40) are depicted "in Flemish bourgeois costume"; see Wittkower, "Marvels of the East: A Study in the History of Monsters," in *Allegory and the Migration of Symbols* (1977; reprint London: Thames and Hudson, 1987), pp. 45–74 and 196–205, at p. 57 (the article was first published in 1942).

27 The leonine-headed people are in John Block Friedman, *The Monstrous Races in Medieval Art and Thought* (Cambridge, MA: Harvard University Press, 1981), pp. 144, 147; otherwise his "monsters" are the more conventional ones like people with dogs' heads or body-length ears or eyes in their chests. On the stereotypical treatment of Africa and Africans, see Adele J. Haft, "Maps, Mazes, and Monsters: The Iconography of the Library in Umberto Eco's *The Name of the Rose*," *Studies in Iconography* 14 (1995): 9–50. On "monstrosities in popular imagery," including "tailed men," see Wittkower, "Marvels of the East," pp. 69–74, 204–05.

28 It is entirely possible that missing parts of the Bell Map were also illustrated, particularly territory in Asia, which is almost completely omitted. Amann's tables and notes record co-ordinates for legends and, apparently, depictions in Asia for Amazons, Prester John, and the shrine of St. Thomas in India. The Walsperger Map has a single representation of a "human": a giant member of the fearsome *anthropophagi* (cannibals) in northern Asia; see Andrew Colin Gow, "Gog and Magog on *mappaemundi* and early printed world maps: Orientalizing ethnography in the apocalyptic tradition," *Journal of Early Modern History* 2, no. 1 (1998): 61–88, at p. 78. Gow concludes with Jonathan Swift's famous quip about the makers of "Afric-Maps" who "o'er uninhabitable Downs / Place Elephants for want of Towns" (p. 88).

29 In both editions, these legends come from the atlas map marked "Quarta Africae Tabula." They also appear in the Holle's reprint, in 1486, and another Italian edition, in 1490.

30 See notes 3 and 4, above. I have been trying to avoid making "the immediate physical area of [my] own experience ... the normative center of the world," a process Braude calls "viciniacentricity" (*Sex, Slavery and Racism*, typescript).

31 This is not so odd as it may seem. While many medieval *mappaemundi* contain the names of the earth's three *partes*, they often accompany a written text that offers this same information; some of the most frequently reproduced of these are diagrammatic maps that appear at, or near, the beginning of Book 14 of Isidore of Seville's *Etymologies* ("De Terra et Partibus"). The reversed locations of the "continental" designations "EUROPA" and "AFFRICA" on the

Hereford Map are, in Valerie I.J. Flint's estimation, "a mistake whose dimensions inspire a certain awe"; see Flint, "The Hereford Map: Its Author(s), Two Scenes and a Border," *Transactions of the Royal Historical Society,* 6th ser. 8 (1998): 19–44 (at p. 23). I might also point out that in the upper half of the Hereford Map, "ASIA" (running vertically) competes for attention with a horizontal "INDIA" (the two words form a T). All four legends are in gold; see Westrem, *The Hereford Map,* pp. 20–21, 26–27.

32 The Vienna-Klosterneuburg corpus is not completely absent of "continentalist" thinking. In his transcriptions of world maps, Fridericus Amann announces proudly in a heading that he had acquired his information from the "cosmographies" of Ptolemy, Honorius (he says "pope" but must mean Augustodunensis), Marco Polo, and Pomponius Mela, the latter being especially valuable for his role as "der welt-ausz tayler" (world divider) in his *De chorographia* (known during the later Middle Ages and the early modern period as *De situ orbis*); see Durand, pp. 176, 371–72.

33 Lewis and Wigen, *The Myth of Continents,* pp. 21–25; citations at pp. 22, 23.

34 Ranulph Higden, *Polychronicon* (ca. 1342), trans. John Trevisa (18 April 1387), edited and extended [from 1358 to 1461] by William Caxton (Westminster: Caxton, 1482); citation here from the second edition (Westminster: Wynkyn de Worde, 13 April 1495), sig. A.7.v^a–b (I.7). I cite this English version not only because it is nearly contemporaneous with the production of the Bell Map, but also because it is relatively comprehensible today. Nevertheless, the following translation into modern English may be helpful:

> [Of the three divisions of Earth] Asia is greatest in size. Europe is lesser [in land area] and similar in its number of people. Africa is the least of all three divisions, both in terms of area and number of people. And therefore some men who were knowledgeable about peoples and lands reckoned only two divisions of the earth: Asia and Europe. And they reckoned that Africa is narrow in width [north-to-south], and that evildoers, corrupt air, and wild and venomous beasts live there. Thus, they who reckon Africa to be a third division [of the earth] reckon not according to land area and measurements of length and width [east-to-west and north-to-south], but according to various natural inclinations—better and worse—and classify Africa from Europe and Asia as a distress-causing member [of the body] that is [separate] from members that are whole and sound and in fine fettle. In addition, Africa, given its natural condition, has less space [that is habitable]. And owing to its inclement climate, it has a greater amount of desolate wilderness. And although Africa is small in size, it has more desolate wilderness and wasteland, on account of the extreme burning of the sun's heat, than does Europe, despite the chill and extreme cold that are found there, since everything that lives and grows can survive better in cold than in heat. Yet moderation rules both (see Pliny, *Natural History,* Book 6). Thus it is that Europe fosters and brings forth good-looking humans whose are larger and taller in body, mightier in strength, hardier and bolder of heart, and better looking in shape than [the people of] Africa. For the sun burns constantly upon the people of Africa and draws out their humours

[essential bodily fluids], and makes them short in stature, black of skin, curly of hair—and by [this] drawing out of spirit, makes them cowardly of heart. The opposite is [true] of northern people. Outside, in the cold, small holes and [skin] pores stop and retain the [body's] heat, and so makes them fatter, taller, and whiter, and, thus, hardier and bolder of heart.

Vilnius, ca. 1685, as depicted in a copperplate by Daniel Pelzeldt, from
Dmytro Stepovyk, *Oleksandr Tarasevyč (Kyiv: Mystectvo, 1975); used by*
permission.

The Bells of Vilnius

Keeping Time in a City of Many Calendars

DAVID FRICK

O n 25 June 1640, King Władysław IV of Poland-Lithuania signed a decree that banned the Calvinist church, school, and hospital from the royal city of Vilnius to a new site, just beyond the walls. In an attempt to explain the measure, the document attributed recent unrest in this royal city to the close proximity of the places of worship attended by the feuding parties:

> And since it is evident that the *situation* [my
> emphasis] of the Calvinist church among Catholic
> churches gave the occasion for both the earlier and
> the current excesses, and since we, by Our royal oath,
> are obliged to avert all occasions for causing disorder,
> to say nothing of violating the peace among dissidents
> in religion, therefore, by Our royal judgment, we
> remove from that place in perpetuity all exercise of
> the faith of the dissidents, both public and private.[1]

The decision and its effects were fraught with ambiguities. On the one hand, the decree was a step toward placing legal barriers against the practice of any Christian confession other than the Roman Catholic; as such it was a landmark in the progress of the Counter-Reformation in Poland-Lithuania. On the other hand, thanks in part to traditions of a practical, everyday toleration in Vilnius, the results did not come close to the goals of the Catholic parties. The Calvinists immediately re-established their complex just outside the city walls, and the Lutherans remained inside the walls, on German Street, both congregations surviving well into the twentieth century. Even the king's ban drew upon the language of Poland's traditions of tolerance: the royal goal, after all, was the maintenance of "peace among dissidents in religion."[2]

I present some preliminary considerations from a larger project that investigates the proximities that were blamed for the unrest in this instance and in others. My attempt will be to uncover details of the day-to-day encounters between people of different ethnicities, religions, and languages, across a range from the amicable to the violent, from matrimony to murder. I will examine how and with what results people of mid-seventeenth-century Vilnius came—or did not come—into contact in a variety of life situations: in rituals of birth and name-giving; in the family; at school; at work; in conversation; in the marketplace; in and before the magistrate; at worship; in neighbourhoods; in public processions and displays; in the service of the nobles; in time-keeping; in sickness and poverty; at death. Here I focus on the question of time-keeping and the tensions caused by the various public and private calendars. But first, I offer a brief historical overview of the city's peoples, religions, and languages.

TOO CLOSE FOR COMFORT?

Visitors to Vilnius remarked—often in neutral or even marvelling tones—upon what the king gave as one reason for his decision to ban the Calvinists beyond the walls: the close proximity of an unusual variety of peoples, religions, and languages. One Samuel Kiechel, citizen of Ulm, who spent eleven days in Vilnius during the summer of 1585, at the beginning of a four-year peregrination to the Holy Lands, noted, in addition to the city's "schlimm wasser, schlecht und gering bier" (poor water, bad and little beer) the following details:

> The houses are generally all built of wood and
> covered with boards, with the exception of two of the
> most fashionable streets or ways, in which to the

greater extent Germans and others live as merchants, who then also have their own church and pastor, whose salary they pay amongst themselves. In addition to the "Martinists" [i.e., followers of Martin Luther], the city has also many sorts of religions and sects, all of whom have their churches and public *exercitia* [exercises], such as papists, Calvinists, Jesuits, Ruthenians or Muscovites, Anabaptists, Zwinglians, and Jews, who also have their synagogue and place of gathering. Then there are also the heathens, or Tatars, and all the religions, companies, and sects have *libertatem conscientiae* [freedom of conscience], in which no one is hindered.[3]

Our Ulmer may have erred a little on the high side, but only slightly, in his estimation of the extent of Vilnius's religious variety;[4] moreover, even in 1585 not all religions and sects enjoyed the same kind of "freedom of conscience." Nonetheless, he was not far wrong, and the picture still had a certain basic validity in 1640.

Vilnius was a mixed city even before the formal Christianization of Lithuania in 1386 under the sponsorship of the Polish Roman Catholic church. At that point, pagan Lithuanians, Orthodox Ruthenians (ancestors of modern Belarusians and Ukrainians), and Catholic Germans inhabited the city. Orthodox culture enjoyed a certain favour in those days: many Ruthenians had moved to the city after Kievan Rus' came under Lithuanian rule in the thirteenth century, bringing with them the Cyrillic-based Ruthenian that would become a language of culture and remain the official chancery language of the Grand Duchy of Lithuania until the end of the seventeenth century; consequently, some of the first individual cases of conversion among the Lithuanian élite were to Orthodox Christianity. At this point, the pagan temple coexisted peacefully with the German Catholic and Ruthenian Orthodox churches. Some scholars have located the origins of Vilnius' traditions of *practical* toleration in these patterns that were established in the pre-conversion period.[5]

The city would always retain a significant Ruthenian presence, and the use of chancery Ruthenian remained a mark of

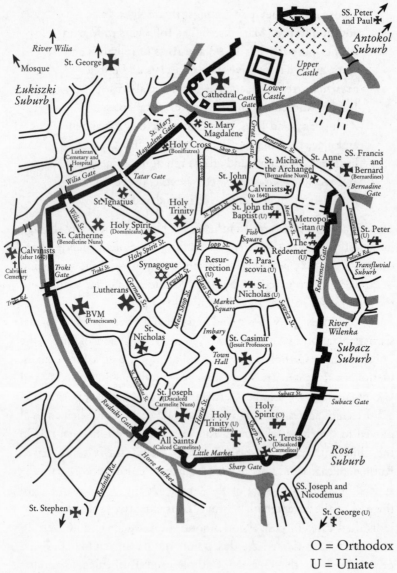

River Wilia

Mosque

Łukiszki
Suburb

St. George

SS. Peter
and Paul

Antokol
Suburb

Upper
Castle

Cathedral

Castle
Gate

Lower
Castle

St. Mary
Magdalene

Lutheran
Cemetary and
Hospital

Holy Cross
(Bonifratres)

Wilia Gate

Tatar Gate

Skop St.

St. Michael
the Archangel
(Bernardine Nuns)

St. Anne

SS. Francis
and
Bernard
(Bernardines)

St. John

Calvinists
(to 1640)

Bernardine
Gate

St. Ignatius

Holy
Trinity

St. John the
Baptist (U)

Metropol-
itan (U)

St. Peter
(U)

St. Catherine
(Benedictine Nuns)

Holy Spirit
(Dominicans)

Fish
Square

The
Redeemer
(U)

Redeemer Gate

Transfluvial
Suburb

Calvinists
(after 1640)

Calvinist
Cemetery

Troki
Gate

Troki St.

Holy Spirit St.

Synagogue

Jopp St.

Resur-
rection
(U)

St. Paras-
covia (U)

St.
Nicholas (U)

Pollock Rd.

River
Wilenka

Lutherans

BVM
(Franciscans)

German St.

Jewish St.

Glass St.

Market
Square

Subacz
Suburb

St.
Nicholas

Imbary

St. Casimir
(Jesuit Professors)

Town
Hall

Subacz Gate

St. Joseph
(Discalced
Carmelite Nuns)

Subacz St.

Holy
Trinity (U)
(Basilians)

Holy
Spirit (O)

St. Teresa
(Discalced
Carmelites)

Rosa
Suburb

All Saints
(Calced Carmelites)

Little Market

Sharp Gate

Rudniki Rd.

Horse Market

SS. Joseph and
Nicodemus

St. Stephen

St. George (U)

O = Orthodox
U = Uniate

Churches in Vilnius, ca. 1640. Courtesy of the author.

Lithuanian identity long after the élite stopped using the language. Nonetheless, the conversion of Lithuania to Roman Catholicism brought with it a change in the attitude of Lithuanian society toward the Ruthenian aspect of its identity. It laid the foundation for four centuries of political federation between the Lithuanian and Polish states, which opened the doors to significant Polish immigration. More important here, it facilitated a linguistic and cultural Polonization of the Lithuanian élite that would eventually reach to the burghers, leaving, by the early seventeenth century, the greatest concentrations of Lithuanian speakers in the countryside.

The late fourteenth century also marked the arrival in the area of Vilnius of numbers of Tatars and Karaim. The Tatars had no legal right to live within city walls; they settled with a wooden mosque and a school, in the adjacent suburb of Łukiszki (in Lithuanian, Lukiškės), and were thus a part of the city's daily life.[6] The Karaim (a medieval Jewish sect that had rejected rabbinical traditions) found a home in Troki (in Lithuanian, Trakai), a day's walk away. They would play a certain role in the life of Vilnius's Jewish community; they thus belong to the margins of the story.[7] Jews were slower to gain a legal footing in Vilnius than in other cities of Lithuania. In 1551 a royal decree exempted the Vilnius houses of the noble élite from the jurisdiction of the magistrate, thus preparing the way for Jews to rent those houses within the city walls, and eventually to buy them. The first synagogue came into being in 1573. And in 1593, in the wake of anti-Jewish riots, King Sigismund III gave the Jews of Vilnius a privilege to live on certain streets and to engage in certain occupations since, as he explained, "we already found the Jews living in Vilnius when we ascended the throne."[8]

After various false starts, the Reformation became a part of the city's life in the second half of the sixteenth century. The Lutherans, dating from 1555, and the Calvinists, from the 1560s, were permanent fixtures in the confessional landscape of Vilnius. An urban anabaptist movement with some levelling tendencies experienced a brief life in the 1570s, but it left no permanent marks on the religious life of the city.[9] The Lutheran church was largely non-noble, comprising a portion of the urban ruling élite, plus merchants and artisans; its two congregations, a German-speaking majority and a Polish-speaking minority, shared the same building and, sometimes, the same bilingual ministers. The Calvinist church was largely noble, although some burghers did appear in its midst; it had a Polish-speaking majority and a German-speaking minority.

In 1596, as a result of the Union of Brest, the majority of the Ruthenian Orthodox church *hierarchy* agreed to enter into communion with Rome, forming what is known as the Greek Catholic or Uniate church. Much of the Ruthenian *flock*, however, rejected the move; they thus, in their view, remained truly Orthodox and heirs to all Greek rights and privileges. All the churches of Vilnius that were Orthodox in 1595 were eventually turned over to the Uniates. In 1598 the Orthodox established a new centre in the Holy Spirit church, monastery, hospital, and brotherhood, just across the street from what was now the leading Uniate church, monastery, hospital, and brotherhood of the Holy Trinity.[10]

In 1640, Poles, Lithuanians, Germans, Ruthenians, Jews, and Tatars peopled this conurbation of approximately 14,000 inhabitants.[11] These peoples worshipped in some twenty-three Catholic and nine Uniate churches, one Orthodox, one Calvinist, and one Lutheran church, one synagogue, and one mosque. They spoke Polish, Lithuanian, Ruthenian, German, Yiddish, and some Tatar; they prayed or wrote learned treatises also in Latin, Church Slavonic, Hebrew, Aramaic, and a little Arabic. The walls of Vilnius stretched for 2.9 km and enclosed an area of 0.8 km^2. (In size the city was not unlike Cracow, whose walls stretched 3.1 km and enclosed an area of 0.6 km^2).[12]

Vilnius received Magdeburg Law in 1387, and eventually members of all the Christian confessions could achieve citizenship. In 1536, after a city council consisting solely of Ruthenians or "Greeks" (that is to say, Orthodox) had been elected, the "Lachs" (a term that usually meant Poles, but here signified all Catholics, including Lithuanians and Germans) sought and obtained from King Sigismund I a privilege that decreed an equal division between Greeks and Romans in all future elections to the city council, including benchers, councillors, and burgomasters.[13] At this point (i.e., before the Reformation and before the Union of Brest), the terms "Roman" and "Greek" exhausted the range of Christian *confessions* represented in city government, although each term might cover more than one *ethnic* group. With the increasing fragmentation of Roman and

Greek Christianity in the course of the sixteenth century, more and more groups would compete for seats under the Roman and Greek quotas. And with the increasing political dominance of Roman Catholicism, some of the groups would find it increasingly difficult to succeed. Nonetheless, the principle of Roman-Greek parity would never be broken, and individuals from marginalized groups would be elected and sworn to office in Vilnius well after the "victory" of the Counter-Reformation.

I turn now to a series of investigations into the tensions caused—and certain accommodations necessitated—by the fact that the various peoples of Vilnius organized portions of their lives according to various calendars.

THE RUTHENIAN MONTH

Sometime soon after 1582 the expression "Ruthenian month" *(ruski miesiąc)* entered into the Polish language. It meant "a good long while," as in "they beat him so thoroughly that he had to salve his wounds a Ruthenian month."[14] The Ruthenian month was long because it was late—ten days in the sixteenth and seventeenth centuries and eleven days in the eighteenth, due to the ever-increasing discrepancy between the old, Julian calendar and the new, Gregorian one. For matters of official record-keeping, the jump was made in Poland-Lithuania sometime between 20 and 22 October, in 1582, the year when the calendar was first introduced by Pope Gregory XIII (and only sixteen to eighteen days behind the official date of 4 October set by the pope). The Catholic church, together with Catholic society in Poland, also made the change at this time.[15] But the new calendar was not imposed in more private matters, including the religious observance of non-Catholics. The Orthodox, the Uniates (after 1596), and *some* Protestants (I will return to this issue later) continued to adhere to the old calendar for varying lengths of time, the Orthodox and Uniates throughout the period in question and beyond.

In some regards, the Ruthenians and any others who remained on the old calendar were in a position similar to that of the Tatars, Jews, and Karaim, who kept time according to their own systems. They were allowed to use their own calendars for internal affairs but were forced to adapt to the dominant norm for any matters that reached beyond the limits of their own community. Life together in the worlds of politics, law, and commerce necessitated constant adaptation on the part of the more weakly situated groups. There were some cases of a certain syncretism. For example, in spite of attempts by the Jewish kahal (community council) to limit such procedures, the Lithuanian Jews sometimes registered business transactions conducted with other Jews not only with the Jewish court (and according to the Jewish calendar), but also with the local Christian courts (according to the new Roman calendar). Lithuanian Tatars, by contrast, sometimes used a hybrid dating system in correspondence with other Tatars—years given AD followed by Arabic months.[16]

If an Orthodox or Uniate individual or polity used the old calendar for some reason in correspondence with the non-Ruthenian world, the usage was clearly marked as such: "in the old fashion" or "according to the old calendar."[17] Otherwise, in dealings with the wider world, the "unmarked" mode of time-keeping usually implied the new calendar. But the fact that Ruthenians would even think of using their own time-keeping in correspondence with the "outside world" reflects a fundamental difference between the situation of this relatively subordinate group and that of the more thoroughly subordinate Jews, Karaim, and Tatars. Ruthenians were engaged in a losing battle *within* a dominant Christian world, and the various sides viewed the situation in this way.

The issue came to the fore soon after the introduction of the new calendar in Poland-Lithuania under King Stefan Bathory in 1582. Bathory directed two decrees specifically at Vilnius in 1586. One of the major sore points was the habit of Ruthenians (and also Jews and Tatars, and apparently some Catholics as well) to conduct business on Catholic holidays. The economic basis for the problem is obvious: if your own religious calendar required a certain number of days during which business could not be conducted, could you afford not to work also on the set of holidays celebrated by the dominant religion(s)? On 29 July 1586 Bathory issued a decree requiring Ruthenian merchants and artisans to rest on Catholic holidays:

> We have come to understand that there in Vilnius, on
> holy days according to the new calendar, which have
> been established by the universal Christian Roman
> Church, you initiate some sort of difference, open
> shops; and some of the merchants and artisans take
> care of other forbidden necessities. Further, people of
> the Ruthenian religion interpret letters published
> from our chancery according to their own intent.
> And thus, opposing this, we command that peace and
> the ancient custom in the celebration of holy days be
> maintained in this matter.[18]

Ruthenians might argue whether "ancient custom" had indeed been maintained in this fashion, but hereafter they could not conduct business on Catholic holy days without fear of punishment.

Vilnians at large, however, were not required by royal decree to have the same sort of regard for Ruthenian holy days. Thus whether or not an Orthodox or Uniate burgher rested according to the Ruthenian calendar remained an issue of discipline within the Orthodox and Uniate church communities. Nonetheless, certain compromises were made. In a decree of 8 September 1586, the king instructed the Vilnius magistrate not to force Ruthenians to appear before the municipal authorities on Ruthenian holidays:

> We command ... that you not cause any problems in
> this matter in this city of Vilnius for people of the
> Greek rite, and that you not make any obstacles in
> the celebration of holy days according to their rite,
> and especially the Birth of the Lord, His Baptism,
> Circumcision, Resurrection, the Lord's Ascension,
> the Descent of the Holy Spirit, the Trinity, all the
> holy days of the Most Holy Virgin Mary, and of the
> other Apostolic Holidays, according to their ancient
> custom and rite, and that, on these above-mentioned
> holy days, the people of the Greek rite not be
> summoned to the Town Hall and submitted to
> judgment by the courts ... and that oaths not be
> rendered by them on these holy days.[19]

Bathory charged the Vilnius magistrate "in the name of Christian love" to take pains that "one side not cause any scandal for the other," so that "the peace might be maintained in this city of ours in all respects."[20] Thus, at least in theory, Ruthenian merchants and artisans rested on Roman and Greek holy days, and the Vilnius magistrate rested on the Roman holy days and did limited business (not involving Orthodox parties) on the Greek.

In this manner, and in a few others, public life in the city of Vilnius took into account the annual cycles of the "Greek" inhabitants (both Uniate and Orthodox). But these accommodations to the Greeks were minimal; the city conducted its affairs largely on Roman time. And since the Greeks were involved at every step in the work of the city as a whole (to a much greater degree than the Jews and the Tatars), they were forced to make constant adjustments.

Consider the city's various guilds. Many of them were highly mixed organizations, and many made provisions for parity in power sharing among the elected officials in ways similar to those established for the magistrate. Typically, this meant a two- or three-way division of authority among a fixed number of "annual elders" (sometimes also among other lesser officials in strict parallelisms).[21] The Tailors' Guild, for example, in a charter of 1665, stipulated that there were to be six annual elders, "three of the Roman, and three of the Greek religion."[22] The Tanners' Guild, in a charter of 1672, specified that its six annually elected elders were to come "two from the Roman faith, another two from the Greek, and two from the German."[23]

In short, Greeks were represented in many guilds, and they often took part in their administration. And while their lives as Greek Christians (again, both Uniate and Orthodox) were governed by the rhythms of the Julian calendar, their lives as Greek tailors and Greek tanners were largely conducted according to the Gregorian calendar. Following traditions that reached well before the introduction of the new calendar, each guild was instructed to meet on established days identified by the saints' feasts. When, for example, the Cobblers' Guild, which shared power between Greeks and Romans, was directed on 9 December 1552 to meet each year on the festival of St. Nicholas to choose its elders, the timing was still one that united citizens of this particular trade.[24] After 1582 all such directions to meet on a particular date were a potential source of division. The Red- and Black-Leather Tanners (in articles dated 27 November 1614) agreed to meet annually on St. Michael's Day.[25] The fishermen (on 28 May 1664) decided to meet on the feast day of the fisher of men, "the Roman St. Peter's holiday according to the new calendar."[26] And the tailors wrote into their statute of 23 March 1665 that they would meet annually to choose their elders (three Romans and three Greeks) on the day of St. Nicholas.[27] All unspecified dates were according to the new calendar.

Guild membership brought with it a number of obligations that had implications for the organization of time. Each guild endeavoured to maintain a particular altar in a particular church, almost always Roman Catholic.[28] Members were required to attend Sunday and holy-day masses at their designated place of worship. Members were also obliged to present the guild colours in public processions ranging from secular events, such as the welcoming of the king to the city, to events that were not only religious but also closely identified with Roman Catholicism, such as Corpus Christi processions.[29] In the course of the seventeenth century a system of "buying out" evolved, whereby non-Catholic guild members could pay into the guild box for the right not to attend *certain* religious ceremonies. (But not all: guild members were generally required to take part in funeral services for their brethren.)[30] These provisions were both onerous and generous. Although they made living together easier, only the wealthier could afford to take advantage of them, and the result was that the non-Catholic guild member ended up supporting both the Catholic altar of his guild and that of his own church.

In addition to telling Vilnius guild members what they should do with their time on Sundays and Catholic holy days, the laws of the city told all inhabitants what they must not do. This concern is already familiar to us from Bathory's decree of 29 July 1586, ordering the Rus' of Vilnius "not to open their shops or to practice their trades on holy days according to the correction of the new calendar."[31] Similar concerns arose in contexts where Roman Catholics and peoples of other calendars came into close daily contact. One such place was in mixed households, which brought together husbands and wives, or masters and their servants, who were of different religions and confessions. Here, too, it was the Ruthenian who had—at least according to law—to make accommodations for the requirements of the new calendar.

And yet, there are certain indications that the Roman calendar was not absolute in its rule over the life of the city. Legal documents often specified that the given reckoning was according to the new calendar; such stipulations appeared throughout the century after the introduction of the Gregorian calendar and beyond.[32] This indicates a situation in which the "unmarked choice" still required a surprisingly frequent marking. It may also indicate an occasional awareness that a divisive and troublesome choice was being made. In 1627 the Goldsmiths' Guild shared power in their new articles equally between Catholics and an unspecified "other religion." An interesting article seems to have allowed for the differences caused by the two calendars: "A priest is to be engaged [*najmować*] for a year, according to agreement with him, but without table, since it would not be proper to include dinners in view of the fasts and vigils of various [brethren] of the other religion."[33] I will return in a moment to the question of which "other religion" was intended here. What interests me at the moment is the fact that this article represents an isolated piece of evidence that the calendar of the "other" figured in the minds of those who lived on the dominant time.

Consider, further, the 1652 inventory of a house previously owned by a certain Jarosz Jabłko, apothecary, on upper Great Castle Street:

> First, from the street, an apothecary with a little chamber, from which the yearly rent brings 80 florins. The payment year begins from the Ruthenian Shrovetide.
>
> From the street, a vaulted tavern chamber with a brewery, an apartment, and a basement, from which dwellings there comes 100 Polish zł in rent. The payment year begins on the Roman Candlemas.
>
> A basement from the street side, for rent, from which 50 zł.

A vaulted chamber, in which a tailor lives, gives in rent 30 złotys. The year begins on the Roman Shrove Tuesday.

An empty shop for rent.

An empty second-storey dwelling for guests, 10 florins per week.

A little chamber in front of the kitchen, where the gate-keeper lives, gives 12 ½ zł. The year begins with Christmas.

A chamber with an apartment on the second floor, where a furrier lives, pays 30 zł in rent. The year begins a week after the feast of saints Simon and Jude.

A chamber with an apartment, where a baker lives, likewise pays 30 zł. The year begins in Advent in December, three weeks before Christmas.

A chamber with a recess, where an embroiderer lives, pays 30 zł. The year for the payment of rent begins with the feast of saints Simon and Jude.

A little chamber in the back is vacant.

A chamber in which a cobbler lives, from which he pays rent of 30 zł. The year begins with the feast of St. Mary Magdalene.

A chamber where a tailor's widow lives, pays 17/15 Polish zł. The rental year begins with the feast of St. Mary Magdalene.

In the back, a chamber for rent, from which 30 zł in rent is to come.

In the back, a ruined chamber.[34]

Here we see clearly that all chambers were potentially habitable, and that at the moment of this particular inventory most were occupied (and presumably not just by the baker, but also by the baker's wife and children). A different sort of inventory (this one from 1646) suggests that in some cases the renters of a given house might have belonged to different churches.[35] Whatever the original reason for the use of the two calendars in determining the rent schedule in this particular house, even under its new ownership (the daughter and son-in-law of Jabłko), the rent for one set of rooms continued to come due according to the Greek calendar.

Which leads to a more general question: did Roman Vilnius know when Greek Vilnius was celebrating its holy days (even if it did not alter its work schedule on those days)? Given the numbers of Uniate and Orthodox inhabitants, the number of Uniate churches, and the importance of the one Orthodox complex, as well as the public nature of preparations for holidays, it would seem likely that Catholics and Protestants (as well as Jews and Tatars) in Vilnius lived with a certain everyday awareness of the Greek calendar. An incident that took place in December of 1683 may shed some light. On the twenty-second of that month, students of the Jesuit academy brought a complaint before the Vilnius magistrate against the Orthodox Holy Spirit Church:

> After the conclusion of the Mass in the parish church
> of St. John [the seat of the Jesuits in Vilnius], they
> [the students] went to the Uniate Holy Trinity
> church, wishing to render veneration to the Most
> Holy Virgin in the miraculous image that is found
> there, since it was the feast of the Immaculate
> Conception according to the old calendar, as well as
> wishing to take a look at the brotherhood helping to
> celebrate that feast with beating on drums and kettles.
> And having tarried there a while, wishing then to take
> a look at the dialogue [play] that was being performed
> in the Dis-Uniate [i.e., Orthodox] church of the Holy
> Spirit, they went to the aforementioned church and
> stood peacefully in it and listened to the entire
> dialogue. There they looked at the first rockets as
> they were set off. Then a few hand rockets were fired
> upon the above-mentioned gentlemen, their lords the
> students of the Academy, and they covered with soot,

sulfur, and burns the hats, cloaks of some; upon His Grace, Lord Duniński, however, they inflicted a harmful wound on the cheek of his face under his left eye, and they also covered with sulfur and burns the eye itself .... Whereby more than once did they make taunts and boasts, *his formalibus* [in this manner]: "we will drink yet of Lach [i.e. Polish, Catholic] and student blood."[36]

This gruesome account of a religious celebration turned violent contains a certain amount of sad humour for readers in the late twentieth century; it may also have raised some eyebrows when it was registered with the court. The students did not enjoy a good reputation with the citizens of Vilnius, in spite of attempts by the Catholic clergy in 1640 to portray Jesuit students as helpless innocents from whom the private Calvinist municipal police of Vilnius palatine Krzysztof Radziwiłł took away their mother's pierogies as they returned to their studies through the city gates from stays at home.[37] The account of events cited above was, of course, the version offered by the Jesuit students themselves to the Vilnius magistrate. The monks of the Holy Spirit Monastery registered a counter-account (which I have not seen); in it they certainly complained of the provocative and violent behaviour of the students during the Orthodox celebration.[38] But the point here is that, whether with innocent or deceitful intent, the Jesuit students came to visit the Uniates and the Orthodox precisely because it was a holy day according to the Greek calendar. And given the Uniate "beating on kettles and drums" and the Orthodox "dialogue" (i.e., theatrical production) and fireworks that accompanied the celebrations in a kind of neighbourhood competition, it seems unlikely anyone in town was unaware of what day it was.

A SAXON MONTH?

In number there were certainly fewer Protestants than Greeks in Vilnius, but nonetheless they were of considerable importance. The Calvinists were still, in 1640, represented by one branch of the powerful Radziwiłł family and would long have a faithful backing in a certain middling *szlachta* (nobility). The Lutherans, on the other hand, were well represented in the urban ruling élite, with wealth and political significance disproportionate to their numbers. In other parts of Europe, some Protestant societies made adherence to the old calendar a defining aspect of their difference from Roman Catholics.[39] What about here? In short, was there a "Saxon month" in Vilnius?

The answer involves certain ambiguities. The question of doctrine and practice in the matter of calendar reform among the various Protestant churches in the Polish-Lithuanian Commonwealth has received next to no scholarly attention. This may be, in part, because it seems to have been a non-issue for the Protestant societies of Poland-Lithuania at the time of the reform. I know of no Polish Protestant defences of the old calendar, and I am aware of few positive statements about the issue. A Protestant synod held in Poznań dated its proceedings Thursday, 5 May 1583.[40] This was a new calendar date, used without apology in this official context by a provincial synod of the Polish church of the Czech Brethren (which conformed to the Calvinists) just half a year after the introduction of the corrected calendar in Poland-Lithuania. I have not been able to establish any use of the old calendar in synod documents at the provincial level after 1582.

Records for the Vilnius Calvinist church begin only in 1611, since its library and archive were destroyed that year in an anti-Protestant tumult. The extant records indicate that, at least by 1611, the Vilnius Calvinist church was using the new calendar. On the other hand, protocols of the annual provincial synods indicate regional variation within the Lithuanian Calvinist church. The Vilnius synod of 1616 stipulated that the new calendar was to be the norm, except in the so-called Ruthenian (i.e., Belarusian) district of the Lithuanian Calvinist church, where, "for the sake of the edification of the Lord's Church," either calendar was to be permitted.[41] This was in spite of increasing pressure for uniformity within the Lithuanian Calvinist church, with Vilnian usage serving as the norm. The provincial synod of 1614 had determined that the "form [of worship] is to be that which is in the Vilnius church."[42] By 1644 the provincial synod meeting in Vilnius declared that *"propter conformitatem* [for the sake of conformity] with other churches of God, holy days should be celebrated there [in the Ruthenian district] from now on according to the new calendar."[43]

Thus, although the Vilnius Calvinist church seems to have been on the new calendar from early on, a certain lack of conformity within the larger Lithuanian church was allowed for some time. In addition to the variance between the Vilnius and Ruthenian districts, we should consider the possibility that certain nobles, including those who played important roles in the life of the Vilnius church, allowed or encouraged use of the old calendar on their estates and among their clientele.

The case of the chief patron of the Vilnius church in 1640, Krzysztof Radziwiłł (1585–1640), Lithuanian hetman and palatine of Vilnius, raises certain questions. A recent study has cited a letter from Radziwiłł as evidence that by 1624 he was dating his private correspondence according to the new calendar.[44] But actually the hetman's letter raises more questions than it answers. In it, Radziwiłł invited his friend and regular correspondent, Eustachy Wołłowicz, the bishop of Vilnius, to attend "the christening of my little son set *pro die 30 Iuni Stilo novo* [for the day of 30 June according to the new style]."[45] Radziwiłł may well have dated his voluminous correspondence *stilo novo* without calling attention to the fact. I would imagine that this was a necessity in order to avoid misunderstandings, especially given that so many of his letters were addressed to Catholics such as the bishop of Vilnius. But the fact that he thought it necessary to inform his good friend the bishop that the christening would take place on a particular day according to the new calendar points rather to a need to be clear. It indicates a sense that the bishop, who knew Radziwiłł well, might otherwise mark the event in his social calendar only after figuring out a new calendar equivalent for a perceived old calendar date. In any event, the specification of the calendar points to a usage that was still in flux.

Concerning the Lutherans across town on German Street, I have only a few pieces of evidence, largely indirect. When Andrzej Schönflissius, long-time Polish pastor of Vilnius' Lutheran congregation, published his Polish-language funeral sermon for Vilnius burgomaster Jakub Gibel, he quietly used the new calendar in giving the date of Gibel's death: Friday, 13 November 1637 is a new-style date.[46] This would seem to indicate that the Lutheran congregation employed the new calendar, at least by this time.

Somewhat contradictory evidence is offered, however, by one of the leading polemicists of the first generation of Vilnius Jesuits, Stanisław Grodzicki, who published *Two Sermons on the Correction of the Calendar* in Vilnius in 1589. These works were directed against both the "heretics" and the Ruthenians. They were an answer "to the allegations of both the people of the Ruthenian rite, who take delight in their Greek errors, and also of the heretics, who, as adiaphorists, are displeased by any sort of order."[47] It is not entirely clear to what extent Grodzicki addressed local Protestants under the rubric "adiaphorists," and to what extent his remarks were aimed at "heretics" in general. Only one passage points directly to the Vilnius Lutheran church: "I know," Grodzicki wrote, "what the heretics of the Saxon faith say, both in Germany (about which books have been published) and also here (about which we know)—that this is a voluntary thing ... adiaphoron."[48] I find significant the lack of specificity in Grodzicki's attack on the local Germans ("about which we know"), and the fact that he attributes to them, not a defence of the old calendar, but an indifferent attitude to the entire issue. This stands in stark contrast to the detail and specificity of his attack on the local Ruthenians.

Other testimony, however, suggests the use of the old calendar by some of Vilnius's Saxons. The above-cited 1627 statute of the Goldsmiths' Guild, which divided power between Catholics and "others," contained some interesting evidence in this regard. It read (once again): "A priest is to be engaged [*najmować*] for a year, according to agreement with him, but without table, since it would not be proper to include dinners in view of the fasts and vigils of various [brethren] of the other religion."[49] In fact, the guild had long been almost entirely "Polish" and "German." It would seem unlikely that the "other religion" in this case referred to the Uniates or the Orthodox. Thus, so it would seem, the "others" were the still strongly positioned Saxons, whose calendar sensibilities were being considered here.[50]

In sum, Polish-Lithuanian Protestants seem to have been using the new calendar from the very beginning, and in a certain official way, since synodal records were kept according to that reckoning. Nonetheless, there are recurring suggestions of a lack of conformity. But above all, I note the dog that didn't bark: I have been unable to find any record of internal discussion surrounding the initial switch—apparently together with the Catholics in 1582—of Protestant society in Poland-Lithuania to the new calendar.

A TIME TO FAST AND A TIME TO FEED

If there was no great public polemic over the calendar between Catholics and Protestants in Poland-Lithuania, there was a certain debate over how the Christian was to make use of his time. The *Agenda* published in Gdańsk in 1637, which was to be normative for all Calvinists and Czech Brethren of Poland and Lithuania, gave a church calendar headed simply "The Calendar, which is commonly called Gregorian."[51] In smaller congregations, there were to be only two services during the work week, on Wednesdays and on Fridays. In the larger congregations, "and where there is a school for this purpose" (this would have been the case at the Vilnius Calvinist church), services were to be held twice a day, morning and evening.[52] Calvinists and Czech Brethren were supposed to celebrate Advent, Christmas, Circumcision, the Appearance to the Magi, Maundy Thursday, Good Friday, Easter, Ascension, Trinity, Transfiguration, and more. In addition, they were to celebrate various commemorations of the Virgin Mary, of the Holy Apostles, martyrs, and other faithful confessors and imitators of Christ the Lord "for the call to imitate them in faith and in a pious life."[53]

This was a calendar unusually full of saints' days and high holy days for Protestant usage. Still, a certain implicit distancing from perceived Catholic attitudes toward the celebration of holy days is evident in notes on how Protestants were to behave on those days. All days, we read in the *Agenda*, are equal in certain respects: "not only on Good Friday is Christ the Lord crucified." On Sundays, the Christian was not to engage "in the labours customary to weekdays."[54] Holy days, on the other hand, were established among Christians, "not for loafing about, nor for drunkenness, dancing, etc."[55] On saints' days, in contrast to Sundays, "having listened to the Word of God, ... [Christians] proceed to the work of their vocation. They do not spend them in excesses, in idolatry, or in superstitions."[56] The *Agenda* warned the pastor against adding to this already full ecclesiastical calendar, "partly because on holy days sins are multiplied more in taverns, dancing, and in other indecencies, which teach idleness, and partly because there are barely enough working days for the poor to take care of the things necessary to life."[57]

Although Calvinists engaged in fasting according to a particular schedule and celebrated certain saints' days, Catholic polemicists derided them on both accounts for engaging in "Catholic" activities in un-Catholic fashion. A leading figure among the Czech Brethren in Great Poland, Szymon Teofil Turnowski, published a *Mirror of the Christian Religion in Poland* in 1594 in Vilnius, as a result of his presence there for a disputation between Protestants and Jesuits. That very year the Vilnius Jesuit Marcin Łaszcz responded to this work with a tract entitled *Eyeglasses for the Mirror of the Christian Religion in Poland*. Łaszcz could not fault his opponent for adherence to the old calendar, because Turnowski not only accepted the new one, but also claimed at one point to have proselytized for it among the Orthodox during his stay in Vilnius.[58] Rather, the Jesuit polemicist attacked what the Protestants had done with the calendar. "I certainly have cause to praise you," he wrote sarcastically, "in that you have received our dear St. Adalbert [Wojciech] and dear St. Stanisław into your Church and, as I hear, have written them into your calendar. And what is more, that you, as you claim, have converted these saints to your faith."[59] Further, Łaszcz defended the Catholic calendar of fasts as the original one: "Poles did not eat meat on Saturday for six hundred years; it has only been during the time of you Lutherans that the gluttony has begun ... You cannot stand to look at fasting. You prefer to look into the kitchen where meat is being cooked. Not so did St. Adalbert, who fasted both Fridays and Saturdays."[60]

The citizens of Vilnius may well have looked into each other's kitchens, and their noses likely told them when their neighbours were preparing the wrong foods at inappropriate times. An instance of alleged Protestant sabbatary carnivorousness gave the Jesuits of Vilnius occasion in 1623 to publish a versified pamphlet deriding the recent death of Pastor Mikołaj Burchardy, their Lutheran colleague across town. The unfortunate pastor had, apparently, fallen from a chicken-coop ladder and broken his neck. In this Jesuit representation, the Lutheran congregation of Vilnius then wrote a letter—in verse—to Martin Luther in heaven, which was to be taken along on the journey by the deceased minister. It turns out, of course, that the addressee lives rather in hell, "where already a third of the devils speaks German."[61] The minister's fall, moreover, had occurred on a Saturday, when, after returning from giving his sermon and "chugging some booze," he asked his wife what was for dinner. Upon hearing that she intended to prepare eggs and some fish, the minister flew into a righteous rage:

> "Well, stupid," he says, "do you intend to become a papist
>> That you feed me scrambled eggs on a
>> Saturday?"

> And so, somewhat enthused by that booze,
>> And raging like a lion over your [i.e., Martin
>> Luther's] decrees,

> Being a true son of you, his father,
>> He bounds up the ladder to the chicken coop
>> for a hen.

> ...

> That head, entirely full of God's Writ,
>> Clattered upon the ground such that the wool
>> flew out of it.

> The tongue, with which he once briskly flogged
> God's Words,

Was cut by his teeth, whereupon his speech
also ceased.

And his little soul, when the doors were closed for it
in his throat,
  Barely escaped, the poor thing, through an
  other end.

Thus if it should smell a bit of musk,
  May Your Grace direct it to the baths; let it
  wash itself.

...

And if he should have missed the road to heaven by a
bit,
  (Which is no cause for surprise with a drunk),

You should indicate to him the straight road.

...

  He wished to eat meat on a Saturday, that true
  martyr.

For, in order not to keep papal fasts,
  He did not begrudge breaking his neck, falling
  from the chickens.[62]

And there are other passages from the polemical literature suggesting that people (or, in any case, confessional polemicists) in Vilnius knew what their neighbours did and when they did it. In a litany of alleged discrepancies between Uniate program and Uniate practice, their observer from across the street, the archimandrite of the Orthodox Holy Spirit Monastery, Meletij Smotryc'kyj, charged in 1622: "You confess, practice, and teach one way *publice* [publicly] and another way *privatim* [privately] ... *Publice* you monks do not eat meat, but *privatim*—hah!" (And he went on to note: "*Publice* you celebrate according to the old calendar, but *privatim* according to the new one.")[63]

Not all months were equal. In addition to being long or late, the Ruthenian month became also backward, second-rate. Rus' was, in the current stereotype, "simple" and "crude," and one of the ways it betrayed this simplicity and crudity was through a "stubborn" adherence to the old calendar. When Vilnius Jesuit Stanisław Grodzicki wrote in 1589 against the heretics and schismatics who favoured the old calendar, he attacked the Protestants on issues of dogma and science. But his words toward the Ruthenians (his most immediate audience, since the Protestants seem to have refused to fight back on this issue) often added elements of derision. The following passage is typical of Catholic polemical postures:

> But our Ruthenians point to the current spells of cold
> weather [in arguing against the new calendar], and
> with them they abuse the simple man. But they
> themselves are much greater simpletons in this matter
> ... If they do not believe me, let them ask those who
> have been there [i.e., in the Holy Lands], or let them
> make a quick trip themselves, even a bit nearer by, to
> Italy or to Spain. Then they will see that there not
> only the fields, but even the trees are already now
> turning green. If they understand that elsewhere it is
> already much warmer, then why do they wish to
> mark the beginning of spring according to the
> warmth of their Lithuania?[64]

The inhabitants of the Ruthenian month were, in this representation, isolated and provincial, ready to make general pronouncements according to experiences limited to Lithuanian latitudes.

In Catholic (and even some Uniate) polemical works, there appeared the figure of the Ruthenian bumpkin, who was unqualified to participate in complicated discussions of calendar reform, and should therefore simply have accepted the findings of the wiser Catholic mathematicians and astronomers. An extreme example of this sort of treatment was published in 1642 by Kasijan Sakovyč. Long-time archimandrite of the Uniate monastery in Volhynian

Dubno, Sakovyč had first converted from Orthodoxy to the Uniate church in about 1624. Nearly twenty years later, around 1640, Sakovyč made what was considered an impossible confessional move, a "conversion" across the supposedly non-existent border between Greek and Roman Catholicism. The "last straw" in this case, at least according to Sakovyč, was a failed attempt to convince the Uniates of the Holy Trinity Monastery in Vilnius that it was finally time for the Uniates to switch to the new calendar.[65]

The work I wish to consider here is entitled *A Dialogue or Conversation between Maciek and Dionizy, the Vilnius Schismatic Pop*. In it, a Catholic, Polish-speaking visitor to Vilnius named Maciek encounters Dionizy, a local, Ruthenian-speaking *pop* (simple priest), whose language is represented, in Latin letters, as a kind of crude, jargon-version of Polish. Dionizy mistakes all of the abstract Polish and Latin technical terms of Maciek's discourse on the calendar for similar Ruthenian words with physical, rustic meanings. *Matematyka* (mathematics) became *motyka* (hoe), and *komput* ("computation," a technical term for handbooks on determining when to celebrate Easter) became *kupiut* (they buy) in the Ruthenian perception and re-rendering. A final argument against celebrating Easter according to the old calendar concerned the "great quantity of rotten fish and herring" Maciek noticed in the Vilnius town square on his way to his conversation with Dionizy.[66] In a piece of charming doggerel, Maciek addressed Rus':

> The poor herrings now roast in the sun,
>> So long have your days of fast dragged on.
>
> Nay, soon even herrings will not stay,
>> If you the Lord's Rising so delay.
>
> Know by such a clear clock at the least,
>> When you ought to celebrate the Feast.[67]

Thus in Sakovyč's portrayal, Rus' was immediately recognized in Vilnius by its adherence to the old calendar, and, typical of this convert's attitude toward his former co-religionists, Orthodox and Uniate, the community was marked by associations with physical degradation. Note further that Sakovyč had simply turned the argument of Grodzicki's Ruthenian "simpletons" on its head: the old calendar cannot be right because it is rather too hot at Ruthenian Easter. And part of the evidence came from a perceived disharmony of diet and time: the Ruthenians were eating their herring and thin soups out of season.

The Ruthenian month thus became a subject for derision on the part of Catholic polemicists and a source of insecurity for Ruthenian élites. In a learned treatise from 1603 on astronomy, astrology, and the calendars, Marcin Łaszcz (also a Jesuit who had spent time in Vilnius and who was a veteran of the pamphlet wars) provided a detailed chart showing the constant slippage of the old calendar. According to him, Greek Easter would be celebrated over the years in all seasons: in AD 23,358, for example, it would be celebrated on 15 October; and by AD 43,574, it would have made its way through the cycle of months back to 15 March.[68] These futuristic calculations also belonged to what would become a kind of favoured genre among Catholic and some Uniate polemicists, that is, the "great absurdities" of Ruthenian usage.

There was a political problem here for Catholic and Uniate polemicists. From 1582 until the Union of Brest in 1596, Catholic polemicists could criticize Ruthenian adherence to the old calendar without any restraints. After 1596, however, the Catholic side was supposed to accept the licitness of Uniate usages, including adherence to the old calendar. There was a clear perception among élites that this aspect of Uniate usage was due to a calculation that switching to the corrected calendar would greatly diminish the ability of the Uniate church to compete for souls among "simple Rus'." This perception put Ruthenian élites in a position of internal conflict.

Vilnius Jesuit Wojciech Tylkowski would write in 1685 that "even the Uniates differ [with respect to the calendar] by permission of the Church for great reasons, but in this it is not a matter of something that belongs to the faith, but to doctrine."[69] The "great reasons" of which Tylkowski wrote probably had to do with the above-mentioned calculation on the part of Catholic and Uniate hierarchies. When, in 1622, Meletij Smotryc'kyj, archimandrite of the Vilnius Orthodox Holy Spirit Monastery, attributed to his Uniate neighbours across the street a secret use of the new calendar, he was alleging that they thought of the calendar as belonging to the category of *adiaphora* (indifferent doctrinal points). And it was only because they risked losing their flocks that the shepherds adhered to the old rather than the new; thus, the Uniate hierarchy, too, believed in the simplicity of Rus'. Writing in 1628, after his conversion, the now Uniate Smotryc'kyj would claim that his former co-bishop and now opponent, Orthodox Metropolitan of Kiev Iov Borec'kyj, had long seen the matter of the calendar as the chief stumbling block for a union of Rus', since the "simple people" could not be made to understand the need for the correction.[70] Uniate polemicist Sakovyč wrote in 1640 of the "shame" involved with the old calendar;[71] in 1644, Uniate polemicist Jan Dubovyč called the variance in the celebration of "the same" holy days a matter of *dyzgust serdeczny* (disgust of the heart).[72]

TENSIONS OF DIFFERENCE AND IDENTITY

How people kept time, and what moments they marked as belonging to the sacred, was one of the most pervasive aspects of difference among the peoples, religions, and confessions of early modern Vilnius. This was a city in which the calls to worship rarely ceased. Think only of the regular weekly and annual Jewish, Islamic, and Christian cycles of services; then add to this the conflict between the Christian calendars. The lists of high holy days I have cited (Bathory's list of days on which the Orthodox were not to be called into court, and the Calvinist calendar set in the *Agenda* of 1637, plus the very full Roman Catholic calendar) suggest that the bells of Vilnius got little rest.[73]

It is clear that the calendars played a role in the succession of religious violence that took place throughout the age. Weekly and annual rhythms provided regular occasions for "tumults and excesses" within the city: every week as the various religions and confessions heeded the call and made their way to their various, closely situated places of worship; every week as the kitchen smells of those who, in the opinion of the other, ought to have been fasting made their way to the noses of those who actually were fasting;[74] every year, as the various confessions celebrated their many and various high holy days, held festivals (often loud), and conducted public processions; every year, at the time of provincial synods.

This multiculturalism of early modern Vilnius was one in which cultures stood in clear hierarchical relationships to each other. Jews and Tatars occupied well-defined spaces of difference. Within that space they lived their lives more or less according to their own rules and calendars; any dealings beyond the community required adapting to the Christian—usually in Vilnius the Roman Catholic Christian—world, although we should consider the possibility that Jews and Tatars who had dealings with Greeks and Saxons also made compromises in the directions of those cultures. Lutherans, Calvinists, Uniates, and Orthodox occupied somewhat less well-defined spheres. All felt a certain pull to conform to what was becoming a Roman Catholic norm, and part of the pull focused on the dominant system of time-keeping. Ruthenians, above all, were caught between a definition of difference that included adherence to the old calendar and a need to conform that was motivated by concerns of economics and cultural prestige.

Uniates left particularly eloquent testimonies to the discontents of difference from the dominant world. They, of course, did not write disinterestedly about Ruthenian difference. Recall that they often presented their program with the words of Christ: "That they all may be ONE" (John 17:21). But these writings are of some use in imagining the kinds of difficulties caused by difference. I again cite two Uniate polemicists: Kasijan Sakovyč and Jan Dubovyč, both of whom had some experience of confessional relations in Vilnius, an important centre for the Uniate church. Sakovyč spent time in the city in 1640 to make his plea for a correction of the Ruthenian month. Dubovyč may have had some relationship with a family of some importance, originally on the Greek side of the city's magistrate. Both men left testimonies to the difficulties of life in a city run on various clocks, and both focused on the "absurdities" of lives lived in close contact between Eastern and Western Christians. Sakovyč wrote in 1640:

> By receiving the new calendar you will avoid those
> difficulties that occur in the married life of a Roman

with a Ruthenian woman, of a Ruthenian with a
Roman woman, in the making of pilgrimages, in going
to sessions of the courts, tribunals, sejms, to weddings
and funerals. Also in the maintaining of servants and
retinue of various religions, in preparing different food
for them, etc., etc. And so you will have one set of
joys from the receiving of the new calendar, in home,
in the Orthodox church, in the Catholic church, on
pilgrimages. But from adhering to the old, only
tribulation of the soul, and a certain shame, and no
little incurring of harms. That, Sir Ruthenian
nobleman, they do not allow you to celebrate your
holy days, but you have to go to court and render
account of yourself ... And you, Sir Merchant, have to
celebrate Roman holy days whether you like to or
not, and your workers are idle, and you have to feed
them, give them to drink, clothe them, pay them, and
all this takes away from, not adds to, your
pocketbook ... It is very improper when the one says
"*Christos woskres,*" and the other will not reply for
five weeks "*Woistinu woskres,*" and your Roman
friend in his rejoicing will be dancing about, but you,
sitting over herring and sour soup, will be in distress.[75]

And Dubovyč wrote in 1644:

The one sings "Christ has arisen from the dead,"
while the other occupies himself with a threnody over
the most dear passion of the Lord. One rejoices at the
coming of the Holy Spirit, but the other is still
preparing for the Lord's Ascension. These celebrate
the festivals of saints Luke the Apostle, George the
Martyr, Stephen the Protomartyr, John the Baptist,
but for the others are now the days of the holy
apostles Simon and Jude, of the Holy Cross,
Epiphany, or of Three Kings, the Birth of the Most
Virgin Mary. And what is worse, the holy days
themselves are broken through various
entertainments, work...[76]

There are, however, certain indications that this distress was not felt equally across the Christian confessions nor across all social groups. The fact that the calendars provided so many occasions for tensions, and that so few of them seem to have given rise to violence, suggests that this multicultural city functioned on a daily basis with some efficiency and with a certain sharing of power across confessional boundaries. Acts of religious violence seem not to have been a constant in the life of the city; officials on various sides often did what they could to prevent them, and their perpetrators—including Catholics—were often punished.

It was the clergy that seems to have been most concerned with the pains of difference and to have taken the greatest pains to preserve certain differences. The constant prohibitions by priests and ministers against intermarriage, against attending the christenings and funerals of the other, against sending one's children to the schools of the other, suggest that the flocks were less strict about keeping their distance from each other.

A counter-voice to the testimonies of Uniate priests Sakovyč and Dubovyč is provided by some of the statutes of the guilds, which seem to have accepted the variety of Vilnius and to have been most concerned with finding practical solutions for preserving the peace among "dissidents in religion." The 1627 statute of the Goldsmiths' Guild, which shared power equally between Catholics and an "other religion," led off with a nice statement of the problem and the goals: "What the soul does in the human body, good order causes in every gathering of people."[77] The Red- and Black-Leather Tanners, in articles of 1614, sought "that we preserve good order among the burghers of this city."[78] And the Tailors' Guild, which shared power equally between Romans and Greeks, provided a detailed handbook on the preservation of that order in their statute of 1665.[79]

Scholars have noted the levelling pull of *szlachta* culture, which erased certain differences between Catholics and Protestants and even initiated some Tatars, Jews, and burghers into its set of values.[80] Perhaps coexistence in the city of Vilnius exercised a similar levelling pull that made life together workable. After all, not all the bells and signals exerted a centrifugal force upon the inhabitants of

Vilnius. The bells summoned a wide spectrum to work in the various guilds, and the night watch announced curfew by "beating the *capa* [or *capstrzyk*, from the German *Zapfenstreich*, "curfew"] on the drums in order to remind [the citizenry] of their obligations."[81]

In this regard, I find telling the dispensations of Vilnians at the time of their death. While a few were partisan in the bequeathing of their worldly goods, giving only to the churches, schools, and hospitals of their chosen confessions, many revealed a kind of civic patriotism that cannot be explained, in my opinion, as a hedging of bets in the face of death.[82] It was not unusual for a burgher, as he or she approached death, to show an interest in the financial well-being of the Uniate Basilians, the Orthodox Basilians, the Jesuits, the Dominicans, and the Franciscans, all of them of the city of Vilnius.

NOTES

1 *Akty, izdavaemye Vilenskoju arxeografičeskoju komissieju,* vol. 20 (Vilnius: 1893), p. 335. On the events of 1640, see Bogumił Zwolski, *Sprawa Zboru ewangelicko-reformowanego w Wilnie w latach 1639–41,* Bibljoteczka wileńska, vol. 6 (Vilnius: 1936); and Henryk Wisner, "Likwidacja zboru ewangelickiego w Wilnie (1639–1646): Z dziejów walki z inaczej wierzącymi," *Odrodzenie i Reformacja w Polsce 37* (1993): 89–102. The story was retold by the nineteenth-century Polish novelist and historian, Ignacy Kraszewski *(Kościół Święto-Michalski w Wilnie: Obraz historyczny z pierwszej połowy XVII wieku* [Vilnius: 1833]), which was in turn the subject of a study by Bogumiła Kosmanowa ("Sprawa wileńskiego kościoła św. Michała [wizja J.I. Kraszewskiego a rzeczywistość historyczna]," *Odrodzenie i Reformacja w Polsce* 40 [1996]: 53–68).

2 *Dissidentes in religione* was, in the Polish-Lithuanian context, a technical term whose history can be traced to the 1573 Confederation of Warsaw, which promised to maintain peace among the confessions. The agreement reached at that time became the basis for the so-called *pacta conventa* to which the elected kings of Poland-Lithuania gave their approval before coronation. The literature on the Confederation of Warsaw and on the theory and practice of religious toleration in Poland-Lithuania is large. Among the more important recent studies, with further bibliography, are Mirosław Korolko, *Klejnot swobodnego sumienia: Polemika wokół konfederacji warszawskiej w latach 1573–1658* (Warsaw: PAX, 1974); Zbigniew Ogonowski, *Z zagadnień tolerancji w Polsce w XVII wieku* (Warsaw: Państwowe Wydawnictwo Naukowe, 1958); Janusz Tazbir, *Państwo bez stosów* (Warsaw: Państwowy Instytut Wydawniczy, 1967); Tazbir, *Dzieje polskiej tolerancji* (Warsaw: Interpress, 1973); and Wisner, *Rozróżnieni w wierze: Szkice z dziejów Rzeczypospolitej schyłku XVI i połowy XVII wieku* (Warsaw: Książka i Wiedza, 1982).

3 Cited according to Edmund Klinkowski, "Grodno, Wilna und das Posener Land in einem deutschen Reisebericht vom Jahre 1586," *Deutsche Wissenschaftliche Zeitschrift für Polen* 30 (1936): 133–38. The entire travel account was edited by K.D. Harszler (*Die Reisen des Samuel Kiechel: Aus drei Handschriften*, Bibliothek des Litterarischen Vereins in Stuttgart, vol. 86 [Stuttgart, 1866]).

4 And not as much as papal nuncio Torres, who wrote in a report to Rome in the early seventeenth century that, although the Reformation had already lost much ground among the *szlachta* (nobility), "there are not few [heretics] among the common people, especially in Vilnius, where one can count up to sixty [*sic*] different sects, and it is often possible to come upon a home in which the father belongs to one, the mother to another, and the children to yet another" (Erazm Rykaczewski, ed., *Relacye nuncyuszów apostolskich i innych osób o Polsce od roku 1548 do 1690* [Berlin: 1864], p. 143). It is unclear to me whether this was papal nuncio to Warsaw Cosmas de Torres (nunciature 1621–22) or Joannes de Torres (nunciature 1645–52). Rykaczewski did not further identify him.

5 See Marceli Kosman, "Konflikty wyznaniowe w Wilnie. (Schyłek XVI–XVII w.)," *Kwartalnik Historyczny* 79 (1972): 3–23; *Reformacja i kontrreformacja w Wielkim Księstwie Litewskim w świetle propagandy wyznaniowej* (Wrocław: Ossolineum, 1973); and *Protestanci i kontrreformacja: Z dziejów tolerancji w Rzeczypospolitej XVI–XVIII wieku* (Wrocław: Ossolineum, 1978). For histories of Vilnius in the late medieval and early modern periods, see Marja Łowmiańska, *Wilno przed najazdem moskiewskim 1655 roku*, Bibljoteczka wileńska, vol. 3 (Vilnius: 1929); Władysław Kowalenko, "Geneza udziału stołecznego miasta Wilna w sejmach Rzeczypospolitej," *Ateneum Wileńskie* 2 (1925–26): 327–73, and *Ateneum Wileńskie* 3 (1927): 79–137; V.G. Vasilievskij, "Očerk istorii goroda Vil'ny," in *Pamjatniki russkoj stariny v zapadnyx gubernijax imperii,* ed. P.N. Batjuškov, vols. 5 and 6 (St. Petersburg: 1872–74); and *Vilniaus miesto istorija nuo seniausių laikų iki Spalio revoliucijos,* ed. J. Jurginis, V. Merkys, and A. Tautavičius (Vilnius: Mintis, 1968). Essential reading is the new study of the Vilnius "ruling élite" in the second half of the seventeenth century: Aivas Ragauskas, *Vilniaus miestos valdantysis elitas XVII a. antrojoje pusėje (1662–1702 m.)* (Vilnius: Diemedžio leidykla, 2002).

6 On Lithuanian Tatars in the early modern period, see Piotr Borawski, "O sytuacji wyznaniowej ludności tatarskiej w Wielkim Księstwie Litewskim i w Polsce (XVI–XVIII w.)," *Euhemer: Przegląd religioznawczy* 4, no. 118 (1980): 43–54; "Tolerancja religijna wobec ludności tatarskiej w Wielkim Księstwie Litewskim (XVI–XVIII wiek)," *Przegląd humanistyczny* 25, no. 3 (1981): 51–66; and "Sytuacja prawna ludności tatarskiej w Wielkim Księstwie Litewskim (XVI–XVIII w.)," *Acta Baltico-Slavica* 15 (1983): 55–76. Also see Borawski and Witold Sienkiewicz, "Chrystianizacja Tatarów w Wielkim Księstwie Litewskim," *Odrodzenie i Reformacja w Polsce* 34 (1989): 87–114; Borawski, "Asymilacja kulturowa Tatarów w Wielkim Księstwie Litewskim," *Odrodzenie i Reformacja w Polsce* 36 (1992): 163–92; A. Muchliński, ed., "Zdanie sprawy o Tatarach litewskich przez jednego z tych Tatarów złożone Sułtanowi Sulejmanowi w r. 1558," *Teka wileńska* 4 (1858): 241–72, *Teka wilenska* 5 (1858): 121–79, and *Teka wileńska* 6 (1858): 139–83; Jacek Sobczak, *Położenie prawne ludności tatarskiej w Wielkim Księstwie Litewskim,* Poznańskie Towarzystwo Przyjaciół Nauk, Wydział Historii i Nauk Społecznych, Prace Komisji Historycznej, vol. 38 (Poznań: 1984); Szymon

Szyszman, "Osadnictwo karaimskie i tatarskie na ziemiach Wielkiego Księstwa Litewskiego," *Myśl karaimska* 10 (1933): 29–36; Leon Krzyczyński, "Historia meczetu w Wilnie. (Próba monografii.)," *Przegląd islamski* 6 (1937): 7–33; Andrzej B. Zakrzewski, "Osadnictwo tatarskie w Wielkim Księstwie Litewskim–aspekty wyznaniowe," *Acta Baltico-Slavica* 20 (1989): 137–53; Zakrzewski, "O asymilacji Tatarów w Rzeczypospolitej w XVI–XVIII w," in *Tryumfy i porażki: Studia z dziejów kultury polskiej XVI–XVIII w.,* ed. Maria Bogucka (Warsaw: Państwowe wydawnictwo naukowe, 1989), pp. 75–96; and Zakrzewski, "Niektóre aspekty położenia kulturalnego Tatarów Litewskich w XVI–XVIII w," in *Wilno–Wileńszczyzna jako krajobraz i środowisko wielu kultur,* vol. 2 (Białystok: 1992), pp. 107–28; and Jan Tyszkiewicz, *Tatarzy na Litwie i w Polsce. Studia z dziejów XIII–XVIII w.* (Warsaw: Państwowe wydawnictwo naukowe, 1989).

7 On Lithuanian Karaim, see Szyszman, "Osadnictwo" and Szyszman, *Le Karaïsme: Ses doctrines et son histoire* (Lausanne: L'age d'homme, 1980); A. Geiger, *Isaak Troki: Ein Apologet des Iudenthums am Ende des sechszehnten Jahrhunderts* (Wrocław, 1853); and Jacob Mann, *Texts and Studies in Jewish History and Literature, Karaitica* vol. 2, (Philadelphia: Hebrew Press of the Jewish Publication Society of America, 1935).

8 Cited according to Israel Cohen, *Vilna* (Philadelphia: Jewish Publication Society of America, 1992), pp. 25–26. On the Jews of Vilnius, see also S.A. Beršadskij, "Istorija vilenskoj evrejskoj obščiny: 1593–1649 g. Na osnovaniju neizdavannyx istočnikov," *Vosxod* 6, no. 10 (1886): 125–38, *Vosxod* 6, no. 11: 145–54, *Vosxod* 7, no. 3 (1887): 81–98, *Vosxod* 7, no. 4: 65–78, *Vosxod* 7, no. 5: 16–32, *Vosxod* 7, no. 6: 58–73, *Vosxod* 7, no. 8: 97–110; and Israel Klausner, *Vilnah: Yerushalayim de-Lita* (Tel Aviv: 1988).

9 See Stanisław Kot, "Aufbruch und Niedergang des Täufertums in Wilna (1563–1566)," *Archiv für Reformationsgeschichte* 49 (1958): 212–26.

10 On the Christian confessions in early modern Vilnius and their interrelations, see Adam Ferdynand Adamowicz, *Kościół augsburski w Wilnie. Kronika* (Vilnius: 1855); Gottfried Schramm, "Protestantismus und städtische Gesellschaft in Wilna (16.–17. Jahrhundert)," *Jahrbücher für Geschichte Osteuropas* 17 (1969): 187–214; Kosman, "Konflikty wyznaniowe"; Kosman, *Reformacja i kontrreformacja;* and Kosman, *Protestanci i kontrreformacja.*

11 This was the best estimate of Marja Łowmiańska (*Wilno przed,* p. 77). The matter deserves new attention.

12 Ibid., p. 17.

13 See Kowalenko, "Geneza udziału," p. 369.

14 See Julian Krzyżanowski, ed., *Nowa księga przysłów i wyrażeń przysłowiowych polskich,* vol. 3 (Warsaw: Państwowy Instytut Wydawniczy, 1972), p. 101.

15 On the Gregorian reform of the calendar and the history of its acceptance and rejection in early modern Europe, see G.V. Coyne, M.A. Hoskin, and O. Pedersen, eds., *Gregorian Reform of the Calendar: Proceedings of the Vatican Conference to Commemorate Its 400th Anniversary 1582–1982* (Vatican City: Specola Vaticana, 1983); and David Ewing Duncan, *Calendar: Humanity's Epic Struggle to Determine a True and Accurate Year* (New York: Avon, 1998).

16 See Zakrzewski, "Niektóre aspekty," p. 122.

17 See the letters from the Vilnius Orthodox Brotherhood of the Holy Spirit to Krzysztof II Radziwiłł (original manuscripts in the Warsaw Archiwum Główne Akt Dawnych, Archiwum Radziwiłłów II, 843 and 889).

18 *Zbiór dawnych dyplomatów i aktów miast: Wilna, Kowna, Trok, prawosławnych monasterów, cerkwi i w różnych sprawach,* part 1 (Vilnius: 1843), p. 138.

19 Ibid., pp. 139–40. See also Piotr Dubiński, *Zbiór Praw i Przywilejów Miastu Stołecznemu W.X.L. Wilnowi nadanych: Na żądaniu wielu Miast Koronnych, jako też Wielkiego Księstwa Litewskiego ułożony i wydany* (Vilnius: 1788), pp. 149–51.

20 *Zbiór dawnych dyplomatów,* p. 140.

21 On the guilds, see the primary sources printed in *Akty, izdavaemye Vilenskoju arxeografičeskoju komissieju,* vol. 10 (Vilnius: 1879); Henryk Łowmiański and Marja Łowmiańska, eds., *Akta cechów wileńskich,* vol. 1 (Vilnius: 1939); and the study by Józef Morzy, "Geneza i rozwój cechów wileńskich do końca XVII w.," *Zeszyty naukowe Uniwersytetu im. A. Mickiewicza,* Seria Historia (Poznań: 1959), pp. 3–93, which also offers more extensive bibliography.

22 Łowmiański and Łowmiańska, *Akta cechów,* p. 321.

23 Ibid.

24 Ibid., p. 45.

25 Ibid., p. 160.

26 Ibid., p. 292.

27 Ibid., p. 321.

28 To choose only one example from the many: in an article confirmed in 1689, the Cobblers' Guild, which shared power among Romans, Ruthenians, and "Saxons," undertook to serve the altar of St. Anne at the Dominicans' Holy Spirit Church. See ibid., p. 452 and *Akty, izdavaemye Vilenskoju arxeografičeskoju komissieju,* vol. 10, p. 108.

29 One example: the Tailors' Guild in statutes of 23 March 1665 required all members ("of both the Roman and the Greek religion") to attend the annual Corpus Christi banquet and to take part, behind the guild banner, in the Corpus Christi procession. See Łowmiański and Łowmiańska, *Akta cechów,* p. 321.

30 The Capmakers' Guild in 1636 declared that whenever any brother should die, "the younger brethren will be required to dig the hole and to place the body in the hole and to bring it on the bier, and the others are to accompany the body honourably, all together, both the Greeks [are to accompany] a Roman to the Catholic church, and, from the Roman side, to the Orthodox church, and to bury [the body] as befits." See ibid., p. 212; *Akty, izdavaemye Vilenskoju arxeografičeskoju komissieju,* vol. 10, p. 29.

31 Łowmiański and Łowmiańska, *Akta cechów,* p. 104.

32 See, for example, *Akty, izdavaemye Vilenskoju arxeografičeskoju komissieju,* vol. 20, pp. 518–19, where a business transaction between a Jew and a Ruthenian concerning a Vilnius property specified repeatedly that various deadlines were according to the new calendar.

33 Łowmiański and Łowmiańska, *Akta cechów,* p. 172.

34 "Description of the house of the now deceased Jarosz Jabłko, apothecary, 9 March 1652, currently owned by daughter Cecylia Jabłkówna and husband Joannes Brentell, canon founder to His Royal Majesty," from the books of the Vilnius magistrate, in the Lithuanian State Historical Archive (Lietuvos valstybės istorijos archyvas = LVIA) SA 5096, fols. 590v–591r.

35 In response to allegations in 1646 that—in spite of the ban placed upon them in 1640—the Calvinists were continuing to meet and to hold religious services and synods at their old seat within the city walls, officials canvassed the "neighbours" (i.e., renters of a given house) to discover what they had seen and heard:

> And first of all, when Mr. Daniel Hanke, a citizen and merchant of Vilnius, was questioned, he testified *sub conscientia* [by his faith] that here, where we have been living for several years, there have never been any church services or congresses or commotions. Then we went to a weaver by the name of Jan Tum, a German, and we asked him about the above mentioned things. And he also testified by his word that he and his journeymen had neither seen nor heard any of those things. Then we went to a tailor by the name of Hendrych Heyn, asking him whether any congresses or church services of the Evangelical religion had taken place from the above mentioned time. He too testified on his word that there had never been any of the aforementioned things. Then we went to a second weaver by the name of Piotr Kant. He too witnessed by his word the same as the others. Finally we went to Iwan Bielski, tailor, also living there in the very gate to the estate, and he testified to the same thing by his word—that there had been neither commotions, nor any sort of congresses, nor Evangelical church services. All the above-mentioned artisans are citizens of Vilnius and guild members, some of the Catholic religion, some of the Saxon, others of the Ruthenian Uniate religion.

(From the *Kwit relacyjny* (official report) of generals Stefan Gromacki and Krzysztof Towżyn, found in the the Mažvydas National Library of Lithuania [Lietuvos nacionalinė Martyno Mažvydo biblioteka = LNMB] F93–1714, fols. 1r–2r.)

36 *Akty, izdavaemye Vilenskoju arxeografičeskoju komissieju,* vol. 9 (Vilnius: 1878), pp. 245–47.

37 See the contemporary Catholic complaint, printed in "Actum Commissiey w Wilnie" *Tygodnik Wileński.* 5, no. 108 (1818): 92: "że Warta u Bram pierogi Studentom od Matek posłane odeymuią, y wozy rewiduią, że spisuią Imiona Studentów."

38 See the description of the "Supplication of the [Orthodox] Father Monks" in *Opisanie dokumentov arxiva zapadnorusskix uniatskix mitropolitov 1470–1700*, vol. 1 (St. Petersburg: Sinodal'naja tipografija, 1897), pp. 361–62.

39 See Duncan, *Calendar*, pp. 209–32.

40 Maria Sipayłło, ed., *Akta Synodów Różnowierczych w Polsce*, vol. 4, Wielkopolska 1569–1632 (Warsaw, 1997), p. 85.

41 *Akta Synodów prowincjalnnych Jednoty Litewskiej 1611–1625*, Monumenta Reformationis Polonicae et Lithuanicae, 4, fasc. 2 (Vilnius: 1915), p. 38.

42 Ibid., p. 22.

43 Manuscript, "Księga druga Aktów Synodów Prowincyalnych Litewskich 1638–1675," from the Library of the Lithuanian Academy of Sciences (Lietuvos mokslų akademijos biblioteka = LMAB) fol. 40–1136, p. 73.

44 Kosman, *Reformacja i kontrreformacja*, p. 259.

45 Autograph manuscripts in the Warsaw Main Archive of Old Documents (Archiwum Główne Akt Dawnych = AGAD), Archiwum Radziwiłłów IV, koperta 311, 365 (12 June 1624).

46 Jędrzej Schönflissius, *Antidotum spirituale: To iest, Lekarstwo Duchowne Na Truciznę Srogiey śmierci Przy obchodzie pogrzebu niegdy pobożnego i Szlachetnego Męża Iego Mści Pana Iakuba Gibla Burmistrza Wileńskiego* (Königsberg: 1638), fol. E3r.

47 Stanisław Grodzicki, *O poprawie kalendarza Kazanie dwoie* (Vilnius: 1589), p. 9.

48 Ibid., p. 27.

49 Łowmiański and Łowmiańska, *Akta cechów*, p. 172.

50 My argument is supported by the list of names of guild members who presented this statute to the Vilnius magistrate. I find here no obvious Greeks, but a few clear Saxons: Hermanus Marquarth, Jan Zalesky Pigulka, Girgex Fertner, Grigier Kolsan, Zygmunt Żeligmacher, Esaias Prus, Dawid Lorencowicz, Joseph Bohaterowicz, Hornus Rantel, Alexander Helmbeg, Karol Libert, Jakub Mor, and Symon Bernatowicz. See Łowmiański and Łowmiańska, *Akta cechów*, p. 173. On the goldsmiths of the Grand Duchy of Lithuania see Edmundas Laucevičius and Birutė Rūta Vitkauskienė, *Lietuvos auksakalystė XV–XIX amžius* (Vilnius: Baltos lankos, 2001).

51 *Agenda albo Forma Porządku usługi świętey, w zborach ewangelickich koronnych y Wielkiego Xięstwa Litewskiego* (Gdańsk: 1637), p. 19.

52 Ibid., p. 252.

53 Ibid., pp. 252–53.

54 Ibid., pp. 246–47.

55 Ibid., p. 244.

56 Ibid., p. 253.

57 Ibid., p. 254.

58 Cited in Jolanta Dworzaczkowa, *Bracia Czescy w Wielkopolsce w XVI i XVII wieku* (Warsaw: Semper, 1997), p. 79.

59 Marcin Łaszcz (Marcin Tworzydło, pseud.), *Okulary na Zwierciadło Nabożeństwa Chrześciańskiego w Polszcze*, (Vilnius: 1594), fol. A1r.

60 Ibid., fols. C3v–4r.

61 Zbigniew Nowak, *Kontrreformacyjna satyra obyczajowa w Polsce XVII wieku*, Gdańskie Towarzystwo Naukowe, Wydział I Nauk Społecznych i Humanistycznych, Seria Źródeł, vol. 9 (Gdańsk: 1968), p. 297.

62 Ibid., pp. 292–93.

63 Meletij Smotryc'kyj, *Obrona verificaciey* (Vilnius: 1621), p. 111. See facsimile edition in *Collected Works of Meletij Smotryc'kyj*, Harvard Library of Early Ukrainian Literature, Texts, vol. 1 (Cambridge, MA: Harvard University Press, 1987), p. 454.

64 Grodzicki, *O poprawie*, pp. 12–13.

65 On Sakovyč, see Mirosław Szegda, "Sakowicz (Isakowicz), Kalikst," in *Polski słownik biograficzny*, vol. 34 (Wrocław: 1994), pp. 343–45; S. Golubev, "Lifos—polemičeskoe sočinenie, vyšedšee iz Kievo-pečerskoj tipografii v 1644 godu," in *Arxiv jugo-zapadnoj rossii, izdavaemyj Kommissieju dlja rabora drevnix aktov*, part 1, vol. 9 (Kiev: 1893), pp. 9–26; David A. Frick, "'Foolish Rus'": On Polish Civilization, Ruthenian Self-Hatred, and Kasijan Sakovyč," *Harvard Ukrainian Studies* 18 (1994): 210–48.

66 Kasijan Sakovyč, *Dialog abo Rozmowa Maćka z Dionizym Popem Schizmatyckim wileńskim* (Cracow, 1642), p. Aiv.

67 Ibid., p. Av.

68 Łaszcz, (1603), pp. 114–15.

69 Wojciech Tylkowski (1685), p. 86.

70 Meletij Smotryc'kyj, *Protestatia Przeciwo Soborowi w tym Roku 1628. we dni Augusta Miesiąca, w Kiiowie Monasteru Pieczerskim obchodzonemu* (L'viv, 1628), fols. B4r–C1r. See facsimile edition in *Collected Works of Meletij Smotryc'kyj*, Harvard Library of Early Ukrainian Literature, vol. 1 (Cambridge, MA: Harvard University Press, 1987), p. 634.

71 Sakovyč, *Kalendarz stary, w ktorym Iawny y oczywisty Błąd vkazuie się około święcenia Paschi, y Responsa na Zarzuty Starokalendarzan* (Warsaw: 1640), fol. E1v.

72 Jan Dubovyč, *Kalendarz prawdziwy Cerkwi Chrystusowey* (Vilnius: 1644), pp. 86–87.

73 In addition to the bells of the Christian churches, there were the appointed "criers" who called Tatars and Jews to their places of worship. A 1558 account of Tatar life drawn up by a Lithuanian Tatar for Sultan Suleiman the Magnificent noted that, contrary to normal practice in Islamic countries, in

Lithuania "before worship, one of our citizens goes around the streets, summoning aloud [the worshippers] to prayer in the mosque." The nineteenth-century editor of this text, A. Muchliński, suggested that this non-Islamic practice was borrowed from Lithuanian Jews, who selected someone to walk through the streets summoning the faithful to the synagogue. See Muchliński, "Zdanie sprawy," pp. 16–17.

74 On this point, Jewish butchers came into conflict with Christian butchers, who complained to the magistrate on 4 June 1667 that "a great *scandalum* must arise in our capital city of Vilnius, when the aforementioned Jewish butchers of Vilnius, on Fridays, and especially during Lent, having established the seat of their slaughterhouse near Roman monasteries and churches, slaughtering cattle in the city *publice* [publicly], and throwing out the *faeces* [remains] near their synagogue, on the path where people of the Roman Catholic faith, and above all monks and priests, are accustomed to go on their way to services at the Reverend Fathers Franciscans ...." See *Akty, izdavaemye Vilenskoju arxeografičeskoju komissieju*, vol. 20, pp. 407–08.

75 Sakovyč, *Kalendarz stary*, fols. E1v–2v. "*Christos woskres*" and "*Woistinu woskres*" represent, in Sakovyč's Latin-letter transliteration, the traditional Church Slavonic greeting and response exchanged by Orthodox Slavs at Easter: "Christ has arisen; He has arisen indeed."

76 Dubovyč, *Kalendarz prawdziwy*, pp. 86–87.

77 Łowmiański and Łowmiańska, *Akta cechów*, p. 171.

78 Ibid., p. 160.

79 Ibid., pp. 321–23.

80 To cite one example, see Tazbir, "Różnowiercy a kult maryjny," in *Świat Panów Pasków. Eseje i Studia* (Łódź: Wydawnictwo łódzkie, 1986), pp. 342–64, on the cult of the Virgin Mary among Polish Protestants and its function in the creation of intra-confessional solidarities among the Polish *szlachta*.

81 *Akty, izdavaemye Vilenskoju arxeografičeskoju komissieju*, vol. 20, p. 383.

82 See, for example, the 1673 testament of Vilnius merchant and burgher Krzysztof Sokołowski, who asked to be buried at the Orthodox Holy Spirit Church, but who also gave money to its arch-competitor, the Uniate Holy Trinity Church. Printed in *Akty, izdavaemye Vilenskoju arxeografičeskoju komissieju*, vol. 8 (Vilnius: 1875), pp. 522–28. Sokołowski was by no means alone in this practice.

Part Two

Identities and Subjectivities

JEWS, BUDDHISTS, CHRISTIANS, AND VAGRANTS

(De) Stabilized Identities in Medieval Jewish-Christian Disputations on the Talmud

STEVEN F. KRUGER

C hristian identity—both the identity of Christianity as a whole and that of individual Christians—depends significantly upon a *historical* relation to Judaism. Christianity is a continuation, a descendant, of Judaism, and it defines itself accordingly, taking Hebrew scripture, as "fulfilled" through Christ's coming and as rethought in the texts of the New Testament, as its starting point and inheritance, defining itself indeed as the "true Israel" ("verus Israel").[1] At the same time, however, the Christian redefinition of the meaning of "Israel," of the "chosen people," signals not just continuity but rupture. Christianity is a descendent of Judaism but a rebellious one, taking its inheritance into a "new" dispensation that rewrites and transvalues the central terms of the "old" religion. Distinct identity is achieved here only by means of a strong movement of *dis*identification, as Christianity insists on becoming something essentially and radically different from Judaism. But it is, of course, the very fact of continuity that necessitates the insistence on *dis*continuity, the attempt to break, deny, or repudiate the historical relationship of affiliation with the "parent."

At the heart of Christian self-definition, then, is an assertion of distinction, newness, rupture that is paradoxically dependent upon the continued visibility and presence of what is left behind.[2] The descendant insists on distinct identity, an insistence that, in its very vehemence, calls attention to the (repudiated) link of parentage. The dynamic here is, moreover, characteristic not just of doctrinal and institutional moves to establish Christianity and the church but also of the ways in which *individuals* are thought to enter the new religion. Conversion is a movement, as in the prototypical conversion of Saul to Paul (Acts 9:1–30), that claims a radical discontinuity with the former self, but at the same time it is a movement legible only in relation to that former self. This is a model that remains intimate to the conception of the Christian self well after the church is firmly established. Individual moral movements continue to be conceived in conversionary terms, as (following the formulations of the Pauline epistles) the turning from the old man to the new, from the flesh to the spirit, from death to life. In each of these turns, the former term is indelibly marked as Jewish, even in contexts where there are no actual Jews. Insofar as each Christian individual contains an old, fleshly, death-defined identity that must be repudiated in a conversion to true faith, each Christian contains a Jewish self to be overcome.

The movements of disidentification—whether in the self-definition of Christianity as a whole or in the moral struggles of individual Christians—depend upon a radical stabilization of Jewish identity as the old, carnal, and death-driven, as a shell or husk left behind via the conversionary metamorphosis into Christian identity.[3] Particularly crucial in such a stabilization of Jewishness is a thinking of *temporality* that, even given the presence of contemporary Jews, constructs Jews, Jewishness, and Judaism as belonging fully to the past, a time before the new dispensation brought by Christ and made radically past by the incarnation. As Kathleen Biddick has argued, medieval Christians "translate[d] the corporeal co-presence of Jews among whom they lived into a temporal absence."[4] Jews stand as a stabilized figure of that which has been repudiated as lifeless, empty, unchangeable—tangible and visible in the present only as the spectre of a past irremediably left behind and against which Christianity's and Christians' self-definitions may operate.[5] Such a stabilization of Judaism as pastness depends, of course, upon a series of denials—of a post-incarnational history of Jewish change; of a contemporary medieval Judaism that might not be, in fact was not, identical to the "old testamentary" Judaism that Christ encountered and lived within and that was repudiated by the first Christians; of Jewish physical, political, and intellectual presences in the contemporary medieval moment. These are, however, denials that medieval Christians and Christianity show themselves quite prepared to make.

But while Christianity tries to put its Jewish ancestor behind it, in part by positioning Christian identity in relation to a rigidly stabilized version of Judaism, Christian ideology can always be disturbed by those elements of the real—both historical and contemporary—it denies. A Jewish history that includes, for instance, divisions *within* Judaism,[6] complex and often contested traditions of biblical exegesis, and new deployments of philosophical and theological thought (often in dialogue with philosophical and theological movements within Christianity's other, and more geopolitically threatening, religious rival, Islam), complicates and calls into question the Jewish absent presence stabilized by Christianity to serve its self-constructions. So, too, does a present of Jews and Jewish communities that manifestly demonstrates the *living* qualities of Judaism.

⚜

This complex relation of Christianity to its Jewish "parent" may help us to understand one of the paradoxes in the history of medieval Jewish-Christian relations. The very period that scholars have identified with a growing persecution of Judaism by Christianity is also a moment when Jewish-Christian communication and collaboration appear to be especially intense. The twelfth and thirteenth centuries saw massacres such as those in the Rhineland (1096, 1146) and England (1189–90), often associated with crusading activity; the segregatory legislation of the Fourth Lateran Council (1215); the inquisition and burning of the Talmud and related Jewish books at Paris (1239–48), echoed repeatedly in the decades that followed, with Jewish books confiscated at Oxford in 1244, burnt at Bourges in 1251, disputed at Barcelona in 1263, and confiscated in Apulia in 1270;[7] waves of expulsion from England (1290) and various parts of

France (1288, 1306, 1334); the rise of the blood libel (from 1235), accusations of ritual murder (from ca. 1150), and host desecration (from 1243).[8] During the same period, however, Jewish and Christian exegetes clearly consulted with each other in such centres of learning as Paris.[9] And the massive intellectual movement of recovering and translating antique knowledge involved significant and complex crossings of Islamic, Jewish, and Christian cultures.[10]

In the Paris disputation of 1240, Rabbi Yeḥiel claimed that Jews "sell cattle to Christians, ... have partnerships with Christians, ... allow ourselves to be alone with them, ... give our children to Christian wet-nurses, and ... teach Torah to Christians—for there are now many Christian priests who can read Hebrew books."[11] Whether or not Yeḥiel's claims represent a common historical reality, they suggest the plausibility of such a vision of interreligious interaction for Yeḥiel's largely Christian audience at the debate. Certainly Christian anxiety about too-intimate relations with Jewish communities was repeatedly expressed in twelfth- and thirteenth-century legislation— against, for instance, Jews keeping Christian servants (and specifically wet-nurses). From the Third Lateran Council (1179): "Jews and Saracens shall not be permitted to have Christian slaves in their homes; neither for the purpose of nursing their children, nor for domestic service, nor for any other purpose."[12] And several times documents suggest that such decrees were ignored and hence needed reiteration. Thus, a papal bull of 1205, addressed to the king of France, notes that, despite the legislation of the Third Lateran, Jews "do not hesitate to have Christian servants and nurses, with whom, at times, they work such abominations as are more fitting that you should punish than proper that we should specify"; a similar claim is made in a papal letter of 1244.[13] The decrees of the Fourth Lateran Council (1215) concerning the Jews arose at least in part from a perception that Jewish and Christian communities had come into too-close contact— through Jewish moneylending, interreligious sexual intercourse (necessitating the distinction of Jews and Saracens from the Christian population by the quality of their clothes), and Jews gaining "preferment in public office."[14]

One might explain the simultaneous rise in persecutory relations and flourishing of interreligious collaboration as separate movements occurring in separate social realms, and this is no doubt in part the case: violence against Jews often took place *despite* ecclesiastical and aristocratic wishes and commands. But there is no way to assign persecution wholly to one social realm and collaboration wholly to another;[15] the two intersect in significant ways—as is clear with persecutory legislation that responds negatively to the perception of close Jewish-Christian interaction. Importantly active at this intersection between the persecutory and the collaborative are Christian ideas of temporality intended to stabilize (and hence neutralize the power of) the older, parental religion. If Judaism is a fossilized system of belief, caught—because of the original Jewish refusal to acknowledge Christ as the Messiah—in a way of thinking once divinely sanctioned but no longer applicable to the post-incarnational world, it should remain static, and that this was not the case must quickly have become clear to those Christians involved in the intellectual work of the twelfth-century "renaissance" and the Aristotelian revival that followed. Jews, most notably the great rabbi, philosopher, exegete, and physician Maimonides (1135–1204), were deeply involved in the latter movement, elaborating Aristotelian ideas on the "cutting edge" of European philosophy, and (like their Muslim counterparts) they strongly influenced thirteenth-century Christian thinking. When a scholastic philosopher-theologian like Thomas Aquinas incorporated Jewish philosophical work into his own thinking, as he did, he must have recognized that "new" knowledge was emerging from the "old," supposedly static, religion.[16]

Scholars like those in Paris working closely enough with Jewish exegetes to be themselves accused of "Judaizing" tendencies, must have recognized, too, that Jewish exegesis was a vital and changing intellectual enterprise. Not the literal-minded and plodding (mis)understanding of scripture constructed by anti-Jewish polemic, Jewish exegetical work, while emphasizing the literal and historical, could involve as complex moves to allegorize and spiritualize the text as did Christian exegesis. Jewish polemical literature suggests that Jews became quite practised in responding to Christian charges that they read the Bible only literally and hence with only partial understanding. Joseph Kimḥi, in his twelfth-century *Book of the Covenant*, turns the charge of literal-mindedness back against

Christian exegetes. Though the Christian unbeliever, the *min*, in Kimḥi's dialogic *Book* accuses his Jewish interlocutor, the *ma'amin* (believer), of "understand[ing] most of the Torah literally while we understand it figuratively," the *ma'amin* advances essentially the same charge against Christian reading practices:

> Here [Genesis 1:26] image and likeness are not to be
> taken literally but metaphorically. Image is dominion
> and likeness is rulership, not a physical image. What
> is the matter with you? On the basis of one obscure
> passage, you deny His unity and expound it as [proof]
> of a plurality.[17]

Rabbi Meir ben Simeon, in mid-thirteenth-century Narbonne, reports a disputation he had "on the subject of moneylending on interest" with a Christian in which Meir, like Kimḥi, calls into question Christian approaches to reading the biblical text: "Why do you not interpret the law on interest figuratively like the other prohibitions and thus allow (following your own exegesis) the lending on interest even to your own people?"[18] Whether Christians commonly attended to such Jewish self-defence and polemic—Kimḥi's text, for instance, was probably *not* widely available[19]—some at least knew enough about medieval Jewish exegesis to recognize that it did not simply reflect, as Christian polemic would have it, an obtuse, unchanging (mis)understanding of scripture.

More disturbing still to Christian constructions of Judaism would have been the increasing knowledge of the Talmud that certain Christians gained during this period.[20] An ancient set of texts incorporating oral rabbinic thought developed over the course of many generations, and itself subject to continual interpretation and reinterpretation, the Talmud makes it obvious that the elaboration of Jewish thought never stopped. With its multiple layers of exegesis and argument, its dialogical qualities, its distinction between legal (*halakhic*) and narrative/homiletic (*aggadic*) material, the Talmud represents a Judaism that is vital and changing, and that, much like Christianity, has spun out a significant body of texts questioning, interpreting, rethinking, and updating the "Old Testament" with which Christianity so firmly identified its parent religion.

Such disturbances to a Christian sense of temporality and of Jewish archaism became centrally important in the anti-Jewish polemic and action of the period. Dominican and Franciscan inquisitors at Montpellier in the early 1230s made, in Jeremy Cohen's words, "an unprecedented intrusion into internal Jewish affairs," condemning and (perhaps) burning the works of Maimonides.[21] The details of the affair are not wholly clear from the historical documents that survive, but the condemnation seems related to the broader early thirteenth-century backlash against Aristotelianism.[22] Unlike the challenges to Christian Averroism, however, the actions at Montpellier are primarily directed not toward Christian self-regulation but toward the control of Jewish intellectual life, a control perhaps at first welcomed by conservative intellectual forces within Judaism. In at least one Jewish account of the events leading up to the condemnation, conservative, anti-Maimonidean Jews are depicted approaching the inquisitors with the call "to guard us from error in the exact same way [you do] yourselves" through the prosecution of heresy.[23] It seems clear that the inquisitors here acted to guard Judaism from internal "error," to keep it a pure witness to the truth of Christianity (in Augustine's words, testifying "that we have not fabricated the prophecies about Christ"), a witness unchanged since the time of Christ.[24]

A similar, if more complex, movement can be seen in Christian attacks on the Talmud in this same period. Most directly, such attacks accuse the Talmud of containing explicitly anti-Christian material; in the words of Pope Gregory IX's 1239 letter calling for the kings of France, England, Aragon, Castile, Leon, Navarre, and Portugal to "seize all the books belonging to the Jews of your Kingdom," the Talmud presents "matter so abusive and so unspeakable that it arouses shame in those who mention it and horror in those who hear it."[25] Thus, Judah M. Rosenthal has suggested, in 1240 at Paris, most of the charges against the Talmud fell into the following four categories: "hostility towards Christians" (including commands to kill and deceive Christians, and the claim that Christians suffer in hell eternally while Jews do not), "blasphemies against God" (including claims that even God has sinned, lied to Abraham, and commanded Samuel to lie; that he curses himself for having destroyed the Temple and enslaved Israel; that he studies the Talmud, was defeated in a legal debate by the Rabbis, and weeps three times each day), "blasphemies against Jesus, Mary and Christianity" (including the use of obscene language to designate the pope and the church, and claims that Mary was an adulteress and that Jesus is boiled in excrement in hell), and "stupidity of talmudic laws and stories" (including accounts of Adam having intercourse with all the animals and the serpent with Eve, Cham abusing his father Noah, and God wearing phylacteries).[26]

Serious as they are, however, such attacks against specific doctrinal claims or against a Jewish hostility to Christianity expressed in the Talmud do not seem to represent the essential Christian concern. In addition to, and overriding, the focus on doctrinal "errors" is the strong polemical suggestion that the Talmud should never have been written, that its very existence violates divine order. Nine of the charges levelled at the Talmud in Paris concern "the authority of the Talmud and the Rabbis":

> They claim that the law which they call the Talmud
> was given by God.
> They say that the talmudic law was transmitted by
> God orally.
> They claim that the Oral Law was implanted in their
> minds (and not written).
> They say that the Talmud was preserved without
> being written down until the day arrived when those
> whom they call scholars and scribes, in order that the
> talmudic Law should not be forgotten among the
> people, put it in writing, the product exceeding in
> length that of the Bible.
> The Talmud contains among other absurdities the
> opinion that the above-mentioned scholars and
> scribes are superior to the prophets.
> These scholars are entitled to abrogate the words of
> the Law.
> It is a duty to follow the scholars even when they say
> that the right is left and that the left is right.
> One who does not observe what they [the sages]

teach deserves the death penalty.
They prohibit children from studying the Bible
because they prefer that they study the Talmud from
which they voluntarily derive laws.[27]

All of these supposed Jewish claims are, of course, seen by the
Christian accusers as false and dangerous, and largely because such
claims suggest a post-biblical elaboration of Jewish religion and
thought unacceptable to a Christian ideology that identifies Judaism
firmly with the "Old Testament." Again from Pope Gregory IX's
letter to the kings of Christendom: "The Jews of France and of the
other lands ... are not content with the Old Law which God gave to
Moses in writing: they even ignore it completely, and affirm that God
gave another law which is called 'Talmud,' that is 'Teaching,' handed
down to Moses orally .... [T]he volume of this by far exceeds the text
of the Bible."[28] Here, as Cohen notes, medieval Jews are seen as
"deliberately forsaking the literal biblical Judaism of their ancestors."[29]
And, as Joel E. Rembaum argues, from the Christian point of view,
"[t]he problem was not simply an internal Jewish matter":

> From the pope's viewpoint this situation had a direct
> impact upon the Church. The Jews had abandoned
> the position and function assigned to them by
> Christian tradition .... Thus, the Jews had perpetrated
> a kind of "heresy." Christian law allowed them to
> keep their Bibles at a time when many Christians
> were prohibited from keeping copies of Scripture.
> But, with this privilege the Jews were *non contenti*,
> for they had elevated the Talmud to a level of
> importance above that of the Bible. The Jews were
> allowed to keep their Bibles; they were not to be
> allowed to keep their Talmuds.[30]

Through the accusations it brought forward concerning the Talmud,
Cohen suggests, "The Church ... depicted the 'living' Judaism of its
own day as a heresy and perversion, a pernicious oral tradition of
religious law and doctrine, a gross deviation from the religion of the
Old Testament,"[31] and pursued, for a time at least, not just the
censoring of individual talmudic passages deemed offensive but the

Talmud's full suppression, attempted most spectacularly in its burning at Paris in 1242.

But while Christianity thus "maintained that it was illegitimate for Jews as Jews to preserve the Talmud and live according to its teaching," what seems a contradictory approach also developed in Christian anti-Jewish polemic.[32] Here, the authority of the Talmud was acknowledged, but now presented both as revealing *Christian* truths and as needing to be read in particular ways known definitely to Christians but not to Jews. Christian disputants thus sometimes acted, as the convert Pablo Christiani did in the Barcelona disputation of 1263, to "prove" the truth of Christian doctrine via talmudic material. From the Latin account of the debate: "it was proved to him [Nahmanides] both by the authority of the Law and the Prophets and by the Talmud, that Christ had in truth come, as Christians believe and preach. To this he was not able to reply."[33] Further, Christian disputants attempted to police acceptable modes of reading the Talmud. Thus, the kind of argument the great Jewish philosopher, scholar, and rabbi Nahmanides, the principle Jewish disputant at Barcelona, presents, distinguishing between *halakhah* (as an authoritative explication of the commandments of Torah) and *aggadah* (as narrative material which, in Nahmanides' words, "if anyone wants to believe in ... well and good, but if someone does not believe in ... there is no harm"),[34] is explicitly prohibited in the Tortosa disputation of a century and a half later. Here, the Christian convert Jerónimo of Santa Fe can argue "that a Jew must necessarily believe the entire contents of the Talmud, whether they are explanations of the Law, or legal decisions, or ceremonies, or homiletic material, or edicts, commentaries, additions or *novelle* made about the said Talmud; nor may a Jew deny anything of it."[35] And he can accuse his Jewish interlocutors of having "committed or perpetrated a great crime when you denied the authoritative passages of your Talmud."[36]

Although very different from the active suppression of the Talmud, such regulation of Jewish thinking from outside nonetheless shares with it the impulse to fix Judaism in place and time: even as Christian polemicists are forced by the witness of the Talmud to admit that Judaism has changed during the Christian era, they deny current Jews any flexibility in the treatment of their own traditions and thus again confine Judaism to a static moment outside the dynamic present. The situation Jews found themselves in with regard to the Talmud is thus at the same time ambivalent—including both the condemnation of talmudic writings and the doctrine of necessary belief in them—and, in a certain incoherent way, coherent—with each seemingly contradictory side of the Christian position reasserting the necessity of Jewish archaism, a Jewish temporality violently removed from the present.

⁂⁂⁂

At stake in Christian attacks on the Talmud, then, is the control of Jewish identity, and consequently of Christian identity as well. The very existence of the Talmud, the authority granted it, its treatment as a sacred text to be studied and interpreted—all suggest an ongoingness to Judaism that threatens Christianity's self-definition as the religion of the present, and the future. To treat Judaism as growing and changing, rather than as a fossilized remnant of a past left definitively behind through the Incarnation, is essentially unthinkable for mainstream medieval Christianity; such a thought, "forced" upon Christianity by an increasing knowledge of Judaism in part the result of closer contact between the two religions, challenges not just Christian conceptions of Jewishness but also Christian self-conceptions insofar as these depend upon a relation of clear distinction from Jewishness.

The intimate connection between Christian concern over the Talmud and both Jewish and Christian identity is dramatized in one of the central means used to call talmudic learning into question—the public debate or disputation. A series of important disputations between Christians and Jews—most notably at Paris in 1240, Barcelona in 1263, and Tortosa in 1413–14—made one of their central concerns the Talmud and its suppression or, alternatively, its correction and control. There were other public disputes as well—for instance, a second dispute at Paris (ca. 1272) between Rabbi Abraham ben Samuel and the convert Pablo Christiani (the main Christian spokesman, too, at Barcelona), and one reported at Narbonne by Meir ben Simeon between himself and an unnamed archbishop—in which talmudic teachings are partly at issue.[37] But the debates at Paris (1240), Barcelona, and Tortosa are particularly noteworthy—in part because of the distinguished character of the participants (the Queen Mother Blanche presided at Paris, King James I of Aragon at Barcelona, and the "Antipope" Benedict XIII at Tortosa), in part because of the extensive literature produced from each (Hebrew and Latin accounts survive of all three, including Naḥmanides' *Vikuaḥ* [Disputation]), in part because the dispute at Paris, instigated by the pope and followed as it was by the burning of the Talmud, set the tone for repeated attacks on Jewish learning in the centuries that followed.

As has been argued, none of these disputations is a debate in the true sense of the word—as Robert Chazan suggests, the disputations do not involve "intellectual confrontation on an equal footing."[38] The terms of discussion are set throughout by the Christian side, which, after all, convenes and presides over the debates, compelling the Jewish discussants to appear. Toward the start of the debate at Paris, Rabbi Yeḥiel addresses the Queen Mother: "Your Majesty, do not compel me to answer him [his opponent Nicholas Donin]."[39] Naḥmanides begins the *Vikuaḥ*: "Our Lord the King commanded me to hold a Disputation with Fray Paul."[40] The Hebrew account of the proceedings at Tortosa similarly describes the genesis of the disputation as involving compulsion: "the leaders of Israel stood in trouble and distress before the Pope at the request of Joshua Halorki, who, after his apostasy, was called among the Gentiles Maestre Geronimo de Santa Fe ... for he asked the Pope that the scholars of Israel should come before him, and he would prove to them that the Messiah has come, and is Jesus, and he would prove this from their own Talmud."[41] Indeed, the proceedings have been read as inquisitorial or trial records rather than as debates, with Jewish speakers testifying as witnesses or defendants rather than as disputants in an evenhanded discussion.[42]

Still, these interreligious confrontations take the *form* of debate, and we might productively ask what is served by setting up the trial of the Talmud *as though* it involved an equal facing-off of Judaism and Christianity. Whether real or fictional, debates—in a well-established tradition dating back to the early years of Christianity—serve as emblematic restagings of Jewish/Christian distinction and division.[43] Posing Christian truth against Jewish error, the Christian debate literature attempts to re-articulate Christian identity by reconfronting the Jewish identity from which Christianity emerged and by resettling that identity as fully superseded. (One might read the Jewish debate literature that responds to Christian polemic as an attempt to take back control of the definition of what it means to be a Jew, and in so doing to unsettle a Christian sense of stability, truth, and chosenness.) One particularly striking example of the debate's concern with questions of religious identity is provided in the twelfth century by the *Dialogi contra Iudaeos*, written by the Jewish convert to Christianity Peter Alfonsi and characterized by one recent scholar as "the most influential and widely read of all medieval anti-Jewish tracts."[44] Here, a fictional debate is staged between Peter and Moses; as the author Peter reveals to us, Moses was his name before baptism, and the dialogue is clearly intended to pose Jewish versus Christian selves. Here, as elsewhere in the Christian debate literature, Christian victory is set up from the start, and Peter forces Moses to concede the point on every significant question. The *Dialogi*, then, resurrects Peter's "old," Jewish self only to put it to rest again and in so doing to reconfirm the identity of the "new," Christian self. But the very fact that Christian identity needs reconfirmation— and that this operates by means of calling the Jewish self left behind by conversion back into play—suggests that the resettling of identity performed by the debate operates in conjunction with destabilizing effects. The debate reaffirms the post-conversion identity of Peter, but that this must occur *over and against* the disavowed identity of Moses, means that the confrontation of Christian and Jewish selves in the debate always has some potential to serve as a site for the disruption of that achieved identity it attempts to stabilize.[45]

More generally, we might read the medieval literature of Jewish–Christian debate as involved in an anxious relation to identity, serving to assure its stability, but at the same time—by bringing "truth" into the forum of debate, by reaffirming "truth" through the consideration of "false" positions, and thus by allowing, in no matter how incomplete, constrained, and confined a way, "falsehood" to speak for itself—the very means of stabilization serves a potential *de*stabilization. The extent to which both Jewish and Christian identity are at stake in the public disputes over the Talmud is emphasized, moreover, by the fact that the main Christian disputants in each of the three—Nicholas Donin at Paris, Pablo Christiani at Barcelona, and Jerónimo de Santa Fe at Tortosa—are Jewish converts to Christianity.[46] Other converted Jews, too, were involved more peripherally in these public debates and the events surrounding them.[47] Though there are obvious pragmatic reasons why Jewish converts to Christianity would be valuable and hence intimately involved in these disputes over talmudic knowledge—they would have fuller access to the Hebrew texts central to the debates than even the most highly educated of Christians—the prominence of converts here perhaps also suggests something significant about precisely what is at stake for the Christian side in the disputations. That debate with Jews is perceived as dangerous to the faith of Christian disputants—even though such debates occur in political situations firmly controlled by Christianity—is clear, for instance, from Pope Gregory IX's decree of 1233 to the prelates of Germany, calling on them "to prohibit most stringently that [Jews] should at any time dare to dispute with Christians about their faith or their rites, lest under pretext of such disputation the simple-minded slide into a snare of error."[48] Christians other than converts indeed participated in these disputations, mainly in roles that kept them out of the debate proper, presiding over the proceedings but only occasionally intervening in the actual discussion. This suggests a certain attempt to keep Christians "pure" of direct contact with Jewish intellectual positions, "safe" from the destabilizing effects that might follow upon a Jewish challenge to Christian positions.

Christian converts themselves were already in a somewhat "impure" position *vis-à-vis* Judaism, no matter how avid they were in the defence of the newly embraced faith (and Nicholas Donin, Pablo Christiani, and Jerónimo de Santa Fe were avid Christians, and Christian polemicists, indeed). The very act of conversion, even as it is crucial to the establishment of Christian conceptions of self, also emphasizes the changeability of self, the potential for moving from one identity to another: in this case from the Jewish identity against which Christian identity was resolutely defined to Christian identity itself. Indeed, though conversion of individual Jews to

Christianity was the goal of much polemical missionary work, and sometimes the result of coercive action, it was not uncomplicatedly seen as a praiseworthy end. Corporate conversion of the Jews is, of course, predicted for the end of time, and the decision of individual Jews to become Christian before that time presented a certain disruption to the Christian ideology of Jewish temporality. If Jews could, before their communal conversion, disagree among themselves, and if some Jews could move beyond their Jewish identities to embrace Christianity, what did this say about the notion that Jews were somehow caught in a static past, that Jewish identity was a stubborn, obtuse, dead substance insensible by its very definition to the living spiritual force of Christian truth? While, on the one hand, Jewish conversion to Christianity was treated as proof of the superiority of Christian belief and identity, on the other hand, Jewish converts were often regarded as somehow not fully Christian, not able completely to leave their Jewish selves behind, and hence remaining in certain important ways trapped in their Jewishness.[49] Moreover, the very possibility of a movement from Judaism to Christianity—demonstrating, as it did, that Jewish identity was neither stable nor static—might suggest, too, the instability of *Christian* identity, the possibility that, in an inverse movement, Christians could become Jewish. "New Christians" were seen as particularly susceptible to such an inverted conversion, and to guard against this possibility the Church repeatedly legislated against the "relapse" or reversion of Christian converts to Judaism. From the Fourth Lateran Council, for instance, comes the following decree that clearly voices the anxiety that the "new" self of the convert might not be wholly cleansed of the "old":

> We have heard that certain ones who had voluntarily approached the baptismal font, have not completely driven out the old self in order the more perfectly to bring in the new. Since they retain remnants of their former faith, they tarnish the beauty of the Christian Religion by such a mixture. For it is written "Cursed be he who walks the earth in two ways" [Ecclesiasticus 3:28], and even in wearing a garment one may not mix linen and wool [Leviticus 19:19, Deuteronomy 22:11].

We decree, therefore, that such people shall in every possible manner be restrained by the prelates of the churches, from observing their old rites, so that those whom their free will brought to the Christian religion shall be held to its observance by compulsion, that they may be saved. For there is less evil in not recognizing the way of the Lord than in backsliding after having recognized it.[50]

While the anxiety here is expressly concerned with the "relapse" of converts, insofar as Christian identity altogether is conceived in terms of individual conversion, we may recognize, too, a broader concern about the maintenance of a stable, "converted" Christian self.[51]

The prominence of converts in the disputations over the Talmud thus richly complicates the involvement of questions of identity in the dynamics of debate. As I have just suggested, this prominence may point to a certain Christian reluctance to engage head-on with Jewish interlocutors, a reluctance that may arise at least in part from an anxiety about the destabilizing effects of debate on Christian identity. Further, the converts themselves, though firmly identified *as* Christians, speak out of necessarily complex and vexed identity positions. All speak for a Christian orthodoxy, but at the same time—because of the debates' talmudic focus—all claim, as well, to speak the truth of Judaism and Jewish texts. Though this puts them in a position of particular authority, it also potentially undermines their standing as full members of the Christian community. Such a situation also means that the *Jewish* disputants are arguing not simply against Christian positions but against positions that their former co-religionists at least try to present as Jewish. The resulting dynamics of debate become extremely complicated—and generally in ways that destabilize *both* Jewish and Christian identity. Thus, even when the Jewish disputant gains the upper hand, the larger movement of the debate tends to call into question Jews' competency to interpret their own texts and traditions. At the same time, Christianity speaks in these disputations at least in part via "Jewish"

voices, and Jewish arguments do not leave Christian positions and claims safely unquestioned.

The texts relating to the Paris, Barcelona, and Tortosa disputations deserve a fuller analysis in terms of the dynamics of identity than I am able to give them here. To stand in for that more complete analysis and to gesture toward the complex (de)stabilizations of identity that occur in these debates, consider, as just one instance, the following complicated moment from the Barcelona disputation (as presented in Naḥmanides' account), in which a prominent rabbi, an anonymous Jew off the street, a former Jew, a Christian cleric, and a Christian king confront each other. Arguing about the time of the coming of the Messiah, in a discussion that depends upon close readings of both biblical and talmudic passages, the convert—once Saul, now Friar Pablo Christiani—argues that "There is no Jew in the world who will not agree that 'day,' in Hebrew [*yom*], means literally 'day'." He claims that his opponent Naḥmanides "changes the meanings of words just as he likes." King James of Aragon, presiding over the debate, has "the first Jew" that his men can find brought in. Asked, "What is the meaning of the Hebrew word *yom*?" the Jew answers, "Day," confirming Pablo Christiani's position. But Naḥmanides responds: "My lord King, this Jew is certainly a better judge of the matter than Fray Paul, but not better than I. The word *yom*, in Scripture, sometimes means 'time.' ... And in the plural *yamim* it can be used to mean 'years.' ... But I am speaking on matters of wisdom to someone who does not know and does not understand, and it is fitting that fools should give judgment for him!" At this point, a second friar, Arnold of Segarra (the Dominican prior of Barcelona), intervenes: "See, Jerome has interpreted 'days' in this passage as meaning 'days of the people'," and Naḥmanides "rejoices," concluding that "You can see from Jerome's words that 'days' here are not to be taken in their literal sense as in other passages, and that is why he felt it necessary to give an interpretation."[52]

The Christian position here depends not just on the argument of the converted Jew Pablo Christiani but also on the testimony of a Jew brought in from the street. And the Christian position here suffers a setback, with one friar indeed supporting the Jewish argument by citing Jerome, the most venerable of patristic authorities on the literal meaning of scripture. But while Naḥmanides scores a certain victory here, this comes only at the expense of the Jew brought in off the street and the former Jew, Pablo Christiani; the Jewish position is confirmed only at the cost of making fellow Jews "play the fool." Naḥmanides' victory means, moreover, ceding interpretive authority both to the Christian friar Arnold of Segarra and to the great Christian "author" of Jewish scripture, Jerome.

Though this is just a moment in the debate, it is a moment that clearly dramatizes the slippery ground that public disputation provided for both Jews and Christians. Of course, the political stakes were by no means equal for the two sides: Christians controlled the terms and results of the debate. Though the Barcelona disputation has often been judged a victory for Naḥmanides,[53] he would be brought to trial by the Dominicans in 1265 for having published his account of the disputation. James I of Aragon seems to have protected Naḥmanides in this prosecution, but Pope Clement IV demanded, in a letter to King James, that Naḥmanides be punished—"let a strict severity manifest itself and, by the example of that one, the audacity of others be restrained."[54] Naḥmanides left Europe for Palestine soon afterward (1267), as had Rabbi Yeḥiel two decades earlier in the wake of the Paris debate (1240). These events surely demonstrate how dangerous it was for Jews to speak Jewish belief publicly in Christian Europe—even when, like Naḥmanides, *compelled* to do so. But these events also suggest how threatening to Christianity the statement of Jewish belief might be felt to be—even by a Christian religious/political order firmly in control of its own material circumstances.

NOTES

I thank Glenn Burger for having read several versions of this essay and for having provided his usual astute advice.

1 On Christianity's claim to be "verus Israel," see Marcel Simon, *Verus Israel: A Study of the Relations between Christians and Jews in the Roman Empire (135–425)*, trans. H. McKeating (Oxford: Oxford University Press, 1986).

2 The need for a continued Jewish presence in relation to the developing Church is stated most influentially by Augustine; see *De civitate dei*, ed. Bernard Dombart and Alphonse Kalb (with emendations by the editors of CCSL), Corpus Christianorum, Series Latina 47–48, vol. 48 (Turnhout: Brepols, 1955),

p. 644; *Concerning the City of God against the Pagans*, trans. Henry Bettenson (Harmondsworth: Penguin, 1984), 18.46, pp. 827–28.

3 The metaphor of conversion via the shedding of a husk or skin is a medieval one. See, for instance, Rabbi Meir ben Simeon's account of an archbishop urging conversion upon him: "throw away the husk and eat the pomegranate" (S. Stein, "Jewish-Christian Disputations in Thirteenth-Century Narbonne," inaugural lecture, University College, London, 22 October 1964 [London: H.K. Lewis, 1969], p. 21). And see the interesting *exemplum* in Joan Young Gregg, *Devils, Women, and Jews: Reflections on the Other in Medieval Sermon Stories* (Albany: State University of New York Press, 1997), pp. 126–27, which involves a woman, penitent before her death, escaping demonic punishment by "shedding her own skin," changing into a serpent, and finally "becom[ing] a lovely lady." Such metaphors, of course, resonate with medieval understandings of allegorical reading, themselves central to Christian self-distinction from Judaism and Jewish "literalness."

4 Kathleen Biddick, "The ABC of Ptolemy: Mapping the World with the Alphabet," in *Text and Territory: Geographical Imagination in the European Middle Ages*, ed. Sylvia Tomasch and Sealy Gilles (Philadelphia: University of Pennsylvania Press, 1998), pp. 268–93, at p. 269.

5 For a fuller discussion of this Christian thinking of temporality and Jewish spectrality, see Steven F. Kruger, "The Spectral Jew," *New Medieval Literatures* 2 (1998): 9–35.

6 Such divisions within Judaism are evident, for instance, in controversy over Maimonides' (Aristotelian) works and in Karaite objections to talmudic tradition. (The Karaites were, and are, a group within Judaism denying the significance of rabbinic and talmudic interpretive traditions, insisting instead on a strict construction of the literal biblical text.) For the suggestion that some of the converted Jews involved in Christian anti-talmudic actions were influenced by Karaite anti-talmudism and rationalism, see Judah M. Rosenthal, "The Talmud on Trial: The Disputation at Paris in the Year 1240," *Jewish Quarterly Review* n.s. 47 (1956): 58–76 and 145–69, at p. 67. Rosenthal also notes that the convert Nicholas Donin, the primary Christian disputant in the Paris debate of 1240, was perhaps "convinced of the truth of Karaism" (p. 69). Also see Solomon Grayzel, *The Church and the Jews in the XIIIth Century: A Study of Their Relations during the Years 1198–1254, Based on the Papal Letters and the Conciliar Decrees of the Period*, rev. ed. (New York: Hermon Press, 1966), pp. 339–40.

7 See Jeremy Cohen, *The Friars and the Jews: The Evolution of Medieval Anti-Judaism* (Ithaca and London: Cornell University Press, 1982), pp. 78–85, on the implications of the 1240 inquisition of the Talmud in Paris. As Norman Golb, *The Jews in Medieval Normandy: A Social and Intellectual History* (Cambridge: Cambridge University Press, 1998), points out, the pope's initial order for the confiscation of Jewish books involved not just the Talmud but "universos libros Judeorum vestre Provincie" [all the books of the Jews of your province] (p. 427), and Golb argues that the attack on Jewish learning included, "*inter alia*, commentaries written by earlier French scholars such as Rashi, Jacob Tam, and Rashbam, and by Tosafists of the following generations" (p. 428). The order to burn the Talmud was renewed by Louis IX in 1254 (Golb gives the

date as 1253) and by his two successors, Philip III and Philip IV; see Cohen, *The Friars and the Jews*, p. 80, and Golb, *Jews in Medieval Normandy*, p. 429.

8 I follow Gavin I. Langmuir's dating of ritual murder accusations and the blood libel; see Langmuir, *Toward a Definition of Antisemitism* (Berkeley and Los Angeles: University of California Press, 1990), especially pp. 266–68. For overviews of the increasing persecution of Jews during the twelfth and thirteenth centuries, see Cohen, *The Friars and the Jews*; R.I. Moore, *The Formation of a Persecuting Society: Power and Deviance in Western Europe, 950–1250* (Oxford: Basil Blackwell, 1987); and Langmuir, *History, Religion, and Antisemitism* (Berkeley and Los Angeles: University of California Press, 1990). For a reading of thirteenth-century materials different from Cohen's, see Robert Chazan, *Daggers of Faith: Thirteenth-Century Christian Missionizing and Jewish Response* (Berkeley and Los Angeles: University of California Press, 1989), especially pp. 169–81.

9 On the value for Christian biblical exegesis in this period of Jewish scholarship, see Beryl Smalley, *The Study of the Bible in the Middle Ages* (Notre Dame, IN: University of Notre Dame Press, 1964 [1952]), especially the chapter on Andrew of St. Victor, pp. 112–95. And on twelfth-century Jewish-Christian intellectual relations, see Aryeh Graboïs, "The *Hebraica Veritas* and Jewish-Christian Intellectual Relations in the Twelfth Century," *Speculum* 50 (1975): 613–34.

10 For a convenient overview of the work of translation undertaken in Islamic, Jewish, and Christian centres during the twelfth century, see Marie-Thérèse d'Alverny, "Translations and Translators," in *Renaissance and Renewal in the Twelfth Century*, ed. Robert L. Benson and Giles Constable, with Carol D. Lanham (Cambridge, MA: Harvard University Press, 1982), pp. 421–62. For a reading of medieval Jewish culture that suggests often close relations between Christian and Jewish communities, see Ivan G. Marcus, *Rituals of Childhood: Jewish Acculturation in Medieval Europe* (New Haven: Yale University Press, 1996).

11 Hyam Maccoby, *Judaism on Trial: Jewish-Christian Disputations in the Middle Ages* (London: Littman Library of Jewish Civilization, 1993 [1982]), p. 32; cf. pp. 160–61.

12 Grayzel, *The Church and the Jews*, pp. 296–97.

13 Ibid., pp. 106–07 and 252–53. The latter letter also calls for the burning of the Talmud. The same documents are available in Shlomo Simonsohn, ed., *The Apostolic See and the Jews: Documents: 492–1404* (Toronto: Pontifical Institute of Mediaeval Studies, 1988), pp. 82–83 and 180–81.

14 Grayzel, *The Church and the Jews*, pp. 306–13.

15 See, for instance, John France's critique of the common idea that, in the First Crusade, "the 'Crusade of the Poor' ... is sharply distinguished from that of the knights [and] is alone guilty of persecuting the Jews" (France, "Patronage and the Appeal of the First Crusade," in *The First Crusade: Origins and Impacts*, ed. Jonathan Phillips [Manchester and New York: Manchester University Press, 1997], pp. 5–20, at p. 7).

16 See the essays collected in *Studies in Maimonides and St. Thomas Aquinas*, ed. Jacob I. Dienstag (New York: Ktav Publishing House, 1975).

17 Joseph Kimḥi, *The Book of the Covenant*, trans. Frank Talmage (Toronto: Pontifical Institute of Mediaeval Studies, 1972), pp. 40–41 and 46–47.

18 S. Stein, "A Disputation on Moneylending between Jews and Gentiles in Me'ir b. Simeon's Milḥemeth Miṣwah (Narbonne, 13th Cent.)," *Journal of Jewish Studies* 10 (1959): 45–61, at p. 51. Stein here translates a section of Meir ben Simeon's *Milḥemeth Miṣwah*.

19 The text of Kimḥi s *Book of the Covenant* survives only in a very late form, in a compendium of polemical treatises, the *Milḥemet Ḥovah*, published in 1710 at Constantinople; see Talmage's introduction to Kimḥi, *Book of the Covenant*, p. 18.

20 Rosenthal, "Talmud on Trial," notes: "[The Dominicans] established special courses in Hebrew and employed Jews and converts as teachers. The number of learned converts in the thirteenth century who put their knowledge of the Talmud and their zeal for conversion at the disposal of the Church was steadily on the increase" (p. 62).

21 The citation is from Cohen, *The Friars and the Jews*, p. 59; Cohen concludes that, given the current state of the evidence, "one cannot be sure about the extent of the actual burning" of Maimonides's texts (p. 58).

22 See ibid., pp. 52–53.

23 Ibid., p. 55. See also Rosenthal's account, "Talmud on Trial," pp. 61–62.

24 Augustine, *De civitate dei*, vol. 48, p. 644; *City of God*, 18.46, p. 827.

25 Grayzel, *The Church and the Jews*, pp. 240–43; the text of these documents is also available in Simonsohn, *The Apostolic See and the Jews*, pp. 171–74.

26 Rosenthal, "Talmud on Trial," pp. 76 and 150–66.

27 Ibid., pp. 76 and 145–50.

28 Grayzel, *The Church and the Jews*, pp. 240–41; also Simonsohn, *The Apostolic See and the Jews*, p. 172. The text of Gregory's letter echoes the charges presented by Nicholas Donin at the later trial in Paris, enumerated above and in more detail by Rosenthal, "Talmud on Trial," pp. 75–76 and 145–66.

29 Cohen, *The Friars and the Jews*, p. 75.

30 Joel E. Rembaum, "The Talmud and the Popes: Reflections on the Talmud Trials of the 1240s," *Viator* 13 (1982): 203–23, at pp. 210–11.

31 Cohen, *The Friars and the Jews*, p. 76.

32 Ibid., p. 75. Rembaum, "The Talmud and the Popes," looks closely at changes in papal attitudes toward the Talmud during the 1240s, and later.

33 Maccoby, *Judaism on Trial*, p. 148.

34 Ibid., p. 115; also translated in Oliver Shaw Rankin, *Jewish Religious Polemic of Early and Later Centuries: A Study of Documents Here Rendered in English* (New York: Ktav Publishing House, 1970), p. 188.

35 Maccoby, *Judaism on Trial*, p. 189. For the original text, see Antonio Pacios Lopez, *La Disputa de Tortosa*, 2 vols. (Madrid and Barcelona: Instituto "Arias Montano," 1957), vol. 2, p. 9.

36 Maccoby, *Judaism on Trial*, p. 209; Pacios Lopez, *Disputa de Tortosa*, vol. 2, p. 457.

37 On the second debate at Paris, see Golb, *Jews in Medieval Normandy*, pp. 495–507. On the debate at Narbonne, see Stein, "Jewish-Christian Disputations," pp. 17–22.

38 Robert Chazan, "The Barcelona 'Disputation' of 1263: Christian Missionizing and Jewish Response," *Speculum* 52 (1977): 824–42, at p. 824 n. 1.

39 Maccoby, *Judaism on Trial*, p. 153.

40 Ibid., p. 102; also translated by Rankin, *Jewish Religious Polemic*, p. 179.

41 Maccoby, *Judaism on Trial*, p. 168. Also see the Catalan translation in Jaume Rieri i Sans, *La Crònica en Hebreu de la Disputa de Tortosa* (Barcelona: Fundació Salvador Vives Casajuana, 1974), p. 29.

42 Rembaum, "The Talmud and the Popes," reviews suggestions "that the 1240 Paris 'disputation' was a form of inquisitorial trial" (p. 204). Also see the account in Rosenthal, "Talmud on Trial," and Stein, "Jewish-Christian Disputations," p. 7.

43 For an overview of ancient and medieval Christian-Jewish debate, see the introduction to David Berger, *The Jewish-Christian Debate in the High Middle Ages: A Critical Edition of the Niẓẓaḥon Vetus* (Philadelphia: The Jewish Publication Society of America, 1979), pp. 3–39, and, for more recent discussions, the essays collected in Ora Limor and Guy G. Stroumsa, eds., *Contra Iudaeos: Ancient and Medieval Polemics between Christians and Jews* (Tübingen: J.C.B. Mohr [Paul Siebeck], 1996).

44 John Tolan, *Petrus Alfonsi and His Medieval Readers* (Gainesville: University Press of Florida, 1993), p. 95. As Tolan notes, seventy-nine manuscripts of the *Dialogi* survive, distributed widely across Latin Europe. The *Dialogi* served as an important source for the Christian arguments brought forth by Jerónimo de Santa Fe in the Tortosa debate; see Tolan, *Petrus Alfonsi*, pp. 126–29. I have consulted the text of Alfonsi's *Dialogi* in the *Patrologia Latina* 157, cols. 535–672.

45 For fuller treatment of the dynamics of identity in Alfonsi's *Dialogi*, see Kruger, "Spectral Jew," pp. 30–32; "Becoming Christian, Becoming Male?" in *Becoming Male in the Middle Ages*, ed. Jeffrey Jerome Cohen and Bonnie Wheeler (New York and London: Garland, 1997), pp. 21–41, at pp. 31–34; and "Conversion and Medieval Sexual, Religious, and Racial Categories," in *Constructing Medieval Sexuality*, ed. Karma Lochrie, Peggy McCracken, and James A. Schultz (Minneapolis and London: University of Minnesota Press, 1997), pp. 158–79, at pp. 173–76. For a detailed discussion of the contents of the *Dialogi* and of the text's broad European influence, see Tolan, *Petrus Alfonsi*, pp. 12–72 and 95–131.

46 On Nicholas Donin, see Grayzel, *The Church and the Jews*, pp. 339–40. On Pablo Christiani, see Cohen, *The Friars and the Jews*, pp. 103–28. On Jerónimo de Santa Fe, see Pacios Lopez, *Disputa de Tortosa*, vol. 1, pp. 40–51.

47 See Rosenthal, "Talmud on Trial": "The charges against the Talmud at the trial of Paris are summarized in thirty-five articles in the appendix to a large collection of excerpts from the Talmud and Rashi. The collection known as *Excerpta Talmudica*, or *Extractiones de Talmud*, was compiled by the convert Thibaut de Sezanne upon the request of Odo of Chateauroux. Thibaut engaged the help of two other converts .... The appendix was the work of Donin and other converts" (pp. 74–75). Also see Maccoby, *Judaism on Trial*, p. 163, and Rembaum, "The Talmud and the Popes," p. 205. In the debate at Narbonne between Rabbi Meir ben Simeon and an archbishop, "one or two unnamed Jewish converts to Christianity are also present, but in contrast to Nicholas Donin of Paris or Pablo Christiani of Barcelona their function is quite subordinate" (Stein, "Jewish-Christian Disputations," p. 17).

48 Grayzel, *The Church and the Jews*, pp. 200–01; the letter is also edited by Simonsohn, *The Apostolic See and the Jews*, pp. 141–43.

49 See Jonathan M. Elukin, "From Jew to Christian? Conversion and Immutability in Medieval Europe," in *Varieties of Religious Conversion in the Middle Ages*, ed. James Muldoon (Gainesville: University of Florida Press, 1997), pp. 171–89; and Kruger, "Becoming Christian" and "Conversion and Medieval."

50 Grayzel, *The Church and the Jews*, pp. 310–11.

51 It is significant that the policing of Jewish texts often coincides temporally and spatially with orthodox Christian concern about "heretical" activity, where, from the perspective of the church, a certain movement of "anti-conversion" is at work within Christianity. Moore, *Formation of a Persecuting Society*, gives an overview of such a pattern of "coincidence."

52 Maccoby, *Judaism on Trial*, pp. 128–29; also translated in Rankin, *Jewish Religious Polemic*, pp. 197–98. On the identity of Arnold of Segarra, see Cohen, *The Friars and the Jews*, p. 123. Similar interventions by the friars attending the debate occur elsewhere as well; see, for instance, the involvement of the Franciscan Peire de Genova, in Maccoby, *Judaism on Trial*, pp. 108–09, and Rankin, *Jewish Religious Polemic*, p. 183.

53 See, for a typical account from a Jewish perspective, the portion of the article on Naḥmanides by Joseph Kaplan in the *Encyclopaedia Judaica* (Jerusalem: Keter; New York: Macmillan, 1971), vol. 12, p. 775: "the disputation ... was a victory for Naḥmanides."

54 The letter is dated ca. 1266 by Simonsohn, *The Apostolic See and the Jews*, pp. 230–32; the citation is at p. 231 (my translation).

Jesuit Missionaries and the Earliest Contact Between European and Japanese Cultures

NAKAI AYAKO

Lively and diverse cross-cultural contacts between the Japanese and the Europeans began in 1549 with the arrival of the first European missionary, Francis Xavier. Such exchanges, which continued through the nineteenth century, comprise three main periods.

The first, in which Catholic missionaries played the main role, took place before the ban on Christianity and the policy of national seclusion:[1] for Japan this was a period of transition that lasted from the Middle Ages to early modernity, with *samurai* (warrior) generals conducting civil wars. The missionaries, mainly from southern Europe, brought Christianity and Renaissance culture to Japan; through their influence the so-called *Namban* (southern barbarian) culture flourished. The second period, which can be perceived as the era of the Dutch merchants,[2] coincided with the Tokugawa shogunate, which not only unified Japan, but also strictly forbade Christianity and controlled all contact with foreign countries. Under this regime, naturalists from different Protestant countries were among the Europeans who played an important role in cultural exchanges,[3] whereas Japanese intellectuals interested in European culture established *Rangaku* (Dutch studies).[4] The third period is associated with the opening of the country in 1854 and the Meiji Restoration in 1868: at this time, political power moved from the shogunate to a new Emperor-centred government whose policies sought to enhance national prosperity and military power, engendering in turn the processes of modernization. The political, legal, and economic systems and cultures of the world's powers—Britain, France, Prussia, the United States, and Russia—became models for Japan's westernization. In this new atmosphere, along with the Catholics, American Protestants began Christian missions in Japan. At the same time, the Japanese government promoted the ideology of state Shintoism, according to which the Emperor was perceived as a religious authority and as the father of the Japanese as one big family. Modernization evolved under the motto *Wakon Yōsai* (Japanese Spirit combined with Western technology).[5]

Although much has changed since the first encounter, certain aspects have remained constant in cross-cultural contacts between Europe and Japan, as they have among many other societies. One such question pertains to the nature of 'identity.' The encounter with another culture always destabilizes one's own identity. As Arnold Toynbee explains, European culture first came to Japan as a total system, in which religion, policy, economy, science, art, and technology could not be discretely separated the one from the other.[6] The policy of isolation during the Tokugawa shogunate, he argues, was a psychological reaction to the impact of foreign cultures.[7] The ban on Christianity resulted in part from the fact that the new authorities, who sought to unify the country, feared that foreign culture would overcome the indigenous one, thus threatening Japanese identity. In the third period, however, the policy of seclusion became untenable. According to Toynbee, one solution to the identity crisis was the separation of technology from religion, a goal which was attainable since by this time Western culture had been already secularized.[8]

What is the consequence of the *Wakon Yōsai* ideology? Can we really separate the "spirit" from technology? I think this is impossible. First, because—along with the adoption of foreign technology—new ways of thinking also begin to take root, albeit perhaps imperceptibly and unconsciously. Japanese intellectuals often regard Western culture as "materialistic," but this is only a projection of their reception of "Western" culture. With the separation of technology from the spiritual side of culture, it becomes difficult to reflect ethically and morally on technology. Second, I think that we cannot isolate *the* Japanese spirit or *the* Japanese culture. Awareness of the uniqueness of one's own "spirit" develops only through encounters with others. The "spirit" is not something natural, but rather an ideological construct. And precisely because it is a construct, the spirit does not have a fixed traditional form. Thus, in my opinion, exchanges at the spiritual level are important in matters of cultural contact.

I see "contact between cultures" as a spiritual and philosophical dialogue that takes place during personal encounters between individuals in concrete situations. Through dialogue, the thinking of each participant expands and is enriched. Contact must be a reciprocal relationship. My vision of contact is different from that of the ideological struggle or war, which is articulated, for example, in a volume within the Japanese series of Comparative Literature and Culture, entitled *The Ideological Struggle between East and West*. The editor of this volume traces an "ideological struggle" against the "monotheistic universalism" of the "West" during the 450 years since Xavier's arrival in Japan.[9] I suggest that a vision of contact between cultures informed by an ecumenical spirit can be more productive than the conceptualization of contact as a religious war or "clash of civilizations."[10]

Scholars must consider two aspects when seeking to uncover the spiritual and philosophical dialogues that took place during past contacts between different cultures: the diversity of reactions between individual participants, and the self-reflection of those individuals. This second aspect is especially important because contact with different 'others' elicits self-criticism, that is, an inner spiritual dialogue with oneself and with the 'others' within the 'self.'

In this article I focus on the diverse attitudes of Jesuit missionaries toward the Japanese during the earliest period of contact.[11] I especially consider why some individuals were able—better than others—to sympathetically understand the cultures of Japan and to communicate with its indigenous people. This period is interesting because of the freshness of the encounter; there were few European preconceptions about Japan, the Japanese and their culture. Thanks to Marco Polo, Japan was already known in Europe as *Zipangu* (island rich in gold). It was not, however, this book that engendered Xavier's desire to open a mission in Japan, but an encounter in Malacca with a Japanese man, Yajirō (alternately, Anjirō), who had fled from his country after having committed a murder. Yajirō wanted to meet Xavier to confess his sin and free himself from his spiritual burden.[12] Impressed by this man's intelligence, Xavier decided to go to Japan, and asked the Portuguese captain Jorge Alvares, who had been to Japan, to write a report for him.[13]

There were remarkable differences between European attitudes toward the Americas they "discovered" and toward Japan in the sixteenth century. Most Europeans felt a sense of superiority over the indigenous cultures of the former; the military, political, and economic aspects of their "conquest" overshadowed all cultural contacts. In contrast, the Europeans found in Japan, and later also in China, societies and cultures that they perceived to be as equally civilized as their own.[14] Consider, for example, the hierarchical classification of "discovered" peoples whom the Europeans might wish to Christianize, which was formulated by José de Acosta (1539/40–1600), a Spanish Jesuit missionary in Peru and Mexico. Acosta defined three categories, placing the Chinese and the Japanese and others like them in the first, because of their highly developed civilizations. The Aztecs and the peoples of India under Portuguese jurisdiction he placed in the second group, because—albeit civilized—they were perceived to be far behind European civilization. In the third group, Acosta lumped together all "barbarians." Interestingly, he recommended that missionaries approach the first group as the Greeks and Romans were approached during the earliest period of Christianity.[15] Today, as we accept the idea of equality of cultures, the model of the contact between European and Chinese or Japanese cultures in the sixteenth and seventeenth centuries can be useful for ecumenical dialogues between various cultures and religions.

Today in Japan the study of the "Christian century"[16] is called *Kirishitan shi* (history of early Japanese Christians) and comprises a highly specialized field for multilingual scholars. European primary sources, mainly letters and reports by the missionaries—whether published or unpublished archival documents—are studied and translated into Japanese.[17] There is a paucity of early Japanese primary sources, especially by Japanese Christians, because of the prohibition of Christianity that lasted approximately 250 years. In addition to the studies by Matsuda Kiichi and Ebisawa Arimichi, important work has been conducted recently. For example, Takase Kōichirō has focused on the economic and political aspects of the Jesuit mission,[18] Ide Katsumi on the intellectual history and reception of Christianity in Japan,[19] and Gonoi Takashi on the *Kirishitan* in the founding period of the Tokugawa shogunate.[20] Murai Sanae has studied the relationship between the prohibition on Christianity and the formation of the *Bakuhan* (shogunate and domain) system, as well as the role played by emperors in the prohibition of Christianity.[21] Also, Kawamura Shinzō has researched Christian lay communities.[22] There are many specialized studies on the influence of the Europeans on *Namban* culture—art, music, architecture, language, literature, clothing, and foods.

My interests concern the ethical and philosophical analysis of cultural contacts on the basis of case histories. Jesuit missionaries in Japan deserve to be studied within the context of European intellectual history. For this I need to construct a "typology of [their] relationships to the others."[23] It is important always to discern who establishes the first contact, who encounters the different culture. The personality of individuals determines whether they can better understand an 'other' people, an 'other' culture, and make more successful contacts. Excellence in one's own culture does not guarantee excellence in another. In this chapter, I will discuss Francis Xavier, Luis Frois, Gnecchi-Soldi Organtino, Francisco Cabral, and Alessandro Valignano as examples in a typology of European relationships to Japanese culture.

XAVIER, THE FIRST MISSIONARY

The Basque missionary Francis Xavier (1506–52) was born to parents of aristocratic background in the kingdom of Navarra, which at that time was politically affiliated with France. After Castile occupied the capital, Pamplona, in 1512, his father and brothers lived in exile in France, while Xavier remained in Navarra with his mother and sisters. In 1521 Xavier's brothers were part of the failed attempt, with French troops, to regain Pamplona. At this time, Ignatius Loyola (1491–1556), another Basque who fought on the Castilian side, was injured, an event that later led him to leave a secular military career and join the religious life.

In 1525, Xavier—seeking a glorious career in the Church—went to Paris to study. After receiving his master's degree in 1530, he taught Latin and philosophy, while continuing to study Aristotelian philosophy. He and Loyola became roommates in college. Loyola was already leading an ascetic life; he had been to Jerusalem and had had a mystic experience in Manresa.[24] According to one biographer, Xavier at first despised Loyola and avoided him.[25] But in the end, Loyola inspired Xavier and taught him through his *Spiritual Exercises*.[26]

Published with papal approval in 1548, *Spiritual Exercises* is a book arising from Loyola's religious experiences and the desire to help others. According to John W. O'Malley, it is one of the "most important institutional factors that, when taken in their full implications, shaped the distinctive character of the Society of Jesus."[27] In 1596, a Latin edition of *Spiritual Exercises* was printed at a Jesuit college in Amakusa, Japan, by a printer brought from Europe.[28] It is a manual of religious training that—according to its introductory "general comments"—seeks to "prepare and dispose our soul to rid itself of all its disordered affections and then, after their removal, to seek and find God's will in the ordering of our life for the salvation of our soul," and it leads individuals toward inner communication with God and toward finding him in all things, and it instructs the practice of prayer in the form of meditation or contemplation.[29] Thus, it helps individuals "to make a determinative choice about the future,"[30] and enables them to engage in "self-reflection and self-critical awareness."[31] The book *Spiritual Exercises* is important for understanding the inner side of the Jesuits and for judging their missionary work from their own point of view. When we read Xavier's letters we see that his active, public work was supported by the inner strength that the *Spiritual Exercises* sought to shape.

In 1534, Loyola, Xavier, and five other friends vowed to go to Jerusalem and live in poverty and chastity. In 1540, Pope Paul III recognized the Society of Jesus as a religious order. Shortly before this, Loyola had commissioned Xavier to go to India, at the request of King John III of Portugal. Xavier arrived in Goa in 1542. After having served as a missionary in India, Malaysia, and Indonesia, Xavier met Yajirō (whom he called "Angero") in Malacca.[32]

In a letter from Cochin to the Jesuits in Rome, dated 20 January 1548, Xavier wrote that Yajirō was very "eager to learn." When Xavier asked whether the Japanese would become Christians, Yajirō replied that they would examine, first through questions, how much Xavier knew, and, then through observation, "whether what he says is supported by what he does." Yajirō also stipulated that the Japanese could be led only by "reason."[33] Xavier took him to Goa where, after obtaining a thorough education in Christian doctrine, he was baptized. Xavier explained to Yajirō that Christ's salvation was for all humankind, and guided him through the *Spiritual Exercises*. Yajirō was "moved, consoled and shed tears."[34]

In Goa, Xavier asked the director of the Jesuit college, Nicolao Lancilloto (born in Urbino, Italy, and died in India in 1558), to write a report on Japan with the information provided by Yajirō.[35] This report was used not only by Xavier, but also by Guillaume Postel (1510–81) in his *Des merveilles du monde* (1553).[36] Postel, who had been a servant at the same college where Loyola and Xavier had studied, learned many languages on his own and travelled to the Orient; he became a professor of Oriental languages in Paris and then a Jesuit in 1544, but was later dismissed because of mental illness. According to Kishino Hisashi, Xavier's attitude to other cultures differed from that of Postel, who believed that Christianity was the origin of all the religions in the world, and uncritically used Lancilloto's information about Japanese religions to prove his theory. Xavier, on the other hand, attempted to understand different religions on their own terms, not within a Christian framework. He also compared the knowledge he obtained through Lancilloto with his own experiences in Japan. Kishino highly appreciates what he designates as the "relativism" and "positivism" of Xavier's understanding of cultures.[37] While Postel was an "orientalist," to borrow Edward Said's expression, Xavier was not.[38]

After long deliberation, Xavier decided to go to Japan, so that "the human creature knows the Creator, [so] that the creature, created in God's image, gives glory to God, and [so that] the realm of the mother Church is expanded."[39] According to Kishino, Xavier's specific purpose in Japan was to prepare for subsequent missionary work by researching the religious situation there.[40] On August 15, 1549, Xavier—together with Yajirō and his servants, and two other missionaries—arrived at Kagoshima, Yajirō's hometown.

Xavier recorded his initial impressions of the Japanese and their culture in a long letter dated in Kagoshima on 5 November 1549 and addressed to the Jesuits in Goa; he combines his own experiences with information provided by Alvares, Lancilloto, and Yajirō.[41] Known as his "Magna Carta," this letter was printed 101 times from 1552 to 1927 in at least eight European languages.[42] It was used not only as a religious text for European Christians, but also as a source of new information about Japan.[43]

Xavier's first impressions of the Japanese people and their culture were very positive. He writes that they are the best "pagans" to have been "discovered"; the Japanese are "sociable, good and honest"(12).[44] Honour is important to them; most people are poor, but they do not think that poverty is shameful, because honour is considered to be more important than wealth (13). They eat little, drink without excess and are monogamous. They have high intellectual ability: most people can read and write, and are eager to obtain new knowledge (14). Xavier was confident that the Christian mission in Japan would succeed. According to him, the Japanese were people with "reason"; they were "delighted with hearing things that conform to reason" (15). Thus, for Xavier, "reason" could serve as a foundation for dialogues between the Europeans and the Japanese. His understanding of "reason" was, undoubtedly, informed by Renaissance humanism.

Xavier also wrote about lifestyles in his host country: the Japanese diet is poor; the people eat a little rice and wheat, sometimes fish, some fruit, and a lot of vegetables. He comments: "The people enjoy marvellously good health, there are many that are elderly. Watching their way of life, I can understand that we are able to survive with little food and live naturally, even when we do not have sufficient food ... We are living in this land in excellent physical health. Would that God [allow] us to be thus in our Souls" (45). Xavier finds in the Japanese lifestyle something of the apostolic, naturally ascetic life, which had been recommended in the *Spiritual Exercises*.[45] While in Malacca, Xavier had determined not to eat meat in Japan, because, according to Yajirō, the Buddhist priests were especially strict regarding the consumption of meat and fish.[46] But the observation that there are many healthy old people is his. Explaining how Western Europe has succeeded in assimilating 'the other' and summarizing the work of Cortés, Tzvetan Todorov writes that the "capacity to understand the other" is the specific feature of Western civilization.[47] I would say that it has been a feature of "modern man" since the Renaissance; an altogether different question is whether modern man uses his knowledge to conquer others or to live peacefully among them. Xavier and some of his fellow Jesuits had this capacity for understanding.

While praising the ordinary Japanese, Xavier criticizes Buddhist priests for their sexual lives, especially for their homosexuality (16–18). Homosexuality among them, as well as among the *samurai*, was not unusual in Japan, a fact that was subsequently noted by other missionaries.[48] It appears that the corruption among the Buddhist priests at that time, in contrast to the exemplary life of the missionaries, was one reason why many Japanese were attracted to the new religion. Xavier, however, also records what he perceives as positive experiences with Buddhist priests, mentioning, for example, one individual with whom he had a discussion about whether or not the soul perishes after the death of the body (19).

Concerning matters of religion, in his letter Xavier writes mainly about what he experienced directly.[49] For example, he tells of a pious picture of the Madonna and child, which impressed the lord of Kagoshima and his mother. She wanted to have a copy of it and to learn what Christians believe (39). Xavier does not use the information provided by Alvares and Lancilloto in this respect.[50]

In the same letter, reflecting upon himself, Xavier admits that at first he had thought to be serving God by spreading belief in Him. But, subsequently he learned that God had led him to Japan and put him through difficult trials in order to examine whether he would rely solely on God, rather than on human assistance (43). Xavier regarded persecutions in Japan as God's mercy (23). Later, in a personal letter to Loyola (who was in Rome), he writes that—through the Japanese—God had led him to know the self more deeply, especially his miserable situation and his need to depend only on God.[51]

As for the missionaries who were yet to come to Japan, Xavier identified humility as the most important quality (21):[52] in missionary work, it is necessary to know what a miserable person one is, and to draw deep humility from this knowledge; it is through this humility that trust, hope, and love toward God and one's neighbours grows in the soul (21–24). Xavier warns missionaries against arrogance, a stance also assumed by Bartolomé de las Casas in his *History of the Indies.* It is important for a missionary to "reflect on himself" (31) and to make progress on the way to salvation and perfect virtue (28). Only a missionary with a soul that has been regenerated through meditation can give off the "aroma of virtue," set a good example, and bring about change in others (25). In short, Xavier believes that dialogue with the self and with God on a spiritual level is necessary, and that this can lead to dialogue with others on a spiritual level. Xavier knows from his experience as a missionary that it is through good example—that is, praxis—that people in a different culture begin to understand a new religion.

As for the practical side of missionary work, Xavier recognizes the need to master Japanese (20, 40, 41). He plans to translate the catechism into Japanese and to publish it (58). He wishes to meet Japanese intellectuals at colleges in Japan (53, 54) and dreams of a disputation between Japanese and European scholars (54). Later, Valignano would accomplish what Xavier envisioned.

Xavier does not eschew financial considerations: he advises a Jesuit priest in Goa to bring much gold and many presents with him if he comes to Japan. He even advises other colleagues not to bring too much pepper, so that it could be sold at a high price.[53] (Missionary work, trade, and politics appear to be inseparable. There is a possibility that trade and politics, originally only the vehicles for missionary work, overshadow the goal. Involvement in the silk trade later became a source of criticism against Valignano.[54])

Xavier stayed in Japan approximately two years and left for Goa on 15 November 1551. Although his first impressions were positive, he must also have had negative experiences; later he wrote that the Japanese were less polite to foreigners than to other Japanese.[55] Xavier died on 3 December 1553, en route China; he had set out to convert the Chinese, because he thought the Japanese respected what had come from China.[56]

SUBSEQUENT MISSIONARIES: FROIS, ORGANTINO, AND CABRAL

After Xavier, approximately 180 European Jesuits were sent to Japan. Somewhat later, Franciscans and members of other orders arrived. Among the Jesuits, Luis Frois, Gnecchi-Soldo Organtino, and Francisco Cabral represent radically different models of approaches to Japanese culture.

Luis Frois (1532–97) was born in Lisbon. After having worked in the royal chancery as a secretary, he joined the Jesuits in 1548 and went to Goa, where he met Xavier and Yajirō. He was ordained there in 1561, worked as a secretary, and wrote annual letters on Jesuit missionary work. He was regarded as a man with a talent for writing and speaking. In 1563, he arrived in Japan. After learning the Japanese language and customs, Frois went to Kyoto, then the capital of Japan. From 1566 to 1576 he served as superior for the central district. He often visited Nobunaga Oda (1534–82), who brought about political unification after a century of civil war, and also his successor, Hideyoshi Toyotomi (1537–98). In 1581 Frois escorted—as an interpreter—the Jesuit Visitor to Japan, Alessandro Valignano, when Nobunaga received him in audience. Frois died at Nagasaki, having lived in Japan for approximately thirty years with an interruption between 1592 and 1595.[57] He contributed to the mission through letters, annual reports, and works of history.[58] He also prepared a comparative study of European and Japanese cultures.[59]

His history of Japan is an enormous chronicle, a manuscript of 2,500 pages. It is also a readable travel book, albeit too long, like those by John Mandeville or Marco Polo. Frois writes in a lively and detailed fashion. His viewpoint is interesting to today's Japanese readers, because he describes—from a foreigner's perspective—those things that were usual to his Japanese contemporaries and which, therefore, they would not have recorded. His is an important work, not only as a record of the Christian mission, but also as a political, economic, social, cultural, and intellectual history of Japan at that time.

Frois' comparative study of European and Japanese cultures was written at 1585 in Kazusa, on Kyūshū, but not published until 1955. He compares European and Japanese cultures by studying the appearance and clothing of men, women, children, and Buddhist priests. He also compares religious practices, food and drink; weaponry and horses; types of illnesses and their medical treatment; written culture, books, papers and letters; drama, dance and music; architecture and gardens; and also the construction of ships. He writes in a laconic style: "The Europeans are usually tall and big; the Japanese are inferior in height and composition. The Europeans appreciate big eyes; the Japanese regard them as awful and appreciate narrow eyes ... We show our politeness by taking off our hats; the Japanese by taking off their shoes ... We eat everything with our hands; the Japanese—men as well as women, from childhood—with two sticks. We eat bread of wheat; the Japanese eat boiled rice without salt."[60]

Frois was interested in detail and had an astonishing talent for observation. His attitude toward Japanese cultures seems neutral; his stance evokes that of today's cultural anthropologist. His manner of recording was unsystematic but, despite some misunderstandings, objective: he did not pass judgement. Valignano criticized him for writing with exaggeration and in excessive detail, offering too many unimportant things.[61] This is perhaps true, but what Frois wrote down remains interesting to read.

Gnecchi-Soldo Organtino (1533–1609) was born into a distinguished family near Brescia in northern Italy, which at that time was under foreign political powers. He joined the Society of Jesus in 1556, after having been ordained as a priest. In 1567 he went to Goa where he became rector of the Jesuit College. He arrived in Japan in 1570 together with Cabral. At first, Organtino assisted Frois in the central district, and in 1576 they built a church in Kyoto, which was called Nambanji (southern barbarian's temple).[62] After

Frois left for Kyūshū in 1577, Organtino became responsible for the mission in Kyoto.

Organtino regarded the Japanese very highly. He wrote that they were the most polite, the cleverest, and the most intelligent people in the world.[63] The Japanese were better than the Europeans in most respects, except for their religion. He wrote that every day he learned a lot from the Japanese.[64] Organtino learned the Japanese language and customs, and also studied Buddhist texts.[65] He sought to understand the Japanese political situation. His observation of the Japanese character is interesting because some of the aspects that he recorded remain the same as today: the Japanese do not like to express anger; they like ceremonial politeness, and if they receive presents or kindness, they feel they must return something equivalent to it; they praise each other, and they do not like to insult others.[66]

Organtino also tried to adopt a Japanese lifestyle: he ate rice instead of bread and meat, and, like the Buddhist priests, wore a silk kimono.[67] Knowing that the Japanese liked new and interesting events, he organized for them gorgeous ceremonies and processions.[68] He befriended Nobunaga, who had fought against Buddhist monks and sects to achieve reunification. Nobunaga's struggle endowed him with sympathy toward the Jesuits, and thus he gave Organtino a piece of land in Azuchi, where his own castle stood. Organtino built a theological seminary there.

Under Frois and Organtino, the missionary work of the Jesuits flourished. Important lords like Takayama Hida-no-kami and his son, Takayama Ukon (1552–1615), became Christians.[69] Takayama Ukon, a supporter of Nobunaga and Hideyoshi and a famous master of *cha-no-yu* (the tea ceremony), led his friends to become Christians.[70] Fukansai Habian [Fabián] (1565–1621) was baptized in 1583, entered the society, and worked with Organtino.[71]

According to his letter dated 15 October 1577,[72] Organtino baptized no fewer than eight thousand people. He was so optimistic that he thought all the Japanese would become Christians within ten years.[73] He wrote: "Any Jesuit who comes to Japan and does not foster a love for this bride of wondrous beauty, not caring to learn her language immediately, not conforming to her ways, deserves to be packed back to Europe as an inept and unprofitable worker in the Lord's vineyard."[74] Because he liked the Japanese, Organtino was popular among them; they even gave him a nickname: *urugan bateren* (Father Organ).[75]

Francisco Cabral's attitude toward Japanese culture differed radically from that of Organtino. Cabral (ca. 1533–1609) was born into an old Portuguese family on São Miguel Island. After studying in Lisbon and Coimbra, he did military service in Asia and fought against the Turkish fleet; in 1556, he joined the Jesuits in Goa; in 1558, he was ordained as a priest. The fact that he held important positions—such as professor of theology and father superior—suggests that he enjoyed a good reputation among his colleagues.[76] Although Cabral was reputed to be stubborn and to have a short temper, he was praised for his deep learning.[77] He was an elite representative of European culture and of the Society of Jesus.

Cabral came to Japan because he had been appointed as the mission's superior. Recognizing the need to reform the discipline and the spiritual life, he summoned the missionaries to a retreat, explained his policies, and led them in the *Spiritual Exercises* and meditations. The missionaries supported his reform and praised him highly as their "shepherd."[78] As superior, Cabral travelled around the missions twice, first in 1571–72 and again in 1574. His views of the Japanese were less than favourable: in one of his later letters, he wrote that he had never seen such arrogant, greedy, anxious, and hypocritical people.[79] According to him, the Japanese were educated to disguise their feelings.[80]

On Kyūshū, Cabral's mission policy sought first to convert the *daimyō* (lords), who would then force their people to accept the new religion. Ōmura Sumitada, who controlled Nagasaki, was baptized in 1563; Arima Yoshisada of the Shimabara peninsula in 1576; and Ōtomo Sōrin of Bungo in 1578. The converted lords would often destroy Buddhist temples and Shinto shrines.[81] They were interested in foreign trade. Because Cabral showed little sympathy toward the Japanese and their culture, they disliked him, and many Japanese moved away from the church.

After Xavier, the most important missionary to Japan was Alessandro Valignano (1539–1606). He was born in Chieti, in the kingdom of Naples, which at that time was under Spanish rule. Members of his family had important positions in the city's administration and were close to the bishop, Gian Pietro Carafa, who later became Pope Paul IV.[82] Valignano studied law in Padua. After having tried unsuccessfully to make a career in the church, he returned to his studies in Padua. In 1562, he caused a scandal by slashing a woman's face and injuring her, an act for which he was imprisoned.[83]

Valignano joined the Society of Jesus in 1566 and was ordained in 1571. While studying in Rome, he made friends with Claudio Acquaviva (who subsequently became general of the society), and supervised Matteo Ricci as a teacher of novices. In 1573 Everard Mercurian, the fourth general of the society, appointed Valignano to the post of Visitor to the East. Valignano then pronounced his Solemn Profession, which made him an elite member of the society.[84] After negotiations regarding mission affairs in Lisbon and visitation to India, Malacca, and Macao, Valignano arrived in Japan in 1579 and remained there until 1582. He returned to Japan in 1590 for a two-year stay. His final visit lasted from 1598 until 1603.

When Valignano arrived in Japan, there were two contradictory strategies of missionary work, the one represented by Organtino, the other by Cabral. First, Valignano visited Kyūshū, which was under Cabral's direction. He found that the situation there was not what he had imagined on the basis of letters from Japan. The European missionaries there could not speak Japanese, because Cabral decided that the language was too difficult to master and could not be learned by studying its grammar.[85] Moreover, Japanese members did not understand Portuguese or Latin. Cabral had opposed the teaching of both Latin and Portuguese to them, because he felt that the Japanese Christians would not respect the European missionaries if they were able to understand what the European missionaries were talking about.[86]

The relations between missionaries and the Japanese were poor. Japanese members were treated in a humiliating manner, in an

"Southern Barbarians in Japan." Pair of six-fold screens, colour on gold-leaf paper, 155.8 x 334.5 cm; Momoyama period, seventeenth century. Courtesy of the Imperial collection; used by permission.

attempt to make them obedient to the European members. Although Cabral recognized the need for Japanese members to be involved in missionary work, he insisted that the Japanese Christians not be consecrated as priests. In his view, the Japanese should serve only as helpers; if they had the same knowledge and status as the missionaries, they would no longer respect them.[87]

Valignano criticized Cabral for adhering to his European lifestyle, and for his discriminatory policies and negative attitude toward Japanese culture. Recognizing that cleanliness was very important to the Japanese, Valignano criticized Cabral for eating meat

at a high table with an unclean napkin. Cabral laughed at Japanese customs.[88] He did not understand Japanese, even though he had been in Japan for ten years. Valignano found that many Japanese Christians had left the Jesuits because of Cabral.[89]

Valignano also criticized Cabral's mission policy. He thought that, inasmuch as they were living *in* Japan, the Jesuits would be well advised to adapt to Japanese customs. Having noted the importance of manners and etiquette to the Japanese, Valignano wrote in 1581 his *Advertimentos e avisos acerca dos costumes e catangues de Jappão* (advice concerning Japanese customs and *katagi* [character]).[90] It was important to him that the missionaries maintain their authority among the Japanese, while simultaneously demonstrating affection toward them. Valignano's observations of Japanese manners and etiquette, body language, and expression of feeling remain of great interest to the Japanese of today.

After Valignano formulated the rules for the Japanese Regional Superior,[91] which were based on accommodation and adaptation, Cabral requested in 1580 that he be removed from his post;[92] he left Japan in 1583.

Valignano was rather optimistic about the mission in Japan when he came to Kyoto in 1581. He found that—under Organtino—the state of the mission in Kyoto differed from that of Kyūshū under Cabral's direction. In the area around Kyoto, Valignano found Japanese Christians who were intellectuals and who had been baptized out of religious motivation. One such individual was Takayama Ukon. Valignano was received in audience by Nobunaga more than five times. Nobunaga was so fond of Valignano that, when the latter left Azuchi, he presented him with a beautiful folding screen.[93]

Although Valignano held Organtino's methods in high esteem, he also recognized his colleague's weak points. In a letter from Cochin, dated 12 December 1584, Valignano explained why he had not appointed Organtino as Cabral's successor: Organtino had devoted himself too much to the promotion of welfare among the Japanese and was too generous in spending money on architecture and various other projects.[94] Valignano must have thought that Organtino was not intellectual enough to lead his European colleagues.[95]

Upon returning to Kyūshū, Valignano held in 1581 a final consultation in Nagasaki and confirmed a mission policy based on accommodation to Japanese culture.[96] The next year he left Japan for Macao, where he wrote a summary of his visitation.[97] What Valignano had envisioned was realized afterwards. He took four Japanese boys to an audience with Pope Gregory XIII in Rome. They returned to Japan with a printing press that was then used to publish dictionaries, Latin and Japanese grammars, religious texts, Aesop's fables, and Japanese classics.

Valignano returned to Japan twice after Toyotomi Hideyoshi issued in 1587 his edict of expulsion.[98] Before he left Japan for the last time in 1602, he witnessed the ordination to the priesthood of two Japanese Christians.

The experiences of the first missionaries in Japan greatly differed from individual to individual, as did their attitudes toward its culture, lifestyles, and the everyday behaviour of its people. Let us take, for example, the missionaries' interpretation of the Japanese preference for expressing one's feelings indirectly: while Valignano understood this as prudence,[99] Cabral saw it as falsehood and hypocrisy.[100]

Because Xavier was the first Jesuit in Japan, he was not faced with practical difficulties in his missionary work. He seems to have had more freedom of thought than did subsequent missionaries. We can find in Xavier's letters more spiritual self-reflection than in those of his successors. For him, the universality of Christianity was not what he already possessed, but what he was searching for in new experiences, in dialogue with God. Such experiences opened a new dimension for understanding himself, the world, and God. He was thus able to be flexible in a new cultural environment.

From the perspective of Valignano, Frois wrote in too much detail and at excessive length. Indeed, Frois went beyond those matters that would be important and useful for the mission. When his history of Japan and comparative study of European and Japanese cultures were published for the first time in the twentieth century, they became an invaluable source for social and cultural history. Frois was a Japanologist whose significance is better recognized in cultural studies today than in the history of the mission.

For Cabral, the European way of life and other aspects of European culture could not be separated from Christianity. His understanding of his religion seems not to have been "free from confinement in European forms."[101] He is said to have taken a policy of renewing spiritual zeal by spiritual exercises and meditations.[102] He criticized Valignano, because the latter's "qualities would be excellent in a great captain or prince, but in a religious they need to be accompanied by the spirit of poverty and religious humility."[103] Cabral seems to have been spiritual and religious, but his spirituality was closed to foreign cultures.

Organtino, on the other hand, accommodated himself to the indigenous culture. However, his desire to cater to his hosts' predilection for gorgeous ceremonies and processions could have posed the danger of attracting the Japanese only by the superficial aspect of Christianity, without understanding its spiritual core. Valignano tried to separate mission from conquest. Through a policy of adaptation, he sought to realize Christianity's potential of development in a different culture. One could make the argument that the Italian humanism of both Organtino and Valignano guarded them from being affected by "the whole 'conquistador' understanding of Christianity and of the world."[104]

In this chapter I have considered only the European side of the encounter between the two cultures. More research needs to be done on the Japanese who came into contact with the Europeans. It is equally important to pay attention to the diversity of reactions among them toward the foreign culture. The Buddhist of Zen, whose thinking is intellectual, behaves differently from the Buddhist of Jōdo-shinshū, for whom one obtains salvation only through belief.[105] Each approached the new religion differently, and reacted differently to the ensuing persecution.[106]

As for the problems of identity that such encounters raised and continue to raise, I suggest that the Japanese need to conceptualize them not so much on the national as on the individual level. Encounters with foreign cultures can shake our own identity, but they can also free us from confinement in a narrow identity. When Valignano's policy of adaptation was criticized, he desperately tried to make his colleagues, who had never been to foreign lands out of Europe, understand how everything was different in Japan.[107]

To live in a foreign country or to study a foreign culture to some extent makes us foreigners in our own country and culture. But it is through the knowledge of the other that we develop self-knowledge and our own identity.

I would also like to suggest the possibility of ethical and philosophical studies of the dialogue between religions or philosophies, in addition to and apart from historical investigations. For such research, I think it is necessary to have a new, ecumenical understanding of religions. Nicholas of Cusa (1401–64), who, like Valignano, studied in Padua, formulated a vision of "Peace among the Faiths."[108] He was active in the quest to reunite the Catholic and Orthodox churches. And, confronted with the conquest of Constantinople by the Islamic

Turks, he presented a vision of peace that placed emphasis on thinking philosophically about the essence of religion. Dialogues between religions can also be studied from a similar ecumenical perspective.

NOTES

I gratefully acknowledge Natalia Pylypiuk, Lesley Cormack, and John Boccellari for their helpful suggestions and advice. In this article, the presentation of all Japanese names, including mine, observes Japanese custom, with the surname in anterior position.

1 The ban on Christianity was a process that began in 1587 with an edict by Toyotomi Hideyoshi banishing the *bateren* (Christian missionaries), and was completed in 1614 with an anti-Christian edict issued by the Tokugawa shogunate. The policy of national seclusion—*sakoku* (literally, "the closing of the country")—was articulated in edicts that were issued several times between 1633 and 1639. After the formulation of *sakoku*, Japan had contact through trade only with Holland and China, and communicated only with Korea and Ryūkyū (Okinawa), whose envoys visited *Shōgun*.

2 In 1600, the first Dutch ship drifted ashore to Japan, bringing William Adams, a British subject, and Jan Joosten, a Dutchman. The Dutch Merchant House was established in 1609.

3 Engerbert Kaempfer (1651–1716), a German, Carl Peter Thunberg (1743–1828), a Swede, and Franz Siebold (1796–1866), a German, were among the naturalists who served as doctors at the Dutch Merchant House.

4 Donald Keene, *The Japanese Discovery of Europe, 1720–1830*, rev. ed. (Stanford, CA: Stanford University Press, 1969).

5 See Hirakawa Sukehiro, *Wakon Yōsai no Keifu* [The genealogy of Wakon Yōsai] (Tokyo: Kawadeshobōshinsha, 1971).

6 See Arnold J. Toynbee, *A Study of History*, vol. 4 (London, New York, and Toronto: Oxford University Press, 1951), p. 57, and vol. 8 (1954), p. 505. On Toynbee, see Ide Katsumi, *Kirishitan shisōshi kenkyū josetsu, Nihonjin no kirisutokyō juyō* [Introduction to the study of the intellectual history of the early Japanese Christians: The reception of Christianity by the Japanese] (Tokyo: Perikansha, 1995), pp. 318–65.

7 Toynbee, *A Study of History*, vol. 8, pp. 476–77, 545, and 592–94.

8 According to Toynbee, in the nineteenth century Western civilization was accepted in the Far East because it was regarded as an "unknown technology"; see his *Civilization on Trial* and *The World and the West* (New York: Meridian, 1958), pp. 267–76.

9 Kobori Keiichirō, "Fuhenshugi no chōsen to nippon no ōtō" [The challenge of universalism and the response of the Japanese], in *Tōzai no shisō tōsō* [The ideological struggle between East and West], Sōsho Hikakubungaku

Hikakubunka [Series in comparative literature and culture], vol. 4, ed. Kobori Keiichirō (Tokyo: Chūōkōronsha, 1994), pp. 9–146 and 589–96.

10 See Samuel P. Huntington, *The Clash of Civilizations and the Remaking of World Order* (New York: Simon and Schuster, 1996).

11 A 1585 papal brief designated Japan as a Jesuit monopoly; this situation was changed in 1600 by a brief from Pope Clement VIII, which allowed the mendicant orders to go to Japan by way of Lisbon and Portuguese India. See C.R. Boxer, *The Christian Century in Japan 1549–1650* (Berkeley and Los Angeles: University of California Press, 1951), pp. 239–40.

12 See Xavier's letter from Cochin to the Jesuits in Rome, dated 20 January 1548, in *Sei Furanshisuko zabieru zen shokan* [All the letters of St. Francisco Xavier] (Tokyo: Heibonsha, 1985), p. 272.

13 See C.R. Boxer, *The Christian Century*, pp. 32–36. See Kishino Hisashi, *Seiōjin no nihon hakken: zabieru rainichi mae nihon jōhō no kenkyū* [The discovery of Japan by the Europeans: A study of information about Japan before Xavier's arrival] (Tokyo: Yoshikawakōbunkan, 1989), pp. 46–76.

14 On European attitudes toward American culture, see Tzvetan Todorov, *The Conquest of America: The Question of the Other,* trans. Richard Howard (New York: Harper and Row, 1984). The Christian mission in Japan and China in the sixteenth and early seventeenth centuries provides another example of European attitudes toward the cultures of 'others.'

15 Ide, *Kirishitan shisōshi*, pp. 98–99. Ide cites José de Acosta, *De procuranda Indorum Salute* (Lima: 1577). For a modern edition of Acosta's work, see *Obras de P. José de Acosta,* Biblioteca de autores españoles, vol. 73 (Madrid, 1954), p. 392.

16 See Boxer, *The Christian Century.*

17 Matsuda Kiichi, ed., *16, 17 seiki Iezusukai nihon hōkoku shū* [Reports and letters from Japan by the Jesuits in the sixteenth and seventeenth centuries] (Kyoto: Dōhōsha, 1987); Takase Kōichirō, ed., *Iezusukai to nihon* [The Jesuits and Japan], Daikōkai sōsho [Series on the age of great voyages], vols. 1 and 2 (Tokyo: Iwanamishoten, 1981–88). The published texts by Xavier, Frois, and Valignano have also been translated into Japanese; see Ebisawa Arimichi, ed., *Kirishitan sho, Haiya sho* [Texts by Christians and texts that "reject" Christianity] (Tokyo: Iwanamishoten, 1970).

18 The works by Takase include *Kirishitanjidai no kenkyū* [A study of the Christian period] (Tokyo: Iwanamishoten, 1977); *Kirishitan no seiki* [The century of Christianity] (Tokyo: Iwanamishoten, 1993); and *Kirishitanjidai taigaikankei no kenkyū* [A study of foreign relations in the Christian period] (Tokyo: Yoshikawakōbunkan, 1994).

19 Ide, *Kirishitan shisōshi.*

20 Gonoi Takashi, *Tokugawa shoki kirishitan shi kenkyū* [A study of Christian history in the early Tokugawa period], rev. ed. (Tokyo: Yoshikawakōbunkan, 1992).

21 Murai Sanae, *Tenno to kirishitan kinsei, 'kirishitan no seiki' niokeru kenryoku tōsō no kōzu* [The emperor and the prohibition of Christianity: The structure of power struggle in the 'Christian Century'] (Tokyo: Yūzankaku shuppan, 2000).

22 Kawamura Shinzō, "Making Christian Lay Communities during the 'Christian Century' in Japan: A Case Study of Takata District in Bungo," Ph.D. thesis, Georgetown University, 1999.

23 See Todorov, *Conquest of America*, pp. 185–201.

24 Sasaki Takashi and A. Evangelista, eds., *Loyola no Ignatio, sono jiden to nikki* [Ignatius Loyola: His autobiography and diary] (Tokyo: Katsurashobō, 1966).

25 Kōno Yoshinori, *Sei Furanshisuko zabieru zen shōgai* [The life of St. Francisco Xavier] (Tokyo: Heibonsha, 1988), pp. 17–19. This biography is based on Georg Schurhammer, *Francis Xavier, his Life, his Times,* trans. M. Joseph Costelloe, vols. 1–4 (Rome: Jesuit Historical Institute, 1973–82).

26 Obara Satoru, *Zabieru* [Xavier] (Tokyo: Shimizushoin, 1998), p. 32, and see Sasaki and Evangelista, *Loyola*.

27 John W. O'Malley, *The First Jesuits* (Cambridge, MA: Harvard University Press, 1993), p. 372.

28 It was Valignano's idea to bring the printing press to Japan. See Obara, *Zabieru*, p. 128–51.

29 O'Malley, *The First Jesuits*, p. 46, 47.

30 Ibid., p. 38.

31 Andrew C. Ross, *A Vision Betrayed: The Jesuits in Japan and China 1542–1742* (Maryknoll, NY: Orbis, 1994), p. 205.

32 On Yajirō, or "Angero," see Kishino Hisashi, *Zabieru no Dōhansha Anjirō. Sengoku jidai no Kokusaijin* [Xavier's companion, Anjiro: An international man during the warring states period] (Tokyo: Yoshikawakōbunkan, 2001). For a discussion about his name, see pp.10–14.

33 Xavier's letter to the Jesuits in Rome, dated 20 January 1548. I used the Japanese translation: Francis Xavier, *Sei Furanshisuko Zabieru zen shokan* [All letters of St. Francis Xavier], trans. Kōno Yoshinori (Tokyo: Heibonsha, 1985), which is based on Georg Schurhammer and Joseph Wicki, eds., *Epistolae S. Francisci Xaverii*, 2 vols. (Rome: 1944–45). See M. Joseph Costelloe, *The Letters and Instructions of Francis Xavier* (St. Louis, MO: Institute of Jesuit Sources, 1992).

34 Xavier's letter from Malacca to the Jesuits in Europe, dated 22 June 1549.

35 Kishino, *Seiōjin no nihon hakken*, pp. 93–194.

36 Peter Kapitza, ed., *Japan in Europa*, vol. 1 (Munich: Iudicium, 1990), pp. 97–99.

37 Kishino, *Seiōjin no nihon hakken*, pp. 210–25.

38 Edward W. Said, *Orientalism* (New York: Vintage, 1979). On Postel, see pp. 51 and 65.

39 Xavier's letter from Malacca to the Jesuits in Europe, dated 22 June 1549.

40 Kishino Hisashi, *Zabieru to nihon: Kirishitan kaikyōki no kenkyū* [Xavier and Japan: A study of the early period of Christianity] (Tokyo: Yoshikawakōbunkan, 1998), pp. 86–102.

41 Kishino, *Seiōjin no nihon hakken*, pp. 226–40.

42 Schurhammer, *Xaveriana*, Bibliotheca Instituti Historici S.I., vol. 22 (Rome, 1964), pp. 609–12.

43 Kishino, *Seiōjin no nihon hakken*, pp. 232–34 and 237.

44 Xavier's letter from Kagoshima to the Jesuits in Goa, dated 5 November 1549. This and subsequent numbers in parentheses refer to this letter's paragraph numbers.

45 Loyola, *Reisō* [Spiritual exercises], translated by Kadowaki Kakichi (Tokyo, 1995), pp. 195–98.

46 Xavier's letter from Malacca to the Jesuits in Europe, dated June 22, 1549; par. 15.

47 Todorov, *Conquest of America*, p. 248.

48 For example, Frois and Valignano also mention homosexuality with disgust, and express dismay at the fact that the Japanese were not as averse to it as they were.

49 Xavier discusses Buddhism in greater detail, and reports on a discussion with Buddhist priests and the reactions of the Japanese to Christian teachings, in his letter from Cochin to the Jesuits in Rome, dated January 29, 1552.

50 Kishino, *Seiōjin no nihon hakken*, p. 230.

51 Xavier's letter from Cochin to Loyola in Rome, dated 29 January 1552; par. 2.

52 On humility, see Loyola, *Reisō*, pp. 165–67.

53 Xavier's letter from Kagoshima to Father Antonio Gomes in Goa, dated 5 November 1549.

54 Ross, *A Vision Betrayed*, pp. 54–55, 66, and 91–91.

55 Xavier's letter from Cochin to the Jesuits in Europe, dated 29 January 1552; par. 3.

56 Xavier's letter from Cochin to Loyola in Rome, dated 29 January 1552; par. 19.

57 Matsuda, "Furoisu" [Frois], in *Nihon kirisutokyō daijiten* [Historical lexicon of Christianity in Japan] (Tokyo: Kyōbunkan, 1988), pp. 634–35.

58 Luis Frois, *Nihon shi* [History of Japan], trans. Yanagiya Takeo, 5 vols. (Tokyo: Heibonsha, 1963–78); translation of Frois, *Die Geschichte Japans (1549–1578)*, übersetzt und kommentiert von G. Schurhammer und E.A. Voretzsch (Leipzig:

1926); Frois, *Nihon shi* [History of Japan], trans. Matsuda Kiichi and Kawasaki Momota, 12 vols. (Tokyo: Chūōkōronsha, 1977–1980).

59 Frois, *Yōroppa bunka to nihon bunka* [European culture and Japanese culture], trans. Okada Akio (Tokyo: Iwanamishoten, 1991); see Frois, *Kulturgegensätze Europa-Japan (1585)*, ed. Josef Franz Schütte (Tokyo: 1955), and Peter Kapitza, ed., *Japan in Europa*, vol. 1 (Munich: Iudicium, 1990), pp. 132–42.

60 Frois, pp. 14, 25, 92.

61 J.F. Moran, *The Japanese and the Jesuits: Alessandro Valignano in Sixteenth-Century Japan* (London and New York: Routledge, 1993), pp. 35–36.

62 Frois, *Nihon shi*, vol. 5 (Tokyo: Heibonsha, 1978), pp. 137–44; and Frois, *Nihon shi*, vol. 4 (Tokyo: Chūōkōronsha), pp. 334–41.

63 Organtino's letter, dated September 20 (21), 1577. In Schütte, *Valignanos Missionsgrundsätze für Japan*, vols. 1–2 (1580–1582), (Rome: 1958), pp. 146–47.

64 Organtino's letter dated 15 October 1577. In Schütte, *Valignanos Missionsgrundsätze*, 1–2, p. 145.

65 Together with Frois, Organtino learned *Hokke-sutra* from a former Buddhist priest (Schütte, *Valignanos Missionsgrundsätze*, 1–2, p. 148).

66 Organtino's letter, dated 20 (21) September 1577 (Schütte, *Valignanos Missionsgrundsätze für Japan*, 1–2, pp. 146–47).

67 Schütte, ibid., p. 149.

68 Frois, *Nihon shi*, vol. 5, (Tokyo: Chūōkōronsha), p. 10.

69 See Ross, *A Vision Betrayed*, p. 52.

70 After the ban on Christianity in 1614, Takayama Ukon refused to deny his faith and was expelled to Manila, where he died.

71 Fabián had been a Zen-Buddhist priest. He was baptized with his mother, who served Hideyoshi's wife. After studying at the college in Amakusa on Kyūshū, he taught Japanese at the college and edited *Aesop's Tales* in Japanese and *Heike monogatari* (Tales of the Heike), which were published by the Jesuits and used as Japanese textbooks. In 1605 he wrote an important apologetic work, *Myōtei mondō* (Dialogue between Myōshū, a Buddhist nun, and Yūtei, a Christian nun), and in 1606 he polemicized against Hayashi Razan (1583–1657), the most important Confucian scholar and ideologue of the Tokugawa shogunate. But in 1608 he left the Society of Jesus with a woman who was preparing to become a nun. In 1620 he wrote *Ha-deusu* (God destroyed), an important and influential anti-Christian tract. See Ide, *Kirishitan shisōshi*, pp. 186–288, and Ross, *A Vision Betrayed*, pp. 86 and 101.

72 Matsuda, "Kaidai" [Comments], in Alessandro Valignano, *Nihon junsatsu ki* [Reports of the visitation in Japan], which is a translation of *Sumario de las cosas de Japón (1585): Adiciones del sumario de Japón (1592)*, ed. José Luis Alvarez-Taladriz (Tokyo: Sophia University, 1954; Tokyo: Heibonsha, 1973), p. 297. Matsuda cites Organtino's letter to the general dated 15 October 1577.

73 Ibid.

74 Ross, *A Vision Betrayed*, p. 111.

75 In anti-Christian folk-tales he was also popular as "the leading and most
    powerful magician and wonder-worker, serving the King of Namban and
    seeking the conquest of Japan." See Ross, *A Vision Betrayed*, p. 111. "Padre
    Organtino" is a main figure in "Kamigami no bishō" (God's smile), a short
    story by Akutagawa Ryūnosuke.

76 Matsuda, *Valignano to kirishitan shūmon* (Valignano and the Christian religion)
    (Tokyo: Chōbunsha, 1992), p. 34.

77 Ibid.

78 Ross, *A Vision Betrayed*, p. 50.

79 See Cabral's letter to João Alvares, the assistant to the general in Rome, dated
    10 December 1596, in Takase Kōichirō, ed., *Iezusukai to nihon* [The Society of
    Jesus and Japan], vol. 1 (Tokyo: Iwanamishoten, 1981), p. 174.

80 Ibid., p. 176.

81 Ross, *A Vision Betrayed*, p. 53.

82 Ibid., pp. 32–33.

83 Ibid.

84 Ibid., p. 34.

85 Schütte, *Valignanos Missionsgrundsätze*, I–1 [1573–1580] (Rome: 1951),
    pp. 320–21.

86 Ibid., pp. 321–31.

87 See Cabral's letter to Alvares, dated 10 December 1596, in Takase, pp. 180–81.
    On Cabral's opinion about the admission of Japanese Christians to the Society
    of Jesus, see Ross, *A Vision Betrayed*, p. 55.

88 Schütte, *Valignanos Missionsgrundsätze*, I–1, p. 326.

89 Ibid.

90 Valignano, *Nihon iezusukaishi reihō shishin* [Guide for the Jesuits in Japan
    concerning manners], trans. Yazawa Toshihiko (Tokyo: Kirishitan bunka
    kenkyūkai, 1970). See Ross, *A Vision Betrayed*, pp. 62–64.

91 Ross, *A Vision Betrayed*, p. 59.

92 Ibid., p. 64.

93 Frois, *Nihon shi*, vol. 5, (Tokyo: Chūōkōronsha), pp. 106–17. See Moran, *The
    Japanese and the Jesuits*, pp. 11–12.

94 Schütte, *Valignanos Missionsgrundsätze*, I–2, pp. 129–33.

95 See Valignano's comments in the 1593 list of members, in *Monumenta Nipponica*, I-2 (Tokyo: Sophia University), p. 278. See Matsuda, "Kaidai" in Valignano, *Nihon junsatsu ki*, p. 349.

96 See Ross, *A Vision Betrayed*, p. 65.

97 Valignano, *Sumario de las cosas de Japón (1583): Adiciones del sumario de Japón (1592)*.

98 See Ross, *A Vision Betrayed*, pp. 69–70.

99 Valignano, *Sumario de las cosas de Japón (1583)*.

100 Schütte, *Valignanos Missionsgrundsätze*. I-1, pp. 308–11.

101 Ross, "Alessandro Valignano: The Jesuits and Culture in the East," in John W. O'Malley, Gauvin Alexander Bailey, Steven J. Harris, and T. Frank Kennedy, eds., *The Jesuits, Cultures, Sciences, and the Arts 1540–1773* (Toronto, Buffalo, and London: University of Toronto Press, 1999), p. 338.

102 See Ross, *A Vision Betrayed*, p. 50.

103 Cabral's letter to Aquaviva from Goa, dated 15 December 1593, in Moran, *The Japanese and the Jesuits*, p. 25.

104 Ross, *A Vision Betrayed*, pp. 205–06.

105 According to Valignano, this teaching is the same as Luther's. See Valignano, *Sumario de las cosas de Japón (1583)*.

106 On a Japanese Christian who had been a Zen-Buddhist, see note 74 above. On Kirishitan and Jōdo-shinshū, see Kawamura, "Making Christian."

107 Valignano's letter from Cochin to the general, dated 20 December 1586; see Matsuda, "Kaidai" in Valignano, *Nihon junsatsu ki*, pp. 261–64.

108 *De pace fidei*, in Nicolai de Cusa, "De pace fidei," in *Opera omnia*, ed. R. Klibansky and H. Bascour, vol. 8 (Hamburg, 1970), pp. 1–63. I have read the Japanese translation by Yamaki Kazuhiko, in *Chūsei makki no shimpishisō* [Mysticism in the later Middle Ages] (Tokyo: Heibonsha, 1992), pp. 584–44. See Birgit H. Helander, *Nicolaus Cusanus als Wegbereiter auch der heutigen Ökumene* (Uppsala: 1993).

Vagrants Meet Nomads

Rogues, Aborigines, and Elizabethan Subjectivity

LINDA WOODBRIDGE

*I*n England, the sixteenth century, during which time the country was making its first contacts with the New World, was a time of recurrent famine, widespread unemployment, and serious homelessness and vagrancy. Texts dealing with vagrancy and its attendant problems include sermons, royal proclamations, statutes, jest books, and a genre that posterity has dubbed "rogue literature"— warnings to the public against the petty crimes and tricks of street people, mainly in a comic vein, with a thin veneer of sober moralizing. Primed by such publicity, when Elizabethans encountered nomadic aboriginal people in the New World, they often identified them with English vagrants. Michael Drayton, in his poem "To the Virginian Voyage" (1619), declares that "as savage slaves be in great Britain here, / As any one that you can shew me there."[1]

English travel writers ascribed to aboriginal peoples character defects stereotypic of English vagabonds: as Karen Kupperman notes, they accused Amerindians of "a great many character defects and vices ... improvidence, vengefulness, treachery, thievery, sexual promiscuity ... The men [were] often said to be lazy."[2] Similarly, writers of rogue literature excoriated laziness in vagrants; anticipating familiar attitudes toward "welfare bums" in our own time, many claimed that the unemployed simply did not want to work. The thievery and treachery of vagrants—like that of New World natives—were also popular themes; but it was upon vagrants' sexual promiscuity that writers of rogue literature dwelt with the greatest relish, and on this point rogue literature looks like a model for descriptions of the sexual habits of native peoples. Observe, for example, the striking similarity between the two following accounts of orgies, the first by Thomas Harman, a leading author of rogue literature, and the second from the 1600 English translation of Leo Africanus's *A Geographical Historie of Africa* (ca. 1526). In his 1566 fantasy of rogue life, Harman pictures a gang of vagrants bedding down for the night in a barn; a vagrant woman, in a parody of domesticity,

> shuffles up a quantity of straw or hay into some
> pretty corner of the barn where she may conveniently
> lie, and well shaketh the same, making the head
> somewhat high, and drives the same upon the sides
> and feet like a bed: then she layeth her wallet, or some
> other little pack of rags or scrip under her head in the
> straw, to bear up the same, and layeth her petticoat or
> cloak upon and over the straw, so made like a bed,
> and that serveth for the blanket. Then she layeth her
> slate (which is her sheet) upon that. And she have no
> sheet, as few of them go without, then she spreadeth
> some large clouts or rags over the same, and maketh
> her ready, and layeth her drowsily down.[3]

But no sooner is she settled than she will become the sexual prey of a bullying sort of rogue called "an upright man," and then (like the leftovers of a sordid meal) she will be enjoyed by rank-and-file rogues: "The rogue hath his leavings."[4] The second orgy occurs not among vagrants but among natives of "the land of Negroes," for whom Africanus describes (or fantasizes) a "brutish and savage life": "when night came [the black Africans] resorted ten or twelve both men and women into one cottage together, using hairy skins instead of beds, and each man choosing his leman which he had most fancy unto."[5]

Harman claimed, in his 1566 book *A Caveat for Common Cursetors, Vulgarly Called Vagabonds*, to have interviewed a number of vagrants who came begging at his country residence. He depicted the women as virtual sex slaves: "These doxies be broken and spoiled of their maidenhead by the upright-men, and then they have their name of doxies ... And afterward she is common and indifferent for any that will use her."[6] (Harman often shifts from singular to plural when discussing vagrants, effacing their individuality.) Vagrants, he maintained, "couch comely together, and [i.e., as if] it were dog and bitch"; "a vagrant woman will never make it strange when [she] be called, although she never knew him before"; "not one amongst a hundred of them are married; for they take lechery for no sin, but natural fellowship and good liking, love"; "they be as chaste as a cow I have, that goeth to bull every moon, with what bull she careth not."[7] Like Africanus' "lemans," these women are picked by the men as sexual partners with no choice in the matter at all. Harman's imagined vagrant sexuality resembles closely the salacious fantasies of unbridled sexuality in lands newly explored by Europeans, such as Africa and North America. As Kim Hall shows, writers drew for sexual information on texts such as Africanus', whose spicy accounts no doubt increased public interest in geographical exploration.[8] In their supposed laziness, thievery, treachery, and sexual excess, then, vagrants and aboriginal peoples as imagined by English Renaissance writers uncannily resembled each other. Teasing out the implications of this strange conjunction will help us understand some features of subjectivity as it was developing in the early modern period.

What did English vagrants have in common with New World nomadic tribes that the Elizabethan mind so easily conflated them? In Elizabethan eyes, they did share a kind of foreignness; in retrospect, we can see that the foreignness of vagrants was artificially imposed. Since it was more comforting to regard vagrants as foreign infiltrators than as natives of England, they were routinely represented as gypsies, Irish, or Welsh, and said to speak what was virtually a foreign language: thieves' cant. But in fact most vagrants were English, thrown out of work by enclosures or by depressions in the textile industry. Thieves' cant, many scholars now believe, was mostly a fabrication by writers of rogue literature.[9] Since most of England's vagrants were English, they really did not share foreignness with North American native tribes. The sexual promiscuity of both vagrants and New World natives was probably, in the main, a salacious fabrication. Harman's claims about female vagrants are wildly speculative: for example, although he claims that female vagrants outnumber male vagrants by two to one, A.L. Beier and other historians have shown that women were greatly in the minority among early modern English vagrants.[10] As Diane Willen and others show, among the settled poor women outnumbered men, but for a variety of reasons were much less likely to take to the road.[11] Harman's visions of hordes of sexually compliant female vagrants, like rogue literature's pronouncements on the foreignness of vagrants, appear to be fantasy, and the sexually voracious native peoples of newly discovered lands were likely cut from the same cloth.

For the remainder of this chapter, I will focus on two traits which vagrants and New World aborigines were thought to share: first, mobility, and second, a mysterious secrecy capable of hiding their true nature. Beliefs about vagrants and aborigines, and the tendency to conflate the two groups, project interconnected kinds of early modern anxiety—anxiety about mobility and anxiety about hidden realities. First, mobility.

As Stephen Greenblatt notes in *Marvelous Possessions: The Wonder of the New World*, Christopher Columbus justified his appropriation of Indian territory by disbarring Indians from full humanity on grounds of their mobility, their nomadism, the fact of their "having no settled dwellings";[12] and to some degree, what is frightening about vagrants to Harman and other writers of rogue literature is mobility itself. Harman's fear wasn't groundless—he lived on a main route into London, and vagrants on the roads were increasing alarmingly, in contemporary eyes. But he also projects onto vagrants what his own text shows to be the worst qualities of himself and the propertied classes—deceit, feigned illness, sexual incontinence[13]—and I suggest that he may well also be projecting onto them a taste for unrestrained wandering. Harman proves geographically mobile himself: despite his initial stance as an invalid confined to his country residence for many years, we presently find him in lodgings in London, overseeing the publication of two editions of the *Caveat for Common Cursetors*, and showing no signs of long-term illness. Indeed, upon overhearing out his window the begging activities of an alleged epileptic, he strides into the street "at a sudden," interrogates the man, then sends to Bethlehem Hospital to interrogate the warden about the man's story, gets two apprentices to shadow the beggar, and employs a printer friend to set him up and betray him into confessing how much money he has made at begging. The next day Harman dashes off to Newington to follow the progress of the case.

And Harman exhibits some social mobility: he is basically a member of the wealthy gentry, a magistrate with a manor house—a solid, respected member of the community. But he has also become an author, and is on good enough terms with a London printer to send him forth as a crime-fighter to make citizens' arrests of phony epileptics.[14] The Harman who goes enthusiastically up to London to oversee the printing of his book has a foot in the new commercial world of print culture, and anxiety over genteel folk dirtying their hands in print has been well documented for this period.[15] His dread of vagrants' mobility seems to project uneasiness about the rapid changes society is undergoing; his scapegoating the vagrants simplifies complex cultural changes by blaming those changes on a visible group. His fear of vagrants, at least in part, projects a fear of social mobility.

To illustrate anxieties about mobility, let us look at Harman's ideas on punishment. As Harman discovers through his energetic detective work, the impostor Nicholas Jennings is not only a phony epileptic, he is even a phony vagrant—as Harman eventually discovers, Jennings actually owns a home. Jennings is then put into the stocks, which Harman calls "condign punishment."[16]

Early modern society sanctioned punishments fitting the crime—thieves had their hands chopped off, gossips' tongues were curbed with bridles. Whipping was often a punishment for vagrants committing sexual offenses, appropriate because of the sexual kinkiness that has so long been connected with spankings and whippings.[17] That whipping also involved stripping underlines its sexual connections—the prurience of the whipper appears in King Lear's oft-quoted "thou rascal beadle, hold thy bloody hand! / Why dost thou lash that whore? Strip thine own back; / That hotly lusts to use her in that kind / For which thou whipp'st her."[18] The sexuality of whipping, then, ties in with the sexual promiscuity attributed to vagrants and to aboriginal peoples. But why were the stocks considered condign punishment for vagrants, along with that even greater immobilizer, the prison-cum-workhouse Bridewell? Because, I suggest, the main crime of vagrants was mobility. Mobility, vagrancy alone, was indictable, without other crimes, and a statute of 1547 instituted a "three strikes and you're out" provision for vagrants. For a first offence, a vagabond was to be "whipped and bored through the ear"; a third offence merited death, and many were hanged under this statute, for vagrancy alone:[19] if they had been guilty of a crime other than vagrancy, they would have been charged with that.

Why was mobility so threatening? Taken literally as geographic wandering, mobility was threatening because it represented a departure from the settled life to which a great proportion of the late medieval and early modern populace was habituated—it had been rare for people to travel more than thirty or forty miles from their birthplace during a lifetime. As rural people began moving into London in great numbers during the sixteenth century, the monarchy and parliament devised (ineffectual) measures to send them back, and the post-Reformation state had a particular stake in encouraging homekeeping: as Lena Orlin shows,

> The state designated the individual household, in the
> absence of the old authoritarian church and of a
> national police, as the primary unit of social control ...
> And it reinforced the preexistent patriarchal hierarchy
> to further empower the father politically and also to
> ensure his accountability ... Political patriarchalism ...
> in the late sixteenth century first analogized the
> household's structures of authority with those of the
> state ... The political branch cannibalized domestic
> ideology in order to advance the doctrine of royal
> absolutism.[20]

As a unit of social control, the household was especially useful, since early modern households, as Peter Laslett has shown, were self-contained, both home and workplace for most people. Using the example of a bakery, Laslett shows how the family lived over the shop, the baker ruling the bakery as senior craftsman and his family as patriarch; apprentices lived in, and were considered family members.[21] Accustomed to such housed staidness, contemporaries were understandably nonplussed when confronted with the lives of English vagrants or of nomadic peoples in newly discovered lands. Though many early modern vagrants seem to have had regular beats, following the harvest or local fairs in search of seasonal work, and although aboriginal nomads too made organized perambulations, following game or plants in season, to the early modern mind both were simply aimless wanderings. Their alienness from ordinary settled life rendered them unreadable.

But mobility was already threatening for less literal, practical reasons: not only did vagrants wander in an age when official ideologies prized settled domesticity, they also shifted roles and identities, in an age officially committed to rigid occupational categories and starting to be concerned about stability of identity. And in a larger sense, the geographical mobility of vagrants came to stand in for social mobility, a new fluidity of social class, and for even larger fluidities and instabilities of the age. The use of the word *place* to mean both social rank and geographical location is telling: in the synecdochic thinking of the age, those with no fixed abode came to represent other cultural dislocations occasioned by the Reformation, humanism, a newly centralized government, demographic shifts from outlying counties into London, proto-capitalism. The judicial punishment of Ben Jonson's Volpone, a *rich* man who plays the vagrant's supposed game of feigned disability, embodies the period's desperate need to pin down any kind of slipperiness with punishments producing immobility: "Since the most was gotten by imposture, / By feigning lame, gout, palsy, and such diseases, / Thou art to lie in prison, cramped with irons, / Till thou bee'st sick and lame indeed."[22] That the punishment for imposture was immobilization underlines the connection between the two kinds of anxiety I will be discussing— anxiety about mobility and about hidden realities.

Though it seems paradoxical to discover deep anxieties about mobility in this great age of world exploration and trade for Europeans, the anxiety is evident in the very efforts Elizabethans made to stabilize slippery ideas about immobility and mobility. One way was to pit "good" mobility against "bad." Bad mobility involved women, foreigners, and foreign travel: for example, this was an age that preached the virtues of staying home, especially to women; that witnessed recurrent riots and violence directed at foreign workers; that produced a substantial body of anti-travel literature, and vigorous propaganda campaigns exhorting consumers to "shop English." But some mobility was good: the English were engaged in extensive international trade, royally sanctioned piracy, and colonization; London was becoming a major international trade centre. Tension between these opposing dynamics was defused, for example, by distinguishing between "good" merchants and "bad," the former including wealthy international traders and settled city and town shopkeepers, and the latter including itinerant salesmen (pedlars, chapmen) and itinerant tradesmen (tinkers, cobblers), who were consigned to the category of vagabond and subject to arrest and prosecution—a particularly clear example of the privileged projecting onto vagrants qualities they felt uneasy about in themselves. Or good mobility could be defined as Englishmen travelling abroad to make money, and bad mobility as foreigners travelling to England to make money.

Another strategy was for each social group or gender to value mobility for itself, but to proscribe mobility in the group just below. Well-to-do merchants engaged in international trade valued their own freedom of travel, but sought to immobilize "illegitimate" travelling merchants like pedlars or chapmen by supporting legislation defining them as vagrants. The male sex cherished its own right to move freely about the streets of London, but assented to preachers who declared that "the duty of the husband is to travel abroad to seek living; and the wife's duty is to keep the house";[23] a huge body of literature satirized women for "gadding" about the streets. No wonder, then, that when Europeans encountered people of nomadic lifestyle in newly discovered lands, all kinds of worries and prejudices were triggered.

In the end, Europeans tried to arrest mobility in the new lands. Colonies which seemed to offer great promise of mobility were from the outset marked by repressive structures of confinement, which only worsened with time—in America, slavery, indentured servitude, and Indian reservations; in Africa, slavery; in Australia, penal colonies. The early modern passion for immobilizing and imprisoning eventually cast its shadow over all the English colonies. Vagrants—and sometimes their kidnapped children—were sent to the colonies; the transporting of undesirables to the colonies began in the sixteenth century. And an early act of New England social policy was a typically Elizabethan solution to the problem of noxious mobility: they built houses of correction.[24] In a sermon advocating the transportation of vagrants to the colonies, John Donne compared the whole New World to England's notorious workhouse/prison: "if the whole country were but such a Bridewell, to force idle persons to work, it had a good use."[25] In his *Discourse of Western Planting*, Richard Hakluyt the younger, extolling the benefits of ridding England of good-for-nothings by turning them into Americans, describes English vagrants as American savages were described by other Elizabethans:

> We for all the statutes that hitherto can be devised,
> and the sharp execution of the same in punishing
> idle and lazy persons for want of sufficient
> occasion of honest employment cannot deliver our
> commonwealth from multitudes of loiterers and
> idle vagabonds ... We are grown more populous than
> ever heretofore: so that now ... they can hardly live
> one by another, nay rather they are ready to eat up
> one another: yea many thousands of idle persons ...
> be either mutinous and seek alteration in the state,
> or at least very burdensome to the commonwealth,
> and often fall to pilfering and thieving and other
> lewdness.[26]

Idleness, pilfering, thievery, and lewdness were features of the newly coalescing stereotype of American Indians. And then there was the readiness to "eat up one another." As Kim Hall comments on this passage of Hakluyt's, "This specter of idleness, civil unrest, and near-cannibalism among the unemployed ... is very close to the conditions travelers claimed to find abroad."[27]

Even in such public documents as vagrancy legislation we can tease out traces of anxiety over unstable identity. For many people, identity was no longer comfortably tethered to a village, a trade, a niche in a well-established social hierarchy, and the psychic disturbances occasioned by this instability were, I argue, projected onto the most visibly untethered: vagrants at home and nomads abroad. The imprisoning structures at home (the stocks, Bridewell) and abroad (houses of correction, prisons, slavery and indentured servitude, Indian reservations) were all attempts to arrest mobility, attempts which I think express a crisis of subjectivity, in which personalities were becoming unmoored from the traditional social structures to which they had so long been fixed.

The second, related kind of endemic early modern anxiety was fear of imposture, of hidden realities. In the opening of the 1567 edition of *Caveat for Common Cursetors*, Harman italicizes his conviction that "*some thing lurk and lay hid that did not plainly appear.*"[28] He refers to the shiftiness and deceit of people on the road—their feigned disability, their exaggeration of their own poverty for purposes of begging, their communicating with each other in thieves' cant so that decent people could not understand them. Other writers of rogue literature conjured images of well-dressed "rogues" who infiltrated polite society so that decent people couldn't even detect that they were rogues. Whether exposing those who pretended to greater poverty and misery than they really experienced, or those who pretended to be of higher social class than they were, writers of rogue literature struck a pose as fearless unmaskers of imposture. The lantern shedding light on dark practices became a central image, as in Thomas Dekker's *Lantern and Candlelight*.[29] The lantern carried by truth-seeking Diogenes came to symbolize the rogue writer's relentless spotlight on hidden evils. Harman's formula "*some thing lurk and lay hid that did not plainly appear*" seems to be an English version of the Latin tag *Aliquod latent quod non patent* (Something is hidden which is not obvious), cited by Jack Wilton as he unveils his secret roguish life at the beginning of Thomas Nashe's "The Unfortunate Traveller."[30] Another version of the saying, *Multa latent quae non patent* (Many things lie hidden which are not exposed), appears at the end of a decoding of thieves' cant in Robert Greene's piece of rogue literature, *A Notable Discovery of Cozenage*.[31] The repetition of this phrase indicates the centrality to rogue literature of the conceit of bringing hidden practices to light.

Anxiety about hidden realities appears too in writings about newly discovered lands. To some extent, New World realities were "hidden" only because of their geographic remoteness and the lack of previous European contact. But just as geographic mobility became a synecdoche for social and other kinds of mobility in early modern thinking, so the "hiddenness" of New World practices owing to historic geographical remoteness seems connected in early modern thinking with mysteriousness and secrecy of personal character— aborigines were routinely accused of "treachery," of harbouring thieving and murderous thoughts under a welcoming exterior.

Exploring the period's fascination with bringing secret things to light, Patricia Parker sees a link between "the anatomist's opening and exposing to the eye the secrets or 'privities' of women and the 'discovery' or bringing to light of what were from a Eurocentric perspective previously hidden worlds," in the age of exploration.[32] Both had elements of prurience and voyeurism. Their "shared language of opening, uncovering or bringing to light" was also a feature of "monster literature," to which the literature of exploration was often related; the 1600 English translation of Leo Africanus's book featured "a map of Africa folded and closed upon itself, which, when opened up, brings before the reader's gaze the land of monsters, of Amazons, of prodigious sexuality and of peoples who expose those parts which should be hid."[33] The homology with the discourse of vagrancy of such texts on newly discovered foreign monstrosities declares itself: Harman and his fellows too bring hidden practices to light; they too find (among half-clothed vagrants in their rags) monstrous human beings, prodigious sexuality and ragged, naked immodesty; and they often exoticize vagrants as un-English. Parker further relates this cluster of ideas to the age's passion for eyewitness accounts and to the growth of domestic informing and spying: "This shared language of 'discovery' as informing or spying on something hid ... [gives] many of these exotic histories their affinities with the ocular preoccupations of the growing domestic network of ... informers and spies, charged with reporting on the secret or hid."[34]

Harman and later cony-catching writers did position themselves as "spies charged with reporting on the secret or hid." But we should be wary of reading this rhetorical posture as a herald of modern empirical methods. Even contemporaries were highly skeptical of the "eyewitness" accounts of monstrosities by foreign explorers, and rogue literature's enterprise of spying into abuses was epistemologically tainted from the start. Writers of rogue literature were themselves impostors. Harman's pose as worldly wise investigator of vagrants' deceits, his stance as a reporter on the underworld scene with direct, firsthand knowledge is undercut by the fact that most of his evidence comes from literary tradition, from earlier literary exposés of vagrancy such as John Awdeley's *The Fraternity of Vagabonds* and ultimately the continental *Liber Vagatorum*.[35] Since the *Liber Vagatorum* was a late fifteenth-century text and Harman wrote in 1567, his claims to up-to-the-minute reporting ring false; even in its own time, the *Liber Vagatorum*'s air of being an exposé of tricks "nowadays" was an artifice—many of its rogue scams were copied from an early fifteenth-century list compiled by the Senate of Basel.[36] Knowing that some of his anecdotes originate in a literary tradition, can we believe anything Harman says? What if he simply stole some of his information and made up the rest, rather than interviewing any vagrants at all? We will never be sure how much of the *Caveat for Common Cursetors* to believe, but enough of it is borrowed from other texts, rather than based on experience as Harman claims, to allow us to conclude that he is living a lie as much as the vagrants are. And this is true of much rogue literature: for example, Robert Greene's exposés of the niceties of cheating at cards and dice, published in the 1590s as gleanings of his own firsthand experience, are heavily plagiarized from Gilbert Walker's *A Manifest Detection of ... Dice-Play* (1552).[37] The world of rogue literature is not at all what it claims to be and has often been taken to be by later social historians—that is, a world of tough investigative reporting by fearless crime-fighters infiltrating a dangerous underworld. Instead, it is a world where texts spawn other texts: a literary world.

No wonder anxiety about hidden realities was endemic in the period—even the unmaskers of imposture were impostors.

As Thomas Kuhn, Brian Vickers, William Eamon, and others have shown,[38] early modern science was often piggybacked on magical beliefs, and it is not at all uncommon to find early modern natural philosophers—forerunners of our "scientists"—applying the same language to the uncovering of nature's "secrets" as their contemporary witch-hunters applied to the unmasking of occult practices of sorcery, as writers of rogue literature applied to the unmasking of underworld practices, and as travel writers applied to the illumination of dark practices on dark continents. William Gilbert, for example, in his pioneering work on the proto-science of magnetic philosophy, used the trope of a lantern illuminating occulted realities when he wrote that "the occult and hidden cause" of magnetic variance had "to be brought to light."[40] It is easy for our science-immersed age to misread as thoroughly rational and scientific the writings of early scientists whose own mentalities were often steeped in the occult—for example, William Harvey, discoverer of the circulation of the blood, treated tumours by laying the hand of a corpse on them. How different in kind from the occult powers of witchcraft did the secret forces of magnetism seem to an early modern mind like Gilbert's? The fact that he performed experiments and used a language of empirical observation may obscure for us the extent to which his mentality still partook of much that we would call superstition.

Harman, like Gilbert, makes empirical claims: he and other writers of rogue literature claim information on vagrants based on direct personal observation; but just as in science, an empirical-sounding language often preceded a fully scientific mentality, so in rogue literature, a prototype of the empirical, direct-observation rhetoric of crime reporting seems to have preceded any real investigative reporting. The period was developing—perhaps through the influence of natural philosophers like Gilbert—the rhetorical habit of appealing to direct observation: for example, Annabel Patterson points out, in *Reading Holinshed's Chronicles*, the chroniclers' devotion to eyewitness testimony.[39] But rogue literature's language of empiricism is really little but rhetorical window-dressing. The sixteenth century did not firmly distinguish between discovery and invention—indeed, several discourses used the two words interchangeably. Rogue literature's extensive plagiarism suggests that most of its discoveries were in fact inventions, as was the case with witchcraft. What has long misled scholars is the modern-sounding empirical language in which these literary variations-upon-a-theme are couched.

This second sort of anxiety (about hidden realities) makes contact with the first sort (about mobility) most visibly where Elizabethans fret about unstable social class. Here we encounter fear of hidden wanderers—people who are concealing the fact that they have strayed out of their proper social station into a higher one. Literature of the period abounds in these Elizabethan Eliza Doolittles—such as Widow Edith, eponymous hero of a jest book by Walter Smith, which relates the wanderings of a vagrant woman. Edith, getting hold of good clothes and adjusting her manners, infiltrates the household of the Lord Chancellor Sir Thomas More, and receives marriage proposals from his young well-born followers.[41] Widow Edith embodies both kinds of anxiety: as a vagrant she reflects anxieties about mobility and as an impostor she reflects anxieties about hidden, dark realities, secret identities. What made England with its vagrants as frightening and barbaric as the New World with its cannibal nomads was that nowadays people were not only always on the move, literally or metaphorically, but once they arrived at a new locale, they were passing as established residents.

Although people had believed in witches and feared occulted realities in the Middle Ages too, it was in the sixteenth and seventeenth centuries that witch persecution reached new heights, that empiricism was born, that the New World was explored, that rogue exposés had a literary vogue, and that the rhetoric of bringing dark things to light blossomed. Is it coincidental that this was also an age of new subjectivity, a new interiority, where Puritans saw God by their own inner light, diary keeping flourished, household architecture began evolving private rooms? That the unmasking of imposture, the shining of a bright light onto veiled identities and hidden practices, is a crucial trope in the period, has much to say about subjectivity. People had secret inner selves to protect, as never before. And if they cherished this inwardness in themselves, they seem to have feared it in others. It was all very well to love thy neighbour, but what secrets was thy neighbour harbouring? This age witnessed the birth of the idea of "passing." In Shakespeare's first tragedy, *Titus Andronicus*, a black husband and his white wife produce a baby so light it can "pass"; the play trades on the anxiety provoked by the presence of secret Moors. There were also secret vagrants, like Widow Edith. And secret beggars. In terms anticipating the 1950s, with that era's nightmare visions of infiltrating Communists, Edward Hext, a Somerset justice, described the infiltration of decent society by well-dressed beggars. His paranoia approaches that of witch beliefs: "They have intelligence of all things intended against them, for there be of them that will be present at every assize, session, and assembly of justices, and will so clothe themselves for that time as any should deem him to be an honest husbandman; so nothing is spoken, done, or intended to be done but they know it."[42] Though sumptuary laws aimed to force people to identify their social class by their attire, many successfully infiltrated a higher class through wearing fine clothes and changing their manners and accents. As Frank Whigham shows, handbooks of civility were a two-edged sword: aimed at buttressing the position of the elite by "describing" polite behaviour, civility manuals became how-to books for imitating the elite in order to insinuate oneself into a higher social level.[43] Fear of the mobility of women, their gadding in the streets among vagrants, reminds us that the age was fanatical in its anxiety about cuckoldry—English Renaissance literature brims over with horn jokes. If wives were always gadding and kept their own secrets close, might not a husband suspect that even his own children were strangers, passing as his own children?

The insistent motif of surveillance in vagrancy literature and other discourses at which I've glanced raises a chicken–egg question about subjectivity and interiority. Foucault famously maintained that surveillance creates a subjectivity wherein publicly sponsored values become internalized and public shame becomes private guilt; but it is also possible that it was the growing sense of the private, guarded heart of one's neighbours that created or fostered the urge to investigate, to spy—that created a culture of surveillance. The sixteenth century was preoccupied with imposture and with infiltration. Impostors were potentially everywhere; you couldn't be sure who anyone was. Was your neighbour a witch, or a rogue/confidence man, or a light-skinned Moor, or at least a social climber who had covered her tracks well? Infiltrators, too, were potentially everywhere—the confidence man who insinuated himself into polite society, the pamphleteer who claimed to have infiltrated the rogue underworld to expose its practices. The proto-scientific urge to probe nature's secrets, to expose the principles underlying the behaviour of magnets or of circulating blood, was a close cousin of the urge to probe other people's secrets, to expose what lay beneath genteel clothes and refined accents. Was it the nosiness of the age, its mistrust of surfaces, that gave rise to a particular closeted heart? Or did the closeting provoke the nosiness? Or were nosiness and closeting mutually constitutive?

Natives of exotic lands, and vagrants at home in England, were thought to observe no privacy in their sexuality. As we have seen, Africanus portrays a "brutish and savage" orgy in a cottage in "the land of Negroes," and Harman depicts an orgy of vagrants in a barn, with vagrant women as public sexual utilities for men on the road. The shock effect depends on the assumption that for decent people, sexuality was to be strictly private; this idea was in fact quite new at the time Africanus and Harman wrote.

Noting that the influential architect Leon Battista Alberti recommended separate bedrooms for husband and wife with a communicating door "to enable them to seek each other's company unnoticed," Mark Wigley argues that domestic architecture was "the agent of a new kind of modesty and ... played an active part in the constitution of the private subject";[44] this period witnessed a shift away from servants sharing bedchambers with masters toward house design allowing more private sexuality. It is against a newly private sexuality that we should view charges that vagrants' or aborigines' sexuality was animal-like in its publicness. And insofar as prurience thrives on inhibition, the impulse to expose the sexual practices of others, whether vagrants or New World natives, must in part have been an artifact of the new, inhibiting imperatives to keep one's own sexual activity hidden, a private matter. Again, closeting and nosiness were mutually constitutive—closeting of one's own sexual practices, nosiness about the sexual practices of others.

That early modern thinkers vacillated, worrying about what was too private and what too public, bespoke the instability of a public–private boundary that was in the process of being renegotiated. Imagining scenes of at least quasi-public sex, in the passages cited above Africanus alludes to sex acts by a group of Africans gathered in a cottage and Harman depicts sex acts by a group of vagrants in a barn. Though the walls of cottage and barn provide privacy against the outside world, the sex is non-private to the Africans and the vagrants grouped within, and the authors make it more public by broadcasting it in print. But despite charging natives and vagrants with making public what should be private, these authors in other contexts charge the same groups with hiding what should be public—hiding their true social class, hiding their treacherous plans, hiding their bodily health under a guise of disability. We are left confused by these charges—are the offending groups being blamed for being too open or too closed in their behaviour? The ambiguity of public sex within a private cottage or barn in itself reflects this contradictory thinking: vagrant and aboriginal sexuality seemed shockingly public because, in European polite society, sex was becoming more private; but the fact that group sex was concealed, in barn or cottage, enacts the stereotype of the devious, occulted personality of vagrants and natives.

Writing of our own period, Eve Kosofsky Sedgwick confronts similar contradictions bedevilling another figure with a hidden life—the modern closeted homosexual. Concerning the 1973 case of a teacher fired for discussing his homosexuality on television and radio, Sedgwick notes that a court upheld the firing "on the grounds that he had failed to note on his original employment application that he had been, in college, an officer of a student homophile organization—a notation that would, as school officials admitted in court, have prevented his ever being hired." Paradoxically, then, "the rationale for keeping [the teacher] out of his classroom was ... no longer that he had disclosed too much about his homosexuality, but quite the opposite, that he had not disclosed enough."[45] What

Sedgwick calls "an excruciating system of double binds"[46] is highly visible in early modern anxieties about aboriginal peoples and vagrants, expressed in conflicted condemnations of the lives of such people as both disgracefully public and suspiciously secretive.

Clothing was to psychological concealment what geographic wandering was to social mobility: a material embodiment of something intangible. And again in the contradictory thinking of the day, vagrants were condemned for both deceptive clothing and nakedness. Accused witches were stripped to search for extra teats and other demonic tokens on their bodies; stripping off of clothing as a prelude to whipping was a common punishment for vagrants. Stripping increased the pain of whipping, but it was likely also an emblem of exposure, since beggars were considered deceitful, and one of their major deceits, feigned disability, involved a lie about their bodies. In exposing the body, stripping exposed the lie. In Widow Edith's signature scams, she obtains a good dress through trickery and then uses it to impersonate higher social class. When her cheats are exposed, she is usually stripped to her petticoat and sent packing. The frequency with which Edith is stripped, given that she never feigns disability, suggests that it is a symbolic disclosure of deceit. But at the same time that they worried about deceptive clothing, contemporaries were scandalized by the semi-nakedness of beggars: in an age when women's dresses were long and concealing, beggars went about in rags, through which bare skin was visible. Like their "public" sexuality, sartorial immodesty marked them as alien, just as the unclothed state of many aboriginal people marked them as savage. Both being clothed and being naked could be offensive: too private or too public.

Pronouncements about vagrant language, too, were contradictory. Professing to believe that vagrants regularly conversed in thieves' cant, Tudor writers explained that canting was meant to make its speakers inconspicuous. Walker explains in *A Manifest Detection of ... Dice-Play* that cardsharks used canting "to the intent that ever in all companies they may talk familiarly in all appearance, and so covertly indeed that their purpose may not be espied."[47] But this makes no sense. If, in a modern-day poker game, two of the players suddenly started addressing each other in pig Latin, even people who couldn't make out the sense of pig Latin would suspect that something was up, that these two players knew each other better than they were pretending to, and were signalling each other in ways they didn't want other players to understand. This would hardly make for inconspicuousness; and given the hype attending Tudor thieves' cant, mentioning a "bousing ken" or "stalling to the rogue" in the midst of any scam would have been a dead giveaway. It wouldn't have mattered whether people knew what the words meant: the point was, people would have known that thieves' cant was being spoken, and been instantly on their guard; therefore, only a numskull thief would ever have used such slang in public. The "inconspicuous" explanation is absurd enough to comprise good evidence that "cant" was largely a literary fabrication. And here again is that strange ambiguity—are the vagrants guilty of hiding their nefarious purposes under a code language, or of parading their underworld affiliations through language that is virtually a public badge of criminality? Are the writers worried about vagrants' concealing too much, or revealing too much?

The language of New World natives was also regarded in contradictory ways—sometimes as meaningless babble rather than a true language (disqualifying the babblers from the status of human), and sometimes as a treacherous secret code enabling plots by tribesmen against Europeans. And again there are points of contact between natives and "rogues": Stephen Greenblatt compares the rogue literature's vocabulary lists of thieves' cant to Thomas Harriot's word list of Algonquian terms in his *Brief and True Report of the New Found Land of Virginia* (1588).[48]

Accounting for these contradictions in thinking about the sexuality, clothing, and language of vagrants and aboriginals would require a much longer study than this one.[49] Among the complexities that would need to be considered are the fact that anxiety about obfuscatory clothing stems from a newly private subjectivity that occasioned worry about what others were concealing, while anxiety about nakedness probably reflected the humanist use of clothing to mark the divide between human and animal—immodestly clothed vagrants who would have sex in a barn are, like "savages," closer to animals and thus an affront to the human dignity extolled by humanists. And anxiety about obfuscatory language again reflects suspicion fostered by newly private subjectivity, while the notion of thieves' cant as readily recognizable and decodable, stemming from the "investigative reporter" rhetoric of rogue literature, may have been paradoxically comforting in contrast to more realistic fears: there were plenty of real class interlopers who didn't use identifiable slang but sounded just like respectable people. This is not the place to sort out all these complexities; suffice it to say here that in the case of sexuality, of clothing, and of language, an "excruciating double bind" repeatedly surfaces: condemnation of both public and private sexuality, both clothedness and nakedness, both concealing speech and revealing speech.

All of these condemnations bear on two groups that were repeatedly scapegoated in similar terms and that seem linked in the imagination of the day: vagrants in England and the natives of newly discovered non-European lands. Though domestic vagrants and foreign nomads seem on the surface an unlikely pairing, qualities attributed to these two groups—mobility, lack of fixed domicile, secretiveness, aberrant sexuality, idleness, non-standard clothing and language, and the rest—played upon and to some extent projected anxieties peculiar to the changing subjectivity of the early modern heart.

The sixteenth century was fascinated by that French *cause célèbre*, the trial of an impostor who for some years successfully impersonated Martin Guerre. Here, combining mobility with imposture, a wanderer infiltrated a village, stole the identity of a man who was once embedded in a family and a tight-knit local social structure, and succeeded in "passing," even with Martin Guerre's wife. When vigorous investigators eventually brought the imposture to light, the language surrounding the case was redolent of wondrous New World monstrosities, continually "brought to light" by investigative travel literature. The 1561 account by the trial judge, Jean de Coras, was advertised in its subtitle as *une histoire prodigieuse* (a prodigious history). As Natalie Zemon Davis notes, "very much in the air these days were collections of 'prodigies'—of wondrous plants and animals, of double suns and monstrous births,"[50] and it is telling that for readers of the day, the story of an impostor husband and heir occupied the same conceptual space as tales about monstrosity. To some degree, figures like sea monsters, two-headed calves, and sexually rampant rogues and nomads, were caricatures projecting some everyday fears: fear of mobility and social change; fear that people you think you know are hiding something terrible. The possibility of a hidden monstrosity below a normal human skin haunted the age, from Spenser's Duessa hiding bestial body parts under fine clothes to Othello's suspecting monstrous sexuality under his wife's devotion and finding monstrous lies under his friend's "honesty." No wonder Othello's cry is "O monstrous! monstrous!"[51] The dark side of cherishing the new privacies of one's own heart was the fear of finding a monster impostor in somebody else's.

In *Passing and the Fictions of Identity*, Elaine K. Ginsberg shows just why the prospect of passing—of a black person for a white, of a female for a male—proves so unsettling to those with any stake in society as presently constituted: "The possibility of passing challenges a number of ... assumptions about identities, the first of which is that some identity categories are inherent and unalterable essences."[52] A terror of those who are passing makes sense only in a society that lives in fear that its traditional boundaries, classifications, and hierarchies will be eroded or penetrated. It is telling that, according to Ginsberg, stories of racial or gender passing almost always involve geographical movement, literal trespassing. Her examples are from a later age, but they resonate with sixteenth-century anxieties that projected social passing onto geographic wanderers, whether vagrants at home or nomads abroad.

When humanists blamed poverty on the poor, for having ruined their own fortunes by profligacy, their comments had the unintended consequence of effacing social boundaries: the poor were not a permanent, fixed group but simply those who had slipped out of gentility through moral weakness. A conception of social order like Sir Thomas Elyot's, which depended on God-given fixed social estates—some fit to rule, others to be ruled—was undermined by the possibility of such effacement.[53] Similar logical strain appears in the period's insistence on God-given heterosexual roles; its simultaneous definition of sodomy as a potentiality, not an identity; its essentialist insistence on fixed gender roles; and its simultaneous belief that a woman could physically turn into a man through over-exertion, or a man psychologically turn into a woman by transvestism. The same contradiction is visible in New World contexts, where belief in the innate superiority of white Europeans sat weirdly side by side with fear that white Europeans might be tempted to "go native" in a land of savages. In each of these cases, early modern society insisted on the fixity and divine sanction of boundaries, at the very moment many writers were expressing anxiety about possible slippage across them. We can make sense of such seeming contradictions by positing that anxiety over whether a heterosexual might slip into the ranks of sodomites, or a man into the status of a woman, or a humanist into the condition of a beggar, or a European into an Indian, actually helps to *produce*, as a defensive strategy, essentialist pronouncements about the immutability of such boundaries.

Anxiety about secrecy and impostors, then, went hand in hand with anxiety about mobility because one of the great secrets people had to keep was their mobility, their movability across boundaries—geographic and social boundaries, gender and racial boundaries, boundaries dividing civilized from savage. To some degree, nearly everybody was passing in the sixteenth century, donning a social mask, protecting a newly privatized heart. As a result, a suspicion was abroad in the land that nobody really knew his neighbour, so devious was people's mobility, so great their protectiveness of the private heart. If you pried open the heart of even a true-born Englishman, held up your lantern and brought its dark secrets to light, who knows but what you might find: witchcraft, vagrancy, or even the land of the Algonquian within?

NOTES

1 Michael Drayton, "To the Virginian Voyage," in *The Works of Michael Drayton*, vol. 2, ed. J. William Hebel (Oxford: Blackwell, 1931–41), p. 363.

2 Karen O. Kupperman, *Settling with the Indians: The Meeting of English and Indian Cultures in America, 1580–1640* (Totowa, NJ: Rowman and Littlefield, 1980), p. 121.

3 Thomas Harman, *A Caveat for Common Cursetors, Vulgarly Called Vagabonds* (London: W. Griffith, 1567; STC 12787); first printed 1566; reprinted in *The Elizabethan Underworld,* ed. A.V. Judges, 2nd ed. ([1930] New York: Octagon, 1964), p. 105). Except where otherwise stated, I use the version reprinted in Judges.

4 Ibid., p. 108.

5 Johannes Leo Africanus, *A Geographical Historie of Africa,* trans. John Pory (London, 1600), pp. 284–85.

6 Harman, *Caveat for Common Cursetors,* p. 105.

7 Ibid., pp. 70, 78, 94, 99.

8 Kim F. Hall, *Things of Darkness: Economies of Race and Gender in Early Modern England* (Ithaca and London: Cornell University Press, 1995).

9 See M.A.K. Halliday, "Antilanguages," in *Language as a Social Semiotic: The Social Interpretation of Language and Meaning* (London: Arnold, 1978); John L. McMullan, *The Canting Crew: London's Criminal Underworld 1550–1700* (New Brunswick: Rutgers University Press, 1984); and Paul Slack, *Poverty and Policy in Tudor and Stuart England* (London and New York: Longman, 1988). A.L. Beier, at times skeptical about canting, at other times treats it as a real historical phenomenon; see, for example, his "Anti-language or Jargon? Canting in the English Underworld in the Sixteenth and Seventeenth Centuries," in *The Social History of Language: Language and Jargon,* vol. 3, ed. Peter Burke and Roy S. Porter (London: Polity Press, 1995), pp. 64–101. See also Linda Woodbridge, *Vagrancy, Homelessness, and English Renaissance Literature* (Urbana and Chicago: University of Illinois Press, 2001), pp. 9–10.

10 A.L. Beier, *Masterless Men: The Vagrancy Problem in England* (London: Methuen, 1985), p. 52, table 3.

11 Diane Willen, "Women in the Public Sphere in Early Modern England," *Sixteenth Century Journal* 19 (1988): 559–75.

12 Stephen Greenblatt, *Marvelous Possessions: The Wonder of the New World* (Chicago: University of Chicago Press, 1991), p. 66.

13 See Woodbridge, *Vagrancy, Homelessness,* chapter 1.

14 Harman, *Caveat for Common Cursetors,* pp. 85–90.

15 See, for example, J.W. Saunders, "The Stigma of Print: A Note on the Social Bases of Tudor Poetry," *Essays in Criticism* 1 (1951): 139–64; Martin Elsky, *Authorizing Words: Speech, Writing, and Print in the English Renaissance* (Ithaca: Cornell University Press, 1989); and Wendy Wall, *The Imprint of Gender: Authorship and Publication in the English Renaissance* (Ithaca: Cornell University Press, 1993).

16 Harman, *Caveat for Common Cursetors,* caption to illustration facing page 97.

17 For a graphic contemporary account of a "whipping Jew" who gets sexual thrills from whipping naked women, see Thomas Nashe's "The Unfortunate

Traveller," in *The Unfortunate Traveller and Other Works*, ed. J.B. Steane (London: Penguin, 1972), pp. 353, 359.

18 William Shakespeare, *King Lear*, in *Complete Works*, ed. David Bevington, 4th ed. (Glenview, IL: Scott, Foresman, 1992), 4.6.160–63. See also Laura Lunger Knoppers, "(En)gendering Shame: *Measure for Measure* and the Spectacles of Power," *English Literary Renaissance* 23 (1993): 450–71.

19 E.M. Leonard, *The Early History of English Poor Relief* (Cambridge: Cambridge University Press, 1900), pp. 70–71.

20 Lena Orlin, *Private Matters and Public Culture in Post-Reformation England* (Ithaca and London: Cornell University Press, 1994), p. 11.

21 Peter Laslett, *The World We Have Lost* (New York: Scribner, 1965).

22 Ben Jonson, "Volpone," in *Ben Jonson*, ed. C.H. Herford, Percy Simpson, and Evelyn Simpson (Oxford: Clarendon, 1937), 5.12.121–4.

23 Robert Cleaver, *A Godly Form of Household Government* (London: F. Kingston, 1598; STC 5383), p. 170.

24 Kupperman, *Settling with the Indians*, p. 123.

25 *The Sermons of John Donne*, ed. Evelyn M. Simpson and George R. Potter, vol. 4 (Berkeley: University of California Press, 1953), p. 272.

26 *The Original Writings and Correspondence of the Two Richard Hakluyts*, ed. E.G.R. Taylor, vol. 2 (London: Hakluyt Society at Cambridge University Press, 1935), p. 234.

27 Hall, *Things of Darkness*, p. 54.

28 Harman, *Caveat for Common Cursetors* (1567 edition), sig. Aii.

29 Thomas Dekker, *Lantern and Candlelight* (London: G. Eld, 1608; STC 6485).

30 Nashe, "Unfortunate Traveller," p. 255.

31 Robert Greene, *A Notable Discovery of Cozenage* (London: J. Wolfe, 1591; STC 12279), p. 177.

32 Patricia Parker, *Shakespeare from the Margins: Language, Culture, Context* (Chicago and London: University of Chicago Press, 1996), p. 240.

33 Ibid.

34 Ibid., p. 241.

35 John Awdeley, *The Fraternity of Vagabonds* ([ca. 1561] London: 1575; STC 994); *The Liber Vagatorum*, translated as *The Book of Vagabonds and Beggars with a Vocabulary of their Language and a Preface by Martin Luther*, ed. D.B. Thomas, trans. J.C. Hotten (London: Penguin, 1932).

36 Natalie Zemon Davis, "Poor Relief, Humanism, and Heresy," in *Society and Culture in Early Modern France* (Stanford: Stanford University Press, 1965), p. 277 n. 29.

37 Judges reprints a selection of Greene's pamphlets in *The Elizabethan Underworld* (see n. 3 above), and Arthur F. Kinney reprints a selection in *Rogues, Vagabonds and Sturdy Beggars: A New Gallery of Tudor and Early Stuart Rogue Literature,* 2nd ed. (1972; Amherst: University of Massachusetts Press, 1990); Gilbert Walker, *A Manifest Detection of the Most Vile and Detestable Use of Dice-Play* (London: Abraham Vele, 1552; STC 24961).

38 Thomas Kuhn, *The Structure of Scientific Revolutions,* 2nd ed. (Chicago: University of Chicago Press, 1970); Brian Vickers, *Occult and Scientific Mentalities in the Renaissance* (Cambridge: Cambridge University Press, 1984); William Eamon, *Science and the Secrets of Nature* (Princeton: Princeton University Press, 1994).

39 William Gilbert, *De Magnete: Magneticisque Corporibus, et de Magno Magnete Tellure; Physiologia Nova, Plurimus and Argumentis, and Experimentis Demonstrata* (London: Peter Short, 1600), trans. P. Fleury Mottelay (1893; New York: Dover, 1958), p. 229.

40 Annabel Patterson, *Reading Holinshed's Chronicles* (Chicago: University of Chicago Press, 1994). The French cosmographer André Thevet spun a whole book about the New World out of a visit to Brazil that lasted only from 15 November 1555 to 31 January 1556; his eyewitness reports of indigenous Brazilian cultures, however, were heavily supplemented by acknowledged and unacknowledged borrowings from ancient Greek and Latin authors and modern authors such as Polydore Vergil (see Frank Lestringant, *Mapping the Renaissance World: The Geographical Imagination in the Age of Discovery* [Berkeley and Los Angeles: University of California Press, 1994], pp. 61–70). Thevet, like Harman, makes no distinction between information gleaned from literary sources and that obtained by firsthand observation. Having read about the hippopotamus of African rivers, Thevet managed to see one in a Brazilian river (Lestringant, *Mapping the Renaissance,* p. 54). As the art historian E.H. Gombrich has shown, the eye tends to assimilate the unfamiliar to the familiar, and even artists drawing from the life can produce wildly inaccurate depictions resembling not what they see before them but what they expect to see, based on models with which they are familiar (Gombrich, *Art and Illusion: A Study in the Psychology of Pictorial Representation* [Princeton: Princeton University Press, 1956]). This tendency was especially strong in the sixteenth century, the beginning (as Gombrich argues) of a representational period when artists were correcting by reference to reality the ready-made schema they had inherited from earlier artists. The same can be seen in documents purporting to be firsthand reportage—experience was only just emerging from the dominance of authority. Therefore, early modern writers who claim to be exposing the dark secrets of vagrants or of New World natives or even of Mother Nature through empirical observation should be regarded with healthy scepticism. Sixteenth-century travel writers have long been subject to such scepticism, but a disconcerting number of modern historians use writers of rogue literature, such as Harman, as sources of information (see Woodbridge, *Vagrancy, Homelessness,* pp. 11, 39–41).

41 Walter Smith, *The Twelve Merry Jests of the Widow Edith* (London: J. Rastell, 1525; STC 22869.7); reprinted in William Hazlitt, *Shakespeare Jest-books,* vol. 3 (London: Willis and Sotheran, 1864), pp. 27–108.

42 R.H. Tawney and Eileen Power, *Tudor Economic Documents*, vol. 2 (London: Longmans, 1924), p. 345.

43 Frank Whigham, *Ambition and Privilege: The Social Tropes of Elizabethan Courtesy Theory* (Berkeley: University of California Press, 1984).

44 Mark Wigley, "Untitled: The Housing of Gender," in *Sexuality and Space*, Princeton Papers on Architecture, ed. Beatriz Colomina (Princeton: Princeton University School of Architecture, 1992), p. 345.

45 Eve Kosofsky Sedgwick, *Epistemology of the Closet* (Berkeley: University of California Press, 1990), p. 69.

46 Ibid., p. 70.

47 Walker, *A Manifest Detection ... of Dice-Play*, p. 35.

48 Greenblatt, "Invisible Bullets," in *Shakespearean Negotiations: The Circulation of Social Energy in Renaissance England* (Berkeley and Los Angeles: University of California Press, 1988), p. 49.

49 I pursue some of these issues in more detail in Woodbridge, *Vagrancy, Homelessness*. Portions of this chapter have been drawn from that book.

50 Natalie Zemon Davis, *The Return of Martin Guerre* (Cambridge, MA: Harvard University Press, 1983), pp. 105–06.

51 Shakespeare, *Othello*, 3.3.442.

52 Elaine K. Ginsberg, ed., *Passing and the Fictions of Identity* (Durham, NC: Duke University Press, 1996), p. 4.

53 Sir Thomas Elyot, *The Book Named the Governour*, ed. Henry H.S. Croft, 2 vols. (1531; New York: Bert Franklin, 1967).

Part Three

Travel to the New World

THE EARLY MODERN AND THE POSTMODERN

Re-Writing the Virginian Paradise

The Conflicted Author(s) of a Late Sixteenth-Century Travel Account

PAUL W. DEPASQUALE

etween 1584 and 1590, the English made six voyages to modern North Carolina, an area called "Virginia" at the time in honour of Queen Elizabeth I, who in 1584 granted letters patent to Walter Ralegh to explore and possess American lands not already occupied by England's rival nations. On 13 July 1584, Philip Amadas and Arthur Barlowe, leaders of the reconnaissance expedition, took possession of Hatarask Island and its surrounding areas. Several days later the crew made contact with the people of Granganimeo, brother of the Carolina Algonquian *weroance* (chief) named Wingina, who treated the English to an elaborate ceremonial banquet. Barlowe, who kept the ship's journal, records that the Virginians entertained their visitors with "all love and kindness and with as much bounty after their manner as they could possibly devise. We found the people most gentle, loving, and faithful," he continues, "void of all guile and treason and such as lived after the manner of the Golden Age. The earth bringeth forth all things in abundance as in the first creation, without toil or labor."[1]

This passage from Barlowe's 1584 narrative, first published in Richard Hakluyt's 1589 edition of the *Principall Navigations*, is the one most frequently cited by historians and critics seeking to demonstrate the classical underpinnings of early modern English New World description. Harry Levin was among the first scholars to point out the similarities between noble savages and inhabitants of the Golden Age in writings of the period, and his work has encouraged analogous approaches. Levin suggested in *The Myth of the Golden Age in the Renaissance* that American travellers experienced little difficulty when representing aboriginal peoples since they could draw from a "rich backlog of fabulous lore about aborigines, namely the myth of the golden age. Hence," he adds, "it is not surprising that, whenever the voyagers undertook to describe the inhabitants of the new lands they had been exploring, the Ovidian *topos* was likely to come into play, almost as if it had been touched off by a reflex action."[2] The implicit ease of New World description is also evident in recent writings that insist on an ongoing thematics as travellers wrote about their American experiences, as if past literatures and epistemologies had unshakably left their marks on the minds of sixteenth- and seventeenth-century voyagers. In her comparative study of *Ceremonies of Possession*, for instance, Patricia Seed examines the lure value of the New World garden for the English, in contrast to the Spanish who were drawn overseas by visions of gold and the Portuguese who were enticed by spices and dyewoods.[3] Seed describes Barlowe's assessment of the Englishmen's initial approach to Virginia in 1584—"The second of July we found shoal water, where we smelt so sweet and so strong a smell, as if we had been in the midst of some delicate garden"—as a paradigmatic and defining example of the English attraction to America, one that instantiates the garden's paradisiacal, biblical derivations.[4]

Keeping in mind that even Jacques Derrida has been forced to admit (rather reluctantly) the impossibility of fully getting rid of what he calls the "imperatives of classical pedagogy"—forging links, justifying trajectories, and re-establishing continuities[5]—I want to suggest that reiterations of a seamlessness and fluidity of ideas in early colonialist discourses, though helpful in giving a rough sketch of the ways various epistemologies were picked up and disseminated in the early modern period, tend to conceal the often shifting, contradictory images of America and its inhabitants. They obscure, as a result, what seem to have been highly complex and diverse representational processes in play as individual writers sought to describe unfamiliar territories and peoples. Like other texts of the period, Barlowe's 1584 account, while evoking a rhetoric of praise grounded in the myth of the Golden Age, suggests at the same time that a conflicting body of nascent colonial policies and instructions encouraged the author's descriptions of the new in ways that would be both recognizable and ideologically serviceable to his patron audience. My chapter thus seeks to supplement a thematic approach to early colonialist materials by making two points, before offering some necessarily tentative concluding remarks: (1) that Barlowe's narrative is, in large part, a response to the policies and instructions written by contemporary colonial theorists, and (2) that the conflicted agendas in such policies and instructions helped to engender highly ambivalent images of the Golden Age in Barlowe's discourse.

Barlowe's text epitomizes what Wayne Franklin describes as the discovery narrative, a narrative that depicts America as a "fund of vegetative symbols, a place of 'superabundance' counterpointed to the implicit wasteland of Europe."[6] The following, for example, is his account of New World grapes, a description which inspired Michael Drayton to write his eleventh ode in celebration of "Virginia / earths onely paradise" where "the golden age / still natures laws doth giue":

> [T]he very beating, and surge of the Sea overflowed
> them ... we founde such plentie, as well there [on the
> shore], as in all places else, both on the sande, and on
> the greene soile on the hils, as in the plaines, as well on
> euery little shrubbe, as also climing towardes the
> toppes of the high Cedars, that I think in all the world
> the like abundance is not to be founde: and my selfe
> having seen those partes of Europe that most abound,
> finde such difference as were incredible to be written.[7]

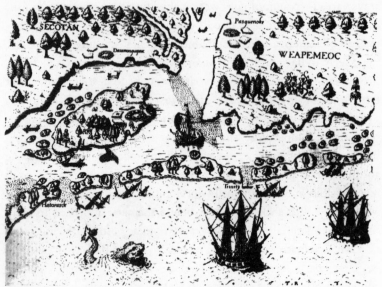

"Virginia," from Thomas Harriot, A Briefe and true Report of the New found land of Virginia *(London: 1588).*

Elsewhere in his narrative, Barlowe catalogues the commodities he anticipates will result in quick gain and long-term profit, with a manic breathlessness that conveys the utter inexpressibility of his American experience. The travellers find deer, rabbits, and fowl "in incredible aboundance." Fruits and vegetables emerge from a soil described as "the most plentifull, sweete, fruitfull, and wholsome of all the world." Cedars are the reddest and tallest in the world, superior to those found in Bohemia, Muscovy, Hyrcania in the Caucasus, the Azores, or India. Pines, cypresses, sassafras, and the lentisk (sweet gum) are other potential commodities possessing outstanding qualities.[8] Throughout, Barlowe's text stresses the unparalleled excellence of Virginia and its peoples, giving weight and breadth to the colonialist fantasy of easy access to a land of plenty which is inhabited, if indeed it must be inhabited, by a loving, honest, and non-militaristic people.

To a considerable extent, such descriptions reflect the ways that travel writers engaged and were in dialogue with the emerging transatlantic policies and instructions of England's colonial theorists. For example, Barlowe's hyperbolic, caricature-like description of

Chief Wingina's brother, Granganimeo, making "all signes of ioy, and welcome, striking on his head, and his breast, and afterwardes on ours, to shewe we were all one, smiling, and making shew the best hee could, of all loue, and *familiaritie*,"[9] serves several functions, not the least of which is its deference to such policies and instructions. It establishes the natives' amicable disposition towards the strangers, an amenability which anticipates favourable trade relations for the English as well as a strategic alliance with Granganimeo, who is a metonymy for Wingina, the person of most power and authority in the region. The use of the word *familiaritie* recalls a formal policy of establishing intimate contact with the inhabitants, first expressed in a set of notes which Richard Hakluyt the elder drafted for Humphrey Gilbert's Newfoundland voyage of 1578 and possibly also for Martin Frobisher's final voyage to Meta Incognita in the same year. Hakluyt the elder, cousin to the more widely known younger editor of the same name, was a lawyer at the Inns of Court who specialized in international trade. "Nothing," he advised Gilbert,

> is more to be indevoured with the Inland people then familiaritie. For so may you best discover al the naturall commodities of their countrey, and also all their wantes, all their strengthes, all their weaknesse, and with whome they are in warre, and with whom confiderate in peace and amitie, &c. whiche knowen, you may woorke many great effectes of greatest consequence.[10]

Hakluyt's notes to Gilbert precipitated the rise of a more systematic approach to Western discovery and reporting than had been previously imagined by those who directed the course of England's American initiatives. Elsewhere in the instructions, the lawyer calls for travellers to make "great observation" and to take "perfect note" of New World phenomena,[11] a call which led to an unprecedented focus on American geography, topography, ecology, and ethnography. A similar preoccupation with knowledge of new lands informs the elder Hakluyt's 1580 instructions to Arthur Pet and Charles Jackman, sent to discover the Northeast Passage by merchants of the Muscovy Company. Here the theorist instructs the travellers "to set downe in plat" any geographic features which might prove useful to future explorers; the two men were also expected to "take a speciall view" and "to note" the inhabitants' military strength and living conditions as fully as possible, even if the explorers had to "give a gesse of many things."[12]

While they were written with specific audiences and voyages in mind, the elder Hakluyt's notes for Gilbert and instructions to Pet and Jackman clearly had potential uses outside those for which they were intended. The younger Hakluyt printed the 1578 guidelines in the *Divers Voyages* (1582), as well as in the first and revised editions of the *Principall Navigations* (1589; 1598–1600), under a heading which assured readers that the document was "not unfitt to be committed to print, considering the same may stirre up considerations of these and of such other thinges, not unmeete in such new voyages as may be attempted hereafter." Likewise, the title of the lawyer's advice to Pet and Jackman (published in the same volumes) includes the clause "not altogether unfit for some other enterprises of discoverie, heerafter to be taken in hand."[13] By printing these originally private instructions in texts intended for public consumption, the two Hakluyts offered a schematic for travellers venturing to all regions previously unexplored. Their explicit, public call for information to do with unfamiliar regions in both the Old and New worlds sought to feed the theorists' main interest in ascertaining what the younger Hakluyt describes in the 1589 *Principall Navigations* as the "speciall commodities, & particular wants" in various parts of the world, "which by the benefit of traffike, & entercourse of merchants, are plentifully supplied."[14] In their collaborative effort to fill empty spaces (or spaces perceived as empty) with English goods and an English presence, the Hakluyts gave little notice to the many discrepancies between Old and New worlds that were the result of vastly disparate geographies and ethnographies; indeed, the younger Hakluyt seems to have considered his cousin's advice for expeditions along the northern coast of Russia and to Asia as perfectly appropriate and translatable to an American experience.[15]

The elder Hakluyt also took part, along with George Peckham, Frobisher, and possibly the younger Hakluyt, in the compilation of the 1582–83 set of instructions for a reconnaissance to southern Norumbega (called New England after 1616) organized by Peckham and Thomas Gerrard, under the joint or several command of William Stanley, Richard Bingham, and Frobisher. Although this voyage failed to take place for some unknown reason, the instructions provide an excellent look at the kinds of American data that travellers around the time of Barlowe's expedition were required to bring home.[16] The captain's instructions set out his responsibility to ensure that all topographical, ecological, geographical, and ethnographical data were meticulously recorded in both journal and "drawen plott" or chart forms. He was further advised to assign one explorer to note the inhabitants' agricultural methods, and another to record

> the statures Conditions apparell and manner of foode,
> which of them be men eaters with the thinges that they
> in every particuler place shall most esteme either of
> their owne Contrye commodyties or of ours. Noting
> also the greatnes and quantetie of every distinct Kinges
> Contryes people and forces ... noting preciselye the
> particuler places where every suche observacions are
> to be made as well in the Journall as platt.[17]

Included in the 1582–83 instructions are guidelines for Thomas Bavin, the artist/surveyor who journeyed with Gilbert, as well as a detailed catalogue of the materials and instruments that Bavin was to carry with him at all times.[18] The instructions provided Bavin with an attendant to make sure he never travelled without at least two writing tables on which to draw and chart, another attendant to keep him supplied with various tools and materials, and "somme others" to accompany him with other instruments and equipment.[19] The fact that Bavin was provided with at least three or four men (compared to, say, the ship's master who was allocated only one) suggests not only that the expedition's organizers considered the position of artist/surveyor to be one of considerable importance, but also that Bavin would have held a relatively prominent status in the voyage.

I focus on these little-known guidelines for two reasons. First, when we consider the belatedness of the English (relative to other European nations) to incorporate graphic description into their accounts of America, the significance and uniqueness of these accounts in the development of early modern English colonial policy and practice becomes even more apparent. Neither the first major non-literary text on America written in English, Richard Eden's 1555 translation of Peter Martyr's *Decades of the Newe Worlde*, nor Richard Hakluyt's *Divers Voyages* of 1582, includes visual depictions of America and its inhabitants, even though such images were commonplace in other European travel accounts and compilations such as Gonzalo Fernandez de Oviedo's *Historia general y natural de las Indias* (1537–47), Giovanni Battista Ramusio's *Navigationi e Viaggi* (1550–59), Girolamo Benzoni's *Historia del Mondo Nuovo* (1565), André Thevet's *Singularitez de la France Antarctique* (1558), and Jean de Léry's *Histoire d'un voyage faict en la Terre du Brésil* (1580). The elder Hakluyt's advice to Ralegh in 1585, that he would do well to follow the example of the Spanish by sending "a skilfull painter" to America,[20] came a full decade after a team of artists working under Franciso Hernandez in Mexico had produced fifteen volumes of illustrations for Philip II of Spain.[21] England, in fact, made no sustained effort to visually depict the New World until Ralegh, following Hakluyt's advice, sent John White on the Grenville expedition of 1585.[22] Also on this voyage was the Oxford-trained scientist and mathematician Thomas Harriot. Together the two men rendered in print and illustration the American phenomena that they witnessed while surveying lands to the north and west of Albermarle Sound with military leader Ralph Lane. In 1590, at the younger Hakluyt's urging, the Flemish publisher Theodore de Bry rendered White's Virginia drawings into engravings for the first part of his *America* series. Accompanied by textual descriptions from Harriot's "A Briefe and true report" (1588), this influential volume publicized England's Roanoke achievements in four languages—English, Latin, French, and German—in what was a risky but highly successful publishing venture.[23]

An examination of the 1582–83 instructions is important for a second, more important reason here, in so far as it might help us to identify possible explanations for Barlowe's adherence to a Golden Age perceptual framework. At first glance, the set of guidelines is a pragmatic call, one reflecting the rudiments of a scientific enquiry, for the types of data which would, colonialists hoped, enable the English to establish a foothold in North America. The 1582–83 instructions, and the ones authored by the elder Hakluyt which preceded them, anticipated a new way of conceptualizing the New World, one that, while hardly a program, edged perceptibly beyond dogma and past authority in order to stress the need for epistemologies based on new experience.[24] As groundbreaking as this set of instructions might appear, however, its inherent contradictions undermine the text at certain critical moments. Calling attention to the fact that Bavin would have to perform his duties within a very limited timeframe, the compilers of the instructions directed the artist to approach his work as a draft which could be more elaborately detailed at a later date: "[Y]ou shall not neede to sett downe any lyne for devision of degrees in any of your first draftes in paper before all your plottes be perfectlye fynished for losse of tyme."[25] One possible consequence of the time restriction was that the artist/surveyor might have been encouraged, had he travelled to the New World as planned, to comprehend and depict American phenomena in terms of broad generic distinctions, and, ironically, sameness. The illustrator was advised, for instance, to "draw to lief one of each kinde of thing that is strange to us in England by the which [Bavin] may alweis garnishe his plott as he shall so course upon his retourne. As by the portraiture of one Cedar Tree he may drawe all the woodes of that sorte and as in this so[rte] may he doe the like in *all thinges ells.*"[26] The ostensible focus on the unfamiliar in this particular instruction, which evidently extended to the inhabitants as well, is subverted by a theoretical emphasis on, and apparent investment in, the sameness of North American phenomena, and what seems to have been the belief that if Bavin had witnessed one cedar or Indian then he had seen them all.[27]

Portraying New World phenomena, especially, as several contemporary European artists had complained, its inhabitants, was a difficult and complex problem. It is likely that the pressures of time exacerbated the complexity of the task for the artist.[28] Given the challenges of representing aboriginals, it is unsurprising that even White, the artist most successful in his efforts to portray Virginians accurately, would include two Timucua Indians among his portraits—

even though none of the English colonists had travelled to Florida. Not only do these illustrations confirm that the artist had copied the work of his mentor, French Huguenot artist Jacques Le Moyne de Morgues,[29] but they also suggest that efforts to depict inhabitants realistically were subordinated to the use of representations sometimes deemed perfectly isomorphic. White's usage of such transplanted (but at least "American") images is, in any case, a step up the ladder of accurate depiction when compared with Le Moyne's savages who look, as Olive P. Dickason points out, "rather as if they had stepped out from the Coliseum", or with the even more chiselled and Europeanized figures that de Bry had rendered (to appeal to audiences that did not, or so the engraver must have believed, possess much desire to know how England's American 'others' actually appeared).[30]

The emphasis on sameness in the 1582–83 instructions seems to anticipate the conclusion of the document, a conclusion that undermines the text still further by asserting what is *already* "knowen by experyence to be in the countryes," according to the authority of Thevet, Giovanni da Verrazzano, and others:

> The soyle ys most excellent plesaunt fertill and of champyon replenished with pastures and meadowes interlarded with woodes most plesaunt to behould as may be imagined of Cedars Cidorus Pynes Firre and Spruce trees ... which yelde most sweet savores the most of them all growing in rowes as yf they had bynne sett artefically by hand, making therby most delicate walkes, there are also grapes of sondrye sortes ... waxe and hony and also spices as Verarsanus thought[.] There are also pease hempe strawberyes blackberyes red and white roses damaske roses parsley rosemary with sondry other good hearbes & flowers Also muske myllion Pompines gourdes Cocombers Violettes Lyllies and sondrye sortes of oderyferous flowers differing from ours ... There ys also Thrushes Stork doves pigeons turtles Cranes Swannes Ducks Geese Fesauntes partheriges black birdes goldfynches ... Bevars Wolfes Foxes red dere Fallowe Deere Martens ... Hares Conyes Otters Weasells Badgers Also a great beast

like a bull ... called a Buffall ... There are also good havens and sondry navigable ryvers ... with great plenty of freshe water fishe ... There is also plenty of copper Sylver and somme gold which they accompt the besest metall. They have also rubies, jaspers, marble, allablaster Freestone and other sondry sortes of Stones of dyvers colours that the place ys like to be most riche and plesaunt. Yt was told Sir Humfrye Gylbart by 2 or 3 of the best sort bothe by office skill and judgment that accompanied Sir Francis Drake in his viage about the world that the most excellentest place that they sawe in all their Vyage bothe for fertilitie pleasure and profytt every kinde of way as well mynnerall as otherwayes was about 45 Degrees of Latitude. And as one of his [presumably Drake's] Quarter masters told him [presumably Gilbert] they sawe an Island in Marii de Sur called de Malco which lay in 46 degrees of Latitude which excelled every kinde of waye all the rest ... that ever they sawe in that their Travaill and Navigation.[31]

According to Quinn and Ryan's map of Drake's circumnavigation in *England's Sea Empire, 1550–1642*, the explorer did not touch anywhere near the eastern coast of North America, although he did sail up the Pacific to the San Francisco Bay area at 37.5 degrees latitude.[32] While W. Kaye Lamb, former Canadian dominion archivist, allows the possibility that Drake came close to the coastline of modern Canada,[33] the two regions identified in the instructions are perhaps better located south of the equator, in either the Golfo San Jorge, Argentina, or southern Chile. What then are references to this "most excellentest place" at 45 degrees latitude and "de Malco" at 46 degrees latitude doing in instructions which relate to a North American journey, particularly in instructions which avoid, until this moment, any kind of promotional hoopla? The equally exaggerated locations—the one described as "the most excellentest place" and the other as a region which "excelled all the rest"—foreground the eagerness of theorists such as the two Hakluyts and Peckham to use dubious eyewitness testimony and hearsay evidence in even their most carefully planned and articulated assessments of North America. The expression of the propagandists' idealized vision of the New World at the conclusion of guidelines which otherwise privilege actual experience in America over authority derived from speculation and dogma is certainly a curious one. The instructions thus seem to embody the often conflicting interests and ideologies of the many key players in the planned expedition so that the hyperbolic conclusion, replete with the standard topoi of the Golden Age, problematizes the intentions of the instructions—the systematic gathering and recording of clear, objective data for the expedition's organizers and sponsors.

The conflicted agenda in such instructions appears to have led to something of a double mission for many travellers, whose attention as they sought American information was oriented toward the new, but in a way reminiscent of the myth of the Golden Age. Barlowe seems to find evidence of such a golden world nearly every-where he turns, most clearly in relation to the Carolina Algonquians whom we have seen described as "most gentle, loving, faithfull, void of all guile, and treason, and such as lived after the manner of the golden age."[34] At the same time, however, depictions of these static, Columbianesque figures do suggest that life in Virginia was not all that the writer had made it seem. At odds with the Golden Age topoi in Barlowe's account is the use of an overt, militaristic idiom and descriptive apparatus which, if not a reflection of anxiety to do with Anglo-American conflict, at least casts serious doubts on the authenticity of the writer's idyllic imagery. After taking possession of Virginia, the English stood on a hill overlooking a valley of "goodly Cedar trees," a panorama which somehow inspired the travellers to fire off their weapons. Barlowe recalls the landscape's reaction to the sound of the harquebus: "[S]uch a flocke of Cranes ... arose vnder vs, with such a crye redoubled by many Ecchoes, as if an armie of men had showted all together."[35] In the writer's description of this, the first recorded gunfire in modern North Carolina, the Virginian landscape reacts to the blast in such a way that celebrates the power and potential of the military technology. The choice of simile, "as if an armie of men had showted all together," suggests, if not a fear of savage ambush, then at least a sensitivity towards the potential militaristic outcome of the English intrusion. Barlowe's depiction of the landscape's response also provides a foretaste of the inhabitants' reaction to guns. "When we discharged any peece, were it but a harquebush, they would tremble thereat for very feare, and for the strangenes of the same."[36] The two passages thus work to convey the impression that America and its inhabitants could easily be subdued by superior European technologies. The trope of the easy containment of the New World and its peoples was, of course, popular in early modern travel writings.[37]

Casual comparisons describing the physical distance between the English and the Indians—descriptions, for instance, of a canoe "foure harquebus shot from our shippes" and of a lone native fishing "two bowe shoote into the water"—evoke a similar sense of the potentially confrontational nature of contact with the indigenes. While such descriptions—idiomatic expressions which reflect the martial-centrism of early modern imperialists—are not uncommon in European travel accounts of the period, they create a jarring effect in a narrative like Barlowe's, which repeatedly disavows signs of conflict with Virginians. Even more discordant is the author's peculiar observation that one of the locals, when greeted onshore by Barlowe and four other top-ranking officials, "never ma[de] any shewe of feare, or doubt,"[38] as if such a reaction was totally unexpected. The remark is perhaps the result of an unwritten but felt contrast between Barlowe's own fear or doubt (to do with his or the Englishmen's arrival on the distant and strange shore, a sense of their own foreignness as it were) and the outward sense of the inhabitant's ease. It may signal as well a kind of disappointment that the arrival of the expedition's five leaders, undoubtedly armed and prepared for conflict should it arise, failed to provoke even the slightest indication of alarm in the lone Indian. Whatever psychology is at work here and elsewhere, a constant factor in Barlowe's portrayals of Virginia and its peoples is a descriptive apparatus which suggests the writer's preoccupation with potential conflict, a preoccupation which throws into serious question his parallel between the Golden Age and America.

A clearer picture of Barlowe's rhetoric of praise emerges when we look at English expressions of approval for natives in the context in which they appear. Notably, Barlowe's comparison of the

Algonquians to inhabitants of the Golden Age follows the account of the travellers' first landing on Roanoke Island, where they were greeted by Granganimeo's wife, whose husband, Barlowe tells us, was absent from the village. She commanded several natives to draw the English boat ashore and to carry the crew to dry ground. Apparently unsure of the honest nature of their hosts, the English expressed concern that some of the Indians might try to steal their oars, so Granganimeo's wife ordered her people to bring them inside her longhouse. The visitors were then led into this dwelling, where, Barlowe writes, she invited them to sit by a fire,

> and after tooke off our clothes, and washed them, and dried them again: some of the women pulled off our stockings, and washed them, some washed our feete in warme water, and shee her selfe tooke great paines to see all thinges ordered in the best manner shee coulde, making great haste to dresse some meate for vs to eate. After we had thus dried our selues, shee brought vs into the inner roome, where shee set on the boord standing along the house, some wheate like furmentie, sodden Venison, and roasted fishe sodden, boyled, and roasted, Melons rawe, and sodden, rootes of diuers kindes, and diuers fruites: their drinke is commonly water, but while the grape lasteth, they drinke wine, and for want of caskes to keepe it all the yeere after, they drinke water, but it is sodden with Ginger in it, and blacke Sinamon, and sometimes Sassaphras, and diuers other wholesome, and medicinable hearbes and trees. We were entertained with all loue, and kindnes, and with as much bountie, after their manner, as they could possibly deuise. We found the people most gentle, louing, and faithfull, void of all guile, and treason, and such as liued after the manner of the golden age. The earth bringeth foorth all things in aboundance, as in the first creation, without toile or labour. [39]

Barlowe's praise of the inhabitants and their land thus appears rather occasion specific, evoked by the memory of the lavish banquet the Algonquians had spread out for their guests. It is probably no coincidence that the inhabitants mentioned here all seem to be female, or at least no coincidence that the writer's descriptive imagination pays particularly close notice to the attentive hospitalities of women, so that a case could be made for the gender specificity of Barlowe's praise for natives. Michael Hattaway's observation that the Virginian narratives are on the whole "notably lacking in sexual content"[40] therefore requires qualification: while Barlowe's depictions of Granganimeo's wife and the other women say little in an explicit way on the subject of male heterosexual fantasy and desire, his images of women unclothing, bathing, feeding, and otherwise attending to the needs of men recall persistent imperialist/ masculinist fantasies at work in travellers' tales of encounters with races of exotic women.[41] At least one Renaissance writer familiar with the Roanoke accounts apparently believed that his contemporaries would readily understand, if not appreciate, a parallel between the female inhabitants of Virginia and a fantasy-like realm of women. Around 1609 John Healey published *The discovery of a new world or A Description of the South Indies*, a translation of Joseph Hall's *Mundus alter* (1605[?]), a fictitious travel work which parodies popular travel narratives. Book Two gives an account of "Shee-landt, or Womandeçoia," a country where, as Healey describes it, "the soil is very fruitful, but badly husbanded." He adds that some people mistake the name and inhabitants of Womandeçoia for the territory and populace of Wingandecoia (the supposed Carolina Algonquian name for the Roanoke areas) and thus make it part of Virginia.[42]

'What is perhaps most important in Barlowe's text is not merely what the writer observes but the fact that he was uninterested in recording either the presence or the actions of the aboriginal males who were also present at the banquet. This "absence" of native men may be due in part to Barlowe's representational practice, which tends to give most discursive attention to persons with greatest authority.[43] The writer's focus on authority is especially strong when the highest-ranking individual present also happens to be female (although Barlowe gives her no name in his text, referring to her only in a way that expresses her substitutive value [e.g. "Granganimeo's wife"]). Barlowe's account of the woman's generosity extends to a celebration of Virginia's bounty and fertility, of what Annette Kolodny terms the "essential femininity of the terrain."[44] The absence of native males augments this celebration, gives it lift, and enables the author to convey an implicit catalogue of the fruits, pleasures, and delights of Roanoke Island that are entirely available to the Englishmen who have been written into the banquet scene, in place, so it appears, of the aboriginal males. The image of Golden Age Virginians is thus an exhilarating, indeed titillating, interpolation aimed at a male audience, one that reflects a set of shared patriarchal assumptions about the benefits of an American conquest and the pleasures awaiting would-be colonialists and settlers.

Events at the banquet quickly turned ugly, as we see in the next scene in which Barlowe's reverie is interrupted by the sudden entrance of two or three men returning from a hunting expedition:

> While we were at meate, there came in at the gates,
> two or three men with their bowes, and arrowes,
> from hunting, whome when we espied, we beganne to
> looke one to wardes another, and offered to reach our
> weapons: but assoone as she [Granganimeo's wife]
> espied our mistrust, she was very much mooued, and
> caused some of her men [i.e. those already present] to
> runne out, and take away their bowes, and arrowes,
> and breake them, and withall beate the poore fellowes
> out of the gate againe. When we departed in the
> euening, and would not tarry all night, she was very
> sorie, and gaue vs into our boate our supper halfe
> dressed, pots, and all, and brought vs to our boates
> side, in which wee laye all night, remoouing the same
> a pretie distance from the shoare: shee perceiuing our
> iealousie, was much grieued, and sent diuers men, and
> thirtie women, to sitte all night on the bankes side by
> vs, and sent vs into our boates fine mattes to couer vs
> from the rayne, vsing very many wordes to intreate vs
> to rest in their houses: but because wee were fewe

men, and if wee had miscarried, the voyage had beene
in very great daunger, wee durst not aduenture any
thing, although there was no cause of doubt: for a
more kinde and louing people, there can not be found
in the world, as farre as we haue hitherto had triall.[45]

What is it about the entrance of these two or three men—members,
supposedly, of an idyllic, pacific community—that causes the English
such considerable anxiety? There is certainly some story hinted at in
the look that the English exchange with their countrymen, but the
author suppresses this narrative.

Similarly, Barlowe does not mention what happened in the
temporal gap between the beating of these two or three men "out of
the gate *againe*" (were they removed more than once?) and the point
at which the visitors decided to break away from their hosts, to
spend a rainy evening in boats put out a good distance from shore,
despite the many gestures of kindness and the frequent entreaties of
Granganimeo's wife to stay the night with the locals. The apparent
reason for their distress has to do with an awareness that the Indians
outnumbered the English, that, as Barlowe puts it, "if wee had
miscarried, the voyage had beene in very great daunger." It does not
require much stretch of the imagination to locate a conceivable sexual
subtext informing Barlowe's fear that his men might "miscarry."
The elisions and gaps in Barlowe's text could thus be seen as an
attempt to conceal or disavow inappropriate, or potentially
inappropriate, relations with the native women. The author's reticence
on the subject of his crew's interaction with their female hosts might
also help to explain the evident surprise, in the following year, of the
people of Granganimeo's brother, the Chief Wingina, when they
observed that the English took no interest in their women, as noted
in Thomas Harriot's *A Briefe and true report*. Harriot describes this
English lack of interest in native women in the context of explaining
the Indian belief that their visitors were immortal because they did
not exhibit any of the traditional urges of mortal men.[46] His
observation may also serve as an affirmation of the commendable
sexual abstinence of the English, and as an indicator of how travel
writers work to legitimize the explicit or implicit claims made in the
texts of fellow writers.

The banquet scene and the tensions with Indian men foreground the patriarchal assumptions that inform images of Algonquians
as living after the manner of the Golden Age. The celebratory mood
of the former scene, which abounds in the generosity of both land
and women, is marked by the exclusion of native men, and this mood
takes a sudden downturn at the appearance of two or three threatening
male 'others.' Even in Barlowe's disjointed, anticlimactic recollection
of the presence of these men—one marked by its resonating
absences—the author can still vividly recall the many kind gestures
of Granganimeo's wife, her various attentions to the Englishmen's
mistrust and doubt, as well as, in contrast to the vague outline of
"diuers men," the precise figure of "thirtie women" sent to sit all
night on the banks closest to the English ships. These are impressive
observations indeed, given that they were apparently made at a
considerable distance, in the dark and rain.

Complicating our reading of Barlowe's text still further is
the fact that in his account—as in other Roanoke narratives, with the
exception of Harriot's report, which exists today in no form outside
Hakluyt's collections—we have no assurance that we are dealing
with an authentic, unmediated text by one particular traveller/author.
In gathering travel materials for his 1589 compilation, the propagandist
Hakluyt the younger evidently had strong material to work with in
Barlowe's journal, which Ralegh had revamped before handing it
over to Hakluyt. David Quinn, Barlowe's most exhaustive twentieth-
century editor, describes the narrative as "a polished one, though
perhaps the polish was applied by Ralegh."[47] Elsewhere Quinn states
that Barlowe's text is "somewhat censored and prettied up," a
"rewritten narrative" which gives an "almost too idyllic picture of the
little Indian world into which he had intruded."[48] E.G.R. Taylor
remarks that Hakluyt, before completing his confidential "Discourse
of Western Planting" (ca. 1584), waited to see the results of the voyage
of Amadas and Barlowe before submitting the document to Queen
Elizabeth.[49] The explorers returned to London and handed Barlowe's
journal to Ralegh around the end of September 1584; Hakluyt
presented the "Discourse" to the queen on October 5. Between these
dates, it is probable that Ralegh had also revised this rough draft,
possibly with the help of his advisor Thomas Harriot, before giving

it to Hakluyt.[50] Numerous persons in the circle of Ralegh and Walsingham undoubtedly read and commented on the manuscript after this date and prior to its revision and publication by Hakluyt in 1589, although we have no manuscript evidence that would help clarify the various stages in the production of "Barlowe's" account.[51] It is conceivable, indeed likely, that anything unpleasant the traveller had written about America was suppressed by Ralegh, Harriot, or Hakluyt. Spanish sources, for instance, relate an initial English arrival at a headland prior to the one at Hatarask Island detailed in Barlowe, where Indians reportedly attacked and ate thirty-eight English.[52] If hostile or unfriendly encounters with Virginians were in fact suppressed, then what I see as contradictions in Barlowe's text, such as an overt militaristic idiom and signs of conflict with Algonquians, may well be traces of the tensions and anxieties that the writer had originally written into his account.

There is good reason to view representations of Golden Age Algonquians as editorial interpolations written and published to convince anxious investors, colonialists, and potential supporters of the beneficence of Virginia and its peoples. By the time Hakluyt first published the Roanoke narratives in 1589, any hardships experienced during the 1584 reconnaissance were well known throughout London. Also well known were the complaints of Ralph Lane's soldiers, who spoke of Virginia's savages and barren landscape, factors which contributed to their near-starvation during the 1585–86 expedition. (It is telling that, of the 108 men who spent the year in America with Lane, only three signed up to return with John White in 1587, and one of these deserted to Spanish Florida.) In his 1588 report, Thomas Harriot alludes to the scathing attacks against Virginia made by Lane's men:

> There haue bin diuers and variable reportes, with
> some slaunderous and shamefull speeches bruited
> abroad by many that returned from thence.
> Especially of that discouery which was made by the
> Colony transported by Sir Richard Greinuile in the
> yeare 1585, being of all the others the most principal,
> and as yet of most effect ... Which reports have not
> done a litle wrong to many that otherwise would
> haue also fauoured & aduentured in the action.[53]

"Let them go where they deserve, foolish drones," Hakluyt the younger ranted around the same time, "who fresh from that place like those whom Moses sent to spy out the promised land flowing with milk and honey, have treacherously published ill reports about it."[54]

As far as is known, these unfavourable reports were not published in print;[55] Mary Fuller suggests that such criticisms of the American initiative exist mainly as moments embedded within the authorized texts.[56] We might add further that official responses, such as Harriot's, to unauthorized and potentially damaging reports help to corroborate, if not authenticate, the voices of protest and dissension that circulated throughout late sixteenth-century London. The construction of Virginia as paradise seems to have arisen partly in response to such voices, although even Hakluyt had to take into account, when he revised the *Principall Navigations* a decade later, the increasing public outcry against England's colonial failures, the severest of which was John White's 110 missing Roanoke colonists.[57] In 1600 it seems that the editor attempted to shift, if only slightly, the mindset of his readers away from the false hopes and delusions he had helped to create. He omitted the sentence, "The earth bringeth foorth all things in aboundance, as in the first creation, without toile or labour" from the description of Virginia and its peoples (with which I began this essay). Consistent with this deletion, Hakluyt also altered the next line, "The people onely care to defend them selues from the cold, in their short winter, and to feede themselues with such meate as the soile affoordeth," by inserting the word *how*, as in, "The people onely care *howe* to...."[58] Not so much counteracting as balancing out or qualifying the image of an American paradise where inactivity and passivity are rewarded is a unique if ephemeral ideal which insists on the need for activity and work. These revisions, when situated within a climate of colonial uncertainty and ambivalence, suggest that Hakluyt, though an indefatigable promotionalist throughout most of his career, was also quite aware of his own potentially undermining rhetoric.

David Quinn has stated that Barlowe's narrative "well deserves its high reputation as one of the clearest contemporary pictures of the contact of Europeans with North American Indians. Its ethnological value is substantial." As well, in the text he finds "many passages" that are "clearly the result of direct personal experience." These are bold claims, given that Quinn himself has been forced to concede that "its omissions are exasperating."[59] His effort to locate a "truth value" in travel accounts is valuable, perhaps even more so in light of Fuller's observation:

> It matters that these things [voyages to America] really happened, and that they were recorded by men who had experienced and witnessed them.... Being written was an important component of their happening, and this is true in a strong sense. The voyage narratives came into being not only as after-the-fact accounts for ideological purposes, but as an integral part of the activities they documented.[60]

Although the geographical, ecological, and ethnographical content of Barlowe's text reflect to some (indeterminable) extent the traveller's American experience, studies of Barlowe's and other early colonial texts require a high degree of caution and scepticism for the reason that the disparate agendas of those who wrote (and edited) them often blur any distinction between fact and fiction.

The ambivalent images of Virginia in the writings of soldier Ralph Lane also come to mind here. In Lane's narrative of the first colony, for example, he expresses the pragmatic though pessimistic view that America would not be worth the trouble to inhabit permanently unless the English discovered either a "good mine" or a "passage to the Southsea."[61] His letter of 12 August 1585 to Francis Walsingham, on the other hand, contains a euphoric account of the commodities available in Virginia, including the observation that in all their search the English had not yet found "one stynckinge weede growing in thys lande."[62] Similarly, in his letter dated 3 September 1585 to the elder Hakluyt and an unidentified "Master H—— of the Middle Temple," Lane emphasizes Virginia's rich commodities and a climate "so wholesome, that we haue not had one sicke, since we touched land here." He concludes, "if Virginia had but Horses and Kine in some reasonable proportion, I dare assure my selfe being inhabited with English, no realme in Christendome were comparable to it."[63] Reminiscing about the 1585 expedition in a letter to Lord Burghley dated 7 January 1592, Lane complains of Virginia's "intemperate clymates" and the "heate and sicknes" that he and his men endured in America. He also alludes to the deaths of thirty-six colonists in the space of three months, although he believes that Virginia on the whole "is a good temperate country [and] that such mortality commeth by the bad fare."[64] A contextual analysis of such inconsistencies would doubtless prove fascinating. Lane's letter to Lord Burghley, for instance, outlines the strict disciplinary measures he considered necessary to soldiers' health at sea and on land. His references to the ill health that he and his men had suffered in 1585, whether or not as widespread as he implies, authenticate the author as credible witness. This letter also takes mild pot-shots at Richard Grenville, leader of the 1585 expedition, in order to hint at Lane's superior leadership capabilities. The soldier's representations of Virginia are a distinct function of his motivations, and the resulting "evidence" can hardly be perceived as reliable. Rather, Lane's images of America foreground the use of discourse as a means of effecting public and private recognition and promotion, a neglected aspect of current examinations of early colonialist writings.

Similarly, Barlowe's narrative suggests its author's eagerness to identify the Golden Age topoi consistent with the colonialist fantasies and aims of his employers; as such, Barlowe's relation is implicated in the struggle, evident in the 1582–83 instructions, to transcend Old World suppositions to do with foreign territories and peoples. And like these guidelines—or, as I have suggested, because of ones like them—Barlowe's narrative fails repeatedly, despite his efforts to document the new, to cast off the insistent European dream of locating a paradise in America. When he wants to speak of potential or actual conflict with Virginians, Barlowe uses instead a rhetoric of praise consonant with imperialist agenda: "[A]lthough there was no cause of doubt," he writes, shrugging off the near skirmish with the native men, "for a more kinde and louing people, there can not be found in the world, as farre as we haue hitherto had triall."[65] Quinn has called Barlowe's observation "[t]he most precise example in Renaissance English of the myth of the gentle savage."[66] Perhaps more to the point, Barlowe's comment is the most stunning example in Renaissance travel writing of an author's effort to manipulate his audience by obscuring the disenchanting realities of Anglo-American contact.[67] And Barlowe's disavowal, needless to say, indicates that the Algonquians had given the English some pause for concern.

Noting the contradictions in Barlowe's text, Greenblatt observes that a "lively interest in swords sits strangely with life in the manner of the Golden Age." However, his view that "[t]here was little reason for Barlowe to construct a coherent, internally consistent account of Virginia," since the report was intended as "a prospectus for potential investors in future voyages," sidesteps the nagging problems of discourses such as Barlowe's—the various details that travel writers suppress and/or disavow in their relations of New World experiences.[68] While no tale can be told in its entirety, as reception theorists as early as Wolfgang Iser have observed,[69] such gaps and elisions strike me as fascinating sites for the exploration of the competing voices brought into play as the writer constructed his version of what he had witnessed in America. Ready-made descriptions of inhabitants as living after the manner of the Golden Age certainly appear with frequency in early modern travel narratives, "touched off," as Levin suggested, "as if by a reflex action," although this reflex action might well be indicative of the conflicting agendas that came into play as travel writers attempted to describe their new and unexpected experiences.[70]

NOTES

I would like to thank the Six Nations of the Grand River Post Secondary Education Office, the Canada–U.S. Fulbright Program, and the Social Sciences and Humanities Research Council of Canada, for their financial support during the researching and writing of this paper.

1 Arthur Barlowe, "Discourse of the First Voyage," in D.B. Quinn, ed., *The Roanoke Voyages*, 2nd ser., vol. 1 (London: Hakluyt Society, 1955), p. 108.

2 Harry Levin, *The Myth of The Golden Age in the Renaissance* (Bloomington, IN and London: Indiana University Press, 1969), p. 60. The "rich backlog of fabulous lore" to which Levin is referring was revived in the Renaissance through such texts as Ovid's *Metamorphoses*, which describes a golden period when "the peoples of the world, untroubled by any fears, enjoyed a leisurely and peaceful existence.... The earth itself, without compulsion, untouched by the hoe, unfurrowed by any share, produced all things spontaneously, and men were content with foods that grew without cultivation" (*The Metamorphoses*,

trans. M.M. Innes [London: Penguin Classics, 1955], 1.2.89–103). Isabel Rivers gives a useful account of the myth of the Golden Age and its Judeo-Christian appropriations in *Classical and Christian Ideas in English Renaissance Poetry* (1979; reprint, London: George Allen and Unwin, 1986), pp. 9–20. For an excellent discussion of the persistent isomorphism of Golden Age topoi in late twentieth-century journalism and travel writing, see David Spurr, "Idealization: Strangers in Paradise," in *The Rhetoric of Empire: Colonial Discourse in Journalism, Travel Writing, and Imperial Administration* (Durham and London: Duke University Press, 1993), pp. 125–40.

3 Patricia Seed, *Ceremonies of Possession in Europe's Conquest of the New World, 1492–1640* (1995; reprint, Cambridge and New York: Cambridge University Press, 1997), pp. 26–27.

4 Ibid., quotation on p. 25; also see pp. 33–35.

5 Jacques Derrida, *The Ear of the Other: Otobiography, Transference, Translation: Texts and Discussions with Jacques Derrida*, trans. Peggy Kamuf, ed. Christie McDonald (1985; Lincoln and London: University of Nebraska Press, 1988), pp. 3–4.

6 Wayne Franklin, *Discovers, Explorers, Settlers: The Diligent Writers of Early America* (Chicago: University of Chicago Press, 1979), p. 21.

7 Barlowe, "Discourse of the First Voyage," p. 95. In his verse addressed to Hakluyt, Michael Drayton writes that "the ambitious vine / Crownes with his purple masse, / The Cedar reaching hie / to kisse the sky." See Drayton, "To the Virginian voyage," in *Poemes lyrick and pastorall: odes, eglogs, the man in the moone* (London: 1606[?]), C4r–C4v.

8 Barlowe, "Discourse of the First Voyage," pp. 96–97, 105–06.

9 Ibid., p. 101, my emphasis.

10 Richard Hakluyt, the elder, "Notes framed by a Gentleman heretofore to bee given to one that prepared for a discoverie, and went not: And not unfitt to be committed to print, considering the same may stirre up considerations of these and of such other thinges, not unmeete in such new voyages as may be attempted hereafter" (ca. 1578), in D.B. Quinn, ed., *New American World: A Documentary History of North America to 1612*, vol. 3 (New York: Arno Press, 1979), p. 24. Christopher Carleill, in "A breef and sommarie discourse upon the entended voyage to the hethermost partes of America" (ca. 1583), similarly advises American travellers to "first grow into familiaritie with the Inland people," since "with freendly entreatie of the people, [the English] may enter into better knowledge of the particuler estate of the Countrey" (Quinn, *New American World*, vol. 3, pp. 30, 33).

11 Hakluyt, in Quinn, *New American World*, vol. 3, pp. 25–26.

12 Ibid., pp. 147, 151–52.

13 Ibid., p. 24.

14 Richard Hakluyt, *The Principall Navigations, Voyages and Discoveries of the English Nation (1589)*, extra ser. 34, vol. 1, ed. D.B. Quinn and R.A. Skelton (Hakluyt Society, Cambridge University Press, 1965), sig. *2.

15 See Mary C. Fuller, *Voyages in Print: English Travel to America, 1576–1624* (Cambridge, MA: Cambridge University Press, 1995).

16 Hakluyt, in Quinn, *New American World*, vol. 3, p. 239. Paul Hulton, *America 1585: The Complete Drawings of John White* (Chapel Hill, NC: University of North Carolina Press, 1984), p. 9, suggests that while Ralegh's 1585 instructions to John White and Thomas Harriot no longer survive, the 1582–83 notes for the artist/surveyor Thomas Bavin were well suited for White and the scientist. Cf. David Beers Quinn, *Set Fair for Roanoke: Voyages and Colonies, 1584–1606*, 2nd ed. (Chapel Hill: University of North Carolina Press, 1986), p. 49. Indeed, the plans and instructions for the 1582–83 expedition would not have been discarded and new ones for the 1584 or 1585 voyages written entirely from scratch, as older instructions (much like letters patent) were in most cases simply retooled and updated to meet the requirements of subsequent voyages. Guidelines for at least the initial voyage to Roanoke certainly did exist, as Barlowe indicates at the beginning of his account addressed to Ralegh: "The 27. day of Aprill ... we departed the west of England [Plymouth], with two barkes, well furnished with men and victuals, hauing receyued our last, and perfect directions by your letters, confirming the former instructions, and commandements deliuered by your selfe at our leauing the riuer of Thames" (Barlowe, "Discourse of the First Voyage," p. 92).

17 Hakluyt, in Quinn, *New American World*, vol. 3, p. 240.

18 The elder Hakluyt's final words of advice to Ralegh in the "Inducements to the liking of the voyage intended towards Virginia" (ca. 1585) likewise articulated the need for a painter on colonial voyages: "A skilfull painter is also to be caried with you which the Spaniards used commonly in all their discoveries to bring the descriptions of all beasts, birds, fishes, trees, townes, &c." (E.G.R. Taylor, ed., *The Original Writings & Correspondence of the Two Richard Hakluyts*, 2nd ser. 56–57, vol. 2 [London: Hakluyt Society, 1935)], p. 338. On the relatively unknown Bavin, see Quinn, *New American World*, vol. 3, p. 239; and D.B. Quinn, *England and the Discovery of America, 1481–1620. From the Bristol Voyages of the Fifteenth Century to the Pilgrim Settlement at Plymouth: The Exploration, Exploitation, and Trial-and-Error Colonization of North America by the English* (New York: Alfred A. Knopf, 1974), pp. 374–75. See also Taylor's unsuccessful efforts to locate a single chart or map drawn by him in "Instructions to a Colonial Surveyor in 1582," *Mariner's Mirror* 37 (1951): 48–62.

19 Hakluyt, in Quinn, *New American World*, vol. 3, p. 242.

20 See note 18 above.

21 Hulton, *America 1585*, p. 3.

22 Around the same time Francis Drake was, according to his Portuguese pilot, "an adept at painting," spending much of his time working away in his cabin on birds, trees, and sea lions (quoted in Michael Alexander, *Discovering the New World: Based on the Works of Theodore DeBry* [New York: Harper and Row, 1976], pp. 7–8). Drake's artist, Baptista Boazio, also made drawings of natural history subjects, and of the Spanish bases attacked by Drake. See Mary F. Keeler, ed., *Sir Francis Drake's West Indian Voyage, 1585–6* (London: Hakluyt Society, 1981), p. 19. On the possibility that White had first travelled to the

Carolina Outer Banks with Amadas and Barlowe in 1584, see Quinn, ed., *Virginia Voyages from Hakluyt* (London: Oxford University Press, 1973), pp. 116, 168 n. 3; Hulton, *America 1585*, pp. 6–15; and David N. Durant, *Ralegh's Lost Colony* (London: Weidenfeld and Nicolson, 1981), pp. 25–26.

23 Cf. Peter C. Mancall, "The Age of Discovery," *Reviews in American History* 26 (1998): 26–53.

24 Whether or not it was possible to achieve knowledge beyond that of the ancient authorities was, of course, a much-debated issue during the Renaissance. Louis LeRoy, professor of Greek at the Université de Paris, argued in *De la vicissitude ou varieté des choses* (Paris, 1575) that new knowledge was not only possible but that its pursuit was intrinsic to human society. LeRoy's work was translated by Robert Ashley, "Of the Interchangeable Covrse, or Variety of Things in the Whole World" (London, 1594). See in particular the twelfth and final book, "Whether it be Trve, or No, that there can be nothing said, which hath not bin said before; And that we must by our owne Inuentions, augment the Doctrine of the Auncients" (pp. Z1–Z2). Anthony Pagden's *European Encounters With the New World: From Renaissance to Romanticism* (New Haven and London: Yale University Press, 1993) is a useful study of the rise of the so-called quarrel between the ancients and moderns which broke out in the late seventeenth century, especially pp. 12, 84, 90, and 92. See also Lesley Cormack's recent discussion of "iconic transformations to modernity," in particular her warning that "[m]any stories and many voices tell different facets of the development [of modernity]; they cannot be blended into a single explanatory tale," in *Charting an Empire: Geography at the English Universities, 1580–1620* (Chicago and London: University of Chicago Press, 1997), p. 11.

25 Hakluyt, in Quinn, *New American World*, vol. 3, p. 243.

26 Ibid., my emphasis.

27 Indeed, John Smith seems to have believed that the natives of Virginia were indistinguishable from those of the Outer Banks. In an insert of several engravings borrowed from Theodore de Bry's renderings of John White's Virginians, Smith writes: "The Countrey wee now call Virginia beginneth at Cape Henry distant from Roanoack 60 miles, where was Sr Walter Raleigh's plantation: and because the people differ very little from them of Powhatan in any thing, I have inserted those figures in this place because of the conveniency" (Smith, "The Generall Historie: New England, & the Summer Isles" [London, 1624] in *Capt. John Smith: Works*, ed. Edward Arber [Westminster: Archibald Constable, 1895], n.p.).

28 While Oviedo wished for the skills of a Leonardo or Mantegna, both friends of his, to help him portray Amerindians in the *Historia*, Jean de Léry elaborated in *Histoire* the problems he had depicting the anatomy of Brazilians: "Although I diligently perused and marked those barbarian people, for a whole year together, wherin I lived amongst them, so as I might conceive in my mind a certain proportion of them, yet I say, by reason of their diverse gestures and behaviours, utterly different from ours, it is a very difficult matter to express their true proportion ... but if anyone covet to enjoy the full pleasure of them, I could wish him to go into America himself" (quoted in Alexander, *Discovering the New World*, pp. 7–8). Cf. Olive P. Dickason, *The Myth of the Savage and*

the Beginnings of French Colonialism in the Americas (1984; reprint, Edmonton: University of Alberta Press, 1997), pp. 16–17.

29 See Hulton, *America 1585*, pp. 8–9, 127.

30 Dickason, *Myth of the Savage*, p. 16. Quinn notes the enduring popularity of de Bry's images: "For generations engravers seeking illustrations for travel books about America, North or even South, lazily went to de Bry and copied and modified for their own purposes [his] engravings" (*Set Fair for Roanoke*, p. 418).

31 Hakluyt, in Quinn, *New American World*, vol. 3, pp. 244–45.

32 D.B. Quinn and A.N. Ryan, eds., *England's Sea Empire, 1550–1642* (London: George Allen and Unwin, 1983), p. 132.

33 W. Kaye Lamb, "Drake," in *Dictionary of Canadian Biography*, vol. 1 (Toronto: University of Toronto Press, 1966), p. 280. My thanks to I.S. MacLaren for pointing out the reference.

34 Barlowe, "Discourse of the First Voyage," p. 108.

35 Ibid., p. 96.

36 Ibid., p. 112.

37 Stephen Greenblatt discusses Thomas Harriot's "A Briefe and true report" as a particularly emphatic account of the European technologies—compasses, mathematical instruments, fireworks, clocks, guns, books, writing, and reading—that Harriot felt endowed the English with God-like capabilities in the eyes of Indians. See Greenblatt, "Invisible Bullets: Renaissance Authority and its Subversion," *Glyph* 8 (1981): 40–61; reprinted in Jonathan Dollimore and Alan Sinfield, eds., *Political Shakespeare: New Essays in Cultural Materialism* (Ithaca: Cornell University Press, 1985), pp. 18–47; and in Greenblatt, *Shakespearean Negotiations: The Circulation of Social Energy in Renaissance England* (Berkeley and Los Angeles: University of California Press, 1988), pp. 21–65.

38 Barlowe, "Discourse of the First Voyage," p. 98.

39 Ibid., pp. 107–08.

40 Michael Hattaway, "'Seeing Things': Amazons and Cannibals," in Jean-Pierre Maquerlot and Michèle Willems, eds., *Travel and Drama in Shakespeare's Time*, (Cambridge, MA: Cambridge University Press, 1996), p. 191 n. 28.

41 See Columbus's relation of Matenino, a supposed island of women in the Caribbean, in his letter to the sovereigns of 4 March 1493, in Margarita Zamora, "Christopher Columbus's 'Letter to the Sovereigns': Announcing the Discovery" (Stephen Greenblatt, ed., *New World Encounters* [Berkeley: University of California Press, 1993], pp. 1–11). Cf. Columbus's provocative descriptions of women in the "Diario," in *The Four Voyages*, trans. J.M. Cohen (Harmondsworth: Penguin, 1992), especially pp. 315, 343, and 347, and Vespucci's "Lettera" described in Susi Colin's "The Wild Man and the Indian in Early 16th Century Book Illustration," in Christian F. Feest, ed., *Indians and Europe: An Interdisciplinary Collection of Essays* (Aachen: Rader Verlag, 1987),

p. 17. The critical literature on the subject is also vast but see in particular Annette Kolodny's first two chapters in *Lay of the Land: Metaphor as Experience and History in American Life and Letters* (Chapel Hill: University of North Carolina Press, 1975): "Unearthing Herstory," pp. 3–9, and "Surveying the Virgin Land: The Documents of Exploration and Colonization, 1500–1740," pp. 10–25. Two of the most important studies to pick up on themes in Kolodny's work are Patricia Parker's rhetorical analysis of the gendering of America as female and waiting for her conqueror or lover in "Rhetorics of Property: Exploration, Inventory, Blazon" (*Literary Fat Ladies* [London and New York: Methuen, 1987], pp. 126–53), and Louis Montrose's discussion of the sexualizing of the exploration, conquest, and settlement of the New World in the context of Ralegh's "The Discoverie of Guiana," in "The Work of Gender in the Discourse of Discovery" (Greenblatt, *New World Encounters*, pp. 177–217).

42 Joseph Hall, *The discovery of a new world or A Description of the South Indies. Hetherto Vnknowne, By an English Mercury*, trans. John Healey (London: 1609) sigs. G7v–H1. Barlowe and Amadas first reported "Wingandacon" as the Virginian name for the Roanoke areas. In the *History of the World* (London: 1614), Walter Ralegh suggests that his employees, like the Spanish explorers in Peru, were somewhat over-zealous in their interpretation of Indian place names: "[S]ome of the Spaniards vtterly ignorant of that language, demaunding by signes (as they could) the name of the Countrie, and pointing with their hand athwart a riuer, or torrent, or brooke that ran by, the Indians answered Peru which was either the name of that brooke, or of water in generall … The same hapned among the English, which I sent … For when some of my people asked the name of that Countrie, one of the Saluages answered Wingandacon which is to say, as you weare good clothes, or gay clothes" (first numeration, pp. 175–76). Ralegh probably learned this more accurate translation from Thomas Harriot, who had worked with the two Algonquians, Manteo and Wanchese, who were brought back to England in 1584.

43 Cf. Karen O. Kupperman, *Settling with the Indians: The Meeting of English and Indian Cultures in America, 1580–1640* (Totowa, NJ: Rowman and Littlefield, 1975) passim; Greenblatt, *Shakespearean Negotiations*, pp. 26–27.

44 Kolodny, *Lay of the Land*, p. 5.

45 Barlowe, "Discourse of the First Voyage" pp. 109–10.

46 Thomas Harriot, "A Briefe and true report" (London, 1588), in Quinn, *Roanoke Voyages, 1584–1590*, vol. 1, pp. 379–80.

47 Quinn, *England and the Discovery*, p. 218.

48 For the first quotation, see D. B. Quinn, *Hakluyt Handbook*, vol. 1, p. 246; for the second quotation, see Quinn, *Set Fair for Roanoke*, pp. 46, 212. Cf. Quinn, *New American World*, vol. 3, p. 276; and Quinn, *Roanoke Voyages*, vol. 1, pp. 9, 11, 17.

49 E.G.R. Taylor, ed., *Original Writings*, vol. 1, p. 34.

50 Ralegh promoted his Roanoke efforts through Hakluyt's "Discourse of Western Planting," which he had asked Hakluyt to write in an attempt to win the reticent queen's support for his Virginian project, and also through a rather

ostentatious parliamentary bill to confirm his letters patent, presented to the House of Commons on 14 December. See Quinn, *Roanoke Voyages*, vol. 1, pp. 15–17, 92, 122; and Quinn, *New American World*, vol. 3, p. 276. Barlowe's text provided key (though somewhat fabricated) evidence in both of these promotions before it became a centrepiece in Hakluyt's 1589 and 1600 compilations.

51 I.S. MacLaren explores such issues as authorship, authenticity, and the stages of a text's composition in the context of eighteenth- and nineteenth-century travel writing, in "Samuel Hearne's Accounts of the Massacre at Bloody Fall, 17 July 1771," *Ariel* 22, no. 1 (1991), especially p. 43, and in "From Exploration to Publication: The Evolution of a Nineteenth-Century Arctic Narrative," *Arctic* 47, no. 1 (1994), especially pp. 40–41, 52.

52 Deposition from the Licentiate Francisco Marqués de Villalobos (Abbot of Jamaica) to the Spanish Crown, 27 June 1586, in I.A. Wright, ed., *Further English Voyages to Spanish America, 1583–94: Documents From the Archives of the Indies at Seville Illustrating English Voyages to the Caribbean, the Spanish Main, Florida, and Virginia* (London: Hakluyt Society, 1951), p. 175. See also Quinn, *Roanoke Voyages*, vol. 1, pp. 81, 94 n. 4, 414–15 n. 5.

53 Harriot, pp. 320–21.

54 Richard Hakluyt, "Epistle Dedicatory to Ralegh" in *De orbe novo Petri Martyris Anglerii Mediolanensis decades octo ... illustratae labore Richardi Hakluyti* (Paris, 1587). In Quinn, *Roanoke Voyages*, vol. 2, pp. 514–15.

55 Quinn, *Roanoke Voyages*, vol. 2, p. 515 n. 1.

56 Fuller, *Voyages in Print*, p. 90.

57 Traces of the 1587 colony were last found by John White in 1590, although Ralegh continued to presume its survival, and hence his entitlement to North American lands, until the loss of his patent in 1603 under James I. See Quinn, *New American World*, vol. 5, p. 159.

58 Quinn, *Roanoke Voyages*, vol. 1, pp. 108–09; my emphasis.

59 Ibid., pp. 1, 15, 17.

60 Fuller, *Voyages in Print*, p. 2. Cf. Philip Edwards, *Last Voyages: Cavendish, Hudson, Ralegh* (Oxford: Oxford University Press, 1988), p. 7; and Richard Helgerson, *Forms of Nationhood: The Elizabethan Writing of England* (Chicago: University of Chicago Press, 1992), p. 151.

61 Ralph Lane, "Discourse on the First Colony: August 17, 1585 to June 18, 1586," in Quinn, *Roanoke Voyages*, vol. 1, pp. 272–73.

62 Lane, "Letter to Sir Francis Walsingham: August 12, 1585," in Quinn, *Roanoke Voyages*, vol. 1, pp. 199–200.

63 Lane, "Letter to Richard Hakluyt the elder and Master H—— of the Middle Temple. September 3, 1585," in Quinn, *Roanoke Voyages*, vol. 1, pp. 208ff.

64 Lane, "Reminiscences of the 1585 Expedition: January 7, 1592," in Quinn, *Roanoke Voyages*, vol. 1, pp. 228–29. According to the Virginia Company of

London's "A true declaration of the estate of the colonie in Virginia, With a confutation of such scandalous reports as haue tended to the disgrace of so worthy an enterprise" (1610), the official death toll of Lane's voyage was set at two (p. E2v).

65 Barlowe, "Discourse of the First Voyage," pp. 109–10.

66 Quinn, *Roanoke Voyages*, vol. 1, p. 110 n. 1.

67 Karen Ordahl Kupperman, in *Roanoke: The Abandoned Colony* (Totowa, NY: Rowman and Allanheld, 1984), observes that such images contributed to deeply unrealistic and ultimately damaging expectations about America (pp. 16–17).

68 Stephen Greenblatt, *Marvelous Possessions: The Wonder of the New World* (Chicago: University of Chicago Press, 1991), p. 94.

69 Wolfgang Iser, "The Reading Process: A Phenomenological Approach," *New Literary History* 3 (1971): 285; Shlomith Rimmon-Kenan, *Narrative Fiction: Contemporary Poetics* (1983; reprint, London and New York: Methuen, 1987), p. 127.

70 Levin, *Myth of the Golden Age*, p. 60.

Stylizations of Selfhood
in Pierre-Esprit Radisson's Voyages

RICK H. LEE

The discovery of Canada by Europeans dates as early as AD 1000 with the Norse. Contact between the Old and New worlds continued throughout the medieval and early modern periods—with the Portuguese and the Basques in the fourteenth century, and the British and the Dutch in the fifteenth and sixteenth. Then came the French, first as fishermen and then as settlers, in the sixteenth and seventeenth centuries.[1] In fact, according to historian Olive Patricia Dickason, by "the turn of the fifteenth century into the sixteenth, the waters of Canada's North Atlantic coast were the scene of intense international activity."[2] But if Canada was the setting of an early form of internationalism at the beginning of the sixteenth century, it soon became transformed as the site of intense competition, mainly between two colonial powers: France and England.

Explorer Pierre-Esprit Radisson (1640–1710) played a crucial role in the drama then unfolding in North America, "where New England [is] already outdoing Old England, and New France outmaneuvering Old France."[3] In particular, Radisson and his brother-in-law, Médard Chouart, Sieur des Groseilliers, navigated their way through uncharted territories in New France. And, just as

Posthumous portrait of Pierre-Esprit Radisson, by Belier (ca. 1785).
Verest, John/National Archives of Canada C–092414, used by permission.

deftly, they manoeuvred through colonial bureaucracies to help establish the Hudson's Bay Company in 1670, a commercial enterprise that secured the British monopoly of the Great Lakes fur trade.[4] In her biography of Radisson and des Groseilliers, *Caesars of the Wilderness*, Grace Lee Nute wryly praises the two men's ability to "slip nimbly between the Sun King and His Britannic Majesty, between Jesuit camp and Recollect clique, between New England and Old England, between New France and Old France, and between Catholicism and Protestantism, giving merry chase to the wits of monarchs, fur-trading barons, governors, and churchmen."[5]

As Nute's observation makes clear, Radisson was highly self-conscious about his identity throughout his life. Finding himself embedded in both New and Old world contexts, he became a social actor who stylized his sense of self accordingly. For example, as one of the first explorers of the Canadian frontier, he represents the protomythical figure of the adventurous *voyageur* or *coureur de bois* (runner of the woods). Almost always identified with hypermasculine virility and alienation from dominant society, *coureur de bois* figures such as Radisson exemplify an early embodiment of the "cultural renegade," whose "transgression of civilized values, plus his willingness to adapt and/or be adopted into native cultures, inspired both the contempt of his fellow whites and the mistrust of French and British colonial authorities."[6] In many ways, the *coureur de bois* was situated in a different sociocultural milieu from his fellow *habitants*—another new social type who in part composed the metropolitan class of *paysan français* in the formative French colonial settlement.

Considering his pivotal role in establishing the Hudson's Bay Company, I would suggest that Radisson represents a hybrid version of these two New World social types, both of whom "had many traits in common: freedom and independence might be regarded as the leitmotif characterizing their actions and their self-image."[7] Moreover, in the context of the Old World, Radisson was equally successful in negotiating his position within the emergent public sphere. He was consistently adept in "cultivating over several decades the patronage networks, courtly and mercantile, English and French, which a man needed in this period to keep his head above water in public life."[8]

To the extent that the "Frenchman" Radisson succeeded in founding a British trading company, he was able to do so because of his ability to perform the various roles available to him in both Europe and the Americas. In addition to hybridizing his professional identity, Radisson also performed a similarly complex hybridization of his national, racial, and ethnic identities during his lifetime. Though he was born a French subject, by the time of his death he had been naturalized as a British one.[9] For him, then, the performing of professional and national identities were mutually constitutive acts. As Michael Warner notes, what remains remarkable about Radisson is that he was "at various times in his life French, Indian, and English."[10] His multiple and shifting subject positions articulate and make more intelligible for us the processes of identity constitution during the early modern period, when "national belonging was more about loyalty to a sovereign than about the birthright of a shared identity with a national people, and his hybrid sense of self may have been typical of many Europeans in the seventeenth-century Atlantic."[11] Paradoxically, Radisson was at once a unique individual and typically representative of his time. Why, then, does he occupy such an undervalued position in Canadian history, and, more generally, in the history of the early modern transatlantic world? Given that the story of his life has so much to teach us about identity formations and re-formations in the seventeenth century, why has he suffered the fate of becoming a "*coureur de bois manqué*" in our current cultural imagination?[12]

Germaine Warkentin, currently the pre-eminent English-language scholar engaged in sustained research on Radisson, provides some answers to these questions. She points out that, even though his "name still produces [today] fused impressions of valour, bravado, and entrepreneurship to glamorize the mining enterprises, hotels, and venture-capital firms that display it," Radisson "always seems to be the centre of someone else's narrative—the historical anecdote, the television series, the children's book—rather than a narrator himself. This is probably because so few of us are aware that he was the first and best teller of his own story"—namely, in his *Voyages*.[13] And even those who are aware of this fact have ostensibly displaced the centrality of both the man and his text for the purpose of narrating the larger story of Canada's past.

A cursory glance at earlier scholarship in literary history and Canadian historiography reveals two methodological tendencies: first, a devaluation of Radisson as a figure worth pursuing; and, second, a politically motivated commitment to imagine Canada originally as either a distinctly anglophone or distinctly francophone community. William John Karr, for example, notes in his history of Canada that "Radisson deserves to be remembered in Canadian history for two reasons: first, because he is a type of the restless, roving trader who did so much to unravel the mysteries of the vast interior of Canada; and second, because he is responsible, Frenchman though he was, for the establishment in Canada of a great English institution, the Hudson's Bay Company."[14] Karr purposely neglects to consider the evidence that documents Radisson's naturalization as a British subject in 1687, twenty-three years prior to his death in 1710. He instead insists on viewing Radisson as a distasteful "Frenchman" whose only claim to glory is in securing the British control of the fur trade during the late seventeenth century. Karr's patronizing tone recirculates the anglocentric rhetoric once used by the British in referring to Radisson and des Groseilliers, as "Mr. Radishes" and "Mr. Gooseberry," *even* as the two men were engaged in their expeditions *for* the British.[15]

While Karr is suspicious of Radisson's political affiliations, literary historian Victor G. Hopwood similarly finds fault with Radisson's *Voyages* for being a non-historical literary document. Noting that because Radisson's "first two voyages deal with his adventures as a youth in the wilds of North America," Hopwood maintains that they are thus "not as important historically as the third and fourth voyages." And when commenting on the possibility that the *Voyages* is an English translation of a French original, he observes that were this the case, "the Hudson's Bay Company paid for a translation of almost dazzling illiteracy."[16] Nor are such ethnocentric biases isolated within the anglophone scholarly tradition, since francophones are also invested in rewriting their own version of Canada's past. Jack Warwick, for one, does not even mention Radisson's *Voyages* in his study on literary themes in French Canada, even as he notes the recurrence and prevailing legacy of the *coureur de bois* figure in the French Canadian literary tradition.[17] Warwick's oversight suggests a larger, more disturbing phenomenon: the figure of the *coureur de bois* did not so much disappear from, as became transformed in, the Canadian cultural imagination, as the English and French both competed to tell their own versions of Canada's past. According to Konrad Gross, by the nineteenth century, "[t]he reputation of the [*coureur de bois*] as a notorious bad man, created by official sources of New France for political reasons, was forgotten when literature, and later historiography, discovered the romantic potential of the fur trade and helped to model [fictional and historical] characters of almost mythic dimensions."[18] And, according to Philippe Jacquin, the Québécois, in tracing their cultural roots to France, often efface from collective memory the ambiguities of the figure of the *coureur de bois*, and transform him into the figure of the pioneer so as to represent Nouvelle-France as a civilized and Catholic settlement.[19]

Both the *coureur de bois* and Radisson have suffered critical neglect. These earlier views indeed confirm Warkentin's claim that "Radisson's very skills as a narrator have left him mistrusted by historians and ethnographers, and [that] the linguistic ambiguity of his text has discouraged literary critics."[20] This critical phenomenon, I would argue, reveals the extent to which earlier scholars failed to acknowledge more fully their own mediated positions as cultural critics and, more specifically, their own investments in identity politics.

According to Jonathan Hart, one of the challenges confronting readers of early modern texts is to "come to terms with the representations of the exchange [between Europeans and Natives] in a way that takes into account the gap between early modern understandings of contact and late twentieth-century views," in order to strike a "balance between the historical record and the ethical interests of the present."[21] It is no coincidence that Karr, Hopwood, and Warwick presented their views in the late 1960s and early to mid- 1970s, a period that witnessed the emergence of intense public debates about the possibility—and viability—of imagining Canada as a "single" nation made up of "two" equal but distinct cultures. In rehearsing their views, I mean to highlight the ways in which cultural memory has informed previous attempts to read—or, rather, *not* to read—Radisson and his *Voyages*. In comparison to the amount of scholarship available on his predecessors and contemporaries—Cartier, de Champlain, de Frontenac, and de La Salle are names that easily resonate in accounts of both New France and pre-Confederation Canada—it seems as if Radisson is deemed less worthy, less significant, as a figure for cultural critique. In effect, the earlier critical reception of Radisson's *Voyages* exposes the truism of Ernest Renan's claim that forgetting and historical error are "crucial factor[s] in the creation of a nation."[22] The failure on the part of these critics to acknowledge their *implicit* engagement with narrating the nation is perhaps evidence of the difficulties involved in—and, as such, the absolute need for—remembering the disconcerting fact that the Law of Nations (*jus gentium*) emerged in Europe during the Age of Discovery.[23] In other words, if Radisson's accounts of his travels were put to political use during his lifetime in the creation of a nation, so they have been put to similar use in our lifetime in the re-creation of Canada's nationhood.

These earlier views are only now being carefully reconsidered by Warkentin and, in the francophone tradition, by Martin Fournier.[24] I share Warkentin's view that "Radisson's literary presentation of himself *is* a historical source, although it has been dismissed,

Radisson greets native chiefs, from a drawing by C.W. Jefferys in the Imperial Oil Collection.

misinterpreted, and trivialized for several centuries."[25] Following her lead, I position Radisson in this chapter at the centre of his own life story and explore his *Voyages* as a literary-historical document. In particular, I discuss the "First Voyage of Pierre-Esprit Radisson," a narrative in which the author recounts his captivity and eventual adoption by a group of Iroquois during the period between April or May 1652 and October 1653.[26] This captivity narrative has to date received little attention, though critics rightly recognize its importance for the study of the literatures of early Canada and the Americas.[27] Warkentin, for example, situates the *Voyages* within the context of an emergent "scribal culture" in New France; though much of her work focuses on the fourth or Lake Superior voyage, she nonetheless maintains that "[a]ll Radisson's accounts of his voyages have to be read with his adoption [and captivity] constantly in view," because so "few of the early explorers of Canada assimilated as fully to Native perspectives as did Radisson."[28] Warner similarly finds the narrative captivating because it "describes one process of acculturation—from French to Iroquois—but it performs another: from French to English."[29] Gordon M. Sayre, in his turn, values Radisson for having been "the lone secular French captivity narrator."[30] Extending these critics' valuable observations, I term Radisson's negotiation and reconstitution of his subjectivities as "stylizations of selfhood." In representing and performing from a rich repertoire of identities in his captivity narrative, Radisson foregrounds the dynamics of cultural mediation between Europeans and Natives, as well as his own complex interpretations of those mediations.

Critics of the early modern period have long recognized the need to explore the dynamics of cultural mediation in encounter and exchange narratives. According to Hart, for example, "[m]ediation is important because from the first contact some Europeans and Natives ignored the divisions between their cultures and found ways of crossing boundaries."[31] Radisson consistently crosses cultural boundaries in his captivity narrative. In what follows, I discuss briefly the manuscript history of his *Voyages*, before continuing with close readings of the captivity narrative. Radisson's strategies in disrupting the structural and temporal logic within his text, I argue, make intelligible the experience of his captivity both to himself and, in different ways, his readers. The narrative articulates Radisson's desire to mediate his own self-understanding of his relationship to his captors on two discursive levels simultaneously. Describing his capture and eventual captivity, Radisson struggles to reconcile the alterity—that is, the relationship between identity and difference—that shapes his relationship with the Iroquois. But his narrative contains a metacommentary that exposes yet another struggle, one that attempts to reconcile the alterity between his present sense of self at the moment of writing his *Voyages* and the past self being remembered and described. Reading the *Voyages* as Radisson's attempt to navigate through the recesses of his memory helps to explain why he "seems to have kept [the first four accounts of his travels] to himself for more than a decade."[32] Mediating between self-representation and self-interpretation, Radisson ultimately demonstrates self-reflexive strategies that are pertinent for contemporary readers of his *Voyages*. His captivity narrative, in particular, foregrounds the possibility of straddling and accommodating two or more cultures, and provides important ways of reading—not only the past but also our current historical moment, as we continue to debate the status of Canada's national identity as both English and French.

Radisson wrote about his explorations during the mid- to late 1660s, but the *Voyages* was not published until 1885. At the end of his first extended stay in England, during the winter of 1668–69, he wrote in English about the first four voyages. The first narrative describes his captivity and adoption; the second, the Onondaga voyage of 1654–55; the third, the Mississippi voyage of 1655–58; the fourth, the Lake Superior voyage of 1659–61. In 1685, Radisson recounted in French his fifth and sixth voyages—those, respectively, of 1682–83 and 1684.[33] The Prince Society of Boston, in an edition of only 250 copies, compiled all six accounts—translating into English the fifth and sixth voyages—and published them as *Voyages of Peter Esprit Radisson, being an account of his travels and experiences among the North American Indians, from 1652 to 1684, transcribed from the original manuscripts in the Bodleian Library and the British Museum* in 1885. Critics share the view that Radisson wrote about his explorations at the request of the Stuart monarch, Charles II, and to persuade the king's cousin, Prince Rupert, and English investors to finance the establishment of the Hudson's Bay Company.[34] Less clear and far more debatable is the issue of whether the manuscripts were originally written in English or in French. Remarking that the manuscripts "have had almost as adventurous a career as their author," Louise Phelps Kellogg explains that they "were written in English, the English of an unaccustomed foreigner."[35] According to Nute in her biography of Radisson, however, the original French manuscripts of Radisson's account of his travels have been lost, and the current archive relies on the English translation, completed in 1669 by Nicholas Hayward, the translator for the Hudson's Bay Company.[36] The issue of language informs any study dealing with Radisson's text, though it remains largely speculative whether Radisson composed his narratives in English, or whether they were later translated from French.

Although the manuscript history of Radisson's *Voyages* is obscure, it implicitly suggests the crucial relationship between author and audience in the production of the narratives. Ian S. MacLaren has recently called for a more careful examination of the evolution of the author in exploration and travel literatures. Sustained analyses of these genres must take into consideration the several stages of writing involved in the production of texts: the shift from field notes to journal, from manuscript to publication. Because of this multistage process, MacLaren insists, we must pay attention to the ways in which the author's "awareness of [potential] readers vitally conditions the narrative, in terms of the way events are structured, plotted and phrased."[37]

Although Radisson's *Voyages* did not necessarily undergo all of these stages, the author, at the time of the narrative's composition, was all too aware of his audience: Charles II. The presupposition of an already established reader thus makes especially clear the "promotional intent" of his narrative.[38] Radisson had to convince Charles II not only that the Great Lakes fur trade would be a profitable venture for the British, but that he, himself, would be the right person to head such an expedition. To succeed, Radisson had to establish in his text two things: a thorough knowledge of the geographical region, plus an intimate familiarity with the Native populations. What better way to describe his expertise than in recounting his captivity? After all, this period afforded Radisson an opportunity to increase his awareness of the Great Lakes area, and, perhaps more importantly, a firsthand opportunity to witness the customs and habits of the Native populations. Although Radisson "was not fundamentally a describer of scenery," since his "natural subject-matter was the world of human beings,"[39] he frequently assigns a correspondence in his captivity narrative between his geographical mapping of regions and the people occupying those regions. He deploys strategies that mark both his place and placement during his captivity and, in doing so, displays an acutely sensitive and cognizant awareness of his subject position in such a predicament. For example, arriving with his captors "[b]y sunsett ... att the Isles of Richelieu," he wryly remarks that it was "a place rather for victors than for captives most pleasant."[40] As we will see, however, the boundary separating "victors" from "captives" is not always clearly demarcated in his captivity narrative.

Radisson begins his text by describing that he was persuaded by two of his companions to accompany them during a hunt. Having agreed to this pastime, he mentions dressing in "the lightest way I could possible"—especially appropriate for the occasion, he adds, because doing so allows him to be "nimbler and not [to] stay behinde" from the others. These precautionary measures, however, articulate more than just pragmatism on Radisson's part. As he explains it, there are really two reasons for dressing in this fashion: not only will it allow him to be more lively or active in order to catch more prey, but it will also enable him to "escape [from any potential] danger ... of an enemy the cruelest that ever was uppon the face of the Earth." Radisson immediately identifies and names the enemy, saying:

> It is to bee observed that the french had warre with a
> wild nation called Iroquoites, who for that time weare
> soe strong and so to be feared that scarce any body
> durst stirre out either Cottage or house without being
> taken or killed, saving that he had nimble limbs to
> escape their fury.[41]

These descriptions in the opening paragraph point to two important details: Radisson's anticipation of an encounter with the Iroquois and, as a consequence, his subtle shifting of the structural logic contained within his text. Being "nimble" no longer simply signifies an ability to travel farther and thus cover more ground in search of prey. Instead, being "nimble" now metonymically signals the ability to escape any potentially hostile encounter with the Iroquois. According to Radisson's logic at the end of the paragraph, apart from those who "had nimble limbs to escape [the Iroquois'] fury," most Europeans did not dare to venture out of their shelters. At the beginning of the paragraph, Radisson positions himself as a hunter seeking prey; by the end of the paragraph, and in articulating his fear of the Iroquois, he has manoeuvred himself into the position of one of "the hunted." He self-consciously displaces his own subject position within the text; he stylizes his own sense of self.

The strategies disrupting the text's structural logic mirror the subtle ways in which Radisson plays with temporal logic as well. If to be "nimble" is to heed one's presentiments, then Radisson is consistent, inasmuch as he already anticipates, right from the start, the appearance of the Iroquois—for the barbaric native "savage" appears always in advance of the savage himself. To the extent that Radisson's intuitive expectations point toward a future present time, and to the extent that this imagined temporality projects and makes manifest an actual encounter with the Iroquois, the beginning of his narrative presupposes the end result—specifically, that of his abduction. This is especially evident in the second paragraph of the narrative, where he says:

> At an offspring of a village of three Rivers we consult
> together that two should go the watter side, the other
> in a wood hardby to warne us, for to advertise us if
> he accidentaly should light [upon] or suspect any
> Barbars in ambush, we also retreat ourselves to him if
> we should discover any thing uppon the River.

The ambiguity of Radisson's use of the subjunctive tense (*should*) in the last part of this sentence assumes a precognition that will ensure his recognition of the Iroquois when an actual cross-cultural contact occurs. What remains peculiar about this strategy, however, is its deviation from Radisson's predominant use of the past tense throughout his narrative. The sentence that follows this one, for example, reads: "Having comed to the first river ... we mett a man who kept cattell, and asked him if he had knowne any appearance of [the] Ennemy, and likewise demanded which way he would advise us to gett better fortune [with the hunt], and [in] what part [of the land] he [e]spied more danger."[42]

Consider, too, the passage that immediately follows Radisson's anticipation of an encounter, in which he describes the hunting party's decision to separate and, more significantly, recounts the occurrence of a nosebleed:

> Priming our pistols, we went where our fancy first
> lead us, being impossible for us to avoid the destinies
> of the heavens; no sooner tourned our backs, but my
> nose fell ableeding without any provocation in the
> least. Certainly it was a warning for me of a
> beginning of a yeare and a half of hazards and of
> myseryes that weare to befall mee.[43]

These sentences encapsulate much of the text's often confusing temporal logic. For Radisson, the inexplicable and sudden nosebleed portends a predestined evil, "a warning for [him]" of things yet to come. Not unlike his earlier introduction of the anticipated appearance of the Iroquois, the nosebleed here functions as a textual trope that prophesies his imminent capture. As such, his use of the past tense in describing a spontaneous bodily affliction conjures up a greater future affliction. The presentation of events is therefore edited out, insofar as "the past tense ... indicate[s] [Radisson's] arrival at the planned destination"—namely, that of his captivity.[44] In her reading of the famine passage described by Radisson in his fourth or Lake Superior voyage, Warkentin notes that "one of Radisson's most persistent stylistic devices [is] narration in the present tense," an indication of his absolute "confidence in the moment" of which he is engaged in describing. For "the point of Radisson's method [of narration] is not to tell us *when* or *where* something happened," she further explains, "but how it was experienced *as* it happened."[45] For the purpose of reading these initial moments in Radisson's captivity narrative, however, I would slightly modify Warkentin's point. Because Radisson is essentially setting up the *Voyages* in the captivity narrative, I would suggest that the temporal shifts evident in his language indicate his confidence in *the potentiality of the future moment*—for the Iroquois inevitably *do* appear and take Radisson as a captive among their tribe.

But, before encountering them, Radisson first discovers that his two companions have been killed; their wounded bodies and mutilated heads serve as evidence for the vicinity of the Iroquois. In graphic detail, he describes finding his companions both "quite naked" and with "their hair standing up, the one being shott through with three bouletts and two blowes of an hatchett on the head, and the other runne thorough in severall places with a sword and smitten with an hatchett. Att the same instance [of looking them over]," he immediately explains, "my nose begun'd to bleed, which made me afraid of my life."[46] It is no coincidence that the sight of his friends lying in a pool of blood should provoke yet another nosebleed for Radisson. The uncanny repetition of the two nosebleeds functions, I would argue, as the first of a series of "centering" moments in Radisson's captivity narrative. According to Vincent Crapanzano in his provocative study, *Hermes' Dilemma and Hamlet's Desire: On the Epistemology of Interpretation*, "centering" moments or "symbolic centers" "exist in all narratives," and "there are always centers embedded within centers—within larger 'centered' and 'centering' units of discourse."[47]

Because my reading of Radisson's captivity narrative derives much of its vocabulary and methodology from Crapanzano, allow me to rehearse his idea of centering at length. According to him, centres are images, events, or theoretical constructs that function "as a nucleus or point of concentration that holds together a particular verbal sequence" or description in narrative, giving "coherence, a semblance of order at least, to what would otherwise appear to be a random, meaningless sequence of expressions" or descriptions. In Radisson's case, the second nosebleed not only fulfills his prophecy that the first was a "warning for [him] of a beginning of a yeare and a half of hazards and of myseryes," but also promises to announce the entrance of the Iroquois. Both events make material his prediction of soon becoming a captive and, in the process, legitimates the function of his captivity narrative. For "[t]he center's force lies in its ability to call forth the legitimation of its own dominant linguistic function," Crapanzano argues. Moreover, to the extent that centering, figuratively speaking, "stops discursive time, at least the discursive display of meaning," where "[t]ime past folds forward; time future folds backwards—into the center from which meaning and order spring," I would also suggest that, at the moment of recalling and describing these details in writing, Radisson is engaged in assigning meaning to his immanent capture by the Iroquois.[48] For Radisson, his nosebleeds represent mnemonic reference points from which to make sense of his past in the present moment of interpreting that very past. These initial descriptions in the captivity narrative—even *prior* to the entry of the Iroquois—expose the author's anxiety to mediate successfully between the present moment of writing and the past moment being recollected in writing. Positioning his nosebleeds as centering events that invite interpretation, Radisson prepares himself to reach an understanding—or, at the very least, the presumption of understanding—of his past experience as a captive.

In preparing himself, moreover, he also prepares his readers for what has thus far appeared to be the delayed appearance of the Iroquois.

Radisson's anxiety is made especially evident in the language he uses to announce the arrival of the Iroquois. Interpreting the repeated occurrence of the nosebleed as a preternatural phenomenon, Radisson continues by describing hearing "a noise" close by and finding himself surrounded. Enter the Iroquois onto the scene of Radisson's recollection:

> Seeing myselfe [en]compassed round about by a
> multitude of dogges, or rather devils, that rose from
> the grasse, rushes and bushes, I shott my gunne,
> whether unawares or purposly I know not, but I
> shott with a pistolle confidently, but was siesed on all
> sides by a great number that threw me downe, taking
> away my arme without giving mee one blowe; for
> afterwards I felt no paine att all, onely a great
> guidinesse in my heade, from whence it comes I doe
> not remember. In the same time they [the Iroquois]
> brought me into the wood, where they shewed me
> the two heads [of my companions] all bloody.[49]

Although somewhat awkward in its prose, this passage displays the rich descriptive mode that characterizes much of Radisson's narrative. In addition to vividly capturing the author's immediate confusion and panic during the encounter, this passage foregrounds two important structuring thematics: memory and identity. The problematics of memory and identity both centre on recognition— on seeing the past in relation to the present, and on seeing 'the self' in relation to 'the other.' Radisson can readily recall, in retrospect, feeling "a great guidinesse in [his] heade," but adds, in qualifying this memory, that "[from] whence it comes [he] doe[s] not remember." To the extent that some memories escape retrospection, they leave just enough impression for Radisson to make some semblance of coherence in reconstructing the past. Radisson's present project of reconstructing the past, moreover, is inextricably linked to the project of reconstructing his identity: that is, to stylize his subjectivities in relation to whatever memories remain available. Describing his capture, he first recalls "seeing [him]selfe [en]compassed round about by a multitude," thereby recognizing himself as different from the Iroquois, his cultural 'others'—or those whom he instead prefers to interpellate as "dogges, or rather devils." But the binary of self/other remains insufficient for Radisson, not least because it fails to maintain the demarcation of the boundary separating Europeans from Natives, and vice versa—for the Iroquois' act of capturing Radisson finally makes material the cross-cultural encounter which Radisson has consistently anticipated within the "contact zones" of his consciousness.[50]

The Iroquois' gesture of showing Radisson his companions' heads constitutes yet another centering moment that marks the dissolution of the boundary separating the two cultures. In other words, this moment shatters the illusion between European and Iroquois; more specifically for Radisson, it collapses the binary of self/other. Unlike his two unfortunate companions, Radisson vaguely remembers being "tak[en] away ... without ... one blowe" from any of his captors. In effect, then, Radisson does not represent an 'other' for those whom he perceives as his cultural 'others.' At least for the moment, the Iroquois see Radisson as somehow different from his two companions, and instead of killing him, they prefer to take him captive. But for the white captive, his recognition of difference does not occur immediately: he requires the intervention of the Iroquois; he must be made to see the difference. According to Crapanzano, in "ethnographic and other cross-cultural encounters where the conventions of centering are not necessarily shared by the parties of the encounter, the negotiation of a 'meaningful' center plays an important role. Each party attempts to center the relationship—the conversation—in terms of his own concerns and conventions," and "though the interest [in centring] is shared, its personal and cultural significance may not be."[51]

In recalling this particular moment, Radisson is essentially describing the cross-cultural negotiation between himself and the Natives, as the two parties attempt to make intelligible the alterity that shapes their relationship with each other. Prior to the encounter, the mutilated heads signify for Radisson the vicinity of the Iroquois, whereas now, these same signifiers function as the visual evidence of his own difference. "At the same time [the Iroquois] brought me into the wood," the captive recalls, "they shewed me the two heads all bloody." Forced by the Iroquois to witness the mutilated heads of his companions, Radisson finally recognizes his difference: a difference not in relation to a cultural 'other,' but to the self—to himself in particular, a white captive who would have been killed but for the grace of the Iroquois.

These centering moments cumulatively destabilize the self/other binary informing Radisson's self-image of his body. In fact, as we have seen, Radisson's captivity narrative often privileges the corporeal—whether it be a nosebleed or a mutilated head. Moreover, references to the body are often grotesque: the removal of someone's heart and the burning of fingers are striking and ubiquitous features of Radisson's text. One graphic passage renders especially explicit some of the torments inflicted on the captives by the Iroquois. In it, Radisson introduces his descriptions as a digression, saying, "I prolong a little from my purpose of my adventure for to say the torments that I have seen suffered att Coutu ..." before going on to narrate:

> They [the Iroquois] tie the prisoners to a poast by
> their hands ... They pluck out their [the prisoners']
> nailes for the most part ... After[ward] they tye your
> wrist with a corde, putting two for this effect, one
> drawing him [the captive] one way, another of
> another way ... Some others cutt peeces of flesh from
> all parts of the body & broyle them, gett you to eat it,
> thrusting them into your mouth, putting into it a
> stick of fire.[52]

By purposely alternating between the third-person *they* and the second-person *you* in his retelling, Radisson makes the scene not only more immediate and grotesque for his readers, but also productively confusing by pulling them into his narrative. Although it can be argued that such descriptions are part and parcel of any captivity narrative—what better way to relate the Indians' barbarity than to magnify their brutalities toward their captives?—a more careful examination of Radisson's narrative yields as many allusions to an aesthetics of the body, especially as it pertains to hair and body adornment. Indeed, to judge by the number of accounts, the Iroquois seem to have entirely fetishized Radisson's hair and body: for example, "they combed my head, and with a filthy grease greased my head, and dashed all over my face with redd paintings"; "the young men tooke delight in combing my head, greasing and powdering out a kinde of redd powder, then tying my haire with a redd string of leather like to a coard"; "a woman ... taking hould on my haire ... combs my head with her fingers and tyed my wrist with a bracelet"; "they cutt off my hair in the front and upon the crowne of the head."[53] With each experience, Radisson gains a more comprehensive understanding of the ways in which the body—specifically *his body*—figures as a legible, cross-cultural signifier of alterity—of identity and difference—for both himself and his captors.

These numerous examples indicate that the Iroquois, regardless of gender, take pleasure in altering their captive's appearance. Their attentions toward Radisson articulate their fondness for him and, additionally, anticipate their later adoption of him into their tribe. One particular passage stands out among the rest. In it, Radisson first describes the group's decision to make camp upon its "arriv[al] in a good and pleasant harbour," then notes the Iroquois' attentions toward him, and, finally, explains his dilemma about attempting to escape from the group. As he recounts it:

> The place round about [was] full of trees. Here they
> kindled a fire and provided what was necessary for
> their food. In this place they cutt off my hair in the
> front and upon the crowne of the head, and turning
> up the locks of the haire they dab'd me with some
> thicke grease. So done, they brought me a looking-
> glasse. I viewing myself all in a pickle, smir'd with
> redde and black, covered with such a cappe, and locks
> tyed up with a peece of leather and stunked horridly,
> I could not but fall in love with myselfe, if not that I
> had better instructions to shun the sin of pride. So
> after repasting themselves, they made them ready for
> the journey with takeing repose that night. This was
> the time I thought to have escaped, for in vaine, for I

being alone feared least I should be apprehended and
dealt with more violently. And moreover I was
desirous to have seene their country.⁵⁴

This passage resonates with Radisson's description of his capture in
its careful regard for details—from the setting of the landscape to the
setting of his hair. More importantly, Radisson's recital here echoes the
rhetoric of the previous passage: here, he notes "I viewing myself ...";
earlier, in describing his capture, he notes "seeing myselfe
[en]compassed ...." Both occasions centre on the agency of the first-
person subjective *I*. But this "I"—the agent—is additionally subjected
to seeing itself as a subject—a self—by the intervention of an 'other.'
Previously, the Iroquois forced Radisson to recognize himself as
different from his companions; here, they again function as mediators
and, by bringing him the "looking-glasse," force him to do the same.

What remains significant, in the end, is Radisson's response
to his mirror image: "I could not but fall in love with myselfe," he
recalls in retrospect. The mirror scene represents the ultimate,
embedded centering moment in Radisson's captivity narrative. To
the extent that the moments I have described each function to mediate
Radisson's conceptualization of his selfhood—his own self-awareness
of his identity as a subject of captivity—the mirror scene registers
not only his "awareness of a contrasting world" but, in effect, also
his "recognition ... of [his] *own otherness* in that world."⁵⁵ The mirror
scene constitutes a double alienation for Radisson: the reflected image
makes intelligible not only the difference between European and
Native but, more interestingly, also the difference between
Radisson's identity as the subject engaged in retrospection *and* as the
object of such retrospection. Even though Radisson recognizes the
need "to shun the sin of pride" at the time of recounting this episode,
he also confesses to a pleasure in having indulged, however
temporarily, his own vanity. And even with the distance of twenty
years, he fondly remembers encountering his visage, "all in a pickle,
smir'd with redde and black." Here, then, Radisson enacts what
Georges Gusdorf identifies to be the ontological problematic that
both conditions and limits the genre of autobiography. On the one
hand, Radisson "looks at himself being and delights in being looked
at—he calls himself as witness for himself." On the other hand,

Radisson's present invitation to bear witness to a prior self belies the transparent self-referentiality that governs all forms of life writing. For, as Gusdorf maintains, "autobiography is condemned to substitute endlessly the completely formed for that which is in the process of being formed."[56]

Radisson's very act of composition attempts to synchronize the past with the present. In other words, he ultimately yearns for a temporality that exceeds the boundaries of text—his captivity narrative—and context, that is, the events conditioning that very narrative. What Radisson essentially remembers is a "white captive" in the process of becoming a "white Indian," a transformation of the self as it begins to embody an 'other.'[57] But that transformation can only materialize with Radisson's recognition and taking possession of his own doubly alienated subjectivity. For, as Crapanzano suggests, an "individual must take possession of his own otherness and not be aware simply of the otherness about him" in order to become a self or subject.[58] Radisson's decision not to try to escape from his captors strongly indicates his attempt to take possession of his own otherness. "And moreover I was desirous to have seene their country," he finally admits. From here on—as his description of the mirror scene implicitly foregrounds—the pronoun referents that differentiate the first-person Radisson from the third-person Iroquois become less and less clear.

In staying faithful to this desire "to have seene their country," Radisson decides to stay with the Iroquois and eventually gets adopted by a family within the tribe. The remainder of his captivity narrative contains fond references to his adoptive family, whose members consistently intervene in his behalf. So strong are his affections for the Iroquois that Radisson "resolve[s] to offer [him]selfe for to serve, and to take party with them" in their tribal war against the Algonquians and, in consequence, against the French. But despite this genuine desire on his part, Radisson remains self-conscious of his insider/outsider status within the Iroquois tribe. He recalls asking his adoptive father about this matter:

> [U]ppon this I venture to aske him what I was. [He]
> presently answers that I was a Iroquoite as himselfe.
> Lett me revenge, said I, my kindred. I love my
> brother. Lett me die with him. I would die with you,

but you will not because you goe against the French. Let me a gaine goe with my brother, the prisoners & the heads that I shall bring, to the joy of my mother and sisters, will make me undertake att my retourne to take up the hattchett against those of Quebecq, of the 3 rivers, and Monteroyall in declaring them my name, and that it's I that kills them, and by that you shall know I am your son, worthy to beare that title that you gave me when you adopted me.[59]

In this passage, Radisson clearly articulates his desire to be identified as a legitimate member of the tribe. He demands that he be named by his adoptive father as "a Iroquoite as himself." Only after this confirmation of his identity does Radisson go on to recite his filial/tribal duties to his family/tribe. He vows "to take up the hattchett against those of Quebecq, of the 3 rivers, and Monteroyall," thereby shifting his political allegiances from the French to the Iroquois. Here, Radisson characteristically aligns his subject position on a geographical/ethnographical trajectory; this example also marks the shifting of Radisson's placement of himself "against"—and hence not in affiliation with—"those of Quebecq, of the 3 rivers, and Monteroyall." But as Radisson quickly discovers in the course of the military expedition, he can never fully "pass" as an Indian. Not coincidentally, the Natives are the ones who once again provoke Radisson to confront his cultural drag. For example, upon the party's arrival at Seneca, a village occupied by another tribe within the Iroquois nation, Radisson describes the Natives' "admir[ation] to see a frenchman accompanying wild men, which [he] understood by their exclamations."[60] Interestingly, in retrospectively recalling this moment, Radisson realigns his subject position as "a frenchman accompanying wild men." But to the extent that the Senecans maintain tribal affiliations with the Iroquois nation, and to the extent that the Iroquois are known to be at war with the French, Radisson's self-conscious positioning of himself as "a frenchman" is strategically misleading.

Significantly, Radisson continues to deploy such strategies in the remainder of his captivity narrative. Claiming to be French on one occasion, and Iroquois on another, he stylizes his subject position to suit the different contexts in which he finds himself embedded. Consider the following two examples, each describing Radisson's arrival at different destinations. Describing his arrival at "the fort of Orange," the Dutch outpost on the site of present-day Albany, New York, Radisson recalls:

> I went into the fort with my brother, and have not
> yett ben knowne [as] a french[man]. But a french
> souldier of the fort speaks to me in [the] Iroquois
> language, & demanded if I was not a stranger, and did
> veryly believe I was French, for all that I was dabbled
> over with painting and greased. I answered him in the
> same language, that no; and then he speaks in
> swearing, desiring me [to tell him] how I fell in the
> hands of those people.[61]

Later, having just succeeded in making his escape from the Iroquois, he remembers his arrival "in a place full of trees cutt," where he meets a Dutchman cutting wood. "I went nearer and called to him," Radisson explains:

> [The man] incontinently leaves his work & comes to
> me, thinking I was Iroquoise. I said nothing to him to
> the contrary. I kept him in that thought ... I tould him
> I was savage, but that I lived awhile among the
> french, & that I had something valuable to
> communicate to the [Dutch] governor.[62]

To the French soldier, Radisson claims to be French rather than Iroquois; to the Dutch woodcutter, he claims to be a "savage" or Iroquois rather than French. Representing the soldier's and the woodcutter's respective responses to his appearance as instances of mistaken identity, Radisson underscores the extent to which cultural assumptions shape *any* European's encounter with others in the New World. But these examples also foreground Radisson's recognition and acceptance that cultural differences have shaped, and will continue to shape, his own relationships with both Natives and Europeans. To the extent that Radisson consistently succeeded in creating and performing from a repertoire of identities, he was able to do so because of his captivity experience with the Iroquois. By orchestrating Radisson's departure from European culture and immersing him in theirs, the Iroquois have led Radisson, figuratively speaking, to reach his final destination—namely, to come to terms with his "stylizations of selfhood."

Among his other discoveries, explorer Pierre-Esprit Radisson deserves to be remembered for discovering his identity *in* difference. As we continue the debate on Canada's conceptualization of its national identity, in the present and for the future, it would serve us well to wonder, in rephrasing Radisson's self-observation as a rhetorical question: as Canadians, could we but fall in love with ourselves?

NOTES

I would like to thank Glenn Burger, Natasha Hurley, Martin Ponce, Raymond Ricketts, Michael Warner, and the editors and readers of this collection for their insightful comments on earlier versions of this chapter. I would also like to acknowledge the generous support of a Social Sciences and Humanities Research Council of Canada Doctoral Fellowship.

1 Olive Patricia Dickason, *Canada's First Nations: A History of Founding Peoples from Earliest Times* (Norman, OK: University of Oklahoma Press, 1992), pp. 11–12.

2 Ibid., p. 12.

3 Grace Lee Nute, *Caesars of the Wilderness: Médard Chouart, Sieur des Groseilliers and Pierre-Esprit Radisson, 1618–1710* (New York and London: D. Appleton-Century, 1943), p. xi. Benedict Anderson argues that "[w]hat is particularly startling in the American namings of the sixteenth to eighteenth centuries is that 'new' and 'old' were understood synchronically, co-existing within homogenous, empty time" (Anderson, *Imagined Communities: Reflections on the Origins and Spread of Nationalism*, rev. ed. [London and New York: Verso, 1991], p. 187). As I will elaborate later on, revisionist tendencies in early Canadian historiography often illustrate a similar desire to recuperate this very synchronicity.

4 The Hudson's Bay Company was set up under the name "The Governor and Company of Adventurers of England, trading into Hudson's Bay," on 2 May 1670. Historian L.C. Green points out that the charters for the Hudson's Bay Company, the Dutch East India Company, and the British East India Company were "drawn up in the same era" (Green, "Claims to Territory in North America," in Green and Dickason, eds., *The Law of Nations and the New World* [Edmonton: University of Alberta Press, 1989], pp. 95–96). It is therefore worth remembering that the Dutch were also major world players during the "scramble" for North America during the mid to late seventeenth century. In fact, Radisson and des Groseilliers were inevitably caught up in the war between England and the Dutch states for the transatlantic trade. Although

the scope of my discussion prevents me from more fully addressing the important role of the Dutch at this time, two examples are worth noting. Radisson concludes his captivity narrative with an account of his trip to Fort Orange, the Dutch outpost on the site of present-day Albany, New York. After declining the Dutch governor's offer to ransom him from the Iroquois, Radisson eventually repented his refusal and defected to the Dutch, with whom he was later employed as an interpreter before returning to Europe in 1654. Father Paul Ragueneau, then in charge of the Jesuit mission in Québec, comments that the conquest of New Holland by New Englanders in 1664 was partially inspired by des Groseilliers, who relied heavily on Radisson's knowledge of the geography of the Iroquois country (Nute, *Caesars of the Wilderness*, pp. 7, 55, 83–84; "Radisson, Pierre-Esprit," p. 537). For a detailed history of the Hudson's Bay Company, see Peter C. Newman, *Company of Adventurers*, vol. 1 (Markham, ON: Viking, 1985).

5 Nute, *Caesars of the Wilderness*, pp. xi–xii.

6 George Lang, "Voyageur Discourse and the Absence of Fur Trade Pidgin," *Canadian Literature* 131 (Winter 1991): 51.

7 Gilles Paquet and Jean-Pierre Wallot, "Nouvelle France / Québec / Canada: A World of Limited Identities," in Nicholas Canny and Anthony Pagden, eds., *Colonial Identity in the Atlantic World, 1500–1800* (Princeton: Princeton University Press, 1987), p. 99.

8 Germaine Warkentin, "Discovering Radisson: A Renaissance Adventurer Between Two Worlds," in Jennifer S.H. Brown and Elizabeth Vibert, eds., *Reading Beyond Words: Contexts for Native History* (Peterborough, ON: Broadview Press, 1996), p. 55. For a shorter version of Warkentin's article, see her "Pierre-Esprit Radisson and the Language of Place," *Queen's Quarterly* 101, no. 2 (Summer 1994): 305–16.

9 According to the *Encyclopedia Canadiana*, Radisson was possibly born in 1636, probably at Paris. Nute, however, dates Radisson's birth in 1640, and places it at Avignon (*Caesars of the Wilderness*, pp. 40–43). Both sources agree that Radisson died in 1710. Nute also notes that Radisson was naturalized as an English citizen in 1687, with the Hudson's Bay Company paying the expenses incurred in the procedure (p. 251).

10 Michael Warner, introduction to "The Relation of my Voyage, being in Bondage in the Lands of the Irokoits," by Pierre-Esprit Radisson, in Myra Jehlen and Michael Warner, eds., *The English Literatures of America, 1500–1800* (New York and London: Routledge, 1997), p. 325.

11 Ibid.

12 Jack Warwick, *The Long Journey: Literary Themes of French Canada* (Toronto: University of Toronto Press, 1968), p. 163.

13 Warkentin, "Discovering Radisson," p. 44; "Pierre-Esprit Radisson and the Language of Place," p. 306.

14 William John Karr, *Explorers, Soldiers, and Statesmen: A History of Canada Through Biography* (Freeport, NY: Books for Libraries Press, 1971), p. 55.

15 In a chapter entitled "Messrs Radishes and Gooseberries," in *Company of Adventurers*, op. cit., Newman explains that the "members of Charles II's court could not or would not pronounce the two men's names correctly and the HBC [Hudson's Bay Company] minutes contain eight different spellings of 'Groseilliers,' with the record keepers eventually settling on 'Gooseberries.' In Radisson's case, the problem was with his first name—which was cited so often as Peter that in his will, written in his own hand, dated July 17, 1710, he refers to himself as Peter Radisson" (p. 62). See, too, R. Douglas Francis, Richard Jones, and Donald B. Smith, eds., *Origins: Canadian History to Confederation* (Toronto and Montréal: Holt, Rinehart and Winston, 1992), p. 109. Although I have been unable to locate specific evidence on the appellation of Radisson as Mr. Radishes, sailing instructions by the backers of the British venture stipulated that the crew members of the *Nonsuch Ketch* and the *Eaglet* "are to take notice that the wampungeage [monetary currency to trade with the Indians] wch [they] carry with [them] is part of our Joynt Cargo wee having bought it for our money of Mr Gooseberry and Mr Radisson and is to be delivered by small quantityes with like Caution as the other goods." The crew members were also instructed to treat Radisson and des Groseilliers "with all manner of Civility and Courtesy and to take care that all [their] Company doe beare a perticular respect Unto them they being the persons Upon whose Credit we have Undertaken this expedition." These instructions illustrate the ambivalent views of the British towards Radisson and des Groseilliers—anglicizing the Frenchmen's names but, at the same time, maintaining a semblance of respectful propriety in order to secure their own self-interests. These passages are cited in Phil Day, "The Nunsuch Ketch," *The Beaver: The Magazine of the North* 299.3 (Winter 1968): 4–17, an essay published on the eve of the tercentenary celebration of the Hudson Bay's Company in 1970. Day's essay provides an entertaining discussion on the reconstruction of the *Nonsuch Ketch*, the ship in which des Groseilliers sailed, and which has since been on permanent exhibition at the Manitoba Museum of Man and Nature.

16 Victor G. Hopwood, "Explorers by Land to 1867," in *Literary History of Canada: Canadian Literature in English*, ed. Carl F. Klinck, 2nd ed., vol. 1 (Toronto and Buffalo: University of Toronto Press, 1976), pp. 23–24, 23.

17 Warwick, *The Long Journey*, n. 12.

18 Konrad Gross, "Coureurs-de-Bois, Voyageurs, and Trappers: The Fur Trade and the Emergence of an Ignored Literary Tradition," *Canadian Literature* 127 (Winter 1990): 77.

19 Philippe Jacquin, *Les Indiens blancs: Français et Indiens en Amérique du Nord (XVIe–XVIIIe siècle)* (Paris: Payot, 1987). My paraphrase of Jacquin's text, which reads, in French: *"[L]es Québécois, en quête de racines françaises, effacent dans le personnage tout ce qui peut rappeler l'ambiguïté du coureur de bois, ils le transforment en pioneer d'une colonisation civilisatrice et catholique"* (p. 240). Jacquin implicitly points to the tendency for nationalist nostalgia within the francophone cultural imagination: it seems that the transformation of the figure of the explorer into that of the pioneer could somehow enable the reconceptualization of New France as a "successful" colonial venture. In quoting from Jacquin, however, my claim does not presuppose a homogenous francophone population in Canada. After all, several provinces—such as Alberta, Manitoba, Ontario, Nova Scotia, and New Brunswick—contain vital

francophonies, communities that share similar cultural traditions but also distinctive regional investments. For provocative discussions of these specificities, see Kenneth McRoberts, ed., *Beyond Québec: Taking Stock of Canada* (Montréal and Kingston: McGill-Queen's University Press, 1995). For a discussion of New France, see Sigmund Diamond, "An Experiment in Feudalism: French Canada in the Seventeenth Century," *William and Mary Quarterly* (1961): 2–34. Unfortunately, my unfamiliarity with francophone scholarship prevents me from more fully elaborating on these points within the body of my chapter.

20 Warkentin, "Discovering Radisson," p. 45.

21 Jonathan Hart, "Mediation in the Exchange between Europeans and Native Americans in the Early Modern Period," *Canadian Review of Comparative Literature/Revue Canadienne de Littérature Comparée* 22, no. 2 (June/juin 1995): 321, 339.

22 Ernest Renan, "What is a Nation?" (1882), trans. Martin Thom, reprinted in *Nation and Narration*, ed. Homi K. Bhabha (London and New York: Routledge, 1990), p. 11.

23 Olive Patricia Dickason, "Concepts of Sovereignty at the Time of First Contacts," in *The Law of Nations*, p. 241 n. 4.

24 Martin Fournier's work on Radisson includes "Le Cas Radisson: Analyse pluridisciplinaire d'une phénomène complexe," *Canadian Folklore Canadienne* 18, no. 2 (1996): 91–109; *Pierre-Esprit Radisson, coureur de bois et homme du monde (1652–1685)* (Québec: Nuit Blanche, 1996); and "Les Quatres couleurs de Radisson," thèse de doctorat en histoire, Université Laval, 1998.

25 Warkentin, "Discovering Radisson," p. 52.

26 Pierre-Esprit Radisson, "The Relation of my Voyage, being in Bondage in the Lands of the Irokoits," reprinted in Jehlen and Warner, *English Literatures of America*, pp. 325–48; *Voyages of Peter Esprit Radisson, being an account of his travels and experiences among the North American Indians, from 1652 to 1684, transcribed from the original manuscripts in the Bodleian Library and the British Museum*, ed. Gideon D. Scull (New York: Peter Smith, 1943). Although I will rely on Jehlen and Warner's anthologized account of Radisson's captivity narrative for its useful modernized transcription, I will also provide corresponding page references to Scull's version of Radisson's text in subsequent references.

27 Although there is abundant scholarship on the captivity narrative genre, most critics have focused their attention on the female captivity experience—most notably, that of Mary White Rowlandson. See, for example, June Namias, *White Captives: Gender and Ethnicity on the American Frontier* (Chapel Hill, NC, and London: University of North Carolina Press, 1993), a 200-page study that devotes only twenty-five pages to the male captivity experience. Although it is beyond the scope of my paper to discuss this scholarly phenomenon at length, I want to suggest that the disappearance of the male captive from the critical landscape reinforces the dominant assumption of exploration as a strictly masculinist venture and, in effect, contributes to the idealization of the male explorer as a mythic figure in our contemporary cultural imagination.

28 Warkentin, "Styles of Authorship in New France: Pierre Boucher, Settler, and Pierre-Esprit Radisson, Explorer," *Papers of the Bibliographical Society of Canada/Cahiers de la Société du Canada* 37.2 (Fall/Automne 1999): 16–34; "Discovering Radisson," pp. 47, 46; "Pierre-Esprit Radisson and the Language of Place," p. 307.

29 Warner, pp. 325–26.

30 Gordon M. Sayre, *Les Sauvages Américaines: Representations of Native Americans in French and English Colonial Literature* (Chapel Hill and London: University of North Carolina Press, 1997), p. 283.

31 Hart, "Mediation in the Exchange," p. 320.

32 Warkentin, "Styles of Authorship," p. 28.

33 For a useful discussion of an alternative chronology of Radisson's *Voyages*, see Arthur T. Adams's foreword to *The Explorations of Pierre-Esprit Radisson* (Minneapolis: Ross and Haines, 1961), pp. ii–xiii.

34 Nute, *Caesars of the Wilderness*, p. 29; Warkentin, "Discovering Radisson," pp. 64–65.

35 Louise Phelps Kellogg, ed., *Early Narratives of the Northwest, 1634–1699* (New York: Barnes and Noble, 1945), p. 31. This view was first put forth by Boston's Prince Society in its reprinting of Radisson's *Voyages* in 1885, a volume edited by Gideon D. Scull. Edmund Slafter, then president of the Prince Society, comments in his introduction that: "The author [*Peter* Radisson, not surprisingly] was a native of France, and had an imperfect knowledge of the English language. The journals ... are, however, written in that language, and, as might be anticipated, in orthography, in the use of words, and in the structure of sentences, conform to no known standard of English composition. But the meaning is in all cases clearly conveyed, and, in justice both to the author and the reader, they have been printed *verbatim et literatim*, as in the original manuscripts" (Scull, *Voyages*, pp. v–vi).

36 Nute, *Caesars of the Wilderness*, pp. 29, 30, 99–100, 121; "Radisson, Pierre-Esprit," pp. 539–40. Other details concerning the manuscript history are less ambiguous. The manuscripts (in English) were later acquired by Samuel Pepys and dispersed some years after Pepys's death, in 1703. Around 1749 or 1750, the collector Richard Rawlinson then chanced upon and purchased the manuscripts. Rawlinson's collection came into the possession of the Bodleian Library at Oxford; the British Museum also houses some of these manuscripts, following a purchase made in 1839. These two archives provide the source for the Prince Society's version of Radisson's *Voyages*. Official documents of the Hudson's Bay Company and of the Jesuits also offer later information on Radisson; both remain important archives for cross-referencing purposes.

37 Ian S. MacLaren, "Exploration/Travel Literature and the Evolution of the Author," *International Journal of Canadian Studies/Revue internationale d'études canadiennes* 5 (Spring/Printemps 1992): 42.

38 Jehlen and Warner, *English Literatures of America*, p. 326. In her most recent article, "Styles of Authorship," Warkentin announces that, based on her extensive archival research, her future work on Radisson will offer evidence to

challenge this accepted view: "For though scholars have argued, and people like myself were taught in school, that Radisson's narratives helped to persuade Charles II to found the Hudson's Bay Company, in fact there is no evidence, either direct or indirect, that the narratives ... completed by Radisson in the late 1660s, were known to anybody but himself until 1686," sixteen years after the establishment of the Hudson's Bay Company in 1670 (pp. 25–26).

39 Warkentin, "Discovering Radisson," p. 48; "Pierre-Esprit Radisson and the Language of Place," p. 309.

40 Radisson, in Jehlen and Warner, *English Literatures of America*, p. 329; in Scull, *Voyages*, p. 31.

41 Ibid., in Jehlen and Warner, p. 326; in Scull, pp. 25–26.

42 Ibid., in Jehlen and Warner; in Scull, p. 26.

43 Ibid., in Jehlen and Warner, pp. 326–27; in Scull, pp. 26–27.

44 I have rephrased MacLaren's argument, which reads, in the original: "If the travels involved adventure, the survival of them will exert its influence on the presentation of events in so far as the past tense will indicate the traveler's arrival at the planned destination" ("Exploration/Travel Literature," p. 42).

45 Warkentin, "Discovering Radisson," pp. 50, 49; "Pierre-Esprit Radisson and the Language of Place," pp. 311, 308.

46 Radisson, in Jehlen and Warner, *English Literatures of America*, p. 327; in Scull, *Voyages*, p. 28.

47 Vincent Crapanzano, *Hermes' Dilemma and Hamlet's Desire: On the Epistemology of Interpretation* (Cambridge, MA, and London: Harvard University Press, 1992), pp. 32, 28.

48 Ibid., p. 28.

49 Radisson, in Jehlen and Warner, *English Literatures of America*, pp. 327–28; in Scull, *Voyages*, pp. 28–29.

50 I obviously borrow this term from Mary Louise Pratt, *Imperial Eyes: Travel Writing and Transculturation* (London and New York: Routledge, 1992), pp. 6–7.

51 Crapanzano, *Hermes' Dilemma*, p. 30.

52 Radisson, in Jehlen and Warner, *English Literatures of America*, p. 339; in Scull, *Voyages*, pp. 52–53.

53 Ibid., in Jehlen and Warner, pp. 328, 329, 330; in Scull, pp. 30, 32, 34.

54 Ibid., in Jehlen and Warner, p. 330; in Scull, p. 34.

55 Crapanzano, *Hermes' Dilemma*, p. 79.

56 Georges Gusdorf, "Conditions and Limits of Autobiography," trans. James Olney, in *Autobiography: Essays Theoretical and Critical*, ed. James Olney (Princeton: Princeton University Press, 1980), pp. 29, 41.

57 On the figure of the "white Indian," see James Axtell, "The White Indians of Colonial America," *William and Mary Quarterly* 32, no. 1 (January 1975): 55–88.

58 Crapanzano, *Hermes' Dilemma*, p. 89.

59 Radisson, in Jehlen and Warner, *English Literatures of America*, p. 343; in Scull, *Voyages*, p. 62.

60 Ibid., in Scull, p. 65.

61 Ibid., in Jehlen and Warner, *English Literatures of America*, pp. 345–46; in Scull, p. 79.

62 Ibid., in Jehlen and Warner, pp. 347–48; in Scull, pp. 83–84.

Re-Reading the Past

Cabeza de Vaca in History, Fiction, and Film

RICHARD A. YOUNG

I n 1513, six years before Cortés entered Mexico, a small group
of Europeans led by Juan Ponce de León reached the Florida
Peninsula. Ponce de León returned there in 1521 and was
followed during the next twenty years by several larger expeditions,
all of which, like his, came and left. Pánfilo de Narváez landed with
four hundred men and eighty horses on the Florida Peninsula in
April 1528. A little over ten years later, Hernando de Soto, with one
thousand men and 350 horses, reached the same area and trekked
into what is today Alabama, Mississippi, and Tennessee, crossing the
Mississippi River into Arkansas and Oklahoma. To the west,
expeditions sailed up the Gulf of California to the mouth of the
Colorado River. The Grand Canyon was sighted and, in the spring
of 1541, Francisco Vázquez de Coronado, travelling overland through
Mexico, crossed Texas into Kansas.

All of these expeditions generated detailed information about
the physical and human geography of the American continent north
of Mexico. Nonetheless, they were also thought to be failures, not
just because of the loss of life and equipment to an inhospitable
environment and hostile inhabitants, but because no immediate
wealth was discovered and no permanent settlements were founded.

The indigenous peoples they contacted were either nomadic or lived in small sedentary communities which could not compare with the great cities found first in central Mexico and later in Peru, and therefore fell far below the expectations of the explorers. The records of these journeys tell their stories.[1]

None is more eloquent on the highs and lows of conquest and exploration than the account of Alvar Núñez Cabeza de Vaca, one of only four survivors who returned to tell what had happened to the 1528 expedition led by Narváez. Lurching from one disaster to another, the remnants of the expedition finally foundered seven months later on the Texas coast in Galveston Bay, where they were at the mercy of the indigenous inhabitants. For the next six years, partly as captive, partly as another gatherer among them, following the food supply with the changing seasons and struggling to survive, Cabeza de Vaca lived among the people into whose presence the sea had literally cast him. Then, with three companions, two Europeans and an African, he embarked on a trek that would take two years. The group walked first northwest across the remaining width of the continent to within a hundred miles of the Pacific coast before turning south and eventually meeting a party of Spanish marauders near Culiacán in Mexico. Cabeza de Vaca spoke of Christianity as he travelled and practised healing among the people he met. But when he was back among his own kind once more, although he had no real tales of wealth and conquest, the rumours of great cities thought to lie to the north of the region he had crossed were fuel enough to ignite the hopes of later expeditions.

The first version of Cabeza de Vaca's experiences was part of a joint account given to the colonial authorities in Santo Domingo in 1537 by the three European survivors. The voice of their African companion is notably silent, or silenced. No original copy of this text has survived, save in a summary included by Gonzalo Fernández de Oviedo y Valdés in his longer history of the Americas.[2] Cabeza de Vaca's own version of his story first appeared separately in a book printed in Zamora (Spain) in 1542. Then, in 1555, two years before his death, he published a slightly corrected edition in a volume that also included an account of his misadventures in Paraguay, as governor of the River Plate province of South America. The story of his journey across the North American continent, generally known as *Los naufragios* [The shipwrecks], as it has come to be called since the 1555 edition, has circulated very widely, has been translated, and remains in print in numerous editions in Spanish.[3] In the last fifteen years or so, stimulated by postcolonial readings of historical texts, postmodern recreations of the past, and the 1992 anniversary of first contact between Europe and the Americas, it has attracted considerable attention and commentary.[4]

For most of its history Cabeza de Vaca's text has been read quite literally, a reflection of reading practices which tended to accept the hegemonic point of view of an imperial culture and which were endorsed by vestigial memories of his presence in the parts of North America he crossed. Well into the seventeenth century, a hundred years after he left, he was still remembered and revered as an evangelist and healer whose peaceful demeanour towards indigenous people contrasted with harsher treatment from the colonial authorities and Spanish soldiers.[5] More recently, accepting the literal truth of *Los naufragios*, he has been recognized as the founder of modern surgery in Texas.[6] Like other conquistadors and expeditionaries, Cabeza de Vaca would also argue that service to the crown was grounds for preferment and reward, and the account of his ordeal was part of representations which eventually earned him the governorship of the River Plate.[7] The credibility attached at the time to his story derives in part from his status as an eyewitness and officer in the Narváez expedition. Another contributing factor was the quasi-judicial nature of a narrative which originated in the joint report he and his companions delivered before the colonial courts in Santo Domingo. The first published editions were each called a *relación*[8] (the title customarily given to such legal declarations); not until later editions, after it had served a plaintiff's purpose, did his text become known as *Los naufragios*. Yet, however self-serving Cabeza de Vaca's text may have been, it clearly differed from other writings of the time of the conquest, not just because of the uniqueness of his experiences, but because of his criticism of aspects of the Spanish imperial project.

The more Cabeza de Vaca became involved in evangelization and healing, the more critical he became of the plunder and enslavement practised by the Spanish. Consider, for example, the following extract from his narrative in which Cabeza de Vaca refers to conflicts he had with the Spanish, whom he refers to as Christians:

> ... we had many and bitter quarrels with the Christians, for they wanted to make slaves of our Indians, and we grew so angry at it that at our departure we forgot to take along many bows, pouches and arrows, also the five emeralds, and so they were left and lost to us. We gave the Christians a great many cow skin robes, and other objects, and had much trouble in persuading the Indians to return home and plant their crops in peace. They insisted upon accompanying us until, according to their custom, we should be in the custody of other Indians, because otherwise they were afraid to die; besides, as long as we were with them, they had no fear of the Christians and their lances. At all this the Christians were greatly vexed, and told their interpreters to say to the Indians how we were of their own race, but had gone astray for a long while, and were people of no luck and little heart, whereas they were the lords of the land, whom they should obey and serve.
> (pp. 139–40)

The conflict between his stance and the conduct of the invaders is increasingly apparent in the last pages of the narrative. There, in addition to his return journey to Spain, Cabeza de Vaca also describes how the negative reputation of the Spanish preceded them and was already felt among the indigenous peoples he encountered in northern Mexico, who had had as yet no other direct contact with the conquerors. Cabeza de Vaca's critical stance enhanced the credibility of his account among later readers, who were focused on the conduct of colonization and aware of the so-called black legend, as the negative consequences of the Spanish conquest and colonization came to be known. This stance was one of the characteristics noted by Beatriz Pastor in a 1983 book examining the ideological trajectory underlying the Spanish discourse of discovery and conquest. In this context, Cabeza de Vaca's narrative is considered to be a discourse of failure, in contrast to the hopeful discourse of Christopher Columbus's diary and the triumphalism of the letters of Cortés. His experiences are seen as cathartic, those of a man who came to colonize but who found himself instead naked among the people he sought to conquer and from the experience learned a lesson quite different from what he had expected.[9]

This narrative of failure, as Pastor has called it, is cast as a Christian journey from darkness and ignorance to enlightenment and self-knowledge. In this respect, a narrative model for Cabeza de Vaca's account might be found in Dante's *Divine Comedy* of the early fourteenth century. As the sixteenth and seventeenth centuries progressed, images of shipwrecks and the castaway would also become topoi for the sense of disillusion and corruption which was the reverse of the more triumphalist vision of the imperial project. From them would also emerge a recycled idealization of the simple life as an antidote to the ills of civilization.[10] Yet others have argued that Cabeza de Vaca's account need not necessarily be read solely as a representation of imperial failure. Pastor emphasized the collapse of the expedition's military objectives and the reduction of Cabeza de Vaca to the condition of the inhabitants among whom he was marooned. Other readers have, in contrast, drawn attention to the dual nature of the Spanish enterprise and the importance of conversion to Christianity and cultural assimilation as the corollaries of subjugation by conquest. In a later analysis by Enrique Pupo-Walker (1987), Cabeza de Vaca's account of his evangelizing and healing is compared with medieval and Renaissance hagiography; his wanderings are seen in relation to pilgrimage narratives and biographies of the saints.[11] When considered from this angle, his representation of the Spanish enterprise acquires a more positive tone and aspects of his narrative will stand comparison with the early histories of the religious orders in the Americas, which, in their way, are as triumphalist as the histories of conquest.

However Cabeza de Vaca's account is read—whether as a quasi-legal declaration or as a vehicle for self-promotion, as an account of self-discovery, an indictment of the conquest, or as promotion of peaceful conversion—his writing was evidently shaped by narrative models in circulation at the time, just as it also consolidated the vision of America and its peoples that had begun to coalesce in Europe immediately after the return of Columbus. This condition, understood in a context where all writing is perceived to be a subjective textualization of experience, regardless of whether it is taken to represent historical or fictional events, is among the principal criteria influencing postcolonial readings of *Los naufragios*. It underlies the essays mentioned and is especially relevant to a commentary on the relation between history and fiction in Cabeza de Vaca undertaken by Robert E. Lewis in 1982. The latter takes positions elaborated by Hayden White as its point of departure, while also noting the degree to which scholarship on Cabeza de Vaca's narrative has traditionally noted the literary qualities of his writing.[12] Yet however much these kinds of readings illuminate why Cabeza de Vaca wrote as he did and how he codified the subjects of his narrative, they do not in the end bring us any closer to those subjects, but tend to make them still more elusive. This is especially so with respect to the people and cultures he wrote about. These have long since disappeared and, at the time that he wrote about them, they had no other spokesperson who could introduce them to the European imaginary or worldview on the basis of so intimate an acquaintance. The point is especially significant in light of two relatively recent attempts to re-create Cabeza de Vaca's experience through fiction and film in ways that focus not so much on the narrative models within which he framed his discourse, as on the ideological constraints that inhibited his ability to express himself freely and openly.

In 1992, the Argentinean writer Abel Posse published *El largo atardecer del caminante* [The long twilight of the wanderer],[13] a novel based on the life of Cabeza de Vaca which was awarded first prize in the Extremadura-America 92 literary competition organized by the Spanish Commission for the Quincentenary. Posse's novel is a fictional account of Cabeza de Vaca's last days and includes a retelling of parts of the narrative produced some 450 years earlier. As in the earlier work, Cabeza de Vaca is also the narrator of his own story, and the text of Posse's novel is presumed to be the product of Cabeza de Vaca's own hand. Thus, in 1557, just a few months or so before his death, now an old man living in Seville, still clinging to his reputation as a peaceful conquistador, he is persuaded to write about his present situation as well as his past. While doing so, Cabeza de Vaca is led to reveal more about his experiences in North America than he had in earlier writings.

The year 1557 coincides with a period in his life when Cabeza de Vaca had, in fact, recently published a revised edition of *Los naufragios* along with a commentary on his experiences in Paraguay, which also figure in Posse's novel. Moreover, there is evidence to suggest that the historical Cabeza de Vaca was conscious of his historical role as a writer and that he may well have produced versions of his experiences that were not destined to see the light of publication.[14] Posse's approach to history and his fictional re-creation of Cabeza de Vaca's confrontation with his life not only take these elements into account, but are evidently circumscribed by the climate of the quincentenary and the focus given at that time to a reassessment of the conquest and its legacy.[15] But, just as Cabeza de Vaca drew upon the narrative models available to him in mid-sixteenth-century Spain, Posse was no less constrained to cast his narrative within the framework of late twentieth-century writing and to use the literary models with which he was familiar and had, indeed, exploited in other contexts.[16]

The so-called new historical novel has been one of the predominant forms of Latin American fiction of the last two decades. It differs from older forms of fictionalized history based primarily on the formula derived from Sir Walter Scott through frequent use of a meta-discourse which questions the validity of traditional beliefs about the past and casts doubts on the value of historical discourse as an authoritative source of representation. For example, the central part of the 1979 novel *El arpa y la sombra* [The harp and the shadow] by the Cuban Alejo Carpentier is a rewriting of the Columbus legend and the diary of the first voyage.[17] Here, while lying on his deathbed and waiting for the friar who will hear his last confession, Columbus rehearses what he will say. This gives his discourse a potentially greater degree of self-revelation than his diaries and letters because

Columbus is no longer addressing the Catholic majesties in Spain, but his maker, who already knows all and is not to be deceived. A similar deconstruction of Simón Bolívar, the hero of the Wars of Independence, is the subject of Gabriel García Márquez's 1989 novel *El general en su laberinto* [The general in his labyrinth]. This work describes (although not from a first-person perspective) the last days of General Bolívar during a journey along the Magdalena River towards Santa Marta in Colombia and offers a retrospective look at his life that considerably diminishes his heroic stature.[18]

Posse's story of a hero afflicted with a last-minute bout of honesty has a familiar sound when compared with other new historical novels in which fiction has served to examine the truth of historical traditions.[19] His approach differs, therefore, from that of writers like Pastor or Pupo-Walker, who found that Cabeza de Vaca represented himself and his experiences in accordance with the discursive models he knew and followed, but they did not suggest he was untruthful. Posse's novel is more akin to the conclusions drawn by Juan Francisco Maura, who has argued in "Veracidad en *Los naufragios*: la técnica narrativa de Alvar Núñez Cabeza de Vaca" that Cabeza de Vaca's account of his experiences in North America is considerably more unreliable than had hitherto been thought.

Given that Posse's *El largo atardecer del caminante* is a work of fiction, it could hardly demonstrate the unreliability of *Los naufragios* by offering in its place a historically more acceptable version of Cabeza de Vaca's experiences.[20] However, by virtue of its status as fiction, it nonetheless invites us to entertain the hypothesis that the historical Cabeza de Vaca knew more than he told and felt obliged by the prevailing ideology of his time to exercise a degree of self-censorship. Thus, the fictional Cabeza de Vaca sheds a light different from that cast by his historical counterpart in *Los naufragios* and confesses not so much to having written untruths about his eight years in America as to having omitted the whole truth. The historical text provides details about the customs and lifestyle of the people, but does not account fully for the six years spent living among those people before beginning the long trek which ended in Culiacán. Above all, it is notoriously silent on the degree to which Cabeza de Vaca might have assimilated their way of life and lived as one of them.

The novel fills these gaps. The fictional Cabeza de Vaca not only describes his understanding and appreciation of the worldview and cultural practices of the people among whom he lived, but also gives an extended account of his relationship with an indigenous woman, with whom he had two children. Moreover, he narrates that when he practised healing as he walked across the continent, he not so much invoked the name of Christ or the Christian God (as described in *Los naufragios*) as applied the shamanistic knowledge he had acquired from living in that region. In the last pages of the novel, Cabeza de Vaca re-encounters his son, who had been captured by slavers and transported to Europe. He obtains his son's release, but is unable to save his life—events which bring a kind of closure to Cabeza de Vaca's existence, at the same time as they symbolically represent consequences of the conquest of America.

From the several occasions in the novel when Cabeza de Vaca refers to *Los naufragios* and explains why he had previously written as he had, it is possible to perceive the conditions that circumscribed his writing and determined what he could say about himself, about the indigenous people among whom he was living, and the degree to which he assimilated their way of life. When, for example, he refers to the ritual that required every man to make a blanket of marten skins when he married, he notes parenthetically that he changed the account of how he came by his blanket:

> (When the other castaways, living among other tribes, became aware of my concubinage, they sent me a blanket made of marten skins, undoubtedly making fun of me, since I had always been critical of such things. I record the incident of the blanket of skins in my book *Los naufragios* and I lie, of course, when I say that they had presented it to me 'on learning I was sick'.) (pp. 96–97)[21]

Cabeza de Vaca comments similarly on having glossed over the six years spent among an indigenous community:

> I had spent almost six years in the new world of a simple plains tribe. Years that ran like seawater through my fingers. (I didn't lie too much in my

Naufragios when I reduced it all to a couple of pages.
How is it possible to understand the contents of a
world that is not understood? Either it is despised or
it is understood and neither of these conditions had
yet worked its effect on me.) (pp. 139–40)

To have said otherwise or to have said more, would, of course, have
placed him in jeopardy, as he comments when describing how he
learned to be a medicine man: "In *Los naufragios* I narrated my
initiation as a witch or medicine man. I did so in a very oblique or
evasive manner in order not to fuel the ever ready fire of the
Inquisition" (p. 107).

Comments such as these cast doubt not just on the particular
incidents and conditions to which they refer, but, by extension,
on everything that Cabeza de Vaca ever wrote. They invite the
supposition that underlying *Los naufragios* are untold omissions and
transformations which irrevocably distance the reader both from the
experiences of the writer and from the peoples of America among
whom he lived. Moreover, it is suggested that the entire historiography
of the conquest and colonization period is similarly affected. The
threat of punishment by the Inquisition is not only represented as
real enough, but is the sanction by which ideological conformity and
an understanding of the New World according to a predetermined
epistemology are ensured. The point is made very early in the novel,
in the context of Cabeza de Vaca's account of a visit paid to him in
Seville by the celebrated historian Gonzalo Fernández de Oviedo.
Historically, their paths had likely crossed years earlier, since Oviedo
had been in the Caribbean in 1537 at the time that Cabeza de Vaca gave
the first account of his captivity and journey to the colonial authorities
in Santo Domingo before returning to Spain. By now, however,
Oviedo is an old man who has become the very embodiment of
history: "It is evident that Don Gonzalo Fernández de Oviedo is
convinced that the Conquest and the Discovery exist only to the
extent that he was able to retrieve, organize, and narrate the events. He
is the proprietor of what we now customarily call 'History.' What
he does not record in his narrative gossip either does not exist or is
false ..." (p. 30).[22] Cabeza de Vaca's characterization of Oviedo also
implicitly draws attention to the constructedness of history, a point

on which he dwells further when reflecting on the transience of all things and the survival of the past only through its textualization:

> Oviedo, who writes fourteen hours a day, will be the conquistador of the conquistadors, the depository of truth, the corral of deeds and persons. He will do much more with the pen than we really did with the sword. Curious fate. But Jehovah himself would not be Jehovah if the Jews had not enclosed him in a book.

> For better or worse, the only reality that survives is that of written history. The King himself ends up believing what the historian says instead of what he is told by the one who conquered the world by his sword.

> Everything ends up in a book or in oblivion. (p. 33)

It is to circumvent this latter fate that the Cabeza de Vaca of Posse's novel has written this newest version of his experiences. He eventually hides it—like a message in a bottle cast into the sea—among the books in the library in Seville where he has been working in the hope of avoiding, as he writes in the last sentence of his manuscript, oblivion, "the worst of all shipwrecks" (p. 262).[23]

This is not to say, of course, that the newest version of Cabeza de Vaca's experiences is not, in its way, any less constructed than the earlier versions, although it pretends to be factually more complete. The notion that underlying any version of a story there is another version of the same story runs through the entire novel. This is especially evident in moments when Cabeza de Vaca offers a critique of the discovery. He views it as an extension of the Spanish worldview to new lands and peoples which merely exposes the ills and brutality of Spain's own ideology and conduct: "We have discovered nothing in the Indies. What we have discovered is Spain" (p. 163), he notes at the beginning of one paragraph on the ideology of conquest. Nothing was discovered, he writes later, because Spain's intention was not to discover, but to conquer and rule: "We did not set out to discover, which is to know, but to refuse to know" (p. 214).[24] Yet even the wily old Oviedo is astute enough to realize that there is more to history than what is told and that official versions in particular often cover more than they reveal. On their first meeting in 1537, Cabeza de Vaca sensed that Oviedo was less interested in his narrative of events than in what was omitted from it (p. 29). Oviedo's visit, thirty years later in Seville, was prompted by rumours that Cabeza de Vaca had another, secret version of his story (p. 30).

The sense of 'otherness' that the existence of another version evokes is precisely what Spain denied by legislating in favour of its own epistemology. This, for the most part, is the central motif of Posse's novel, where the idea of another version is not merely a new configuration of old facts or the revelation of new ones, but a new worldview, a different version of the conquest and the conquered. This sense of otherness is also captured in the novel at moments when Cabeza de Vaca expresses his awareness of other versions of himself or is conscious of the degree to which he has become an 'other,' an alien within his own culture. On one occasion, sorting through his wardrobe, his old clothes serve to remind him of the different existences he has led:

> Why can't we slough off these solemn and prestigious
> corpses? It isn't easy to escape their tyranny. They are
> the only visible corpses of our successive deaths. The
> body is adept and tends to hide its deaths. Only the
> suits of clothes remain, lamely proclaiming their
> nonentity, like the sheaths of those Sinaloan snakes,
> dried out skins losing their colours in the burning
> desert. Successive versions of ourselves that die on us
> along the way. (p. 24)

On another occasion, prompted by Oviedo, Cabeza de Vaca refers to himself as belonging to neither of the two racial groups that confronted each other in the new empire:

> "I must confess that what most convinced me in your
> story is when you speak of three different categories:
> you speak of Christians, of Indians, and of a
> mysterious us. Who is this mysterious us?"

"You've caught me by surprise. I'm at odds to explain it…. It's as if I had written it without working it out properly. Perhaps I wanted to refer to those of us who can no longer be either Indians or Christians…." (p. 32)

In his article on Posse's novel, Seymour Menton has read Cabeza de Vaca's reply to Oviedo as a reference to himself as a cultural mestizo.[25] There is something, perhaps, to Menton's suggestion, but Cabeza de Vaca's condition is not quite that of an individual who combines two races in his being and is a pariah to both. He is afflicted by a series of contradictions that are impossible to resolve, consequences of his belonging to one culture while having experienced another and being unable to speak of it. He embodies the sense of the 'other' which the Spanish refuse to admit and which he cannot publicly acknowledge. Thus, the new version of his life in America will remain secret and the one circulating publicly is still the one that has been officially endorsed. In Spain, Cabeza de Vaca is appointed to the tribunal of the Inquisition, a body which would condemn as heresy the very life he had led in America; although he had experienced the worldview of the indigenous people of America as an alternative to European civilization, he is unable to proclaim its validity.

This is all fiction, of course, but it does have some implications for historiography. Like many postmodern works of fiction, especially the Spanish American new historical novel, Posse's *El largo atardecer del caminant* is about writing; it reveals the textual construction of the "real" at the same time as it constructs an alternative version of reality. As such, his creative response to *Los naufragios* serves an end similar to that pursued by academic enquiries in search of the sixteenth-century narrative models adopted by the historical Cabeza de Vaca, for it also shows why he wrote in the way that he did and why, in effect, he had little alternative. For these reasons, Posse's novel also has much in common with Nicholas Echeverría's *Cabeza de Vaca*, a 1990 Spanish-Mexican film version of the conquistador-turned-wanderer's experiences which adopts an equally creative approach to the examination of these questions.

Strictly speaking, the film is not an adaptation of *Los naufragios*. It makes no pretense about fidelity to the sixteenth-century text; the opening credits include the statement that it was "inspired by the book by Cabeza de Vaca." The director is highly selective in his choice of incidents. He introduces new ones, and those taken from the book are developed in entirely new directions. The viewer of the film who is familiar with the book will recognize the differences between the two, but the question of narrative constructions of experience, although clearly evident, is not addressed as directly or in as great a length in the film as in Posse's novel. The events represented in the film are conveyed retrospectively. Its opening sequences show Cabeza de Vaca after he has ended his trek, once he and his companions have encountered their compatriots and entered territory already under the control of the Spanish. As he reflects on his eight lost years, there is a flashback to their beginning, showing the shipwreck and collapse of the Narváez expedition, from which the story then unfolds, and we are in due course returned to the present from which the film began. But Cabeza de Vaca is not the narrator. The camera now and again adopts the point of view of a character, but the story is seen for the most part through an eye external to it. The meta-discursive elements of the film—the degree to which it includes a commentary on the very story it is telling—are contained in the speech and conduct of the characters.

Towards the end of the film, Cabeza de Vaca and his two companions come across a burned-out settlement showing evident signs of having been recently attacked. When he ministers to a dying man and extracts a musket ball from his wound, they all become aware of the proximity of the Spanish. However, delighted as they are at reaching the end of their journey, the more immediate concern of Cabeza de Vaca's fellow travellers, Andrés Dorantes and Alonso del Castillo Maldonado, is for the story they will tell the authorities. Fearful lest their life among the native people be subjected to too close a scrutiny or that they be considered mad and returned to Spain in chains, his companions realize that they must say nothing about having adopted the customs of the people among whom they lived and practised native medicine. In the end, enhancing rumours they have picked up on their travels and pandering to the expectations of their listeners, they weave an embroidered tale of great cities and magical kingdoms appropriate to the age of Cortés and Pizarro, in which America was the home of the fabulous. Around the campfire at night, Dorantes, in particular, captures the imagination of the Spanish soldiery with tales of women with three breasts, of ointments that gave him great sexual power, and of cities of gold that gleamed in the sunlight.

The viewer of the film is aware, of course, that these stories are a fabrication, simply by comparing them to what the film has represented. For the viewer, the truth of the film does not lie in the soldiers' dreams of wealth but in the story of contact in an unknown world between a few Europeans and an unknown culture. Yet the reality constructed by Dorantes, and perhaps even by Cabeza de Vaca himself when he eventually published his story as *Los naufragios*, is in many ways more plausible to their contemporaries because it corresponds to a prevailing worldview. Given this context, looking back from the end of the film to the events narrated earlier, it is clear why Cabeza de Vaca and his companions are anxious to avoid too close an examination of the previous eight years, for the film is essentially a story of how they adopted the culture of the people who had held them captive. As in Posse's *El largo atardecer del caminante*, it is the "secret" version of Cabeza de Vaca's exploits that are told. The film does not show Cabeza de Vaca living with a wife and children, as does the novel, but, in common with Posse's text, does show his having learned the shaman's art from his captor, who also introduced him via hallucinogens into the mystic world of his tribe. The bond formed between Cabeza de Vaca and his captor is, in fact, stronger than any cords that bind him or bars that contain him: he is free to wander without restraint, but is held in check by the shaman's power.

On one occasion, Cabeza de Vaca attempts to escape, taking advantage of his captor's apparent lack of vigilance. But his disappearance has been noted; his escape is thwarted. The shaman knots a cord around the neck of a lizard and ties the other end of the cord to a stake in the ground. Images of the lizard, struggling to get free, but helplessly running in circles around the stake, are alternated with views of Cabeza de Vaca running over the waterlogged terrain, buffeted by low branches, and falling down—as if re-enacting the treatment of the lizard by the shaman—eventually to collapse on the ground by his captor. Like the lizard, he has run in circles, all escape frustrated by the link that ties him to the shaman. *Los naufragios* contains no such incident that clearly demonstrates how Cabeza de

Vaca is made part of the world into which he has been cast. When he finally ends his captivity, it is not because he escapes, but, as in Posse's novel, because his native mentor gives him the knowledge to survive and eventually sends him out to practise it. Yet even then, through the transformation of an incident that is indeed described in *Los naufragios*, the film shows that the bond has not been broken.

In *Los naufragios*, Cabeza de Vaca narrates an occasion during his captivity when he was separated from the group of native people with whom he had been foraging for fruit. He describes the incident as follows:

> As soon as we were settled we went out to hunt for
> the fruit of certain trees, which are like spring
> bittervetch (orobus), and as through all that country
> there are no trails, I lost too much time in hunting for
> them. The people returned without me, and starting
> to rejoin them that night I went astray and got lost. It
> pleased God to let me find a burning tree, by the fire
> of which I spent that very cold night, and in the
> morning loaded myself with wood, took two burning
> sticks and continued my journey. Thus I went on for
> five days, always with my firebrands and load of
> wood, so that in case the fire went out where there
> was no timber, as in many parts there is none, I
> always would have wherewith to make other torches
> and not be without firewood. It was my only
> protection against the cold, for I went as naked as a
> newborn child. (pp. 84–85)

The episode is described in the rather laconic style characteristic of *Los naufragios* in general without any accounting for the burning tree. For some readers, however, the incident is strongly reminiscent of the Bible and the encounter of Moses with the burning bush from which he heard the voice of God.[26] Thus, for Cabeza de Vaca, the flames are sent from above and are a symbol of his Christian faith and the presence of God in a hostile land among primitive people. As such, it is one among other allusions and affirmations by Cabeza de Vaca of his fidelity to his beliefs and of the distance he claimed to have maintained with respect to indigenous life and culture. By contrast, in the film *Cabeza de Vaca*, the episode is reconstructed as a demonstration of the degree to which he continued to be subject to the practices of native culture, even after his mentor had sent him on his way.

In the film, Cabeza de Vaca is alone and lost at night, as in *Los naufragios*, and fearful that he will die of cold. However, the burning tree by which he warms himself is sent by a source different from the one recorded in his narrative. Using the same technique as in the episode with the lizard, images of Cabeza de Vaca alternate with those of his mentor blowing on a burning ember, which catches fire at the same moment that the tree bursts into flames. Thus, in this new land in which Cabeza de Vaca finds himself, it is not the God of Moses who comes to his aid, but the mystic power of his native mentor. Similarly, as he later makes his way across the land, the medicine he practises is partly indebted to European know-how, but it depends largely on what he had learned in America and is more akin to the practices of American shamanism than Christian faith. In comparison with how it is told in *Los naufragios*, the episode in which Cabeza de Vaca restores a dead person to life is significantly changed in the film: the funereal rites are elaborated much more; the dead person is a young woman rather than a man; and the body language and speech of Cabeza de Vaca are ostensibly more those of the culture to which he has assimilated than those of the culture from which he came. Small wonder that, once returned to a Spanish domain and required to give an account of their journey and their time in captivity to authorities decidedly intolerant of any deviation from orthodoxy and likely to react to even the slightest odour of witchcraft, Cabeza de Vaca and his companions chose to accommodate their narrative to a model to which they knew their listeners would be receptive rather than risk being more open about the character of their conduct.

The movie critic of the *Los Angeles Times* (cited on the jacket of the English video edition of the film) described *Cabeza de Vaca* as "A more mystical and less sentimental *Dances with Wolves*." This comment, interestingly enough, also reveals an inability to describe 'the other' except in terms of 'the self'—but the film does lapse in some moments into Hollywood cliché. It, too, resorts to familiar narrative models, not the least of which is derived from a new-age interest in native cultures and their supposed ability to live in harmony with their natural environment. In this regard, the film *Cabeza de Vaca* confirms the difficulties that circumscribe any epistemology and the difficulty of obtaining knowledge of one culture when it is mediated by another. But it is not just that. What the film, the novel, and, to some extent, the academic analyses all affirm is that we cannot be confident of the content of a book like Cabeza de Vaca's *Los naufragios* because we cannot be certain of its writer. The jacket of the English video edition of the film, with a generous touch of commercial hype, describes it as "The true and amazing adventure of the legendary Spanish explorer that will dazzle your mind and move your soul." In the end, notwithstanding the discrepancies between Cabeza de Vaca's text and the film, the latter is perhaps as true, or maybe truer in a certain way, than any of the other versions, including his own, given that even his original work may be understood to be not so much as his experiences as he lived them, but his experiences as he constructed them in narrative form and chose to have them remembered.

Although belonging to two different periods of history, the three texts examined in this essay nevertheless require us to confront similar problems with respect to how we view contacts made with other cultures and how we endeavour to make contact with the past. For all three sources of the narratives of first contacts between Europeans and Americans in the present-day southern states of the United States—Alvar Núñez Cabeza de Vaca the explorer, Abel Posse the novelist, and Nicolás Echeverría the film director—the events narrated have suffered the fate of all events and are irretrievably lost. This condition leaves us in a state of uncertainty, knowing that any representation of the past is dependent on a reconstruction undertaken on the basis of memory and prevailing epistemology. Even for Cabeza de Vaca himself, the representation of his experiences must contend with whatever tricks his memory plays, on willful omissions, and on the inevitable consequence of writing within the frame of the world view he shared with his contemporaries. For later reconstructions of events, that is, for Posse and Echeverría, we must not only contend with how the tale was originally told, but with who told it: the figure of Cabeza de Vaca, who has also long since disappeared, but whose image remains as an icon of the past. Moreover, from the time between the original narrated events and our present, a tradition of interpretation has accrued, some of which may be compatible with our worldview, some of which may not. Under the circumstances, perhaps the best that we can aim for in any attempt to make contact with the past is a sense of what we perceive to be true. Not veracity, but verisimilitude, a feeling that what we are told sounds right—remembering, of course, that what sounded right for Cabeza de Vaca and his contemporaries hardly does so now, just as what sounded right for the conquerors invariably seemed less so for the conquered.[27]

NOTES

1 For a brief account of contacts with the region by Juan Ponce de León, see Charlton W. Tebeau, *A History of Florida* (Coral Gables: University of Miami Press, 1971), pp. 19–22. For early histories and chronicles of the de Soto and Coronado expeditions, see *The Florida of the Inca*, ed. and trans. John Grier Varner and Jeannette Johnson Varner (Austin: University of Texas Press, 1951); and George Parker Winship, *The Coronado Expedition 1540–1542* (Chicago: Río Grande Press, 1964).

2 Gonzalo Fernández de Oviedo y Valdés, *Historia general y natural de las Indias: islas y Tierra-Firme del Mar Océano*, Biblioteca de Autores Españoles, vol. 4, no. 120, edited and introduced by Juan Pérez de Tudela Bueso (Madrid: Ediciones Atlas, 1959), pp. 287–318.

3 The two early editions of Cabeza de Vaca's narrative are, respectively: *La relación de lo acaescido en las Indias en la armada donde yva por gobernador Panphilo de Narváez desde el año de veynte y siete hasta el año de treynta y seys* [Relation of what happened in the Indies to the armada of the Governor Pánfilo de Narváez from the year 26 to the year 36] (Zamora: 1542), and *La relación y comentarios del gobernador Alvar Núñez Cabeza de Vaca de lo acaescido en las dos jornadas que hizo a las Indias* [Relation and commentaries by the Governor Alvar Núñez Cabeza de Vaca of what happened during the two journeys he made to the Indies] (Valladolid: 1555). The edition cited in this chapter is *The Narrative of Alvar Núñez Cabeza de Vaca*, translated by Fanny Bandelier and introduced by John Francis Bannon (Barre, MA: Imprint Society, 1972). It includes a translation of Oviedo's summary of the joint report.

4 See Margo Glantz, ed., *Notas y comentarios sobre Alvar Núñez Cabeza de Vaca* (México: Grijalbo, 1993). A total of seventeen essays, first published between 1962 and 1992, are reprinted in this volume covering many of the issues prompted by readings of Cabeza de Vaca's text.

5 On Cabeza de Vaca's early reputation, see Jacques Lafaye, "Les miracles d'Alvar Núñez Cabeza de Vaca (1527–1536)," *Bulletin Hispanique* 64 (1962): 136–52.

6 See Juan Francisco Maura, "Veracidad en *Los naufragios*: la técnica narrativa de Alvar Núñez Cabeza de Vaca," *Revista Iberoamericana* 170–71 (January–June 1995): 192.

7 In the *proemio* (prologue) to the first two editions of *Los naufragios,* Cabeza de Vaca emphasizes his service to the crown. Robert E. Lewis pays particular attention to it in "*Los naufragios* de Alvar Núñez Cabeza de Vaca: historia y ficción," *Revista Iberoamericana* 48 (July–December 1982): 681–94.

8 See note 3 above.

9 See Beatriz Pastor, *Discurso narrativo de la conquista de América* (La Habana: Casa de las Américas, 1983), pp. 294–337.

10 The idea already appears in Dante, but among notable examples from the literature of imperial Spain are the elegiac poem "Vida retirada" of Luis de León (1527–91) and the *Soledades* of Luis de Góngora (1561–1627).

11 Enrique Pupo-Walker, "Pesquisas para una nueva lectura de *Los naufragios*, de Alvar Núñez Cabeza de Vaca," *Revista Iberoamericana* 53 (July–September 1987), pp. 517–39.

12 On Lewis, see note 7 above. The text by Hayden White cited by Lewis is "The Historical Text as Literary Artifact," in *Tropics of Discourse* (Baltimore: Johns Hopkins University Press, 1978), pp. 81–100.

13 Abel Posse, *El largo atardecer del caminante* [The long twilight of the wanderer] (Buenos Aires: Emecé Editores, 1992). All references are to this edition and in my translation.

14 See Pupo-Walker, "Pesquisas," pp. 537–38.

15 As an example of the kinds of scholarly reassessments undertaken at that time, see two anthologies of essays, both edited and introduced by René Jara and Nicholas Spadaccini: *1492–1992: Re/Discovering Colonial Writing* (Minneapolis: University of Minnesota Press, 1989) and *Amerindian Images and the Legacy of Columbus* (Minneapolis: University of Minnesota Press, 1992).

16 An earlier novel by Abel Posse, *Daimón* (Barcelona: Librería Editorial Argos, 1978), draws on accounts of the South American rebellion of Lope de Aguirre (1513?–16) against Philip II and the first voyage of the Spanish along the Amazon from Peru to the Atlantic.

17 Alejo Carpentier, *El arpa y la sombra* (Mexico: Siglo XXI, 1979); *The Harp and the Shadow,* trans. Thomas Christensen and Carol Christensen (San Francisco: Mercury House: 1990).

18 Gabriel García Márquez, *El general en su laberinto* (Madrid: Mondadori, 1989); *The General in his Labyrinth*, trans. Edith Grossman (New York: Alfred A. Knopf, 1990).

19 For further discussion of the new historical novel, see Seymour Menton, *Latin America's New Historical Novel* (Austin: University of Texas Press, 1993) and María Cristina Pons, *Memorias del olvido: la novela histórica de fines del siglo XX* (México: Siglo Veintiuno Editores, 1996). In the broader context, it should also be kept in mind that the new historical novel is part of debates that have emerged in relation to postmodernism and the so-called new history. See, for example, Linda Hutcheon's discussion of "historiographic metafiction" in *A Poetics of Postmodernism: History, Theory, Fiction* (New York: Routledge, 1988) and Keith Jenkins' introduction in Keith Jenkins, ed., *The Postmodern History Reader* (New York: Routledge, 1997).

20 In "La verdadera historia de Alvar Núñez Cabeza de Vaca en la última novela de Abel Posse, *El largo atardecer del caminante*" (*Revista Iberoamericana* 52 [April–June 1995]: 421–26), Seymour Menton examines this proposition, focusing specifically on the fictional dimensions of the novel and its engagement with history.

21 Parentheses are used repeatedly in the novel for this kind of meta-textual commentary.

22 For a general view of the life and work of Fernández de Oviedo, see Francisco Esteve Barba, *Historiografía indiana* (Madrid: Editorial Gredos, 1964), pp. 59–75.

23 The notion of narrative as a form of survival is interestingly developed in a novel by another Argentinean, Juan José Saer, titled *El entenado* (Buenos Aires: Folios Ediciones, 1983), which has several parallels with the Cabeza de Vaca story. It is an account of the experience of a young boy, written in old age. As the sole survivor of a Spanish landing party, the members of which were massacred and consumed in an act of ritual cannibalism by a South American tribe, the boy lives with the tribe for several years until he is released upon the arrival of a larger party of marauding Spaniards. After his return to Spain, he eventually realizes that he had been spared and sheltered solely that he might bear witness to the life and existence of the tribe, a role made more significant in light of the tribe's extinction due to conquest.

24 In the Spanish original—"No fuimos a descubrir, que es conocer; sino a desconocer"—the play between the two verbs *conocer* (to know) and *desconocer* (to ignore, or refuse to know) succinctly captures the epistemological inflexibility of the Spanish and the willfulness with which it was followed.

25 See note 20 above.

26 See Maura, "Veracidad en *Los naufragios*," p. 193.

27 A somewhat different version of this essay has appeared in Spanish under the title "Cabeza de Vaca en la literatura y el cine: lectura y representación de un relato histórico" in *Anclajes* (Santa Rosa, Argentina: Revista del Instituto de Análisis Semiótico del Discurso) 4, no. 4 (December 2000): 177–206.

Afterword

Making Contact: Maps of Identity

JONATHAN HART

aking Contact: Maps, Identity, and Travel challenges some of the categories that are by now so familiar: the Middle Ages and the early modern, Europe and its other, East and West, ethnic groups and nation, dominant and marginal cultures. The volume belongs to a body of recent work that helps to question presumptions about race, continentalism and ethnicity. In seeking to complicate historical interpretations and theories of culture, geography, history, ethnology and literature over more than five hundred years, from the thirteenth century well into the seventeenth, this book focuses on various ways of making contact. "Making" involves craft, construction, work, a goal while "contact" suggests a coming together, sometimes in peace, other times in friction. "Making contact" represents a significant event, a new network or relations and an impact between two sides that were independent or who might have wished to remain separate. The contact shakes up both sides and alters them, especially in the first instance, irrevocably.

Contact between now and then has its own benefits and problems. The past shifts, so that periodicity sometimes seems unstable and tentative while heuristic and suggestive. The division between the Middle Ages and the early modern period becomes complicated when in matters of space and time, identities and subjectivities, colonization and travel they are discussed together. The medieval and after share traces and continuities as well as differences. Literal mapping of the world and the use of many calendars in one location unsettle the maps of identity of people in the period under discussion. Mapping, then, as one would expect, has a more definite and "literal" meaning, such as the charts and maps that are the work of mapmakers, comprise cartography, and interest geographers, which are themselves representations and abstractions of a "concrete" world, but mapping also has an interpretative and metaphorical dimension that literary scholars have used in terms of reading, philosophers in terms of epistemology or possible world theory, and historians to discuss exploration or cause, effect and influence in ideas. This doubleness of the so-called literal and figurative allows for a richness as well as for some confusion. While this Afterword, and even more this volume, can be suggestive about this richness and complexity of "mapping" in the different aspects of making contact, they cannot be definitive in defining the concept of mapping.

Making contact raises issues about the vexed question of identity, which is often multiple and changes over time, a kind of mapping of time that historical interpretation often reads back on an earlier period late in the day or after the fact. The various ways of measuring or interpreting time affect discussions of these identities. It does not take a declaration of the "rights of man" during the French Revolution or the adumbration of the postmodern condition in the past two decades to raise questions of cultural identity and contact. These are ancient themes in the lives of persons and peoples. *Making Contact* explores the early tentativeness, fluidity, anxiety and destabilization of cultures. One of the main contributions of this collection, although it is just one part in a body of work that explores the lines of periodization, is to bring the Middle Ages and the early modern period together, to explore the shifting boundaries between them, the new perspectives each provides for the other.

Late in the fifteenth century, scholars described as the middle age (*medium aevum*) the period of western European history between the fall of Rome (fifth century AD) and the revival of classical learning and the flourishing of cities in the time in which the "humanists" were living. This term, which became known in English as the Middle Ages, shared much with the period after it, including, for instance, the central role of Christianity, the influence of classical antiquity, the revival of cities and the development of vernacular literatures. As is well-known, Jules Michelet's *Histoire de France* (1833–67; translated early on as *The History of France*, 1844–46) and Jacob Burckhardt's *Die Kultur der Renaissance in Italien* (1860; translated as *The Civilization of the Renaissance in Italy*, 1878) did a great deal to encourage the study of the "Renaissance." The "Renaissance," or the "early modern period," is something that travels from Italy to other countries and that, depending on the place in question, is often said to start in the late 1300s or early 1400s and end in the 1700s. On the Continent, the "Baroque", as a term, takes up much of what is generally taken in the English-speaking world to be the late Renaissance. There is also the question of the cultural contact in the late Middle Ages and early Renaissance with other places where the Europeans had seldom ventured or, as in the New World, had never visited. People in the Middle Ages did not construe themselves as betwixt and between antiquity and a still unheard of Renaissance. The early modern is a term that has as many limitations as the "Renaissance": the one looking too much forward to modernity in teleological fashion, the other to a pastoral or nostalgic revisiting of the classical past. It is an important reminder, especially for those of us who learned about high European culture, that the "Middle Ages" and the "Renaissance" (no matter how flawed these terms) involved much more than Europe in trade and cultural contact. Africa, Asia and the Americas were all part of these periods, even from a European point of view.

Possibly, while European trade along the silk road had been important in the Middle Ages and the Portuguese had already made their way down the coast of Africa, it was Columbus' landfall in a world new to Europeans that began the early modern period as it might be construed as a moment of recognition of something new. Whether this event would count as being important in a period that nineteenth-century scholars characterized as the Renaissance, as something reborn from the ancients, is questionable or, at least, even more intricate. Acosta's laughter at Aristotle's misguided notion of the Torrid Zone, as Anthony Grafton has noted, is momentous: yet this moment of something modern is a correction of the classical learning and not something upheld because it is traditional.[1] Whether Copernicus or Galileo defined a movement from the medieval to the early modern period or the Renaissance has been long debated. Even though the essays in *Making Contact* do not focus on periodization, they assume an overlap between the Middle Ages and the Renaissance at the beginning of the period and between the Renaissance and the Enlightenment at the end.[2] Few categories are seamless, so a medieval idea or practice can overlap with a humanist one during early modern period or Renaissance. The challenging of stereotypes in the period under study and in our own ways of seeing today is a key aspect of this volume.

Stereotyping the past is both a necessity and a danger. In interpreting culture and the texts that make and remake it, interpreters in the present, whether historians, literary scholars, ethnologists, theologians or others, must do what artists do—select and order. This choice creates a narrative shape, logic of explanation, clear argument or rhetorical take, often necessary options or ways into texts. The danger arises when interpreters are not restless about their understanding of the past, in terms of evidence from the earlier times and points of view or engagement in the present. The selection necessary for an interpretation of the past, or a collection of methods or hermeneutics that might comprise an interpretive 'school', can become a *doxa* or dominant ideology in a field. Even refreshing readings and schools can become a hardening repertoire of rules and moves. To stereotype the past, then, is to rest with a given interpretation rather than to see each vital interpretation or cluster of interpretations as an ongoing reconfiguration of a field, period, text, or of the past more generally. The "stereotype" might be necessary but only in a discipline that reconfigures itself and guards, ironically, against its own excesses. One of those excesses would be hardening of positions without ample regard for new evidence, an adherence to what Parmenides of Elea (5th century BC), the founder of Eleaticism, in a philosophical poem called *doxa*, the everyday world of belief.[3] To insist too much on a theory or ideology without evidence or, conversely, to resolve on a frozen constellation of facts in an empiricism that represses the theory on which it is based, might produce what might playfully be called "doxic waste." *Making Contact* is one attempt to question prevailing certainties about the division between these periods before the modern. In a metaphorical sense, the volume, like Rabelais' Pantagruel, is on a quest for truth amid the fixed islands on the journey.[4] Among the Greeks, the decree of the assembly and the opinions of the philosophers constituted dogma, but, later in Christian doctrine, became the right opinion about things, or orthodoxy.[5] This ideological setting may have little to do with the intentions of the individual scholars or school: their very success can lead to imitation and a proliferation that actually blurs or obscures the insights of the groundbreaking texts. Other interpretations will, however, lead the discussion to evocative avenues. In the study of past lives, places and fictions, there is a play among doxa, paradox and orthodoxy. In attempting to understand the complexities of the past, new maps and identities will emerge, which, in turn, will have to be revised.

Revision of the stereotype moves between encrustation and breaking new ground: the stereotype itself can seduce in the act of uncovering it. In an understanding of stereotyping there is room for hope and caution. The hope is in the avoidance of stasis in the study of identity and other cultures: the caution resides in the blind glare of self-congratulation in which the unmasking of stereotypes is actually a set of imitations that appear to be more variable than they are. Roland Barthes' *Le Plaisir du texte* is a case in point: it raises the issue of whether the unmasking of the stereotype is natural and sufficient in various contexts.[6] Quite possibly, the ideological operation of such a realistic sign is an imitation that effaces its imitation of nature and thereby presents itself as natural. The sign can then be double and blind itself with ideology in the unmasking of the ideological. Can re-telling the story of the past, or reconfiguring the argument of the past, through new evidence or new readings of old texts, some central and others neglected, help to break up the encrustations of cliché and received opinion? While returning to Barthes, years after his following crested, I think that his notion of stereotyping is useful for suggesting what are the hopes of, and concerns for, reconfiguring the Middle Ages and early modern period.

This reconfiguration often says much about the periods that come after: the "Renaissance," for instance, was, as we have seen, a term that was used long after the period it was made to describe. Paradoxically, the future may wish to join in sympathy with the past by ordering and shaping it, but that very wish for jointure can suggest rupture. A sympathetic estrangement, in which the historical imagination approaches the past for understanding but in which that very act reveals or reaffirms the strangeness of the anterior, implies an ambivalence, a double movement, in revisiting earlier periods. Although the past and present are estranged from each other, the one being distant and seemingly dead and the other examining what went before from a point of view that begins from different premises than those that prevailed in the earlier time, they can read each other productively. Apparently inconvenient evidence from the archive can challenge theory on the edge of tomorrow while the theoretical approach can present a vision or shape to see the mass and tangle of the past in an innovative way. History and theory benefit from each other, which is good because they are entangled. No history can be written without a historiography or theory of history, whether implicit or explicit, and no theory can endure long that evidence does not support. Both help to shake up typecasting.

In some ways stereotyping is a means of limiting the number of behaviours and kinds of events over time, creating a transhistorical view that connects past and present. This possibility of communication across the ages has benefits but it can also make explanations stock and can work against the very historical differences that history and historical methods are supposed to define. Time has a theoretical framework behind it, what was once called a philosophy of history, but which might now be described as a theory of temporality. Time is something that is central to many fields of study: physics, astronomy, biology, psychology, philosophy, literature and history to name a few. Some in the humanities, like Paul Ricœur, have devoted themselves to its study and have related it to narrative just as Stephen Hawking has connected time and mathematics in cosmology. Historians, as Dale H. Porter once noted, have not spent the time on the theoretical dimension of time that one might expect.[7] Literary theory has discussed history but has not done much to consider the temporal nature of texts. Sequence and analysis in historical narrative coexist and seem but may not be, as Porter notes, contradictory: in fact, they might be intricate and reciprocal.[8] The same should be true for literary studies, where the movement of narrative and poetics of literary texts, which by definition were composed in the past and are revived and performed in the present, coincides with the analytical and dialectical. As I have said elsewhere, story and argument become story-argument while time and history are not identical as history is human time in action, its representation and interpretation.[9]

Narrative and explanation entwine. Analogy, for instance, is a mode of story and analysis. Traditionally analogy, a form of comparison, can be viewed poetically and as an aspect of argument. Analogy as poetic comparison lives in metaphor, which is the identity of two parts, animate or inanimate, a yoking that can be so spectacular, for instance in metaphysical poets like John Donne, that its comparative nature can be forgotten or occluded. Argument by analogy was long used in theological and philosophical discussions of the existence of God. Here the metaphor is not meant to dazzle and revive or perform the animistic connection between the living being and the world, the apparently animate and the inanimate, but, through a parallelism in logic, is designed to shed light on a problem or move the argument forward in an enthymene or syllogism. The blurring of narrative and analysis in the case of analogy suggests that history and literature, like philosophy and perhaps mathematics and logic, involve a blurring of the movement between narrative and argument. How we visualize time and the past might just involve "another" and not resolve or define the contradictions and reciprocity of the coexistence of story and explanation. In literary studies the texts of literature contain both elements in differing measures as does close reading and theory.

In one view, history is a story about the past, and, to create a story, selection and order are necessary. Such shaping can involve a kind of typecasting, which relies on a focus, a field of recognition, beyond which is a blurred view or blindness. Seeing stereoscopically, or observing one solid image from two images from different points of view, differs from seeing through stereotypes, or repeating from a simulacrum without apparent change. The one is double-eyed and expansive; the other is blind to anything beyond its own repetition or field and is single-minded. The stereotype, like the stereoscope, cannot escape analogy. Other terms related to analogy, like comparison, doubleness, duplicity, ambivalence and ambiguity, are part of the means of repeating the type as a natural sign for a people, nation, gender, race or historical period. Stereotyping of the past suggests the importance of comparisons and the making and breaking of stories and arguments by various means, including analogy, which, for the sake of space, is the case provided here. If this pursuit of analogy might seem distant to historians—anyone studying Rabelais, Cervantes, or Woolf would have a hard time denying the importance of metaphor and the analogical—I cite a passage from Carlo Ginzburg on analogy. Here is how he begins his essay "The Inquisitor as Anthropologist":

> The analogy which is the subject of this brief essay
> struck me for the first time several years ago in Bologna
> while I was attending a colloquium on oral history ....
> Suddenly it occurred to me that even historians of
> early modern Europe—a noncontemporary society
> which has left enormous amounts of written evidence—
> sometimes use oral sources, or, more precisely,
> written records of oral speech. For instance, the
> judicial proceedings of lay and ecclesiastical courts
> might be comparable to the notebooks of
> anthropologists, recording fieldwork performed
> centuries ago. It should be interesting to test this
> analogy between inquisitors and anthropologists,
> as well as between defendants and 'natives.'[10]

For Ginzburg, the comparison between different times, disciplines and types of sources needs to be tested. While Ginzburg concludes that the historian is not the same as the anthropologist and inquisitor, in the interpretation of evidence he or she has something to learn from both.[11] The analogy proved useful in a heuristic attempt to understand the relation among fields and between past and present. This is a call to examine old texts and various periods, like the Middle Ages and early modern period, in new ways—to ask new questions of familiar material and to come up with dormant or obscure evidence in the archive.

The relations among history, literature and ethnography have found effective expression in the work of Keith Thomas, Peter Burke, Clifford Geertz, Natalie Zemon Davis, Stephen Greenblatt, and others as well as in studies by Ginzburg and Robert Darnton.[12] Darnton discusses the differences between the history of culture or ethnography, which examines the manner in which people make sense of the world, and the history of ideas, which sets out the connections of formal thought among philosophers. In comparing these sub-fields of history, Darnton distinguishes "ordinary people" from philosophers—the former think with things and the latter with logical propositions. He asks:

> What things are good to think with? Claude
> Lévi-Strauss applied that question to the totems and
> taboos of Amazonia twenty-five years ago. Why not
> try it out on eighteenth-century France? Because
> eighteenth-century Frenchmen cannot be interviewed,
> the skeptic will reply; and to drive the point home, he
> will add that archives can never serve as a substitute
> for field work. True, but the archives from the Old
> Regime are exceptionally rich, and one can always put
> new questions to old material. Furthermore, one
> should not imagine that the anthropologist has an
> easy time with his native informant. He, too, runs
> into areas of opacity and silence, and he must interpret
> the native's interpretation of what the other natives
> think. Mental undergrowth can be as impenetrable in
> the bush as in the library.[13]

Darnton arrives at an analogical method between history and anthropology not too different from Ginzberg's and comes to a similar conclusion. Evidence as a test of method is something that *Making Contact* emphasizes. A hypothesis or a flexible thesis need not lead to stereotyping: theory and historiography need not be unbending dogma. In this collection a new generation of scholars explores the questions of stereotypes and of interdisciplinarity, especially as they relate to history and literature. The "Native" becomes a problematic notion in *Making Contact*. Who is at home? Who is in exile? Participant and observer are not sealed from their environment. The ethnological or cultural lens is turned back on the dominant culture, on Europe in some cases, on Europeans as visitors or intruders in others, for instance, in the New World. The scholars in this volume try to shake up received opinion and to destabilize set points of view.

This merging and de-merging of disciplines in all their instability is nothing new, but it is their reconfiguration that is of interest. History and literature, which have performed a long dance together, are expressing new forms that at once distinguish and connect the two disciplines. Lionel Gossman gives an apt summary of the divergence of the two fields:

> For a long time the relation of history to literature
> was not notably problematic. History was a branch
> of *literature*. It was not until the meaning of the word
> *literature*, or the institution of literature itself, began
> to change, toward the end of the eighteenth century,
> that history came to appear as something distinct
> from literature.[14]

Both implicitly and explicitly, *Making Contact* contributes to the debate on the relation between literature and history. That this relation is problematic does not mean that it is not productive. The very friction between literature and history, as well as between the mythological and ideological in both disciplines, that is the story and the argument, provides some exciting possibilities.

Another difficult but suggestive relation with which this collection engages is that between theory and history. At the beginning of the 1990s, Lynn Hunt set out a divide between history and social theory that still has considerable resonance and that also applies to the division between history and literary theory:

> History's relationship to social theory is now
> radically in doubt. Before this contention can be
> developed, however, it must be admitted that history's
> relationship to theory of any sort has always been

problematic, especially for those who actually
research and write history as professional historians
(rather than as historiographers or philosophers of
history). Book reviews of theoretically inspired work,
history department promotion meetings, and graduate
seminars all provide evidence of this ingrained
resistance to thinking theoretically. Only art history
can compare to history in its fundamental hostility to
the intrusion of theory into the discipline; both share
as disciplines, moreover, a similar self-definition based
on the common denominator of the connoisseurship
of documentary evidence.[15]

Theory and practice, then, affect the discipline of history as much as
they do literature, sometimes representing a divide, whether division
is necessary or not. The archive and the theoretical overview are
thought to be mutually exclusive, whereas what this Afterword is
arguing for, and the essays in this collection are suggesting, is a
mutuality. Archive and theory adjust each other into something
more telling about the topic and time in question. This is one of the
key aims and contributions of *Making Contact*. The division between
history and theory, archival practice and historical method, is one of
the fixed ideas, intellectual clichés or disciplinary stereotypes that
this collection is attempting to explore and break down.

   Making Contact: Maps, Identity, and Travel is divided into
three categories ranging from questions of time and space through
identities and subjectivities to travel to the New World. The first
section, "Spatial and Temporal Maps: *Mappaemundi* and Calendars,"
ranges from medieval cartography to calendars in the seventeenth
century. This question of mapping, which has geographical and
temporal implications, meant different things at different times. John
Dee, an Elizabethan geographer, captured this sense of multiple aims
in mapping and in those who had maps and globes in their houses:
"some, for one purpose: and some, for another, liketh, loveth, getteth,
and vseth, Mappes, Chartes, and Geographicall Globes."[16] Maps as
conceptions of the world, as palimpsests of ideology, as markers and
secrets of trade, embodied a sense of the boundaries of those who
commissioned, made and read them.[17]

It is appropriate the collection opens with an essay on Africa, a continent that has been subject to different degrees of European colonization since the Portuguese set up trading posts there in the fifteenth century and a continent still feeling the effects of the colonial divisions of its territory in the nineteenth and early twentieth centuries. Scott D. Westrem begins his essay on Africa in a European *mappamundi*, or map of the world, of about 1450 with Félicité, a character from Jean Genet's play, *Les Nègres: clownerie* (1959), as a means of asking about different representations of Africa in a global context. Westrem explores this example of an early recovery of Ptolemaic geography and of an old and worn representation of Africa. How do these stereotypes occur, even in something that is forward-looking or avant-garde, be it Genet's drama or this world map from the late Middle Ages? Westrem's essay observes in this fragment of a *mappamundi* this European recuperation of Ptolemaic cartography, Arabic empirical geography and the first stirrings of colonization in the Atlantic.

Europeans also used many forms of calendars, which "simultaneously" mapped out time, often in the same locale, in a variety of ways. Calendars are a spatial arrangement of temporality, another form of knowledge. They can suggest a great deal more about a community than the way they ostensibly mark time. David Frick explores the relation between the city walls and many calendars of Vilnius in the 1640s. He begins with a decree that banned the Calvinist church, school and hospital to a place beyond the city walls, an ambivalent move as it allowed legal barriers to be set up against a Christian denomination other than the Roman Catholic Church while it also constituted a significant step in the counter-Reformation in Poland-Lithuania. This decree, partly framed in the language of tolerance, did not have all its desired effects, and the Lutherans, who remained within the walls and the Calvinists, who remained henceforth beyond, survived into the twentieth century. Frick investigates proximities among different ethnic, religious and linguistic groups in Vilnius and how their various calendars caused tensions in the city. Time and space, even in the rituals of the day and of life, have political dimensions. In death the Vilnians often bequeathed their worldly goods to different confessions as long as they were in Vilnius, so that this civic pride might be at the root of this complex multiculturalism.

The second section, "Identities and Subjectivities: Jews, Christians, Vagrants and Nomads," moves from Jewish subjects in the Middle Ages to the identities of rogues and indigenes in the Elizabethan era. Groups at the margins or that are excluded often suggest as much about those who would keep them outside or off-balance as about themselves. What is it about the movement of peoples, about the apparently marginal or different, that challenges the definition and power of the established group?

Jews, for instance, embodied this anxiety over identity in medieval Europe. Judaism had a complex relation to Christianity in the Middle Ages, for it was seminal but revised, repudiated, and scapegoated.[18] Steven F. Kruger argues that the identity of Christians, as individuals and as a body, depends on a historical relation to Judaism in terms of a paradox that involves continuity and rupture: Christianity breaks with Judaism but must define itself in relation to a visible and present Jewishness. Conversion embodies discontinuity from the former self, but a break that is defined against that earlier state. Kruger maintains that Christianity must stabilize Judaism as something old, associated with the flesh and death, in order to contrast it against the redemptive transformation of the Christian. In the Middle Ages the Jew was spatially and corporeally there but transformed typologically and was, therefore, temporally absent. Discussing a moment in the thirteenth century in which Jews and Christians engaged in public disputation, Kruger suggests how dangerous it was for Jews to speak about Jewish belief publicly in Europe even when they were compelled to do so and how challenging that was to the well-ensconced Christian powers, religious and political.

Christianity also came into contact with other religions with which it had much less direct ties with than it did with Judaism. Centuries later than the time Kruger discusses, Christian missions in Japan provided a radically different context for religious contact and confrontation. In an analysis of the meeting of Christians with a complex Asian culture, Ayako Nakai gives a suggestive account of European missionaries in sixteenth-century Japan, especially in regard to the role of Francis Xavier. This past example also faces Japan now: Nakai questions whether it has been possible for the Japanese to combine their spirit with European learning as they have contended. Spirit, for Nakai, is ideologically constructed and is defined in encounters with others, so that there can be no traditional form of spirit. Through Xavier's own writings, spiritual exercises and meditation, he explores himself as well as the Japanese. By the time Alessandro Valignano, the next major missionary, arrived, there were 100,000 Japanese Christians, and his work conflicted with another important figure in the Christian mission to Japan: Francisco Cabral. What is interesting about Xavier, Nakai implies, is that in new experiences he sought, but did not possess, the universality of Christianity: his journey was an ongoing dialogue with God. This way, according to Nakai, is an example for Japanese and Westerners today and something better than Cabral's identification of Christianity with European culture and than Organtino's too many compromises with the native culture of Japan.

Sometimes conflicts occur within a culture and can arise from, or be parallel to, frictions between that culture and other cultures. Contact and conflict could happen in terms of class in England as much as embodied through religious events in Japan. Linda Woodbridge's essay discusses sixteenth-century England, a period when England was building on the voyages of Giovanni Caboto or John Cabot and seeking permanent settlements in the New World, when famine, unemployment, homelessness and vagrancy were widespread at home. Woodbridge makes a significant connection between the Old World and the New: when Elizabethans came upon nomadic indigenous peoples in America, they frequently identified them with vagrants in England. English travel writers and authors of rogue literature both excoriated the laziness, treachery and thievery of their "subjects," aboriginal peoples for the one group and vagrants for the other. The English insisted on the fixity of identity and divinely authorized boundaries in the face of authority, because, as Woodbridge asserts, the anxiety over the slippage of borders helps to produce pronouncements about the essence and immutability of such lines. Mobility threatened this sense of immutable identity and created anxiety in English culture about errancy and transgression, in the air of England and the dust of America. Woodbridge implies, then, that in identity or subjectivity in English culture at this moment a tension, if not a disjunction, existed between insistent fixity and anxious slippage.

Identity and subjectivity are also concerns of the third section, "Travel to the New World: The Early Modern and the Postmodern." The essays in this part move from the English rewriting of the Virginian paradise through stylizations of selfhood, particularly in the *Voyages* of the seventeenth-century French explorer Pierre-Esprit Radisson, to "writing" the past, especially in regard to how Cabeza de Vaca is portrayed in history, fiction and film. The emergence of the modern meets the time that would be after the modern. Modernity is a vexed question because the "Renaissance" is a largely nineteenth-century term that reads retroactively the rebirth of classical learning onto a period centuries earlier, whereas the term now in fashion, and much favoured by historians, "early modern," is just as retrospective but frames the likes of Ariosto, Erasmus, and Rabelais as all looking ahead to those they prefigure: the moderns. There is a touch of triumphalism or hubris in this for people of recent times. This retrospective teleology, while different from a retroactive nostalgia for Socrates and Cicero, calls attention to the problematics of nomenclature and periodicity. The "modern" in "early modern" and "postmodern" is as problematic as the prolepsis and epigone that use prefixes to assert and deny its fixity.

This section begins with an essay in which Paul W. DePasquale seeks to revise modernist views of the early modern exploration. He examines the utopian impulse in English writing about North Carolina during the 1580s and begins with a passage from Arthur Barlowe, an author much appropriated by those seeking out the classical foundations of early modern descriptions of the New World by the English, most particularly in the identification of America with the golden age. For DePasquale, it is important to expose, rather than to conceal, the shifting and contradictory images of America and its peoples. By analyzing Barlowe as a test case, DePasquale is able to qualify this classicism and most especially the golden age thesis, most notably expounded by Harry Levin. While DePasquale does not deny the myth of the golden age in Barlowe, he wants to demonstrate its coexistence with conflicting materials that would not serve or be recognized by the official ideology of Barlowe's patrons. Barlowe's descriptions of the new, DePasquale implies, create what might be called colonial dissonance, something ethnological, cultural and political as well as cognitive. DePasquale aptly notes that official responses, like Thomas Harriot's, to unofficial and potentially detrimental reports emphasize dissension and protest among the English. The making of Virginia into a paradise might have been an answer to such opposition to colonization but it also had to respond to that protest. Even Richard Hakluyt the younger, for instance, a great promoter of empire, made editorial changes that softened the rhetoric of expansion and hope lest it work against the very colonization he called for.

Other conflicts in identity emerged in the settlement of North America. The French in America provided their own examples of the blurring of boundaries and identities. Rick H. Lee discusses Radisson as a hybrid of two emerging social types in New France, a *coureur de bois* and a *habitant*, a woodsman and farmer. Radisson crossed national boundaries and mixed identities: he played a key role in the establishment of the Hudson's Bay Company in 1670 and, although born French, died an English subject. This mobile identity is, in Lee's view, most evident in the text concerning Radisson's first voyage. How Radisson disrupts the temporal and spatial logic of his text suggests ways in which he perceives himself in relation to his captors. The slippage in Radisson's subjectivity is also related to the complexity of the construction of his text, for instance the question of whether he wrote in French and was translated into English or whether he composed in English. Lee sees Radisson's text, which has been undervalued, as a useful model for revaluing identity politics, particularly in connection with Canada, and in terms of a cultural mediation that accommodates two or more cultures. This kind of cultural critique would, then, become an embracing of hybridity, something that an age that calls itself postmodern and postcolonial has come to value. The self-presentation and the myth of the captive achieving freedom again as an explorer and as a writer applies as much to Cabeza de Vaca as it does to Radisson.

The section shifts from French to earlier Spanish explorations of America partly because Richard Young brings us back from the future to the past: he discusses the early modern through the lens of the postmodern. Young examines the expedition of 1528 to Florida, which Cabeza de Vaca, one of four survivors, recorded. This voyage was one of many to the mainland of North America in the twenty years, from 1521, when Juan Ponce de León returned to Florida after his first journey there in 1513, to 1541, when Coronado sighted the Grand Canyon. Young discusses the various versions of Cabeza de Vaca's experiences, from the first account in 1537 through his own text in 1542 and its corrected version of 1555, to postmodern and postcolonial interpretations and recreations of this story. Until recently, Young notes, Cabeza de Vaca's text was interpreted in light of the hegemony of empire. This conquistador was considered reliable: his story was thought true partly because its first form was a joint report with his companions delivered to the colonial courts in Santo Domingo and his own published accounts deemed themselves part of the quasi-legal genre of *relación*. Young makes an intriguing point that while Cabeza de Vaca's text may have been self-interested, it also distinguished itself in its criticism of Spanish imperialism. The film *Cabeza de Vaca*, the novel and, to some degree, the academic interpretations suggest, according to Young, that it is difficult to be confident in the content or author of *Los naufragios*. What the problem revolves around, in the early modern and the postmodern, is, for Young, narrative. How Cabeza de Vaca constructed his experiences in a story, how he made his memorial, and how fiction and film have remade him in history and story, are in the middle of this dilemma.

This relation between history and fiction, mediated through rhetoric and narrative, is something that is as much alive in the Middle Ages and early modern period as it is in our time. Images and representations, whether textual or visual, involve an intricate transmission from author or artist to reader or viewer. Plato's Socrates, especially in the tenth book of *The Republic*, was skeptical of poets because they could represent the world but do little useful within it, except sing hymns to the republic. This ideological impulse has often tried to use art and poetry, and Plato seems to have been suspicious of the power of images to move their audience. Aristotle was more tolerant of mimesis than his teacher was, and his *Poetics* allowed poets a window through which to escape into their craft without political justification. In the ninth article of *The Nature and Domain of Sacred Doctrine* Thomas Aquinas answered the objection that Holy Scripture should not use metaphors with the view that it is right to put forth divine and spiritual truths through comparisons with material things because humans attain intellectual truths through sensible things because their knowledge comes from sense: God provides according to the capacity of everything's nature. In his *Apology for Poetry* Philip Sidney argued that the concrete and sensible nature of poetry, which includes images, moves the reader to moral action. Poetry now, and not philosophy, was the bearer of the universal. *Making Contact* begins and ends by bringing twentieth-century concerns to medieval and early modern maps and texts, those images of understanding and misunderstanding.

The collection also shows an awareness of postmodernist and postcolonial conditions that deny fixity of identity and the universality that European culture claimed for itself. The essays deny that "man" also represents woman, that Africa, Asia and America are projections of Europe, that multiculturalism is something new. Mediation and ambivalence, conflict and coexistence all prevail in these encounters during the Middle Ages and early modern period. While that time is not ours, there are traces and unofficial versions that this volume, and others like it, is excavating. What excites me most about *Making Contact* are the surprising connections the authors have discovered in diverse topics about Africa, Asia, Eastern and Western Europe and America in several fields such as geography, history, ethnology and literature. What is fascinating about the past is that it moves and is recalcitrant, and if, as the scholars in this collection show, one looks again and again, something splendid and difficult will emerge as we move with it, and those recognitions will not necessarily find the official versions, or the ideological positions, the present prizes. Identities are fluid and multiple, then and now, however fixed people wanted and want them to be. Even the universal has its particularities. Poetry is and is not ideological, and the study of the past, in whatever discipline, has similar qualities. The mapping of the past is as complex and strange as it was to those medieval makers of maps with which we began: the story in history is never done.

NOTES

1 See Anthony Grafton with April Shelford and Nancy Siraisi, "Introduction," *New Worlds, Ancient Texts: The Power of Tradition and the Shock of Discovery* (Cambridge, MA: Harvard University Press, 1992), pp. 1–2.

2 See Hart, "Reading the Renaissance: An Introduction," *Reading the Renaissance: Culture, Poetics, and Drama* (New York: Garland, 1996), pp. 1–4.

3 See W.J. Verdenius, *Parmenides: Some Comments on His Poem*, A. Fontein, trans. (Groningen: J.B. Wolters, 1942).

4 See Daniel Ménager, "The 16th Century: French literature," in *The New Encyclopedia Britannica*, 15th ed. (Chicago: Encyclopedia Britannica, 1991), p. 545.

5 See Reinhold Merkelbach, *Roman und Mysterium in der Antike* (München: Beck, 1962).

6 See Roland Barthes, *Le Plaisir du texte* (Paris: Éditions du seuil, 1973) and Mireille Rosello, *Declining the Stereotype: Ethnicity and Representation in French Cultures* (Hanover, NH: University Press of New England, 1998).

7 Dale H. Porter, *The Emergence of the Past: A Theory of Historical Explanation* (Chicago: University of Chicago Press, 1981), p. ix.

8 Porter, *Emergence of the Past*, pp. 1–3.

9 See Hart, "Afterword," *Theater and World: The Problematics of Shakespeare's History* (Boston: Northeastern University Press, 1992).

10 Carlo Ginzburg, *Clues, Myths, and the Historical Method*, John and Anne Tedeschi, trans. (Baltimore: Johns Hopkins University press, 1989), p. 186.

11 Ginzburg, *Clues*, p. 164.

12 Robert Darnton, *The Great Cat Massacre and Other Episodes in French Cultural History* (New York: Vintage, 1985), p. 283, n. 4.

13 Darnton, *Great Cat Massacre*, p. 4.

14 Lionel Gossman, *Between History and Literature* (Cambridge, MA: Harvard University Press, 1990), p. 227.

15 Lynn Hunt, "History Beyond Social History," in *The States of "Theory": History, Art, and Critical Discourse*, David Carroll, ed. (New York: Columbia University Press, 1990), pp. 95–111.

16 In an interesting study of mapping, Jerry Brotton highlights Dee's work and this passage (p. 20); see John Dee, *Preface to Euclid's "Elements of Geometrie"* (London: 1570), p. aiiij; and Jerry Brotton, *Trading Territories: Mapping the Early Modern World* (London: Reaktion, 1997).

17 See J.B. Hartley, "New England Cartography and the Native Americans," in *American Beginnings: Exploration, Culture, and Cartography in the Land of Norumbega*, Emerson W. Baker et al., eds. (Lincoln: University of Nebraska Press, 1994), pp. 286–313, 363–71.

18 See René Girard, *Le bouc émissaire* (Paris: B. Grasset, 1982).

Bibliography

PRIMARY SOURCES

"*Actum Commissiey w Wilnie.*" ["The Proceedings of the Commission in Vilnius."] *Tygodnik Wileński.* 5, no. 106 (1818): 1–28, no. 107: 49–66, no. 108: 81–93.

Adamowicz, Adam Ferdynand. *Kościół augsburski w Wilnie. Kronika.* [The Lutheran Church in Vilnius: A Chronicle.] Vilnius, 1855.

Agenda albo Forma Porządku usługi świętey, w zborach ewangelickich koronnych y Wielkiego Xięstwa Litewskiego. [Agenda, Or the Form of the Order of Holy Service in the Evangelical Churches of the Crown and the Grand Duchy of Lithuania.] Gdańsk, 1637.

Akta Synodów prowincjalnnych Jednoty Litewskiej 1611–1625. [The Acts of the Provincial Synods of the Lithuanian Calvinist Church, 1611–1625.] Monumenta Reformationis Polonicae et Lithuanicae, series IV, fascicle II. Vilnius, 1915.

Akty izdavaemye Vilenskoju Kommissieju dlja Razbora Drevnix Aktov. [Acts Published by the Vilnius Commission for the Edition of Ancient Acts.] Vol. 8, vol. 9, vol. 10, vol. 20. Vilnius, 1875, 1878, 1879, 1893.

Alfonsi, Peter. *Dialogi contra Iudaeos.* In *Patrologiae cursus completus, Series latina.* Edited by J.-P. Migne, vol. 157, cols. 535–672. Paris, 1841–79.

Anonymous. *The Book of Vagabonds and Beggars with a Vocabulary of their Language and a Preface by Martin Luther.* (*Liber Vagatorum.*) Translated by J.C. Hotten. Ed. D.B. Thomas. London: Penguin, 1932.

Augustine. *Concerning the City of God against the Pagans.* Translated by Henry Bettenson. Harmondsworth: Penguin, 1984.

Augustine. *De civitate dei*. Edited by Bernard Dombart and Alphonse Kalb (with emendations by the editors of CCSL). *Corpus Christianorum*, Series Latina, 47–48. Turnhout: Brepols, 1955.

Awdeley, John. *The Fraternity of Vagabonds*, ca. 1561. London: John Awdeley, 1565, STC 993, title page only; version of 1561 presumed lost; earliest extant full version, London 1575, STC 994.

Barlowe, Arthur. "Discourse of the First Voyage" (c. 1584–85). *The Roanoke Voyages, 1584–1590*. Edited by David Beers Quinn, vol. 1, pp. 91–116. London: Hakluyt Society, 2nd Ser., 104–05, 1955.

Bell Map. Minneapolis, James Ford Bell Library, University of Minnesota, MS 1450 mMa.

Berger, David. *The Jewish-Christian Debate in the High Middle Ages: A Critical Edition of the Nizzahon Vetus*. Philadelphia: The Jewish Publication Society of America, 1979.

Carpentier, Alejo. *El arpa y la sombra*. Mexico: Siglo XXI, 1979.

Carpentier, Alejo. *The Harp and the Shadow*. Translated by Thomas Christensen and Carol Christensen. San Francisco: Mercury House Inc., 1990.

Cleaver, Robert. *A Godly Form of Household Government*. London: F. Kingston, 1598. STC 5383.

Dee, John. *Preface to Euclid's "Elements of Geometrie"*. London: 1570.

Dekker, Thomas. *Lantern and Candlelight*. London: G. Eld, 1608. STC 6485.

Donne, John. *The Sermons of John Donne*. Edited by Evelyn M. Simpson and George R. Potter. 10 vols. Berkeley: University of California Press, 1953.

Drayton, Michael. "To the Virginian Voyage," 1619. *The Works of Michael Drayton*. Edited by J. William Hebel. Vol. 2. 363–364. Oxford: Blackwell, 1931–41.

Dubiński, Piotr. *Zbiór Praw i Przywilejów Miastu Stołecznemu W.X.L. Wilnowi nadanych. Na żądaniu wielu Miast Koronnych, jako też Wielkiego Księstwa Litewskiego ułożony i wydany*. [A Collection of the Laws and Privileges Granted to Vilnius, the Capital City of the Grand Duchy of Lithuania, Gathered and Published at the Demand of Many Cities of the Crown and of the Grand Duchy of Lithuania.] 1788.

Dubovyč (Dubowicz), Jan. *Kalendarz Prawdziwy Cerkwi Chrystusowey*. [The True Calendar of the Church of Christ.] Vilnius, 1644.

Elyot, Sir Thomas. *The Book Named The Governour*, 1531. Edited by Henry Herbert Stephen Croft. 2 vols. New York: Bert Franklin, 1967.

Ebisawa, Arimichi. *Kirishitan sho, Haiya sho* [Texts by Christians and Texts that "Reject" Christianity]. Tokyo: Iwanamishoten, 1970.

Fernández de Oviedo y Valdés, Gonzalo. *Historia general y natural de las Indias, islas y Tierra-Firme del Mar Océano*. Edited and introduced by Juan Pérez de Tudela Bueso. Biblioteca de Autores Españoles, pp. 117–121. Madrid: Ediciones Atlas, 1959.

Frois, Luis. *Nihon shi* [History of Japan]. Translated by Matsuda Kiichi and Kawasaki Momota. 12 vols. Tokyo: Chūōkōronsha, 1977–1980.

Frois, Luis. *Nihon shi* [History of Japan]. Translated by Yanagiya Takeo. 5 vols. Tokyo: Heibonsha, 1963–1978.

Frois, Luis. *Yōroppa bunka to nihon bunka* [European Culture and Japanese Culture]. Translated by Okada Akio. Tokyo: Iwanamishoten, 1991.

García Márquez, Gabriel. *El general en su laberinto*. Madrid: Mondadori, 1989.

García Márquez, Gabriel. *The General in his Labyrinth*. Translated by Edith Grossman. New York: A.A. Knopf, 1990.

Genet, Jean. *Les Nègres: clownerie*. Edited by Marc Barbezat. Décines [Isère]: L'Arbalète, 1960.

Genet, Jean. *The Blacks: a clown show*. Translated by Bernard Frechtman. New York: Grove Press, 1960.

Gilbert, William. *De Magnete: Magneticisque Corporibus, et de Magno Magnete Tellure; Physiologia Nova, Plurimus and Argumentis, and Experimentis Demonstrata*, London: Peter Short, 1600. Translated by P. Fleury Mottelay, 1893. Reprint New York: Dover, 1958.

Greene, Robert. *A Notable Discovery of Cozenage*. London: J. Wolfe, 1591. STC 12279.

Grodzicki, Stanisław. *O poprawie kalendarza Kazanie dwoie*. [Two Sermons on the Correction of the Calendar.] Vilnius, 1589.

Hakluyt, Richard (the elder). "Instructions for the North-East Passage" (c. 1580). *The Original Writings & Correspondence of the Two Richard Hakluyts*. Edited by E.G.R. Taylor. Vol. 1, pp. 147–58. London: Hakluyt Society, 2nd Ser., 56–57, 1935.

Hakluyt, Richard (the elder). "Notes framed by a Gentleman heretofore to bee given to one that prepared for a discoverie, and went not: And not unfitt to be committed to print, considering the same may stirre up considerations of these and of such other thinges, not unmeete in such new voyages as may be attempted hereafter" (c. 1578). *New American World: A Documentary History of North America to 1612*. Edited by David Beers Quinn. Vol. 3, pp. 23–26. New York: Arno Press, 1979.

Hakluyt, Richard (the elder); Frobisher, Martin; Peckham, George; and Hakluyt, Richard (the younger). "Instructions for a Voyage to Southern Norumbega" (c. 1582–83). *New American World: A Documentary History of North America to 1612*. Edited by David Beers Quinn. Vol. 3, pp. 239–45. New York: Arno Press, 1979.

Hakluyt, Richard (the younger). *Discourse of Western Planting. 1584.* In *The Original Writings and Correspondence of the Two Richard Hakluyts.* Edited by E.G.R. Taylor. Vol. 2, Document 46, pp. 211–326. London: Hakluyt Society at Cambridge University Press, 1935.

Hakluyt, Richard (the younger). "Epistle Dedicatory to Ralegh". From *De orbe novo Petri Martyris Anglerii Mediolanensis decades octo...illustratae labore Richardi Hakluyti* (Paris, 1587). *The Roanoke Voyages, 1584–1590.* Edited by David Beers Quinn. Vol. 2, pp. 513–515. London: Hakluyt Society, 2nd Ser., 104–5, 1955.

Hakluyt, Richard (the younger). *The Principall Navigations, Voyages and Discoveries of the English Nation (1589).* 2 vols. Edited by D.B. Quinn and R.A. Skelton. Hakluyt Society, Extra Ser., 34. Cambridge: Cambridge University Press, 1965.

Hall, Joseph. *The discovery of a new world or A Description of the South Indies. Hetherto Vnknowne, By an English Mercury.* Translated by John Healey. London, 1609[?]. Translation of *Mundus alter.* London, 1605[?].

Harman, Thomas. *A Caveat for Common Cursetors, Vulgarly called Vagabonds.* London: W. Griffith, 1567. STC 12787; first printed 1566. Reprinted in *The Elizabethan Underworld,* edited by A.V. Judges, 2nd edition, pp. 61–118. New York: Octagon, 1964.

Harriot, Thomas. "A Briefe and true report" (London, 1588). *The Roanoke Voyages, 1584–1590.* Edited by David Beers Quinn. Vol. 1, pp. 317–87. London: Hakluyt Society, 2nd Ser., 104–5, 1955.

Harszler, K.D., ed. *Die Reisen des Samuel Kiechel. Aus drei Handschriften.* [The Travels of Samuel Kiechel, From Three Manuscripts.] Bibliothek des Litterarischen Vereins in Stuttgart 86. Stuttgart, 1866.

Higden, Ranulph. *Polychronicon.* Translated by John Trevisa, edited by William Caxton. 2nd ed. Westminster: Wynkyn de Worde, 13 April 1495.

Jonson, Ben. *Volpone.* In *Ben Jonson.* Edited by C. H. Herford, Percy Simpson, and Evelyn Simpson. Vol. 5, pp. 15–136. Oxford: Clarendon, 1937.

Kapitza, Peter, ed. *Japan in Europa.* Vol.1. Munich: Iudicium, 1990.

Kimḥi, Joseph. *The Book of the Covenant.* Translated by Frank Talmage. Toronto: Pontifical Institute of Mediaeval Studies, 1972.

Lane, Ralph. "Discourse on the First Colony. August 17, 1585 to June 18, 1586". *The Roanoke Voyages, 1584–1590.* Edited by David Beers Quinn. Vol. 1, pp. 255–94. London: Hakluyt Society, 2nd Ser., 104–5, 1955.

Lane, Ralph. "Letter to Richard Hakluyt the elder and Master H—of the Middle Temple. September 3, 1585". *The Roanoke Voyages, 1584–1590.* Edited by David Beers Quinn. Vol. 1, pp. 207–210. London: Hakluyt Society, 2nd Ser., 104–5, 1955.

Lane, Ralph. "Letter to Sir Francis Walsingham. August 12, 1585". *The Roanoke Voyages, 1584–1590.* Edited by David Beers Quinn. Vol. 1, pp. 199–204. London: Hakluyt Society, 2nd Ser., 104–5, 1955.

Lane, Ralph. "Reminiscences of the 1585 Expedition. January 7, 1592." *The Roanoke Voyages, 1584–1590.* Edited by David Beers Quinn. Vol. 1, pp. 228–31. London: Hakluyt Society, 2nd Ser., 104–5, 1955.

Le Canarien. Edited by Elías Serra Rafols and Alexandre Cioranescu. 3 vols. Las Palmas: La Laguna, 1959–65.

Leo Africanus, Johannes. *A Geographical Historie of Africa.* Translated and edited by John Pory. London: 1600.

Loyola, Ignatius. *Reisō* [Spiritual Exercises]. Translated by Kadowaki Kakichi. Tokyo: Iwanamishoten, 1995.

Loyola, Ignatius. *Loyola no Ignatio, sono jiden to nikki* [Ignatius Loyola, his Autobiography and Diary]. Edited and translated by Sasaki Takashi and A. Evangelista. Tokyo: Katsurashōbō, 1966.

Łaszcz, Marcin (pseud. Tworzydło, Marcin). *Okulary na Zwierciadło Nabożeństwa Chrześciańskiego w Polszcze.* [Spectacles for the Mirror of the Christian Religion in Poland.] Vilnius, 1594.

Łaszcz, Marcin (pseud. Żebrowski, Szczęsny). *Zwierczadło roczne, Na trzy części rozdzielone. Pierwsza, na czas Kościelny, y Politycki opisany. Wtóra, respons na skript Latosów. Trzecia, co trzymać o wróżbie gwiazdarskiey.* [An Annual Mirror, Divided into Three Parts: The First, Written for Ecclesiastical and Secular Time; The Second, A Response to the Writing of Latos; The Third, What to Hold Concerning Astrology.] Cracow, 1603.

Łowmiański, Henryk and Łowmiańska, Marja, eds. *Akta cechów wileńskich.* [Acts of the Vilnius Guilds.] Vol. 1. Vilnius, 1939.

Matsuda, Kiichi, ed. *16, 17 seiki Iezusukai nihon hōkoku shū* [Reports and Letters from Japan by the Jesuits in the Sixteenth and Seventeenth Century]. Kyoto: Dōhōsha, 1987–1994.

Nashe, Thomas. *The Unfortunate Traveller.* In *The Unfortunate Traveller and Other Works.* Edited by J.B. Steane. Pp. 251–370. London: Penguin, 1972.

Nicolaus Cusanus. *De pace fidei.* In *Nicolai de Cusa, Opera omnia.* Edited and commented by R. Klibansky and H. Bascour. Vol. 8, pp. 1–63. Hamburg, 1970. Japanese translation by Yamaki Kazuhiko, in *Chūsei makki no shimpishisō* [Mysticism in the later Middle Ages]. Tokyo: Heibonsha, 1992.

Nowak, Zbigniew. *Kontrreformacyjna satyra obyczajowa w Polsce XVII wieku.* [The Counter-Reformation Social Satire in Poland in the Seventeenth Century.] Gdańskie Towarzystwo Naukowe, Wydział I Nauk Społecznych i Humanistycznych, Seria Źródeł 9. Gdańsk, 1968.

Núñez Cabeza de Vaca, Alvar. *La relación de lo acaescido en las Indias en la armada donde yva por gobernador Panphilo de Narváez desde el año de veynte y siete hasta el año de treynta y seys.* Zamora: 1542.

Núñez Cabeza de Vaca, Alvar. *La relación y comentarios del gobernador Alvar Núñez Cabeza de Vaca de lo acaescido en las dos jornadas que hizo a las Indias.* Valladolid: 1555.

Núñez Cabeza de Vaca, Alvar. *The Narrative of Alvar Núñez Cabeza de Vaca*. Translated by Fanny Bandelier and introduced by John Francis Bannon. Barre, MA: The Imprint Society, 1972.

Pacios Lopez, Antonio, ed. *La Disputa de Tortosa*, 2 vols. Madrid-Barcelona: Instituto "Arias Montano," 1957.

Posse, Abel. *Daimón*. Barcelona: Librería Editorial Argos, 1978.

Posse, Abel. *El largo atardecer del caminante*. Buenos Aires: Emecé Editores, 1992.

Quinn, David Beers, ed. *New American World: A Documentary History of North America to 1612*. 5 vols. New York: Arno Press, 1979.

Quinn, David Beers, ed. *Richard Hakluyt, Editor: A Study Introductory to the facsimile edition Of Richard Hakluyt's* Divers Voyages *(1582)*. 2 vols. Amsterdam: Theatrum Orbis Terrarum Ltd., 1967.

Quinn, David Beers, ed. *The Roanoke Voyages, 1584–1590*. 2 vols. London: Hakluyt Society, 2nd Ser., 104–5, 1955.

Radisson, Pierre-Esprit. "The Relation of my Voyage, being in Bondage in the Lands of the Irokoits." In *The English Literatures of America, 1500–1800*. Edited by Myra Jehlen and Michael Warner, pp. 325–48. New York and London: Routledge, 1997.

Radisson, Pierre-Esprit. *Voyages of Peter Esprit Radisson, being an account of his travels and experiences among the North American Indians, from 1652 to 1684, transcribed from the original manuscripts in the Bodleian Library and the British Museum*, Edited by Gideon D. Scull. New York: Peter Smith, 1943.

Rieri i Sans, Jaume, ed. *La Crònica en Hebreu de la Disputa de Tortosa*. Barcelona: Fundació Salvador Vives Casajuana, 1974.

Rykaczewski, Erazm, ed. *Relacye nuncyuszów apostolskich i innych osób o Polsce od roku 1548 do 1690*. [Reports Concerning Poland by Apostolic Nuncios and Other Individuals, 1548 to 1690.] Berlin, 1864.

Saer, Juan José. *El entenado*. Buenos Aires: Folios Ediciones, 1983.

Sakovyč, Kasijan (Sakowicz, Kassian). *Kalendarz stary, w ktorym Iawny y oczywisty Błąd vkazuie się około święcenia Paschi, y Responsa na Zarzuty Starokalendarzan*. [The Old Calendar, in Which is Demonstrated the Manifest and Obvious Error Concerning the Celebration of Easter, and a Response to the Censures of the Old-Calendar-ites.] Warsaw, 1640.

Sakovyč, Kasijan (Sakowicz, Kassian). *Dialog Abo Rozmowa Maćka z Dyonizym Popem Schizmatyckim Wileńskim*. [A Dialogue, Or the Conversation of Maciek with Dionizy, the Vilnius Schismatic Pop.] Cracow, 1642.

Schönflissius, Jędrzej. *Antidotum spirituale. To iest, Lekarstwo Duchowne Na Truciznę Srogiey śmierci Przy obchodzie pogrzebu niegdy pobożnego i Szlachetnego Męża Iego Mści Pana Iakuba Gibla Burmistrza Wileńskiego*. [Antidotum Spirituale: That is, Spiritual Medicine for the Poison of Harsh Death at the Funeral of the Pious and Noble Man, His Grace, Mr. Jakub Gibl, Mayor of Vilnius.] Königsberg, 1638.

Schurhammer, Georg. *Xaveriana*. Rome: Bibliotheca Instituti Historici, 1964.

Schütte, Joseph Franz. *Valignanos Missionsgrundsätze für Japan. 1573–1583*, I–1 , I–2. Rome: Edizioni di storia e letteratura, 1951, 1958.

Shakespeare, William. *Complete Works*. Edited by David Bevington. Fourth edition. Glenview, IL: Scott, Foresman, 1992.

Simonsohn, Shlomo, ed. *The Apostolic See and the Jews. Documents: 492–1404*. Toronto: Pontifical Institute of Mediaeval Studies, 1988.

Sipayłło, Maria, ed. *Akta Synodów Różnowierczych w Polsce*. [Acts of the Heterodox Synods in Poland.] Vol. 4. Wielkopolska 1569–1632. [Great Poland, 1569–1632.] Warsaw, 1997.

Smith, Walter. *The Twelve Merry Jests of the Widow Edith*. London: William Williamson, 1573. STC 22870. Reprinted in William Hazlitt, *Shakespeare Jest-books*. Vol. 3. 27–108. London: Willis and Sotheran, 1864.

Smotryc'kyj, Meletij. *Obrona verificaciey*. [Defense of the Verification.] Vilnius, 1621. Facsimile edition: *Collected Works*, pp. 399–462.

Smotryc'kyj, Meletij. *Protestatia Przeciwo Soborowi w tym Roku 1628. we dni Augusta Miesiąca, w Kiiowie Monasteru Pieczerskim obchodzonemu*. [Protestation Against the Council that Took Place This Year, 1628, in the Days of the Month of August, In the Caves Monastery in Kiev.] L'viv, 1628. Facsimile edition: Collected Works, pp. 627–42.

Smotryc'kyj, Meletij. *Collected Works of Meletij Smotryc'kyj*. Harvard Library of Early Ukrainian Literature, Texts, vol. 1. Cambridge, MA, 1987.

Takase, Kōichirō, ed. *Iezusukai to nihon* [The Jesuits and Japan], *Daikōkai sōsho* [The Age of Great Voyages Series], vol. 1 and 2. Tokyo: Iwanamishoten, 1981/1988.

Tawney, R.H., and Power, Eileen. *Tudor Economic Documents*. London: Longmans, 1924.

Taylor, E.G.R., ed. *The Original Writings & Correspondence of the Two Richard Hakluyts*. 2 vols. London: Hakluyt Society, 2nd Ser., 56–57, 1935.

Tylkowski, Wojciech. *Zarzuty dissidenskie około wiary y na nie odpowiedzi katolickie*. [The Censures of the Dissidents Concerning the Faith, And the Catholic Answers to Them.] Vilnius, 1685.

Valignano, Alessandro. *Nihon iezusukaishi reihō shishin* [Guide for the Jesuits in Japan Concerning Manners], translation of *Advertimentos e avisos acerca dos costumes e catangues de Jappão* by Yazawa Toshihiko. Tokyo: Kirishitan bunka kenkyūkai, 1970.

Valignano, Alessandro. *Nihon junsatsu ki* [Reports of the Visitation in Japan], translation of *Sumario de las cosas de Japón (1585). Adiciones del sumario de Japón (1592)*. Edited by José Luis Alvarez-Taladriz, Tokyo: Sophia University, 1954 by Matsuda Kiichi. Tokyo: Heibonsha, 1973.

Verdenius, W.J. *Parmenides: Some Comments on His Poem*. Translated by A. Fontein. Groningen: J.B. Wolters, 1942.

Walker, Gilbert. *A Manifest Detection of the Most Vile and Detestable Use of Dice-Play.* London: Abraham Vele, 1555. STC 24961.

Walsperger Map. Vatican City, Biblioteca Apostolica Vaticana, MS Pal. lat. 1362b.

Xavier, Francis. *Sei Furanshisuko Zabieru zen shokan* [All the Letters of St. Francis Xavier]. Translated by Kōno Yoshinori. Tokyo: Heibonsha, 1985.

Zbiór dawnych dyplomatów i aktów miast: Wilna, Kowna, Trok, prawosławnych monasterów, cerkwi i w różnych sprawach. [A Collection of Old City Privileges and Acts: Vilnius, Kaunas, Trakai, Orthodox Monasteries, Churches, and Various Matters.] Part 1. Vilnius, 1843.

Zeitz Map. Zeitz, Stiftsbibliothek, MS Lat. Hist. 497, fol. 48r.

SECONDARY SOURCES

Adams, Arthur T., ed. "Foreword." *The Explorations of Pierre-Esprit Radisson,* by Pierre-Esprit Radisson, pp. i–xxviii. Minneapolis: Ross & Haines, 1961.

Alexander, Michael. *Discovering the New World: Based on the Works of Theodore DeBry.* New York: Harper & Row, 1976.

Almagià, Roberto. *Planisferi, carte nautiche e affini dal secolo XIV al XVII esistenti nella Biblioteca Apostolica Vaticana.* Vol. 1 of *Monumenta Cartographica Vaticana,* edited by Roberto Almagià. Vatican City: Biblioteca Apostolica Vaticana, 1944.

Alpers, Svetlana. *The Art of Describing: Dutch Art in the Seventeenth Century.* Chicago: University of Chicago Press, 1983.

Anderson, Benedict. *Imagined Communities: Reflections on the Origins and Spread of Nationalism,* rev. ed. London and New York: Verso, 1991.

Axtell, James. "The White Indians of Colonial America." *William and Mary Quarterly* 32.1 (January 1975): 55–88.

Barthes, Roland. *Le Plaisir du texte.* Paris: Éditions du Seuil, 1973.

Beazley, C. Raymond. *The Dawn of Modern Geography.* London, 1897–1903; rpt. New York: Peter Smith, 1949.

Beier, A.L. "Anti-language or Jargon? Canting in the English Underworld in the Sixteenth and Seventeenth Centuries." *The Social History of Language: Language and Jargon.* Edited by Peter Burke and Roy S. Porter, vol. 3. 64–101. London: Polity Press, 1995.

Beier, A.L. *Masterless Men: The Vagrancy Problem in England.* London: Methuen, 1985.

Beier, A.L. *The Problem of the Poor in Tudor and Early Stuart England.* London: Methuen, 1985.

Beršadskij, S.A. "Istorija vilenskoj evrejskoj obščiny. 1593–1649 g. Na osnovaniju neizdavannyx istočnikov." ["The History of the Vilnius Jewish Community, 1593–1649. On the Basis of Unpublished Sources."] *Vosxod* 6, no. 10 (1886): 125–38, no. 11: 145–54 and 7, no. 3 (1887): 81–98, no. 4: 65–78, no. 5: 16–32, no. 6: 58–73, no. 8: 97–110.

Biddick, Kathleen. The ABC of Ptolemy: Mapping the World with the Alphabet." In *Text and Territory: Geographical Imagination in the European Middle Ages*. Edited by Sylvia Tomasch and Sealy Gilles, pp. 268–93. Philadelphia: University of Pennsylvania Press, 1998.

Borawski, Piotr. "Asymilacja kulturowa Tatarów w Wielkim Księstwie Litewskim." ["The Cultural Assimilation of Tatars in the Grand Duchy of Lithuania."] *Odrodzenie i Reformacja w Polsce* 36 (1992): 163–92.

Borawski, Piotr. "O sytuacji wyznaniowej ludności tatarskiej w Wielkim Księstwie Litewskim i w Polsce (XVI–XVIII w.)." ["On the Confessional Situation of the Tatar Population in the Grand Duchy of Lithuania and in Poland (XVI–XVIII Centuries)."] *Euhemer. Przegląd religioznawczy* 4, no. 118 (1980): 43–54.

Borawski, Piotr. "Sytuacja prawna ludności tatarskiej w Wielkim Księstwie Litewskim (XVI–XVIII w.)." ["The Legal Situation of the Tatar Population in the Grand Duchy of Lithuania (XVI–XVIII Century)."] *Acta Baltico-Slavica* 15 (1983): 55–76.

Borawski, Piotr. "Tolerancja religijna wobec ludności tatarskiej w Wielkim Księstwie Litewskim (XVI–XVIII wiek)." ["Religious Toleration Toward the Tatar Population of the Grand Duchy of Lithuania (XVI–XVIII Century)."] *Przegląd humanistyczny* 25, no. 3 (1981): 51–66.

Borawski, Piotr, and Sienkiewicz, Witold. "Chrystianizacja Tatarów w Wielkim Księstwie Litewskim." ["The Christianization of Tatars in the Grand Duchy of Lithuania."] *Odrodzenie i Reformacja w Polsce* 34 (1989): 87–114.

Boxer, C.R. *The Christian Century in Japan 1549–1650*. Berkeley, Los Angeles, London: University of California Press, 1951.

Braude, Benjamin. "The Sons of Noah and the Construction of Ethnic and Geographical Identities in the Medieval and Early Modern Periods." *The William and Mary Quarterly*, 3rd ser. 54[1] (January 1997): 103–41.

Breckenridge, Carol and Arjun Appadurai. "On Moving Targets." *Public Culture* 2, No. 1 (1989): 1–4.

Brotton, Jeremy. *Trading Territories: Mapping the Early Modern World*. London: Reaktion Books, 1997.

Burckhardt, Jacob. *The Civilization of the Renaissance in Italy*. Translated by S.G.C. Middlemore. New York, Macmillian, 1890.

Burke, Peter. *Popular Culture in Early Modern Europe*. London: T. Smith, 1978.

Chazan, Robert. "The Barcelona 'Disputation' of 1263: Christian Missionizing and Jewish Response." *Speculum* 52 (1977): 824–42.

Chazan, Robert. *Daggers of Faith: Thirteenth-Century Christian Missionizing and Jewish Response.* Berkeley, Los Angeles, and London: University of California Press, 1989.

Cohen, Israel. *Vilna.* Philadelphia: Jewish Publication Society of America, 1992. (Facsimile reprint of edition of 1943.)

Cohen, Jeffrey Jerome, ed. *The Postcolonial Middle Ages.* London: St. Martin's Press, 2000.

Cohen, Jeremy Jerome. *The Friars and the Jews: The Evolution of Medieval Anti-Judaism.* Ithaca and London: Cornell University Press, 1982.

Coyne, G.V.; Hoskin, M.A.; and Pedersen, O., eds. *Gregorian Reform of the Calendar: Proceedings of the Vatican Conference to Commemorate Its 400th Anniversary 1582–1982.* Vatican City: Specola Vaticana, 1983.

Crapanzano, Vincent. *Hermes' Dilemma and Hamlet's Desire: On the Epistemology of Interpretation.* Cambridge, MA, and London: Harvard University Press, 1992.

Crosby, Alfred W. *Ecological Imperialism. The Biological Expansion of Europe, 900–1900.* Cambridge: Cambridge University Press, 1986.

d'Alverny, Marie-Thérèse. "Translations and Translators." In *Renaissance and Renewal in the Twelfth Century.* Edited by Robert L. Benson and Giles Constable, with Carol D. Lanham, pp. 421–62. Cambridge, MA: Harvard University Press, 1982.

Darnton, Robert. *The Great Cat Massacre and Other Episodes in French Cultural History.* New York: Vintage, 1985.

Davis, Natalie Zemon. *Society and Culture in Early Modern France.* Stanford: Stanford University Press, 1965.

Davis, Natalie Zemon. *The Return of Martin Guerre.* Harvard: Harvard University Press, 1983.

Day, Phil. "The Nunsuch Ketch." *The Beaver: The Magazine of the North* 299:3 (Winter 1968): 4–17.

Derrida, Jacques. *The Ear of the Other: Otobiography, Transference, Translation: Texts and discussions with Jacques Derrida.* First edition 1985. Translated by Peggy Kamuf. Edited by Christie McDonald. Lincoln and London: University of Nebraska Press, 1988.

Destombes, Marcel. *Mappemondes A.D. 1200–1500. Catalogue préparé par la Commission des Cartes Anciennes de l'Union Géographique Internationale.* Vol. 1 of *Monumenta Cartographica Vetustioris Aevi A.D. 1200–150.* Edited by Roberto Almagià and Marcel Destombes. *Imago Mundi,* supp. 4. Amsterdam: Israel, 1964.

Diamond, Sigmund. "An Experiment in Feudalism: French Canada in the Seventeenth Century." *William and Mary Quarterly* (1961): 2–34.

Dickason, Olive P. *Canada's First Nations: A History of Founding Peoples from Earliest Times*. Norman, OK: University of Oklahoma Press, 1992.

Dickason, Olive P. "Concepts of Sovereignty at the Time of First Contacts." In *The Law of Nations and the New World*, pp. 141–295. Edmonton: University of Alberta Press, 1989.

Dickason, Olive P. *The Myth of the Savage and the Beginnings of French Colonialism in the Americas*. First edition 1984. Edmonton: University of Alberta Press, 1997.

Dienstag, Jacob I., ed. *Studies in Maimonides and St. Thomas Aquinas*. New York: Ktav Publishing House, 1975.

Duncan, David Ewing. *Calendar: Humanity's Epic Struggle to Determine a True and Accurate Year*. New York: Avon Books, 1998.

Durand, Dana Bennett. *The Vienna-Klosterneuburg Map Corpus of the Fifteenth Century. A Study in the Transition from Medieval to Modern Science*. Leiden: Brill, 1952.

Dworzaczkowa, Jolanta. *Bracia Czescy w Wielkopolsce w XVI i XVII wieku*. [The Czech Brethren in Great Poland in the Sixteenth and Seventeenth Centuries.] Warsaw: Semper, 1997.

Eamon, William. *Science and the Secrets of Nature*. Princeton: Princeton University Press, 1994.

Ebisawa, Arimichi. *Nihon kirishitan shi* [History of Christianity in Japan]. Tokyo: Hanawashobō, 1966.

Edwards, Philip. *Last Voyages: Cavendish, Hudson, Ralegh*. Oxford: Oxford University Press, 1988.

Elsky, Martin. *Authorizing Words: Speech, Writing, and Print in the English Renaissance*. Ithaca: Cornell University Press, 1989.

Elukin, Jonathan M. "From Jew to Christian? Conversion and Immutability in Medieval Europe." In *Varieties of Religious Conversion in the Middle Ages*. Edited by James Muldoon, pp. 171–89. Gainesville: University of Florida Press, 1997.

Eriksen, Thomas Hylland. *Ethnicity and Nationalism. Anthropological Perspectives*. London and Boulder, CO: Pluto Press, 1993.

Esteve Barba, Francisco. *Historiografía indiana*. Madrid: Editorial Gredos, 1964.

Flint, Valerie I.J. "The Hereford Map: Its Author(s), Two Scenes and a Border." *Transactions of the Royal Historical Society*, 6th ser. 8 (1998): 19–44.

Fournier, Martin. "Le Cas Radisson: Analyse pluridisciplinaire d'une phénomène complexe." *Canadian Folklore Canadienne* 18.2 (1996): 91–109.

Fournier, Martin. *Pierre-Esprit Radisson, coureur de bois et homme du monde (1652–1685)*. Québec: Nuit Blanche, 1996.

Fournier, Martin. *Les Quatres couleurs de Radisson*. Thèse de doctorat en histoire, Université Laval, 1998.

France, John. "Patronage and the Appeal of the First Crusade." In *The First Crusade: Origins and Impacts*. Edited by Jonathan Phillips, pp. 5–20. Manchester and New York: Manchester University Press, 1997.

Francis, R. Douglas; Jones, Richard ; and Smith, Donald B. eds. *Origins: Canadian History to Confederation*. Toronto and Montréal: Holt, Rinehart and Winston of Canada, 1992.

Franklin, Wayne. *Discovers, Explorers, Settlers: The Diligent Writers of Early America*. Chicago and London: University of Chicago Press, 1979.

Frick, David A. "'Foolish Rus'": On Polish Civilization, Ruthenian Self-Hatred, and Kasijan Sakovyč." *Harvard Ukrainian Studies* 18 (1994): 210–48.

Friedman, John Block. *The Monstrous Races in Medieval Art and Thought*. Cambridge, MA: Harvard University Press, 1981.

Friedman, Jonathan. "Myth, History, and Political Identity." *Cultural Anthropology* 7 No. 2 (1992): 194.

Fuller, Mary C. *Voyages in print: English travel to Ameria, 1576–1624*. Cambridge, MA: Cambridge University Press, 1995.

Gautier Dalché, Patrick. "Le souvenir de la *Géographie* de Ptolémée dans le monde latin médiéval (VIe–XIVe siècles)." *Euphrosyne. Revista de Filologia Clássica*, n.s. 27 (1999): 79–106.

Gautier Dalché, Patrick. "Pour une histoire du regard géographique. Conception et usage de la carte au XVe siècle." *Micrologus* 4 (1996): 77–103.

Geertz, Clifford. *The Interpretation of Cultures*. New York: Basic Books, 1973.

Geiger, A. 1853. *Isaak Troki. Ein Apologet des Iudenthums am Ende des sechszehnten Jahrhunderts*. [Isaak Troki. An Apologist for Judaism at the End of the Sixteenth Century.] Wrocław, 1853.

Gillies, John. *Shakespeare and the Geography of Difference*. Cambridge: Cambridge University Press, 1994.

Ginsberg, Elaine K., ed. *Passing and the Fictions of Identity*. Durham and London: Duke University Press, 1996.

Ginzburg, Carlo. *Clues, Myths, and the Historical Method*. Translated by John and Anne Tedeschi. Baltimore: Johns Hopkins University Press, 1989.

Glantz, Margo, ed. *Notas y comentarios sobre Alvar Núñez Cabeza de Vaca*. México: Grijalbo, 1993.

Golb, Norman. *The Jews in Medieval Normandy: A Social and Intellectual History*. Cambridge: Cambridge University Press, 1998.

Golubev, S. "Lifos—polemičeskoe sočinenie, vyšedšee iz Kievo-pečerskoj tipografii v 1644 godu." ["Lithos, A Polemical Work Issued by the Kiev Caves Printing House in 1644."] In *Arxiv jugo-zapadnoj rossii, izdavaemyj Kommissieju dlja rabora drevnix aktov*, part 1, vol. 9. Kiev, 1893.

Gombrich, E.H. *Art and Illusion: A Study in the Psychology of Pictorial Representation.* Princeton: Princeton University Press, 1956.

Gonoi, Takashi. *Tokugawa shoki kirishitan shi kenkyū* [A Study of Christian History in the Early Tokugawa Period], rev. ed. Tokyo: Yoshikawakōbunkan, 1992.

Gossman, Lionel. *Between History and Literature.* Cambridge, MA: Harvard University Press, 1990.

Gow, Andrew Colin. "Gog and Magog on *mappaemundi* and early printed world maps: Orientalizing ethnography in the apocalyptic tradition." *Journal of Early Modern History* 2[1] (1998): 61–88.

Graboïs, Aryeh. "The *Hebraica Veritas* and Jewish-Christian Intellectual Relations in the Twelfth Century." *Speculum* 50 (1975): 613–34.

Grafton, Anthony, April Shelford and Nancy Siraisi. *New Worlds, Ancient Texts: The Power of Tradition and the Shock of Discovery.* Cambridge, MA: Harvard University Press, 1992.

Grayzel, Solomon. *The Church and the Jews in the XIIIth Century: A Study of Their Relations during the Years 1198–1254, Based on the Papal Letters and the Conciliar Decrees of the Period*, revised ed. New York: Hermon Press, 1966.

Green, L.C. "Claims to Territory in North America." In *The Law of Nations and the New World*, pp. 1–139. Edmonton: University of Alberta Press, 1989.

Greenblatt, Stephen. "Learning to Curse: Aspects of Linguistic Colonialism in the Sixteenth Century." In *First Images of America*. Edited by Fredi Chiapelli. vol. 2, pp. 561–580. Berkeley: University of California Press, 1976.

Greenblatt, Stephen. *Marvelous Possessions: The Wonder of the New World.* Chicago: University of Chicago Press, 1991.

Greenblatt, Stephen, ed. *New World Encounters.* Berkeley: University of California Press, 1993.

Greenblatt, Stephen. *Shakespearean Negotiations: The Circulation of Social Energy in Renaissance England.* Berkeley and Los Angeles: University of California Press, 1988.

Gregg, Joan Young. *Devils, Women, and Jews: Reflections on the Other in Medieval Sermon Stories.* Albany: State University of New York Press, 1997.

Gross, Konrad. "Coureurs-de-Bois, Voyageurs, and Trappers: The Fur Trade and the Emergence of an Ignored Literary Tradition." *Canadian Literature* 127 (Winter 1990): 76–91.

Gudziak, Borys A. *Crisis and Reform. The Kyivan Metropolitanate, The Patriarchate of Constantinople, and the Genesis of the Union of Brest.* Cambridge, MA: Harvard Ukrainian Research Institute, 1998.

Gupta, Akhil and Ferguson, James. "Beyond 'Culture': Space, Identity, and the Politics of Difference." *Cultural Anthropology* 7, no. 1 (1992): 7.

Gusdorf, Georges. "Conditions and Limits of Autobiography." In *Autobiography: Essays Theoretical and Critical.* Translated and edited by James Olney, pp. 28–48. Princeton: Princeton University Press, 1980.

Haft, Adele J. "Maps, Mazes, and Monsters: The Iconography of the Library in Umberto Eco's *The Name of the Rose.*" *Studies in Iconography* 14 (1995): 9–50.

Hall, Kim F. *Things of Darkness: Economies of Race and Gender in Early Modern England.* Ithaca and London: Cornell University Press, 1995.

Halliday, M.A.K. "Antilanguages." In *Language as a Social Semiotic: the Social Interpretation of Language and Meaning.* London: Arnold, 1978.

Hart, Jonathan. *Theater and World: The Problematics of Shakespeare's History.* Boston: Northeastern University Press, 1992.

Hart, Jonathan. "Mediation in the Exchange between Europeans and Native Americans in the Early Modern Period." *Canadian Review of Comparative Literature/Revue Canadienne de Littérature Comparée* 22:2 (June/juin 1995): 319–43.

Hart, Jonathan. "Reading the Renaissance: An Introduction." In *Reading the Renaissance: Culture, Poetics, and Drama.* Pp. 1–13. New York: Garland, 1996.

Hartley, J.B. "New England Cartography and the Native Americans." *American Beginnings: Exploration, Culture, and Cartography in the Land of Norumbega.* Edited by Emerson W. Baker, et al., pp. 286–313, 363–371. Lincoln: University of Nebraska Press, 1994.

Hattaway, Michael. "Seeing things': Amazons and cannibals." In *Travel and Drama in Shakespeare's Time.* Edited by Jean-Pierre Maquerlot and Michèle Willems, pp. 179–92. Cambridge, MA: Cambridge University Press, 1996.

Hayles, N. Katherine. "Deciphering the Rules of Unruly Disciplines: A Modest Proposal for Literature and Science." In *Literature and Science.* Edited by Donald Bruce and Anthony Purdy. Vol. 14 of *Rodopi Perspectives on Modern Literature.* Amsterdam-Atlanta GA: Rodopi, 1994.

Helander, Birgit H. *Nicolaus Cusanus als Wegbereiter auch der heutigen Ökumene.* Uppsala, 1993.

Helgerson, Richard. *Forms of Nationhood: the Elizabethan Writing of England.* Chicago: University of Chicago Press, 1992.

Hirakawa, Sukehiro. *Wakon Yōsai no Keifu* [The Genealogy of Wakon Yōsai]. Tokyo: Kawadeshobōshinsha, 1971.

Hopwood, Victor G. "Explorers by Land to 1867." In *Literary History of Canada: Canadian Literature in English.* Edited by Carl F. Klinck. 2nd ed., vol. 1, 19–53. Toronto and Buffalo: University of Toronto Press, 1976.

Hulton, P.H. *America 1585: The Complete Drawings of John White.* Chapel Hill, NC: University of North Carolina Press, 1984.

Hunt, Lynn. "History Beyond Social History." In *The States of "Theory": History, Arts, and Critical Discourse.* Edited by David Carroll, pp. 95–111. New York: Columbia University Press, 1990.

Huntington, Samuel P. *The Clash of Civilizations and the Remaking of World Order.* New York: Simon & Schuster, 1996.

Hutcheon, Linda. *A Poetics of Postmodernism: History, Theory, Fiction.* New York: Routledge, 1988.

Ide, Katsumi. *Kirishitan shisōshi kenkyū josetsu, Nihonjin no kirisutokyō juyō* [Introduction to the Study of the Intellectual History of the Early Japanese Christians: The Reception of Christianity by the Japanese]. Tokyo: Perikansha, 1995.

Iser, Wolfgang. "The Reading Process: A Phenomenological Approach." *New Literary History* 3 (1971): 279–99.

Jacquin, Philippe. *Les Indiens blancs: Français et Indiens en Amérique du Nord (XVIe–XVIIIe siècle).* Paris: Payot, 1987.

Jara, René, and Nicholas Spadaccini. *1492–1992: Re/Discovering Colonial Writing.* Minneapolis: University of Minnesota Press, 1989.

Jara, René, and Nicholas Spadaccini. *Amerindian Images and the Legacy of Columbus.* Minneapolis: University of Minnesota Press, 1992.

Jenkins, Keith, ed. *The Postmodern History Reader.* New York: Routledge, 1997.

Kaplan, Joseph. "Naḥmanides." In *Encyclopaedia Judaica*, vol. 12. Jerusalem: Keter; New York: Macmillan, 1971.

Karr, William John. *Explorers, Soldiers, and Statesmen: A History of Canada Through Biography.* Freeport, NY: Books for Libraries Press, 1971.

Kawamura, Shinzō. "Making Christian Lay Communities during the 'Christian Century' in Japan: A Case Study of Takata District in Bungo." Ph.D. thesis, Georgetown University, 1999.

Kellogg, Louise Phelps, ed. *Early Narratives of the Northwest, 1634–1699.* New York: Barnes & Noble, 1945.

Keene, Donald. *The Japanese Discovery of Europe, 1720–1830,* rev. ed. Stanford: Stanford University Press, 1969.

Kishino, Hisashi. *Seiōjin no nihon hakken, zabieru rainichi mae nihon jōhō no kenkyū* [The Discovery of Japan by the Europeans, a Study of Information about Japan before Xavier's Arrival in Japan]. Tokyo: Yoshikawakōbunkan, 1989.

Kishino, Hisashi. *Zabieru no Dōhansha Anjirō. Sengoku jidai no Kokusaijin* [Xavier's Companion, Anjiro. An International Man during the Warring States Period]. Tokyo: Yoshikawakōbunkan, 2001.

Kishino, Hisashi. *Zabieru to nihon, Kirishitan kaikyōki no kenkyū* [Xavier and Japan, A Study of the Early Period of Christianity]. Tokyo: Yoshikawakōbunkan, 1998.

Klausner, Israel. *Vilnah, Yerushalayim de-Lita*. [Vilnius: The Jerusalem of Lithuania.] Tel Aviv, 1988.

Klinkowski, Edmund. "Grodno, Wilna und das Posener Land in einem deutschen Reisebericht vom Jahre 1586." ["Hrodno, Vilnius, and the Poznań District in a German Travel Report from the Year 1586."] *Deutsche Wissenschaftliche Zeitschrift für Polen* 30 (1936): 133–38.

Knoppers, Laura Lunger. "(En)gendering Shame: Measure for Measure and the Spectacles of Power." *English Literary Renaissance* 23 (1993): 450–71.

Kobori, Keiichirō. "Fuhenshugi no chōsen to nippon no ōtō [The Challenge of Universalism and the Response of the Japanese]." In *Tōzai no shisō tōsō* [The Ideological Struggle between East and West], *Sōsho Hikakubungaku Hikakubunka* [Series in Comparative Literature and Culture], vol. 4, edited by Kobori Keiichirō. Tokyo: Chūōkōronsha, 1994.

Kolodny, Annette. *Lay of the Land: Metaphor as Experience and History in American Life and Letters*. Chapel Hill, NC: University of North Carolina Press, 1975.

Kōno, Yoshinori. *Sei furanshisuko zabieru zen shōgai* [The Life of St. Francis Xavier]. Tokyo: Heibonsha, 1988.

Korolko, Mirosław. *Klejnot swobodnego sumienia. Polemika wokół konfederacji warszawskiej w latach 1573–1658*. [The Jewel of Free Conscience: The Polemic Over the Confederation of Warsaw in the Years 1573–1658.] Warsaw: PAX, 1974.

Kosman, Marceli. "Konflikty wyznaniowe w Wilnie. (Schyłek XVI–XVII w.)." ["Confessional Conflicts in Vilnius (End of the Sixteenth Century–Seventeenth Century)"]. *Kwartalnik Historyczny* 79 (1972): 3–23.

Kosman, Marceli. *Protestanci i kontrreformacja. Z dziejów tolerancji w Rzeczypospolitej XVI–XVIII wieku.* [Protestants and the Counter-Reformation: Aspects of the History of Toleration in the Republic of the XVI–XVIII Century.] Wrocław: Ossolineum, 1978.

Kosman, Marceli. *Reformacja i kontrreformacja w Wielkim Księstwie Litewskim w świetle propagandy wyznaniowej.* [The Reformation and the Counter-Reformation in the Grand Duchy of Lithuania in the Light of Confessional Propaganda.] Wrocław: Ossolineum, 1973.

Kosmanowa, Bogumiła. "Sprawa wileńskiego kościoła św. Michała (wizja J.I. Kraszewskiego a rzeczywistość historyczna)." ["The Affair of the Vilnius Church of St. Michael (J.I. Kraszewski's Vision and Historical Reality."] *Odrodzenie i Reformacja w Polsce* 40 (1996): 53–68.

Kot, Stanisław. "Aufbruch und Niedergang des Täufertums in Wilna (1563–1566)." ["The Rise and Fall of Anabaptism in Vilnius (1563–1566)."] *Archiv für Reformationsgeschichte* 49 (1958): 212–26.

Kowalenko, Władysław. "Geneza udziału stołecznego miasta Wilna w sejmach Rzeczypospolitej." ["The Genesis of the Participation of the Capital City Vilnius in the Diets of the Republic."] *Ateneum Wileńskie* 2 (1925–1926): 327–73; 3 (1927): 79–137.

Kraszewski, Ignacy. *Kościół Święto-Michalski w Wilnie. Obraz historyczny z pierwszej połowy XVII wieku.* [The St. Michael Church in Vilnius: An Historical Picture from the First Half of the Seventeenth Century.] Vilnius, 1833.

Kretschmer, Konrad. "Eine neue mittelalterliche Weltkarte der vatikanischen Bibliothek." *Zeitschrift der Gesellschaft für Erdkunde zu Berlin,* 3rd ser. 26 (1891): 371–406.

Kruger, Steven F. "Becoming Christian, Becoming Male?" In *Becoming Male in the Middle Ages.* Edited by Jeffrey Jerome Cohen and Bonnie Wheeler, pp. 21–41. New York and London: Garland, 1997.

Kruger, Steven F. "Conversion and Medieval Sexual, Religious, and Racial Categories." In *Constructing Medieval Sexuality.* Edited by Karma Lochrie, Peggy McCracken, and James A. Schultz, pp. 158–79. Minneapolis and London: University of Minnesota Press, 1997.

Kruger, Steven F. "The Spectral Jew." *New Medieval Literatures* 2 (1998): 9–35.

Krzyczyński, Leon. "Historia meczetu w Wilnie. (Próba monografii.)." ["The History of the Mosque in Vilnius (An Attempt at a Monograph)."] *Przegląd islamski* 6 (1937): 7–33.

Krzyżanowski, Julian, ed. *Nowa księga przysłów i wyrażeń przysłowiowych polskich.* [A New Book of Polish Proverbs and Proverbial Expressions.] Vol. 3. Warsaw: Państwowy Instytut Wydawniczy, 1972.

Kuhn, Thomas. *The Structure of Scientific Revolutions.* Second edition. Chicago: University of Chicago Press, 1970.

Kupfer, Marcia. "The Lost Wheel Map of Ambrogio Lorenzetti." *Art Bulletin* 78[2] (June 1996): 286–310.

Kupperman, Karen Ordahl. *Settling with the Indians: The Meeting of English and Indian Cultures in America, 1580–1640.* Totowa, NJ: Rowman and Littlefield, 1975.

Kupperman, Karen Ordahl. *Roanoke: The Abandoned Colony.* Totowa, NJ: Rowman and Allanheld, 1984.

Lafaye, Jacques. "Les miracles d'Alvar Núñez Cabeza de Vaca (1527–1536)." *Bulletin Hispanique,* 56 (1962): 136–52.

Lamb, W. Kaye. "Sir Francis Drake." In *Dictionary of Canadian Biography/ Dictionnaire Biographique du Canada,* Vol. 1, p. 280. Edited by George W. Brown, Marcel Trudel, and Andre Vaclon. Toronto and Laval: University of Toronto Press and Les Presses de l'université Laval, 1966.

Lang, George. "Voyageur Discourse and the Absence of Fur Trade Pidgin." *Canadian Literature* 131 (Winter 1991): 51–63.

Langmuir, Gavin I. *History, Religion, and Antisemitism*. Berkeley, Los Angeles, and Oxford: University of California Press, 1990.

Langmuir, Gavin I. *Toward a Definition of Antisemitism*. Berkeley, Los Angeles, and Oxford: University of California Press, 1990.

Laslett, Peter. *The World We Have Lost*. New York: Scribner, 1965.

Laucevičius, Edmundas and Vitkauskienė, Birutė Rūta. *Lietuvos auksakalystė XV–XIX amžius*. [Lithuanian Goldsmithery in the XV–XIX Centuries.] Vilnius: Baltos lankos, 2001.

Leonard, E.M. *The Early History of English Poor Relief*. Cambridge: Cambridge University Press, 1900.

Lestringant, Frank. *Mapping the Renaissance World: The Geographical Imagination in the Age of Discovery*. Translated by David Fausett. Berkeley and Los Angeles: University of California Press, 1994.

Levin, Harry. *The Myth of The Golden Age in the Renaissance*. Bloomington and London: Indiana University Press, 1969.

Lewis, Bernard. *The Muslim Discovery of Europe*. New York: Norton, 1982.

Lewis, Martin W. and Kären E. Wigen. *The Myth of Continents: A Critique of Metageography*. Berkeley: University of California Press, 1997.

Lewis, Robert E. "*Los naufragios* de Alvar Núñez Cabeza de Vaca: historia y ficción." *Revista Iberoamericana* 48 (July–December 1982): 681–94.

Limor, Ora, and Guy G. Stroumsa, eds. *Contra Iudaeos: Ancient and Medieval Polemics between Christians and Jews*. Tübingen: J.C.B. Mohr [Paul Siebeck], 1996.

Livingstone, David. *The Geographical Tradition. Episodes in the History of a Contested Enterprise*. Oxford: Blackwell, 1992.

Lowenthal, David. *Possessed by the Past: The Heritage Crusade and the Spoils of History*. New York: The Free Press, 1996.

Łowmiańska, Marja. *Wilno przed najazdem moskiewskim 1655 roku*. [Vilnius Before the Muscovite Invasion of 1655.] Bibljoteczka wileńska 3. Vilnius, 1929.

Maccoby, Hyam. *Judaism on Trial: Jewish-Christian Disputations in the Middle Ages*. London: The Littman Library of Jewish Civilization, 1993 [1982].

MacLaren, Ian S. "Exploration/Travel Literature and the Evolution of the Author." *International Journal of Canadian Studies/Revue internationale d'études canadiennnes* 5 (Spring/Printemps 1992): 41–67.

Malkki, Liisa. "National Geographic: The Rooting of Peoples and the Territorialization of National Identity Among Scholars and Refugees." *Cultural Anthropology* 7 No. 1 (1992): 37.

Mancall, Peter C. "The Age of Discovery." *Reviews in American History* 26 (1998): 26–53.

Mann, Jacob. *Texts and Studies in Jewish History and Literature.* Vol. II. *Karaitica.* Philadelphia: The Hebrew Press of the Jewish Publication Society of America, 1935.

Marcus, Ivan G. *Rituals of Childhood: Jewish Acculturation in Medieval Europe.* New Haven: Yale University Press, 1996.

Matsuda, Kiichi. "Kaidai [Comments]." In *Nihon junsatsu ki* [Reports of the Visitation in Japan], by Alessandro Valignano, pp. 235–365. Tokyo: Heibonsha, 1973.

Matsuda, Kiichi and Jolissen, E. *Furoisu no nihon oboegaki* [Frois's notes on Japan]. Tokyo: Chūōkōronsha, 1983.

Matsuda, Kiichi. *Valignano to kirishitan shūmon* [Valignano and the Christian Religion]. Tokyo: Chōbunsha, 1992.

Maura, Juan Francisco. "Veracidad en los *Naufragios*: la técnica narrativa de Alvar Núñez Cabeza de Vaca." *Revista Iberoamericana* 170–171 (January–June 1995): 187–96.

McMullan, John L. *The Canting Crew: London's Criminal Underworld 1550–1700.* New Brunswick: Rutgers University Press, 1984.

McRoberts, Kenneth, ed. *Beyond Québec: Taking Stock of Canada.* Montréal and Kingston: McGill-Queen's University Press, 1995.

Ménager, Daniel. "The Sixteenth Century: French Literature." In *The New Encyclopaedia Britannica: 15th Edition. Macropaedia.* Pp. 543–545. Chicago: Encyclopaedia Britannica, 1991.

Menton, Seymour. "La verdadera historia de Alvar Núñez Cabeza de Vaca en la última novela de Abel Posse, *El largo atardecer del caminante.*" *Revista Iberoamericana* 52 (April–June 1995): 421–26.

Menton, Seymour. *Latin America's New Historical Novel.* Austin: University of Texas Press, 1993.

Merkelbach, Reinhold. *Roman und Mysterium in der Antike.* München: Beck, 1962.

Michelet, Jules. *The History of France.* Translated by Walter K. Kelly. London: Chapman and Hall, 1844–46.

Monmonier, Mark. *How to Lie with Maps.* Chicago: University of Chicago Press, 1991.

Moore, R.I. *The Formation of a Persecuting Society: Power and Deviance in Western Europe, 950–1250.* Oxford: Basil Blackwell, 1987.

Moran, J.F. *The Japanese and the Jesuits, Alessandro Valignano in sixteenth-century Japan.* London and New York: Routledge, 1993.

Morzy, Józef. "Geneza i rozwój cechów wileńskich do końca XVII w." ["Genesis and Development of the Vilnius Guilds to the End of the Seventeenth Century."] *Zeszyty naukowe Uniwersytetu im. A. Mickiewicza, Seria Historia.* Pp. 3–93. Poznań, 1959.

Muchliński, A. ed. "Zdanie sprawy o Tatarach litewskich przez jednego z tych Tatarów złożone Sułtanowi Sulejmanowi w r. 1558." ["A Report on Lithuanian Tatars, Rendered by One of Those Tatars to Sultan Suleiman in 1558."] *Teka wileńska* nos. 4 (1858): 241–72, 5: 121–79, and 6: 139–83.

Murai, Sanae. *Tenno to kirishitan kinsei, 'kirishitan no seiki' niokeru kenryoku tōsō no kōzu* [The Emperor and the prohibition of Christianity. The Structure of the Power Struggle in the 'Christian Century']. Tokyo: Yūzankaku shuppan, 2000.

Namias, June. *White Captives: Gender and Ethnicity on the American Frontier.* Chapel Hill and London: University of North Carolina Press, 1993.

Neumann, I.B. and J.M. Walsh. "The Other in European Self-Definition: A Critical Addendum to the Literature on International Society." *Review of International Studies* 17, no. 4 (1991).

Newman, Peter C. *Company of Adventurers*, vol. 1. Markham, ON: Viking, 1985.

Nihon kirisutokyō daijiten [Historical Lexicon of Christianity in Japan]. Tokyo: Kyōbunkan, 1988.

Nute, Grace Lee. *Caesars of the Wilderness: Médard Chouart, Sieur Des Groseilliers and Pierre-Esprit Radisson, 1618–1710.* New York and London: D. Appleton-Century Company, 1943.

Nute, Grace Lee. "Radisson, Pierre-Esprit." In *Dictionary of Canadian Biography/Dictionnaire Biographique du Canada*, vol. 2, 535–40. Edited by David M. Hayne and Andre Vaclon Toronto and Laval: University of Toronto Press and Les Presses de l'université Laval, 1969.

Obara, Satoru. *Zabieru* [Xavier]. Tokyo: Shimizushoin, 1998.

Ogonowski, Zbigniew. *Z zagadnień tolerancji w Polsce w XVII wieku.* [Aspects of the History of Toleration in Poland in the Seventeenth Century.] Warsaw: Państwowe Wydawnictwo Naukowe, 1958.

O'Malley, John W. *The First Jesuits.* Cambridge, MA: Harvard University Press, 1993.

Opisanie arxiva zapadnorusskix uniatskix mitropolitov, 1470–1700. [A Description of the Archive of the West-Russian Uniate Metropolitans, 1470–1700.] Vol. 1. St. Petersburg: Sinodal'naja tipgrafija, 1897.

Orlin, Lena Cowen. *Private Matters and Public Culture in Post-Reformation England.* Ithaca and London: Cornell University Press, 1994.

Pagden, Anthony. *Lords of All the World: Ideologies of Empire in Spain, Britain and France, c. 1500 – c. 1800.* New Haven: Yale University Press, 1995.

Pagden, Anthony. *The Fall of Natural Man.* Cambridge: Cambridge University Press, 1982.

Paquet, Gilles, and Jean-Pierre Wallot. "Nouvelle France / Québec / Canada: A World of Limited Identities." In *Colonial Identity in the Atlantic World, 1500–1800*, edited by Nicholas Canny and Anthony Pagden, pp. 95–113. Princeton: Princeton University Press, 1987.

Parker, John. "A fragment of a fifteenth-century planisphere in the James Ford Bell Collection." *Imago Mundi* 19 (1965): 106–7.

Parker, Patricia. *Shakespeare from the Margins: Language, Culture, Context.* Chicago and London: University of Chicago Press, 1996.

Pastor, Beatriz. *Discurso narrativo de la conquista de América.* La Habana: Casa de las Américas, 1983.

Patterson, Annabel. *Reading Holinshed's Chronicles.* Chicago and London: University of Chicago Press, 1994.

Pons, María Cristina. *Memorias del olvido: la novela histórica de fines del siglo XX.* México: Siglo Veintiuno Editores, 1996.

Porter, Dale H. *The Emergence of the Past: A Theory of Historical Explanation.* Chicago: University of Chicago Press, 1981.

Pratt, Mary Louise. *Imperial Eyes: Travel Writing and Transculturation.* London and New York: Routledge, 1992.

Pupo-Walker, Enrique. "Pesquisas para una nueva lectura de *Los naufragios*, de Alvar Núñez Cabeza de Vaca." *Revista Iberoamericana* 53 (July–September 1987): 517–39.

Quinn, David Beers. *England and the Discovery of America, 1481–1620. From the Bristol Voyages of the Fifteenth Century to the Pilgrim Settlement at Plymouth: The Exploration, Exploitation, and Trial-and-Error Colonization of North America By the English.* New York: Alfred A. Knopf, 1974.

Quinn, David Beers. *Set Fair for Roanoke: Voyages and Colonies, 1584–1606.* 2nd ed. Chapel Hill: University of North Carolina Press, 1986.

Quinn, David Beers., ed. *The Hakluyt Handbook.* 2 vols. London: Hakluyt Society, 2nd Ser., 144–45, 1974.

Quinn, David Beers and A.N. Ryan, eds. *England's Sea Empire, 1550–1642.* London: George Allen & Unwin, 1983.

"Radisson, Pierre-Esprit." *Encyclopedia Canadiana*, vol. 8, pp. 397–398. Ottawa: The Canadiana Company Limited, a subsidiary of The Grolier Society of Canada Limited, 1958.

Raguaskas, Aivas. *Vilniaus miesto valdantysis elitas XVII a. antrojoje pusėje (1662–1702 m.)* [The Ruling Elite of the City of Vilnius in the Second Half of the Seventeenth century (1662–1702).] Vilnius: Diemedžio leidykla, 2002.

Rankin, Oliver Shaw. *Jewish Religious Polemic of Early and Later Centuries, A Study of Documents Here Rendered in English.* New York: Ktav Publishing House, 1970.

Rembaum, Joel E. "The Talmud and the Popes: Reflections on the Talmud Trials of the 1240s." *Viator* 13 (1982): 203–23.

Renan, Ernest. "What is a Nation?" (1882). Translated by Martin Thom. In *Nation and Narration.* Edited by Homi K. Bhabha, pp. 8–22. London and New York: Routledge, 1990.

Ricoeur, Paul. *Temps et récit.* Paris: Seuil, 1985.

Rimmon-Kenan, Shlomith. *Narrative Fiction: Contemporary Poetics.* London and New York: Methuen, 1983; rpt. 1987.

Rosello, Mireille. *Declining the Stereotype: Ethnicity and Representation in French Cultures.* Hanover, NH: University Press of New England, 1998.

Rosenthal, Judah M. "The Talmud on Trial: The Disputation at Paris in the Year 1240." *Jewish Quarterly Review* n.s. 47 (1956): 58–76, 145–69.

Ross, Andrew C. *A Vision Betrayed, the Jesuits in Japan and China 1542–1742.* Maryknoll, NY: Orbis Books, 1994.

Ross, Andrew C. "Alessandro Valignano: The Jesuits and Culture in the East." In *The Jesuits, Cultures, Sciences, and the Arts 1540–1773.* Edited by John W. O'Malley, S.J., Gauvin Alexander Bailey, Steven J. Harris, and T. Frank Kennedy, S.J. Toronto, Buffalo, London: University of Toronto Press, 1999.

Said, Edward. *Orientalism.* 1978; rpt. New York: Vintage, 1979.

Saunders, J. W. "The Stigma of Print: A Note on the Social Bases of Tudor Poetry." *Essays in Criticism* 1 (1951): 139–64.

Sayre, Gordon M. *Les Sauvages Américaines: Representations of Native Americans in French and English Colonial Literature.* Chapel Hill and London: University of North Carolina Press, 1997.

Schramm, Gottfried. "Protestantismus und städtische Gesellschaft in Wilna (16.–17. Jahrhundert)." ["Protestantism and Urban Society in Vilnius (16 to 17 Century)."] *Jahrbücher für Geschichte Osteuropas* 17 (1969): 187–214.

Sedgwick, Eve Kosofsky. *Epistemology of the Closet.* Berkeley and Los Angeles: University of California Press, 1990.

Seed, Patricia. *Ceremonies of Possession in Europe's Conquest of the New World, 1492–1640.* New York: Cambridge University Press, 1995; rpt. 1997.

Simon, Marcel. *Verus Israel: A Study of the Relations between Christians and Jews in the Roman Empire (135–425).* Translated by H. McKeating. Oxford: Oxford University Press, 1986.

Slack, Paul. *The English Poor Law 1531–1782.* Cambridge: Cambridge University Press, 1995.

Slack, Paul. *Poverty and Policy in Tudor and Stuart England.* London and New York: Longman, 1988.

Smalley, Beryl. *The Study of the Bible in the Middle Ages.* Notre Dame, IN: University of Notre Dame Press, 1964 [1952].

Sobczak, Jacek. 1984. *Położenie prawne ludności tatarskiej w Wielkim Księstwie Litewskim.* [The Legal Situation of the Tatar Population in the Grand Duchy of Lithuania.] Poznańskie Towarzystwo Przyjaciół Nauk, Wydział Historii i Nauk Społecznych, Prace Komisji Historycznej. Vol. 38. Poznań, 1984.

Soja, Edward W. *Postmodern Geographies: The Reassertion of Space in Critical Theory.* Verso, 1989.

Stein, S. "A Disputation on Moneylending between Jews and Gentiles in Me'ir b. Simeon's Milḥemeth Miṣwah (Narbonne, 13th Cent.)." *Journal of Jewish Studies* 10 (1959): 45–61.

Stein, S. *Jewish-Christian Disputations in Thirteenth-Century Narbonne.* Inaugural Lecture, University College, London, 22 October 1964. London: H.K. Lewis, 1969.

Szegda, Mirosław. "Sakowicz (Isakowicz), Kalikst." In *Polski słownik biograficzny.* Vol. 34. Pp. 343–45. Wrocław, 1994.

Szyszman, Simon. "Osadnictwo karaimskie i tatarskie na ziemiach Wielkiego Księstwa Litewskiego." ["The Karaim and Tatar Settlements on the Lands of the Grand Duchy of Lithuania."] *Myśl karaimska* 10 (1933): 29–36.

Szyszman, Simon. *Le Karïsme. Ses doctrines et son histoire.* [Karaism: Its Doctrines and History.] Lausanne: L'age d'homme, 1980.

Takase, Kōichirō. *Kirishitanjidai no kenkyū* [A Study of the Christian Period]. Tokyo: Iwanamishoten, 1977.

Takase, Kōichirō. *Kirishitan no seiki* [The Century of Christianity]. Tokyo: Iwanamishoten, 1993.

Takase, Kōichirō. *Kirishitanjidai taigaikankei no kenkyū* [A Study of Foreign Relations in the Christian Period]. Tokyo: Yoshikawakōbunkan, 1994.

Tazbir, Janusz. *Dzieje polskiej tolerancji.* [The History of Polish Toleration.] Warsaw: Interpress, 1973.

Tazbir, Janusz. *Państwo bez stosów.* [State Without Stakes.] Warsaw: Państwowy Instytut Wydawniczy, 1967.

Tazbir, Janusz. "Różnowiercy a kult maryjny." ["The Heterodox and the Marian Cult."] In *Świat Panów Pasków. Eseje i Studia,* 343–64. Łódz: Wydawnicto łódzkie, 1986.

Tebeau, Charlton W. *A History of Florida.* Coral Gables: University of Miami Press, 1971.

Thomas, Keith. "Anthropology and History." *Past and Present* 24 (1963): 3–24.

Todorov, Tzvetan. *The Conquest of America, The Question of the Other.* Translated by Richard Howard. New York: Harper & Row, 1984.

Tolan, John. *Petrus Alfonsi and His Medieval Readers.* Gainesville: University Press of Florida, 1993.

Tomasch, Sylvia and Sealy Gilles, eds. *Text and Territory. Geographical Imagination in The European Middle Ages.* Philadelphia: University of Pennsylvania Press, 1998.

Toynbee, Arnold J. *A Study of History,* vols. IV and VIII. London, New York, Toronto: Oxford University Press, 1951, 1954.

Toynbee, Arnold J. *Civilization on Trial* and *The World and the West*. New York: Meridian Books, 1958.

Tyszkiewicz, Jan. *Tatarzy na Litwie i w Polsce. Studia z dziejów XIII–XVIII w.* [Tatars in Lithuania and Poland: Studies from the History of the XIII–XVIII Centuries.] Warsaw: Państwowe Wydawnictwo Naukowe, 1989.

Varner, John Grier, and Jeannette Johnson Varner, eds. and trans. *The Florida of the Inca*. Austin: University of Texas Press, 1951.

Vasil'evskij, V.G. "Očerk istorii goroda Vil'ny." ["A Sketch of the History of the City of Vilnius."] In *Pamjatniki russkoj stariny v zapadnyx gubernijax imperii*. Edited by P.N. Batjuškov. Vols. 5 and 6. St. Petersburg, 1872–1874.

Vilniaus miesto istorija nuo seniausių laikų iki Spalio revoliucijos. [The History of the City of Vilnius from the Oldest Times to the October Revolution.] Ed. J. Jurginis, V. Merkys, and A. Tautavičius. Vilnius: Mintis, 1968.

Wall, Wendy. *The Imprint of Gender: Authorship and Publication in the English Renaissance*. Ithaca: Cornell University Press, 1993.

Warkentin, Germaine. "Discovering Radisson: A Renaissance Adventurer Between Two Worlds." In *Reading Beyond Words: Contexts for Native History*. Edited by Jennifer S. H. Brown and Elizabeth Vibert, pp. 43–70. Peterborough, ON: Broadview Press,1996.

Warkentin, Germaine. "Pierre-Esprit Radisson and the Language of Place." *Queen's Quarterly* 101/2 (Summer 1994): 305–16.

Warkentin, Germaine. "Styles of Authorship in New France: Pierre Boucher, Settler, and Pierre-Esprit Radisson, Explorer." *Papers of the Bibliographical Society of Canada/Cahiers de la Société du Canada* 37.2 (Fall/Automne 1999): 16–34.

Warner, Michael. "Introduction" to "The Relation of my Voyage, being in Bondage in the Lands of the Irokoits," by Pierre-Esprit Radisson. In *The English Literatures of America, 1500–1800*. Edited by Myra Jehlen and Michael Warner, pp. 325–26. New York and London: Routledge, 1997.

Warwick, Jack. *The Long Journey: Literary Themes of French Canada*. Toronto: University of Toronto Press, 1968.

Westrem, Scott D. *The Hereford Map. A Transcription and Translation of the Legends with Commentary*. Terrarum Orbis 1. Turnhout: Brepols, 2001.

Westrem, Scott D. *Learning from Legends on the James Ford Bell* Mappamundi. The James Ford Bell Lectures 37. Minneapolis: The Associates of the James Ford Bell Library, 2000.

Whigham, Frank. *Ambition and Privilege: The Social Tropes of Elizabethan Courtesy Theory*. Berkeley: University of California Press, 1984.

White, Hayden. *Tropics of Discourse*. Baltimore: The Johns Hopkins University Press, 1978.

Wigley, Mark. "Untitled: The Housing of Gender." In *Sexuality and Space*. Edited by Beatriz Colomina, pp. 327–389. Princeton Papers on Architecture, Princeton University School of Architecture, 1992.

Willen, Diane. "Women in the Public Sphere in Early Modern England." *Sixteenth Century Journal* 19 (1988): 559–75.

Winship, George Parker. *The Coronado Expedition 1540–1542*. Chicago: The Río Grande Press, 1964.

Wisner, Henryk. "Likwidacja zboru ewangelickiego w Wilnie (1639–1646). Z dziejów walki z inaczej wierzącymi." ["The Liquidation of the Evangelical Church in Vilnius (1639–1640): From the History of the Battle with the Heterodox."] *Odrodzenie i Reformacja w Polsce* 37 (1993): 89–102.

Wisner, Henryk. *Rozróżnieni w wierze. Szkice z dziejów Rzeczypospolitej schyłku XVI i połowy XVII wieku.* [Dissidents in Faith: Sketches from the History of the Republic from the End of the XVI to the Middle of the XVII Century.] Warsaw: Książka i Wiedza, 1982.

Wittkower, Rudolf. "Marvels of the East: A Study in the History of Monsters." In *Allegory and the Migration of Symbols*, pp. 45–74, 196–205. London: Thames and Hudson, 1977, rpt. 1987 [originally published in 1942].

Woodbridge, Linda. *Vagrancy, Homelessness, and English Renaissance Literature.* Urbana and Chicago: University of Illinois Press, 2001.

Woodward, David. "Medieval *Mappaemundi*." In *Cartography in Prehistoric, Ancient, and Medieval Europe and the Mediterranean*. Vol. 1 of *The History of Cartography*, edited by J. B. Harley and David Woodward, pp. 286–370. Chicago: University of Chicago Press, 1987.

Zakrzewski, Andrzej B. "Osadnictwo tatarskie w Wielkim Księstwie Litewskim— aspekty wyznaniowe." ["The Tatar Settlement in the Grand Duchy of Lithuania: Confessional Aspects."] *Acta Baltico-Slavica* 20 (1989): 137–53.

Zakrzewski, Andrzej B. "O asymilacji Tatarów w Rzeczypospolitej w XVI–XVIII w." ["On the Assimilation of Tatars in the Republic of the XVI–XVIII Century.] In *Tryumfy i porażki. Studia z dziejów kultury polskiej XVI–XVIII w.*, edited by Maria Bogucka, pp. 75–96. Warsaw: Państwowe Wydawnictwo Naukowe, 1989.

Zakrzewski, Andrzej B. 1992. "Niektóre aspekty położenia kulturalnego Tatarów Litewskich w XVI–XVIII w." ["Certain Aspects of the Cultural Situation of Lithuanian Tatars in the XVI–XVIII Century."] In *Wilno— Wileńszczyzna jako krajobraz i środowisko wielu kultur*. Vol. 2. Pp. 107–28. Białystok, 1992.

Zhiri, Oumelbanine. *Les Sillages de Jean Léon l'Africain du XVIᵉ au XXᵉ siècle.* Casablanca: Wallada, 1996.

Zhiri, Oumelbanine. *L'Afrique au miroir de l'Europe, fortunes de Jean Léon l'Africain à la Renaissance.* Geneva: Droz, 1991.

Zwolski, Bogumił. *Sprawa Zboru ewangelicko-reformowanego w Wilnie w latach 1639–41.* [The Affair of the Evangelical Reformed Church in Vilnius in the Years 1639–1641.] *Bibljoteczka wileńska* 7. Vilnius, 1936.

Index

NOTE: *Page numbers for illustrations are in italics*

cannibals, 123, 128
Carafa, Gian Pietro, 101
Caribbean, 212
Carpentier, Alejo, 209
Cartier, Jacques, 178
cartographers, xx, 6, 11
cartographic depictions. *See* maps;
    narrative, of cartographic
    depictions
cartographic innovations. *See* maps,
    and cartographic
    innovations
Castile, 69, 91
Castillo Maldonado, Alonso del, 216
Catalan Atlas, 16 n. 8
Catholic Church, 23–24
Caucasus, 146
Cervantes, Miguel de, 232
Cham, 70
Champlain, Samuel de, 178
Charles II (king of England), 182
Chazan, Robert, 74
Chieti, 101
Chile, 153
China, 90, 97
Christ, Jesus, 41, 49, 67, 69–70, 93, 211
Christian missions in Japan, 88
Christiani, Pablo, 72–73, 76, 79–80. *See
    also* Paul, Fray
Christianity, ban on, 87, 91, 107 n. 1
Church Slavonic language, 28
Cicero, Marcus Tullius, 239
Clement IV, 80
climatic theory, 13–14
Cochin, 93, 104
Cohen, Jeremy, 69, 71
Coimbra, 100
Colombia, 210
colonial failures, 161–64
colonial theorists, 145–51, 160–61
colonization, 122–23
colonizer and colonized. *See* conflict,
    dominant and subjugated
    cultures
Colorado River, 203
Columbus, Christopher, xxxiii, 17
    n. 15, 118, 207–10, 227

Commonwealth men, xxvi
conceptual models, xvii, 176, 225
    comparative framework of, xxviii
    and crossed boundaries, xviii, 235
    epistemology of, 212, 220, 223 n. 24
    history of
        past as other in, xxxii, 213–14,
            220
        reinterpretation of, xxxii, 205
    and ideological conformity,
        176, 208
    literary history as, 177
    temporal frameworks of, xvii, xix,
        xx
conflict
    dominant and subjugated cultures,
        xviii, xxv, xxxii, xxxiii
    and erasure of identity. *See* identity,
        erasure of
    with natives, 158–61, 164
    in Old and New worlds, xviii, 148,
        155, 157, 242
    religious (*see also* Jewish
        persecution), 9, 18 n. 21, 63,
        65, 69–74
conquest, xxv
    and brutality of Spain's ideology,
        211, 213
    as commercial enterprise, 173
    discourse on
        as failure narrative, 204,
            207, 213
        as triumphalist narrative, 197
            n. 19, 207
    evangelization as corollary to
        subjugation of, 207
    historiography of, as predetermined
        epistemology. *See*
        conceptual models,
        epistemology of
    as imperial project, xxx
    indictment of, xxxi, 205–7
    as plunder and enslavement, 205
Constantinople, 6, 107
contact, xxii, xxiv, xxix–xxx, 217, 225
    as contamination, xxii
    control of, among the Japanese, 88

Dee, John, 235
Dekker, Thomas, 124
Derrida, Jacques, 144
des Groseilliers, Médard Chouart,
    Sieur, 173–74, 177
Destombes, Marcel, 5
Dickason, Olive P., 152, 173
discovery, xxv
disputations (*see also* polemics), xxiii,
    xxiv, 73–76, 78–80
dissidents in religion, 23, 52 n. 1
Donin, Nicholas, 74, 76
Donne, John, 123, 231
Dornates, Andrés, 216–17
Drake, Sir Francis, 153, 167 n. 22
Drayton, Michael, 115, 145
Dubno, 46
Dubovyč, Jan, 48–51
Durand, Dana Bennett, 8–9
Dutch, in the Americas, 196 n. 4

Eamon, William, 127
early modern period, xxxiv n. 4
Eastern Europe, 242
Ebisawa, Arimichi, 91
Echeverría, Nicholas, 215, 220–21
Eden, Richard, 150
Egypt, 11
Elizabeth I (queen of England),
    143, 160
Elizabethan, 128
Elyot, Sir Thomas, 135
England, 65, 69, 115, 117, 122–23,
    146–47, 150–52, 162, 173,
    238–39
English language, 239
epistemology and conceptual models.
    See conceptual models,
    epistemology of
Erasmus, Desiderius, 239
ethnic, xxxiv n. 10
ethnic communities, xxii, 27–29
Europe, 5–8, 10–13, 38, 80, 88, 90, 92,
    100, 145, 205, 208, 211, 225,
    234, 237, 242
Eve, 80

expeditions
    human geography and, 203
    as masculinist venture, idealization
        of male explorer, 177
exploration, 121, 125, 143–44, 148, 153
    Portugese, 144
    Spanish, 144
explorers, xviii, xxviii
    expectations of, 204
    and transformation of the image in
        francophone culture, 177

Fabián. *See* Fukansai, Habian
Fernandez de Oviedo y Valdés,
    Gonzalo, 150
Florida, 152, 241
    Peninsula, 203
    Spanish, 161
folk tales, 10–11
Foucault, Michel (Paul), 129
Fournier, Martin, 178
Fourth Lateran Council, 77
France, 66, 69, 88, 91, 173, 177,
    227, 233
Franklin, Wayne, 145
Frobisher, Martin, 147–49
Frois, Luis, 91, 97–99, 105
Frontenac, Comte de (Louis de
    Buade), 178
Fukansai, Habian, 99
Fuller, Mary, 162

Galileo, Galilei, 228
Galveston Bay, 204
García Márquez, Gabriel, 210
Gdańsk, 41
Geertz, Clifford, 233
gendered behaviour, xxviii
Genet, Jean, 3–4, 14, 236
Gentiles, 74
geographers, xx
German language, 28
German Street, 24, 39
Germans, xxi, 6, 28
Germany, 40

Ichthophagi Aethiopes, 11
Ide, Katsumi, 91
identity, xix, 229
    anxieties about, xxiii, xxv, xxvii, 46,
        75–76, 118–19, 121, 124–30,
        133–35, 238
    Christian, xxiii, xxiv, xxxi, 63–65,
        73, 75–80, 237
    collective, xxiii, xxv
    construction of, xix, xxvi, xxxiii,
        63–65, 73, 75, 89, 133
        linguistic, xx, 133–34
        social, xx
        temporal, xx
    creation of, contact and, xxxii
    and culture, through
        acculturation/assimilation,
        xxv, xxvii, xxix–xxxi, 34, 51,
        99, 175, 194, 210
    and discovery of difference,
        106, 180
    erasure of, xxx, 100, 215
    hidden, xxiv–xxvii, 44, 78, 85,
        118–19, 121, 124–36, 238
    hybridization of, 240
    individual, xxiii, xxv
    Jewish, xxiii–xxiv, 63–65, 71–73,
        75–80, 237
    and language usage and/or
        linguistic ambiguity, xxix,
        27–28
    as loyalty to sovereign, 175
    and the measuring of time, 29–31,
        33–34, 37–38, 40, 50
    multiple, xxix–xxx
    mutable nature of, xxiv–xxv, xxxii,
        76–79, 124, 136, 226, 237,
        240, 242
    religious, xxii
    and repertoires, xxix, 180, 194
    and self consciousness, 50, 88, 174,
        187
    and sexual promiscuity, 133
    shared, xxii
    and (shifting) political allegiance,
        27, 29, 175, 194

    transgressive, xx, 128–29, 132, 136,
        238
imposters, 126–27
India, 93, 101, 146
Indian reservations, 124
Indians. See natives and under specific
        tribes and nations
indigenous. See natives
Indonesia, 93
inquisitors, 69
intellectual history, 233
interaction, unmediated (see also
        narrative, mediated,
        translated)
interdisciplinary, xvii–xviii
interiority, xxvi
Irish, 116
Iroquois Indians (see also natives), xxix
Iser, Wolfgang, 165
Isidore of Seville, 10
Isle of the Dead, 6
Isles of Richelieu, 182
Israel, 74
Italy, 93, 227

Jabłko, Jarosz, 30, 36
Jackman, Charles, 147–48
Jacquin, Philippe, 177
James I (king of Aragon), 74, 79–80
James Ford Bell Library, 5
Japan, 87–97, 99–101, 103–5, 237–38
Jennings, Nicholas, 119
Jerome (an ordinary Jew), 79–80
Jerónimo de Sante Fe, Maestre, 74, 76
Jerusalem, 92
Jesuits (see also missionaries), 25, 45,
        47, 89, 196 n. 4
Jesus. See Christ, Jesus
Jewish culture (see also cultural
        practices, Jewish), 237
Jewish intellectual life, 69
Jewish persecution, 65–67, 80
Jewish synagogue, 27–28
Jewish-Christian relations.
        See relations, Jewish-
        Christian